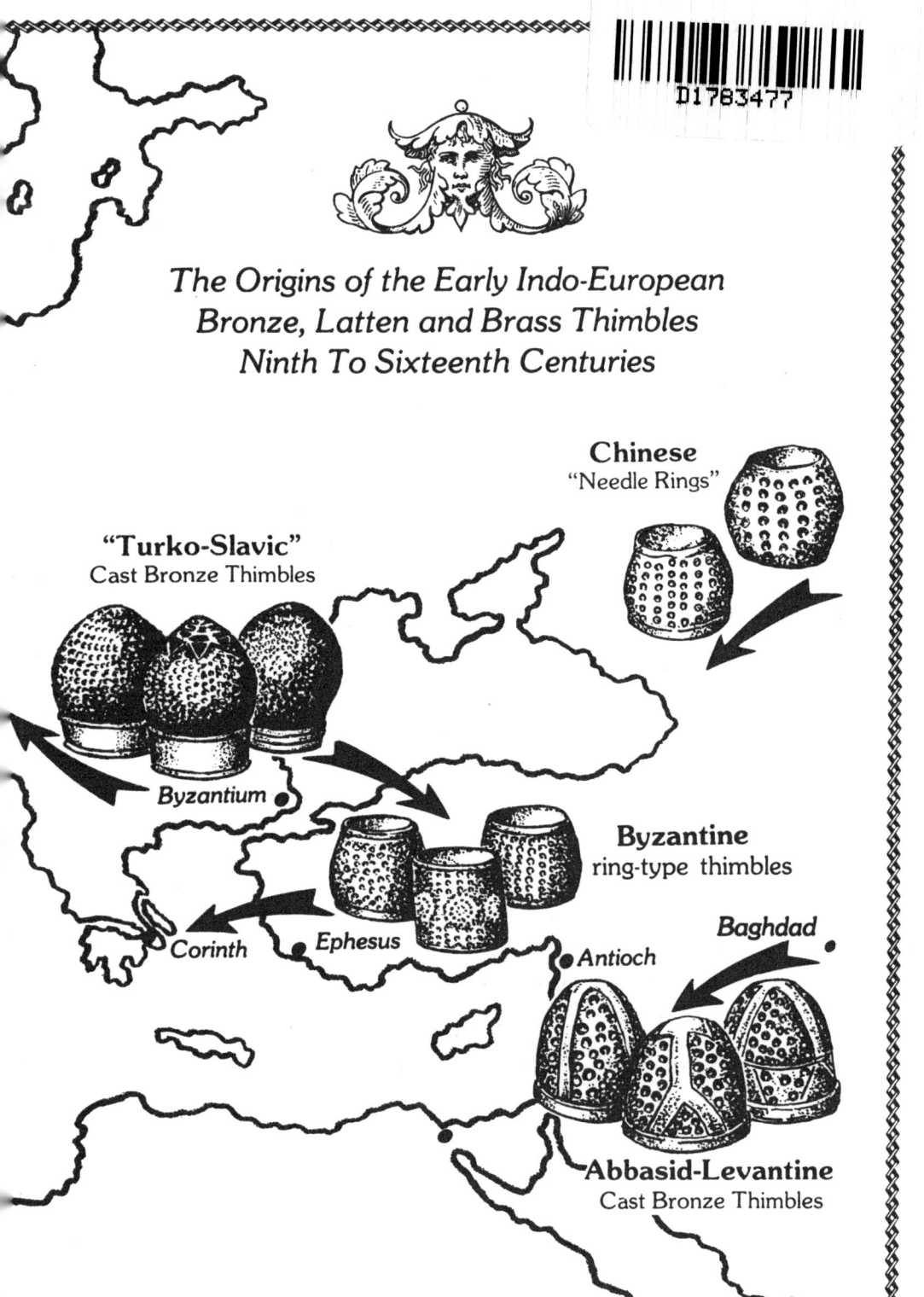

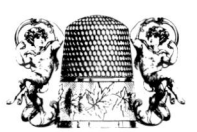

Thimble Collector's Encyclopedia

New International Edition
Thimble Collector's Encyclopedia

John J. von Hoelle

Other books by John von Hoelle:

The Family Simons, 1839-1969: *Thimblers to America for 130 Years*

The Story of Stern Brothers & Co., 1868-1932: *The American Thimblers Who Added Integrity to Our Golden Dreams*

Benjamin Halsted, 1734-1817: *America's First Thimble Manufacturer*

Charles Iles & Company: Thimblers to the British Empire Since 1840

Photography, line art, typesetting, and format by Dine-American, 7 Westbrite Court, Wilmington, DE 19810

Library of Congress Catalog
Card Number 86-71683

ISBN 0-87069-484-7

Third Edition
Copyright © 1986
John von Hoelle

10 9 8 7 6 5 4 3 2 1

All rights reserved. No part of this publication may be reproduced, stored in a retrieval system, or transmitted in any form or by any means, electronic, mechanical, photocopying, recording or otherwise, without prior permission of the copyright owner or the publisher.

Published by

Wallace-Homestead Book Company
580 Waters Edge
(312) 953-1100
Lombard, Illinois 60148

One of the
ABC PUBLISHING
Companies

This work is dedicated to the five women who have brought me much laughter and love... the most precious of all gifts.

    Susan Anne Taylor-Lewis
    Virginia M. Prince
    Kathleen D. McLaughlin
    Janice Ellen Behringer
    Ellen Ann von Hoelle

Contents

Foreword	8
Acknowledgments	9
Introduction	10
In Search of the Origin of the Thimble	13
Thimbles of Aluminum	46
American Indian Thimbles	49
The Thimbles of Austria	52
Thimbles of Bone	58
Thimbles of Brass	60
Thimbles of Central America	64
Chinese Cloisonne Thimbles	68
English Commemorative Thimbles	72
Corozo Nut Thimbles and Cases	73
Cut Glass Thimbles	74
English Silver-Clad Steel Thimbles	80
Dutch Thimbles	82
Enameled Thimbles	84
The Thimbles of Great Britain	86
Filigree Thimbles of the World	94
The Thimbles of France	98
The Thimbles of Gabler Brothers	102
The Wizardry of Gadget Thimbles	104
The Thimbles of Greece	110
The Thimbles of Benjamin Halstead	114
Thimbles of Horn	117
The Thimbles of British India	122
Thimbles of Ivory	124
Thimbles of Ironstone and Earthenware	127
Thimbles of Ketcham & McDougall	132
The Thimbles of Meissen	138
The Thimbles of Muhr	141
Niello Thimbles	144
The Thimbles of Norway	145
The Wacky World of Novelty Thimbles	146
Nuremberg Thimbles	147
American Paneled Thimbles	150
Pewter Thimbles	152
Political Thimbles	157
List of Porcelain Thimble Manufacturers	159
Thimbles of Porcelain and Bone China	160
Artisan Thimbles in Porcelain	165
Thimbles of Portugal	166
Pseudo Thimbles	169
Thimbles with Religious Themes	172
The Thimbles of Royal Worcester	179

List of Royal Worcester Artists	180
The Thimbles of Imperial Russia	181
American Scenic Thimbles	184
The Thimbles of Simons Brothers	192
The Thimbles of South America	194
South Staffordshire Thimbles	196
Souvenir Thimbles	197
Thimbles in Semi-Precious Stone	200
Wooden Tunbridge Thimbles	209
Vegetable Ivory Thimbles	212
Waite-Thresher Thimbles	214
The Thimbles of Wedgwood	215
Thimbles in Wood	216
Whistle Thimbles	218
Thimbles of the Near East	219
The Thimbles of Spain	220
Thimbles from Private Collections	221
Antique Enameled Thimbles in Color	225
Antique Thimbles in Gold and Jewels	226
Thimbles in Ivory with Gold and Jewels	231
The Legendary Thimbles of Meissen in Color	237
Victoria's Collection	232
The Louise D. Alden Collection	246
A "Thimble" in Other Lands	250
A Word About Reproductions	251
Thimbles That Never Were	254
How Thimbles Are Made	255
The Manufacturing of Sewing Thimbles	262
The Creation of an Ivory Thimble	265
Thimble Sources	267
Thimble Patents	268
A Visit to Charles Iles	270
Old Thimble Catalog Pages	276
Early Thimble Advertisements	283
Early American Silversmiths of New England	294
Tokens of Love	296
Thimble Poetry	297
Thimble Markings	298
Mrs. Sickels . . . I Presume?	302
On Thimbles	305
The World's Most Expensive Thimble	310
How Much Is a Thimble Worth?	311
Thimble Condition	312
Index of Illustrated Thimbles	313
Bibliography	329
Epilogue	331
About the Author	333

Foreword

We are proud to bring you this third expanded edition of Thimble Collector's Encyclopedia. Since the last edition, a great deal of new research has come to light about thimbles from archaeological records, metallurgical treatise, and reviews of important archival information by concerned collectors around the world.

To better capture the beauty and elegance of some of the world's most stunning thimbles, we have added hundreds of examples in full color for your enjoyment.

In the past, Europe and the United States were the major thimble informational centers. Recently, China and the Near East have become a new theater of research.

The introductory chapter, *In Search of the Origin of the Thimble,* is the cutting edge of research on this collectible. For the first time, Mr. von Hoelle has organized the types, and identified the regions responsible for our earliest bronze thimbles. Using his unique style of historical perspective, John unfolds the fascinating story, with words and illustrations, of the evolution of the crude stone needle-pushers of our Neolithic ancestors to the beautiful thimbles of the European Renaissance.

It is our hope that you will enjoy reading and using this book as much as we did in bringing it to you. We thank you, the international thimble collecting fraternity, for making this encyclopedia the most popular and foremost reference guide on the subject in the world.

B. David Behringer

Acknowledgments

This preliminary work is a composite of a great mass of information published in diverse scholarly research papers and books in the United States, Europe, and the Orient. The illustrations used were dispersed in the archives of many nations, museums, and private collections. The gathering of this information has proved be to a challenging task and was made possible only by the fine efforts of the many people involved.

At this time, I wish to gratefully recognize the contributions of the following scholars whose opinions, knowledge and extensive research I have relied on heavily: Mr. Joseph Farrell, Head of Classical Studies, University of Pennsylvania; Dr. Gladys Weinberg, Professor Emeritus, Museum of Art and Archaeology, University of Missouri; Mr. Robert Guy, Curator of the Princeton University Museum; Carl W. Bishop; Associate Curator, Smithsonian Institute; Dr. H. C. Chang; T. K. Ung; Dr. Nancy Bookidis, Curator of the American School of Classical Studies, Athens, Greece; Zhao Puchu, President of the Chinese Historical Research Society; Mrs. Doris Bowman, Textiles and Sewing Implements Specialist, Smithsonian Institute; Mrs. Priscilla Sarah of the Metropolitan Museum of Art, New York; Mr. Conrad Kohl, Helmut Greif, and Barbara Rohler for translations from the Nuremberg City Archives; and Dr. W. A. Robertson, for technical information on ancient and medieval metallurgy.

For technical data on the manufacturing of thimbles and the histories of their companies, I wish to express my gratitude to Mr. Gerhard Dannenhauer, Works-Manager for Gabler Brothers, Schorndorf, Germany; Mr. Richard Mealings, owner of Charles Iles and Gomms, Ltd., and Mr. Edward Cox, his Works-Manager. These men spent many hours with me explaining thimblemaking equipment and techniques, and allowed me to gain invaluable "hands-on" experience using their unique machinery.

A special thanks to the following friends and collectors who have allowed us to share, via photography, their unique thimbles and needle-pushers which have added so much to our explanations: Irmgard von Traitteur, Ann Blakeslee, Doris Ramstead, Matthew F. Regine, Christa Sommerkorn, Elizabeth G. Sickels, Elizabeth and Janusz Waciorski.

Last, my warm appreciation to the very special friends who helped to prepare this work for publication: Virginia Weaver, Sarah Anne Weisbrot, Ronald Giordano, Marian Lipsius, Evelyn Eubanks, Kay Gardner, Debbie Fuller, Jeannine Conner, Marjorie Perkins and Evelyn DerMarderosian.

Introduction

The evolution of the thimble from a basic sewing aid to one of today's most collected miniature art forms is a fascinating story. Museums around the world have among their collections, crude thimbles of stone, bronze and ivory from many civilizations. These are displayed side by side, with ornate and precious thimbles created by some of the finest craftsmen in the world.

In years gone by, thimbles were made to order by silversmiths or firms which specialized in common mass-produced thimbles. Your source depended on your station in life; servant or woman of position and wealth. While the common people sewed with thimbles of iron or brass, the great ladies of yesteryear embroidered their prized art needlework with thimbles of great beauty and value. Superb thimbles of silver and gold, set with precious stones, pearls and coral were part of many noble women's most cherished possessions.

The Industrial Revolution brought silver and gold thimbles with machine-made knurling and die-stamped designs within the reach of the middle class. Thus, the nineteenth century became the "Golden Age" of thimbles.

Historical writings are full of accounts of famous people giving special thimbles as gifts to loved ones. Queen Elizabeth I of England is said to have given her ladies-in-waiting silver thimbles made from Sir Francis Drake's plunder of the Spanish Main. One of these thimbles has been handed down through the women of the deGraue family. Both Queen Ann and Queen Victoria continued this practice, with Victoria on record as a generous giver of thimbles. She firmly believed "idle hands have need of needle and thread."

Paul Revere, the American patriot, revolutionary, and master silversmith, made thimbles to order, as did most colonial silversmiths. A lovely gold one he designed for his daughter, Maria, is on display in the Boston Museum of Fine Arts. Historical thimbles are the Rembrandts of thimble collectors' dreams. When one of these rarities finds its way into the great auction houses, many thousands of dollars are bid before the hammer falls!

This little tool has been with us for almost two thousand years. A study of its evolution from a simple sewing aid to an object of intrinsic beauty is a study of the progress of our own civilization. The thimble became an art form, and should be more widely recognized as one of the most collectible miniature art forms known to us today. It is also my desire to one day inspire fellow collectors to further research and organize the vast amount of information known today about this little, but remarkable, object.

This book is intended to be an introduction into the fascinating world of today's collectors' thimbles. It contains an illustrated glossary of terminology used by advanced collectors.

Only definitions which apply directly to thimbles are used. Many of these same words have other meanings which have been omitted. Companies listed may have made many other items besides thimbles, but only their association with the thimble is mentioned.

Persons listed in this volume are the "Who's Who" of thimble collecting society. Each has, in his own way, contributed to our present knowledge; some by writing books, articles, or research papers, others by founding study groups. Regional thimble clubs and newsletters are also noted. Many designers, craftsmen, and artists whose skills have included the making of the beautiful thimbles we collect are mentioned. There is another group of collectors whose vision and drive were channelled into originating the early conventions, which led to the birth of Thimble Collectors International. Officers of this great organization deserve a special recognition. But all deserve our deepest appreciation for their contribution to this fascinating field.

Welcome into this remarkable little world, and remember — our thimbles today are the descendants of generations of ever-changing styles and interpretations. Welcome to a hobby where one can still find a silver antique at less than twenty dollars, or for you big spenders, a tiny porcelain treasure at $18,000.

Thimble collecting may be enjoyed by persons on a limited budget who find their treasures at local flea markets and mail order catalogs, or by wealthy collectors at prestigious international auctions and quality antique dealers.

Thimbles, be they plastic politicals or precious gold, are all important to the true collector; some are just more expensive than others. Thimble collecting is for all ages and all budgets. Enjoy!

John J. von Hoelle

In Search of the Origin of the Thimble

A study of the evolution of the
Acutrudium and the Digitabulum

Prologue

Few objects come to mind which have contributed so quietly to the betterment of our civilization than the common thimble. This little sewing aid has been part of the personal accessories of needlewomen and sewers for countless generations. It enjoyed its greatest expression as a valued object of art from the late sixteenth to the early twentieth century. The thimble, which had its beginning in our most distant past, was passing into almost unnoticed oblivion by the mid-twentieth century. It had become, to many people, an obsolete, but quaint, little tool of yesteryear.

Only in the past twenty years, among advanced collectors, has there been expressed a genuine interest in thimble history and its social significance. Since then, most of the prominent eighteenth and nineteenth century manufacturers and their marks have been researched. Pioneers like John Lofting, Benjamin Halstead, Johann Gabler and others have had their remarkable contributions published. Yet the origins of the thimble have been clouded in the mist of antiquity, legend, and conjecture. Thus, I have avoided the early writings of Andere, Bond, Groves, Syer Cuming, Whiting, and Holmes on ancient thimbles.

This work, using the latest research and opinions of leaders in the fields of anthropology, archaeology, and metallurgy, is an attempt to trace the main evolution of the thimble for the serious collector.

One of our first observations is that the basic metal thimble evolved from a pre-historic group of pressure tools called "needle-pushers," or by the Latinized word "Acutrudium."

To better understand the origin of the thimble or the digitabulum, it is best to become familiar with the function of its predecessor, the needle-pusher, and thereby learn why a tool of more finesse was required. Knowing what an object is and not wondering or seeking the why, the where, the when or the how is, I believe, the indefinable mystique which separates the enthusiastic accumulator from tomorrow's discerning collector.

Courtesy, Fingerhutmuseum, Creglingen, Germany

The Magdeburg Acutrudium

Two Neolithic "Groove-Type" Acutrudia

In Search of the
Origin of the Thimble

Prior to the development of "true" sewing, prehistoric women "laced" animal skins together with blunt-pointed bodkins of wood, bone, or ivory. Thin strips of leather or sinews were used as thread. A sharp-pointed awl-type tool was used to pre-punch holes for the "threaded" bodkin to pass through. Thus, clothing, tents, and sacks were "laced" together. This Stone-Age method required no pressure tool, for the bodkin was first inserted and then pulled through the pre-formed holes to join the two hides.

Approximately twelve thousand years ago during the Neolithic or New-Stone Age, a new, quicker and more accurate method of sewing emerged. The blunt bodkin with its large eye evolved into a sharp pointed needle. These pre-historic needles were usually made of bone, ivory or even long thorns. They were a bit thinner and more polished than their earlier cousin, the bodkin.

This new sewing technique required strong pressure to push the crude needles through the tough leather hides. Born of necessity, there evolved the tool we call the needle-pusher. The earliest needle-pushers could have been any small piece of wood or rock. Later, stones were selected and drilled for this specific purpose. These crude sewing tools have been found at many neolithic sites in Europe, southern Russia, Africa, and China.

One such tool was found recently in Eilsleben, near Magdeburg, Germany. It is believed to be a unique example of a neolithic stone needle-pusher. This pressure tool, made of black amphibolite, measures about two-by-three inches. The large drilled hole near the top fits a small finger comfortably. Notice the small drilled indentations to catch the needle below the large thumb hole. Although a bit awkward, it was effective.

Other interesting examples of early neolithic needle-pushers have been found in several North African cave excavations. This type of sewing-stone differs from the Magdeburg acutrudium in that they have a deep trough or groove to better hold the needle when applying pressure. They measured about three inches long and, although rather crude, fulfilled their task quite well.

The next major development in sewing was the discovery of woven textiles. It is believed among leading anthropologists that weaving of long grasses and wicker for baskets, fishnets, and mats set the stage for this technological breakthrough.

Stone and Leather Sewing Implements

A Neolithic needle-pusher

Ancient Egyptian hybrid needle-pusher circa 1200 B.C.

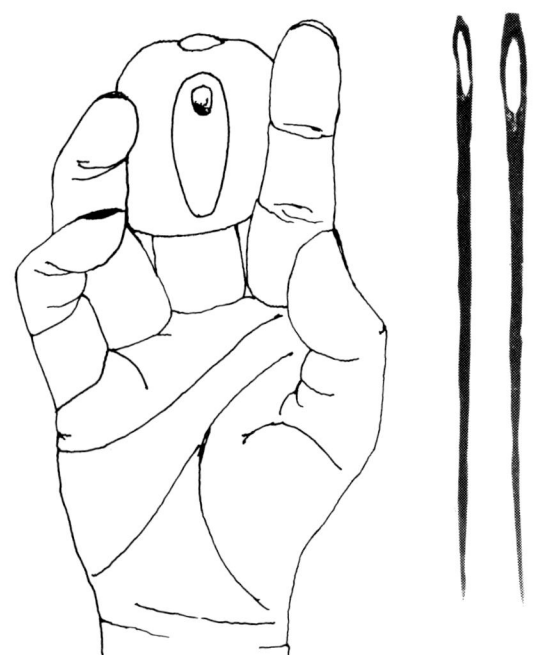

Courtesy Metropolitan Museum of Art

A leather finger-shield used by American Indians for sewing. Pre-1700.

As early as seven thousand years ago, flax, a grass-like plant indigenous to the Nile Valley, was being woven into linen cloth by the Egyptians. With the new, improved bronze needles which came into being approximately 2000 B.C., sewing this strong fabric with spun linen thread required far less effort.

The strong pressure of the palm of the hand was no longer required when sewing the light-weight fabrics. Another type of pressure tool must have evolved, one which could be worn on the finger or thumb.

During the centuries which saw the dawn of the Age of Textiles, it is believed that the most common form of needle protection was a simple piece of leather wrapped about the finger to absorb the pressure of the needle. However, other types of hybrid pressure tools, which were half thimble, half needle-pusher, also evolved.

On display in the Metropolitan Museum of Art in New York, is a curious example of what is believed to be this type of ancient Egyptian hybrid pressure tool. Found in 1915 during museum excavations at El Lisht, this composite stone pressure tool dates about 1200 to 1000 B.C. I believe this unique piece is an important link in the evolution of the thimble. Notice its similarity to the stone grooved-style needle-pusher of earlier origin.

From 5000 to 2300 B.C. an ever growing variety of material became available to our ancestors. While linen was the primary fabric in ancient Egypt and the Tigris-Euphrates civilization, wool and hair were being woven or pressed into felt in the colder climates to the north. In India along the Indus valley, cotton was spun and loomed as early as 3000 B.C. Far to the east, the Chinese had mastered the art of weaving silk by 2300 B.C.

The makeshift leather wrapping of this era may have given way to little sewn caps of leather, or even longer-length sheaths with some embroidery or tassels, as used by aboriginal inhabitants of Siberia and Alaska prior to contact with the early explorers. Positive proof of shape or decoration on these ancient leather thimbles is, for now, but simple conjecture.

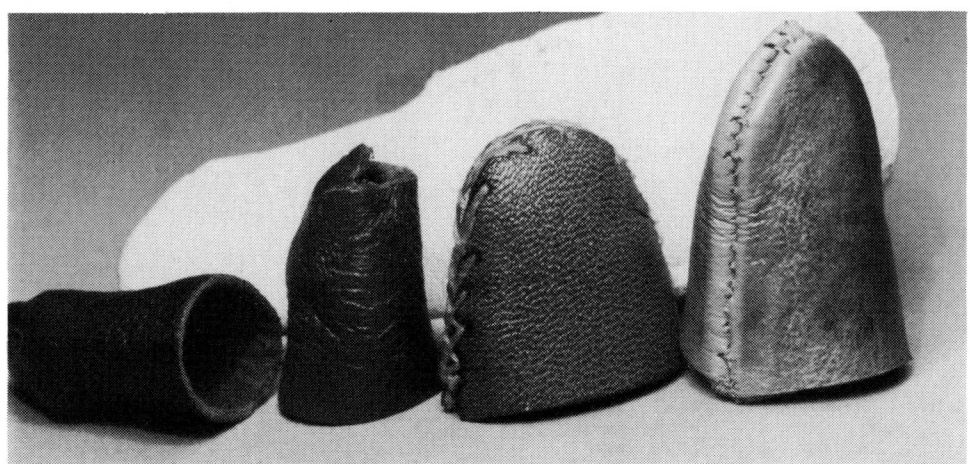

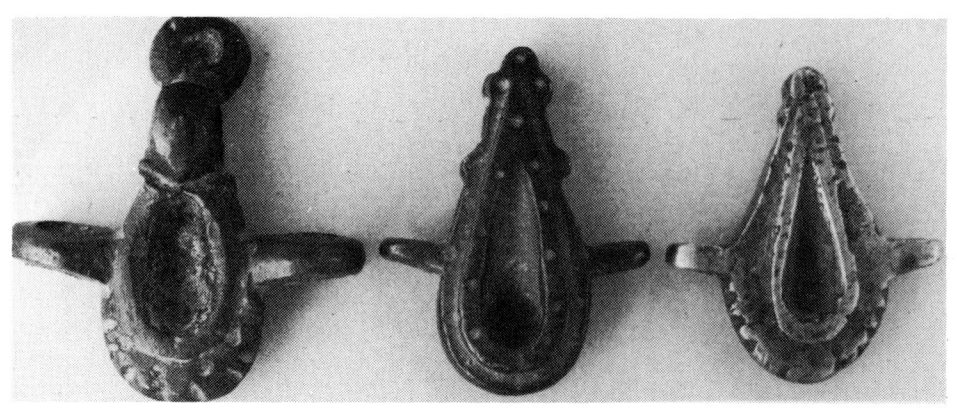

Cast Bronze Acutrudia
from the Roman, Byzantine and Ottoman Empires

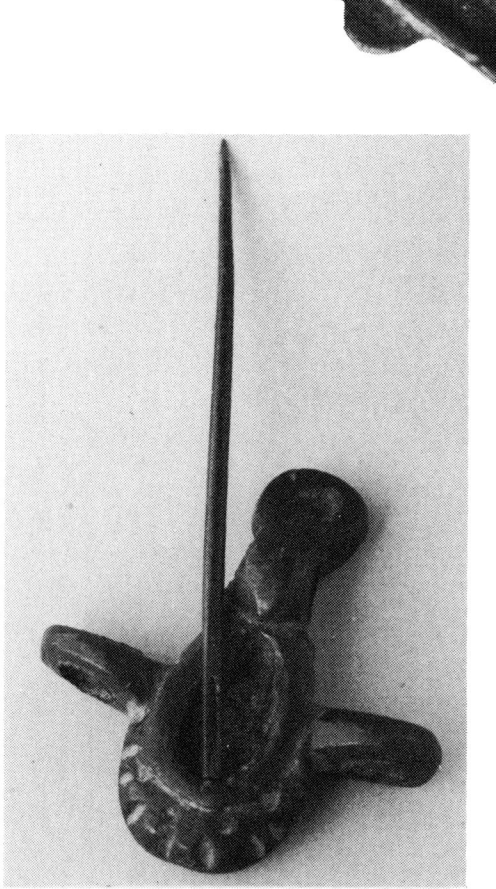

Courtesy von Traitteur Collection

Unfortunately, no leather sewing thimbles of ancient provenance are known to have survived. Also, no word for "sewing thimble" seems to have been found in any of the ancient languages of the Egyptians, Romans, or Greeks.

With the advent of the Bronze Age, we find that the old palm-held needle-pusher had evolved into another curious, but interesting shape. Now made of cast bronze and fitted with leather thongs, it fit comfortably in the palm. Examples of this type of pressure tool have been found at sites throughout the Roman, Byzantine, and Ottoman Empires. Many have subtle forms of decorations on their palm side.

It is believed that this tool was used primarily by men who stitched heavy canvas for sails and tents, carpet makers, leather workers and those who sewed heavy woolens. This type of bronze pressure device was used in some parts of the Middle East with little change until the late eighteenth century. A version of this ancient sewing aid is still used today in the form of a "sailor's palm." It can still be purchased at marine supply houses and is used to hand sew thick sail canvas when machines are not available.

We are now able to assume sewing during classical times was divided into two basic methods: in the first, women sewing light or medium-weight fabrics used leather wrapping to protect their fingers; in the second, men used bronze needle-pushers to sew heavy canvas and leather.

We owe to the ancient Chinese the next two major improvements in sewing: the steel needle and the sewing ring. Silk, a valuable and delicate material, could not be sewn satisfactorily with the thick ivory, bone or bronze needles of the day without leaving unsightly needle holes all along the seams.

The Chinese discovery of alloying carbon with iron produced a new metal, steel. This was the material the silk workers needed for ultra-thin needles that were able to hold a sharp point and give extreme durability. Centuries before the birth of Christ, steel needles were being used throughout the Oriental silk industry.

The legendary silk routes developed as the fame of this wondrous cloth reached the western civilizations. Through India and Persia to the dominions of the Egyptians and the Romans, it traveled by caravan and by ship. Along with the costly silks came the precious steel needles needed to properly sew them. Thus, the steel needle was introduced to the western world before the first century B.C.

Chinese Needle-Rings

Bronze needle-rings excavated at Xu Fu, Tang Dynasty

Bronze needle-rings excavated at Kai-Feng, Sung Dynasty

Chinese silver needle-rings, Manchu Dynasty

Chinese needle-rings excavated at Taxkorgan, Han Dynasty

The second major improvement was the introduction of a new type of pressure tool. There is strong evidence the Chinese were using metal "needle-rings" or "Zen-Huan" as early as the second century A.D. Numerous bronze, brass, and silver ring-type thimbles have been found in excavated sites throughout China. According to research materials in the National Baijing University archives: "The most common style was made 'in the flat' and rolled to form a ring, sometimes with the ends overlapping. The ring was left unsoldered for easy sizing. Some form of decoration was often rendered where the two ends met. Others were casted in one piece."

Dr. Zhao Puchu, a noted authority on Chinese archaeology, stated: "This type of sewing ring is of ancient origin with known examples dating back to the late Han dynasty (A.D. 100-220)." I have been informed by other Chinese scholars, such as Dr. H. Chang and T. K. Ung, who also hold this common belief which seems to be curiously absent from Western knowledge. The needle-ring is characteristically Chinese: practical, easy to make, and easy to use. It allowed rapid sewing with minimal pressure and, due to its open-end design, permitted good air circulation. This unique feature prevented the buildup of perspiration which occurred in the copper-alloy, closed-end thimbles of Western design. In these closed-end thimbles there formed a greenish substance called verdigris. Verdigris could become deadly poison if a needle should pierce the copper-alloy thimble and prick the finger, injecting the dangerous substance into the blood stream. High fever and death sometimes resulted from this common accident.

The Chinese needle-ring was so perfect in concept; it changed very little over the next two milleniums as it traveled westward, reaching the Persians before the seventh century and the Byzantines by the ninth century.

This statement is based on the observation that few metal thimbles have been found with good provenance, which date before the ninth century A.D. in Europe, although it is believed some imported Chinese-style sewing rings could have followed the great silk routes with the steel needles at an earlier date. Several curious finds of thimbles near Roman towns have been reported, but upon close examination, these, too, may be attributed to the Byzantines or in some cases early Nuremberg.

Byzantine Bronze Sewing Rings

Courtesy American School of Classical Studies

Sewing-rings excavated at Corinth, Greece

The Oldest European Thimbles Known

Byzantine cast-bronze thimble rings like the ones excavated from Ephesus and Antioch. Note the similarity to the Chinese needle-rings.

Byzantine bronze thimbles excavated in Turkey

Excavations of the Byzantine sections of the ancient cities of Antioch, Ephesus and Corinth have yielded dozens of bronze ring-type thimbles, curiously similar to earlier Chinese examples. These have been dated by noted archaeologists to be from the ninth to the thirteenth centuries. Excavated sites in the older Roman and Greek sections in these same cities have yet to uncover a single thimble! This observation and the scarcity of any other documented finds of metal thimbles in the ancient Roman world before the ninth century leads us to the conclusion that the "ring-type" pieces of Chinese origin are the earliest known style of metal sewing thimble.

All efforts by me to discover the location of the legendary "Herculeaneum" thimbles in the "Genevieve collection" or any other authentic "Gallo-Roman" metal thimbles, as mentioned by several noted British writers, have proven fruitless. Many old bronze thimbles found in museums and purported to be "Roman" are Byzantine, Islamic or medieval at best, and most are being re-attributed by conscientious curators.

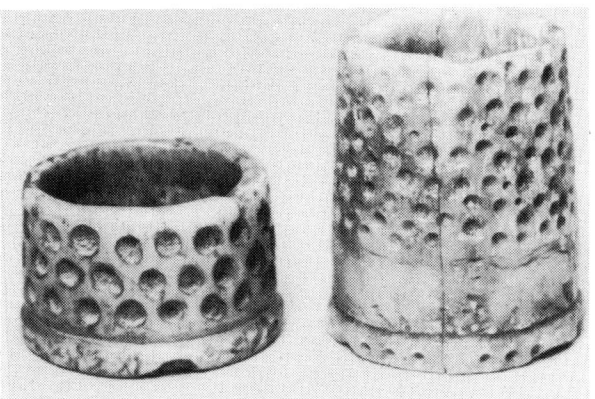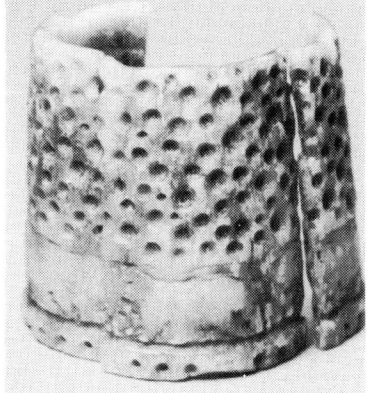

Bone thimbles excavated at Ctesiphon

Extensive excavations of the Sassanian city of Ctesiphon, near modern Baghdad, have uncovered no metal thimbles, but two interesting ring-type examples were found. Both thimbles were made from a cross section of camel bone. The first piece looks very much like a common sewing ring. The second, a remarkable tall ring-type, has four animals carved in bas-relief, walking about the band. If their provenance proves correct, these thimbles would be the earliest known examples to have survived in the Middle East. The city of Ctesiphon was destroyed by an Arab army in the seventh century and never re-occupied.

Cast Bronze Turko-Slavic Thimbles

Courtesy Smithsonian Institute

In the faith of Islam and the armies of Allah, there arose another power which would establish an empire from Istanbul, across North Africa to Spain. Arab, Turk, Persian, Egyptian, and Moor were united by religion, ruled by Sultan and Caliph, and became the dread of the western world.

From their impressive civilization came many innovations, not least among them, a new type of thimble for heavy sewing. It was rather large, heavy, cast in bronze, and, for the first time, completely covered the tip of the finger or thumb.

These early Islamic thimbles can be divided into three distinct styles. The first style known as "Turko-Slavic," has a large bulbous dome, suggesting a Persian or Turkish influence. Many have some kind of rudimentary line decoration about the band and sometimes on top of the dome. Their large size, 1¼ inch to 1¾ inches, suggests that they may have been worn on the thumb. However, one example examined by me had the remains of a leather shell inside the thimble, thus down-sizing the inside diameter to fit a large finger.

These Turko-Slavic thimbles have been found in the eastern Mediterranean countries and up through Bulgaria, Rumania, and Hungary. They date from the thirteenth century to the eighteenth century, and were cast in bronze using the lost-wax method. The indentations usually seem to have been hammered in.

Turko-Slavic Thimbles

Note the "star pattern" on the apex of the above bronze thimble and the one on the facing page, bottom right. Also the ventilation holes on top of many Turko-Slavic thimbles.

Courtesy von Traitteur Collection

Courtesy: Azzah-ben Sura

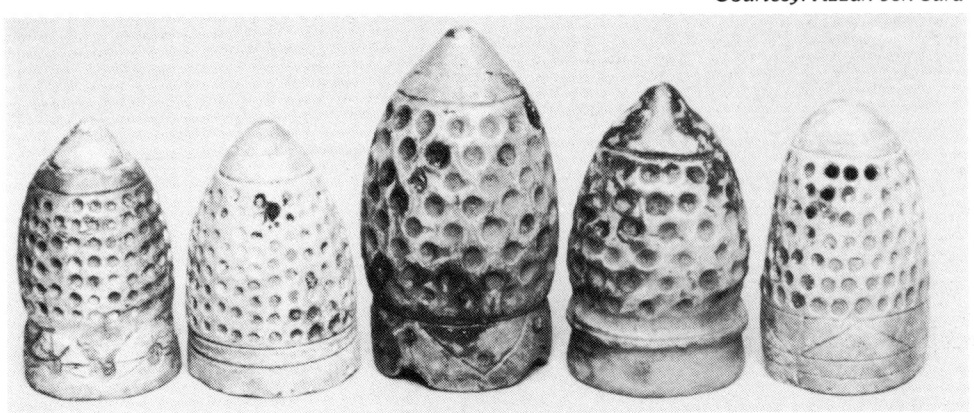

Cast Bronze
Hispano-Moresque Thimbles

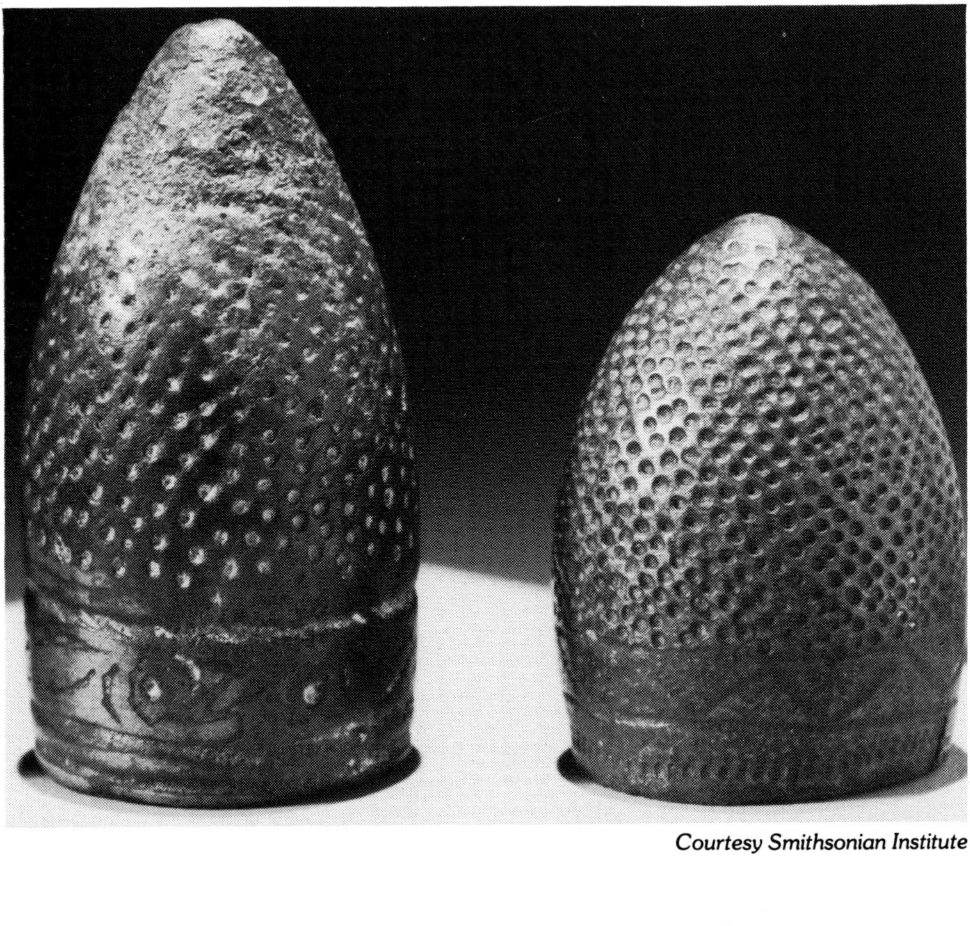

Courtesy Smithsonian Institute

The second style of early Islamic thimble is known as "Hispano-Moresque." These thimbles, with their unique, pointed tops, date from the tenth to the fifteenth century. They have been found primarily in western North Africa and Spain, but a few have also been found in France and in Viking settlements as far north as Denmark.

These heavy, but more graceful, thimbles were also cast in bronze. They often have an attractive floral, leaf, or vine motif about their band and top, as well as simple incised line decorations. Another unusual feature of many of the Hispano-Moresque pieces is the indentations. These thimbles were often cast with the indentations already carved into the wax model.

The third style of early Islamic thimble is the "Abbasid-Levantine" style. These thimbles often had a distinctive "ledge-type" rim jutting out from the base of their dome-shaped silhouette. A unique series of "chevron" motifs usually separated the hand-punched indentations. They were not "bulbous" like their Turko-Slavic cousins, nor pointed at the top like the Hispano-Moresque pieces.

These interesting thimbles have been found in sites throughout Asia Minor, particularly in Israel, Syria, Trans-Jordan, Iraq and Iran. They seem to date a bit earlier than the other cast bronze Islamic thimbles, circa ninth to the twelfth century. and are the rarest of the Islamic styles.

These early Islamic thimbles were used primarily by men who stitched heavy canvas, leather or carpets.

Abbasid-Levantine Thimbles

Courtesy: Azzah-ben Sura

It is my belief that among the many innovations created by the Islamic Saracens, it was the Abbasid-Levantine style thimble which the returning Crusaders introduced to pre-Renaissance Europe.

Our earliest western European thimblers seem to have adopted this shape as opposed to the bulbous Turko-Slavic or the pointed Hispano-Moresque thimbles.

The Origins of the Early Indo-European Bronze, Latten and Brass Thimbles Ninth To Sixteenth Centuries

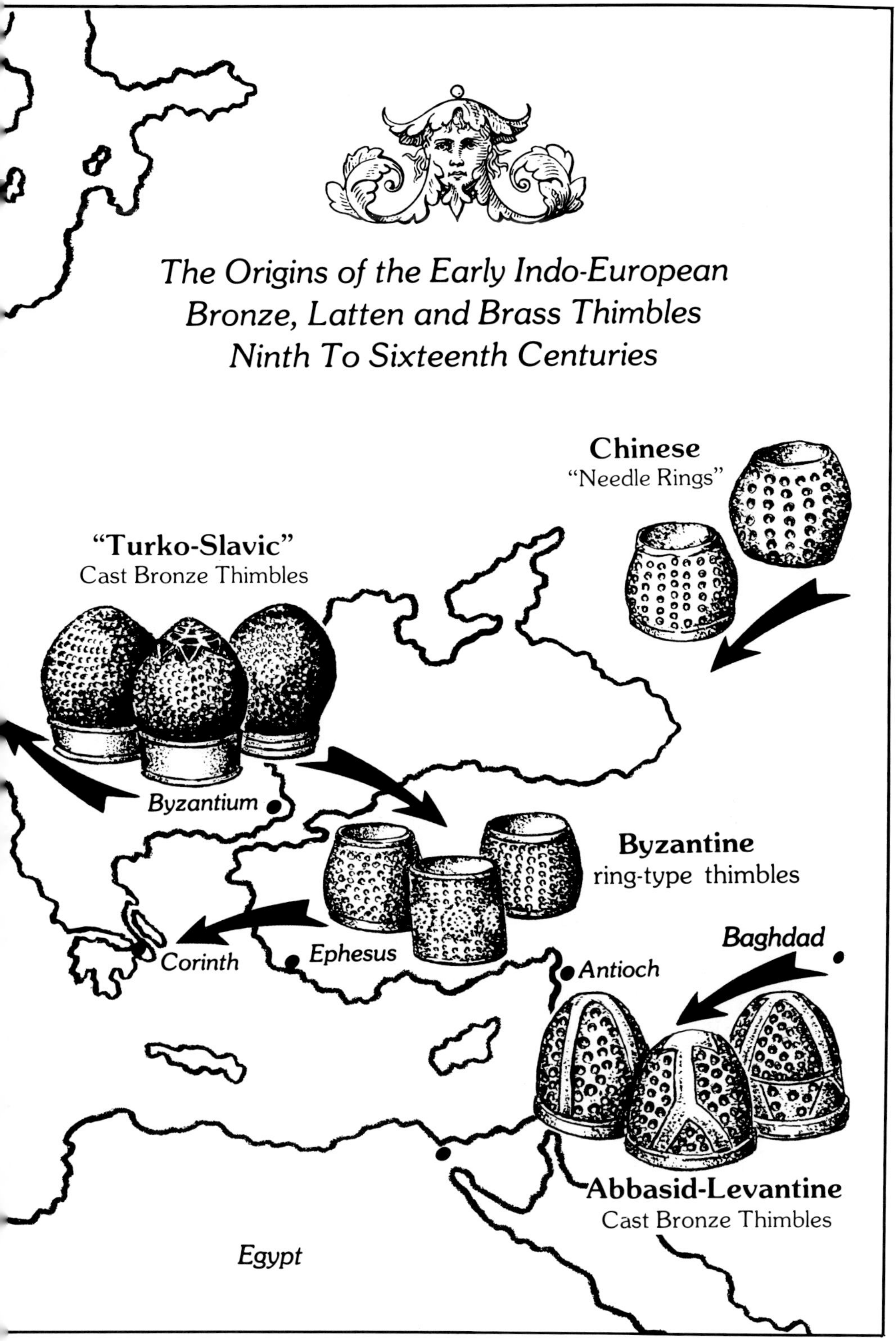

Chinese "Needle Rings"

"Turko-Slavic" Cast Bronze Thimbles

Byzantium

Byzantine ring-type thimbles

Baghdad

Corinth   *Ephesus*   *Antioch*

Abbasid-Levantine Cast Bronze Thimbles

Egypt

Pre-Renaissance European Thimbles

Cast latten (laiton) thimbles, 12th to 15th centuries

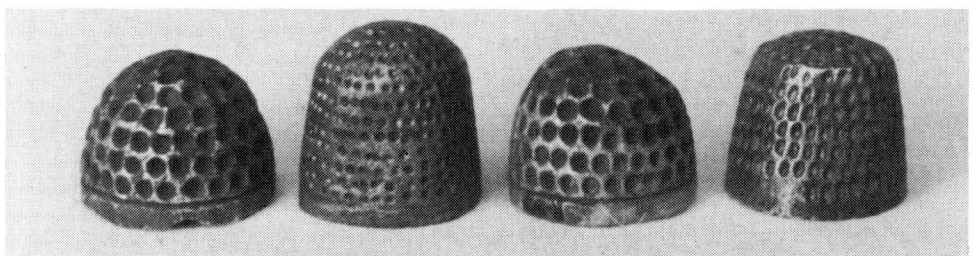

Courtesy Nuremberg Archives

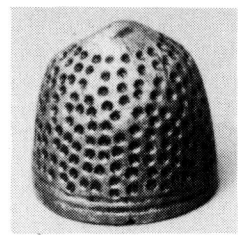

Oldest known drawing of a thimblemaker

Until about the thirteenth century in the more progressive societies, seamstresses working with light and medium-weight fabrics still used the bronze ring-type thimbles side by side with leather ones. In the still awakening dominions of western and northern Europe, the leather thimble remained the primary finger protector used by women. As late as A.D. 1150, the word zieriskranz, old German for "ornamental wreath," was used by Saint Hildegard von Bingen to describe a metal sewing ring in her commentaries. Obviously, the late German word for thimble, fingerhut, had yet to be coined.

Before the Dark Ages gave way to the early Renaissance, we find the first traces of a new smaller, lighter thimble, made of a material called latten, covering the fingertip. This metal, an alloy of copper and calamine, is the predecessor of modern brass. Latten, due to the impurities of the unrefined zinc in the calamine, was often porous, and one can sometimes notice color differences of reddish and yellowish copper in the texture. Latten was not very malleable due to poor crystalization, and was difficult to hammer or press without cracking. Most of the early latten thimbles were cast in sand molds, but a few are known to have been hammered into a shallow die to obtain their shape. Some thimbles of this type were also still being cast in bronze.

These early latten pieces tended to be a bit thicker and somewhat squat in form during the twelfth to the fifteenth century and gradually became taller and thinner by the late 1400s due to improved casting techniques.

The cradle of latten thimble production seems to have been Germany, and one city, Nuremberg, reached an early preeminence. In Nuremberg's public library there is a hand-tinted drawing of a monk drilling indentations into thimbles using an Archimedean drill. This illustration of an early knurling technique dates just before A.D. 1400. A cast latten thimble, very similar to the ones shown in the drawing, is on exhibit in the collection of the Kam Museum in Nijmegen, Germany. This thimble has been dated with good provenance to be pre-A.D. 1400. Similar thimbles are also in private collections such as the ones in the illustration below. The early latten thimbles gradually began to replace their leather counterparts in Western Europe from about the 12th century, although in remote parts of the British Isles and Northern Europe leather thimbles were still being used until the late nineteenth century.

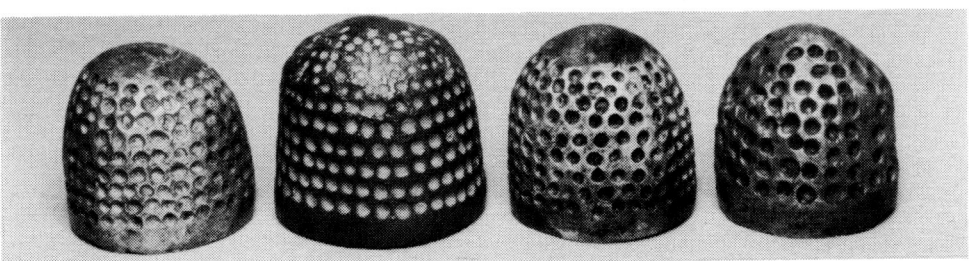

French woodcut of a medieval thimble and button-maker's workshop.

Tools of a Medieval Thimblemaker

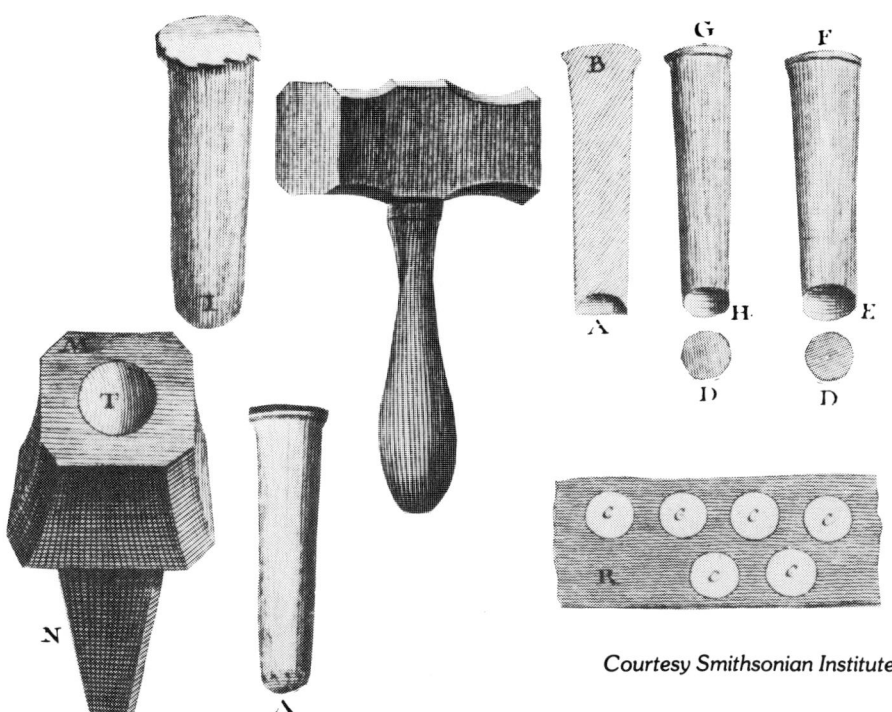

Courtesy Smithsonian Institute

In France, during the thirteenth century, thimbles were made by two separate guilds. The buckle-makers (Fermailliers) were allowed to make only latten thimbles via the sand casting method. The button-makers (boutonniers) guild had the rights to make theirs in copper and iron. Copper, being very malleable, could be "deep drawn" using an iron dapping block, dapping die, and hammer. This old French woodcut shows several "boutonniers" using this method for forming buttons as well as thimbles.

A variety of shapes were produced during this time depending on the place of origin, but the overall appearance of most of these early western European thimbles suggests the short dome-type was the predominant style. The indentations were either drilled or hammered. Many have a small hole in the top to help facilitate in the sand casting. Others have a small notch or two in the rim which was used to help secure the thimble to the lathe. This procedure was necessary, for the lathe removed the roughness and irregularities of the thimbles due to the sand casting method.

This technique continued until the second quarter of the sixteenth century when the metalsmiths of Nuremberg discovered the secrets of refining zinc from calamine. This wondrous new alloy of copper and pure zinc gave to the thimblemakers of Nuremberg a new and very malleable material which could be easily hammered into a thimble form, indented and polished to shine like gold, and not mottled like the earlier latten pieces.

Courtesy Nuremberg City Archives

Woodcut of a Nuremberg thimblemaker, circa 1564

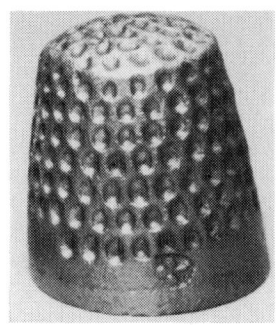

Note maker's mark

Early 16th century

This method known as "deep drawn" created a new, longer, thinner shape. The above wood block engraving by Jost Amman, published in 1564, depicts this new method of thimblemaking. Notice that the man on the left is using a hammer and dapping die to press a disc of metal into the thimble stamp (dapping block). On the right, the master is hammering in the indentations with a punch. The slower drilling method for creating the indentions was now discontinued.

Until the early sixteenth century, the coppersmith guild cast the thimble shells for the thimblemakers, who just indented and finished them off. These skills were minimal and the thimblemakers enjoyed little prestige. They did not even have the protection of their own guild. All this changed by 1537, when the thimblemakers of Nuremberg, armed with a new metal, a new technique, and new-found skills, were allowed to form their own guild and codify their laws, which were rigorously maintained. A record of this early constitution is still preserved in Nuremberg. It was recently translated into English and published in Helmut Greif's excellent book, *Talks About Thimbles*, which offers a detailed look into medieval thimble making.

Brass Nuremberg Thimbles - Late 16th Century

The thimbles of Nuremberg, from the middle of the sixteenth to the eighteenth century, had a distinctive style all their own. The indentations usually began at the top of the band and worked their way around the body of the thimble until they reached the top. There was a noticeable angle divergence from the side of the thimble to where the top began. The "domed" look was gone. Also, many thimbles had a maker's mark stamped on the outside of the thimble just before the start of the knurlings. These maker marks were in the form of clover leaves, goblets, keys, stars, etc.; each master had his own mark. It is our hope to one day trace these marks to their owners.

These new, longer thimbles now gave the celebrated craftsmen of Nuremberg some space below the indentations for ornamentation. Thus, for the first time since the Hispano-Moresque thimbles, decorative designs began to be incorporated into thimbles. By the late sixteenth century, a great profusion of mottoes, dates and motifs enhanced the city's thimbles.

Nuremberg was not just making thimbles of brass, but also of precious gold and silver, beautifully engraved and enameled. The thimble was being transformed from a basic sewing tool into a beautiful object of art, nurtured and treasured by the needlewomen of the Renaissance.

Just beyond the old city walls is the medieval cemetery of St. Johannes. Here, under great blocks of stone, crested with elaborate bronze epitaphs, lie some of the master thimblers of 16th century Nuremberg.

On their epitaphs, cast in high-relief are the thimbles they made. So detailed are these thimbles that the designs on the bands and the different types of knurlings are still clear after four centuries! Thimble designs once believed to be ancient Roman can be found here, and we are now able to positively attribute them as being from Nuremberg.

*Author examining epitaph of the
master Nuremberg thimblemaker Matthes Kessler*

*The epitaph of Hans Tober, 1580
Master Nuremberg fingerhuter*

The Medieval Cemetery of St. Johannes

The resting place of many Nuremberg master thimblemakers

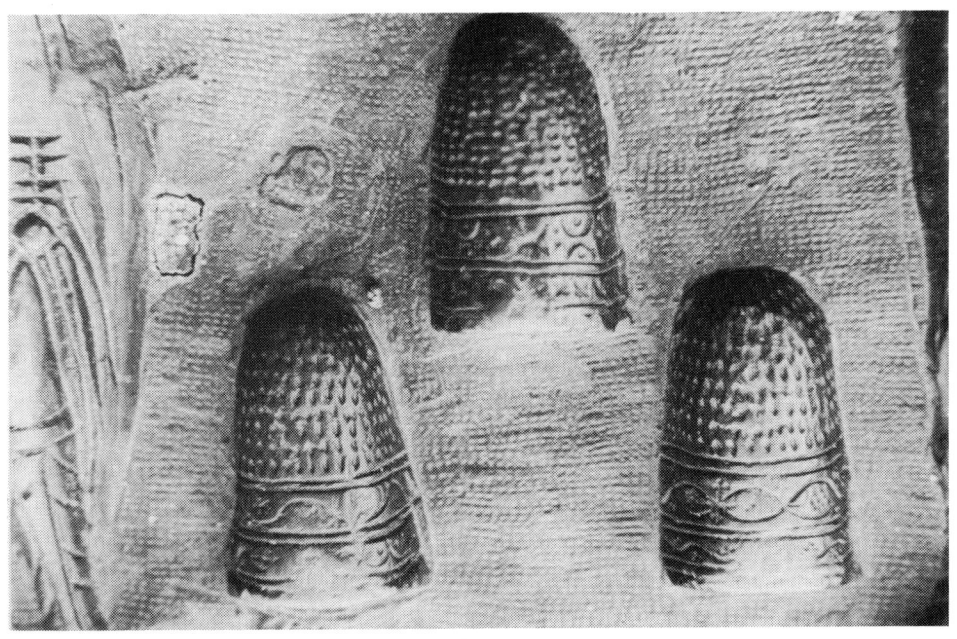

Enlargement of the thimbles on epitaph of Hans Tober

Silver Renaissance thimble, dated 1577

Courtesy Metropolitan Museum of Art

Nuremberg 16th century

Thimble on the epitaph of Matthes Kessler

The Medieval city of Nuremberg, 16th century

Dutch Brass Thimbles - Late 17th Century

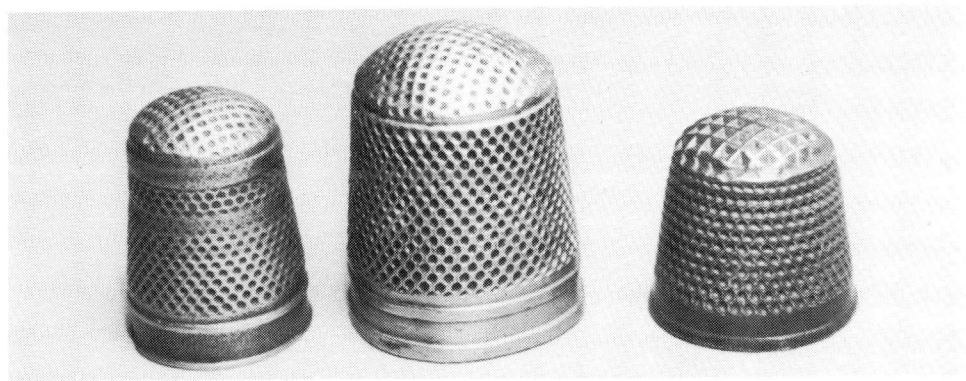

In Holland, England and Sweden, thimblemakers continued the primitive sand casting method, with some refinements, until the early eighteenth century. The use of this outmoded process for two centuries after a faster, less costly method had been discovered in Germany has puzzled researchers for years. One theory suggests the national conservatism in these countries, plus the lack of skilled craftsmen with a knowledge of brass metallurgy, perpetuated the obsolete sand casting technique of making thimbles. This ended in the early eighteenth century when the secret of how to refine zinc became generally known throughout Europe. The "deep drawn" method, using power presses, is the process adopted by all the major mass-production thimble manufacturers of the nineteenth and twentieth centuries.

During the next four centuries, master artisans around the world created thimbles in a bewildering array of styles and materials never equaled by any other sewing tool. By the late nineteenth century, thimbles had reached their zenith in variety and popularity, with millions being produced annually. Within fifty years, they would be regarded as a quaint little tool of another era, but their rich history is being preserved and cherished by private collectors the world over.

Today, thimbles are a highly collectible object of art with a long and fascinating history to appreciate. The next time we, as collectors, admire a tall, elegant, French, nineteenth century gold thimble with a delicate line of seed pearls about its beautifully chased band, its machined knurlings finished in perfect precision, let's remember our pre-historic seamstress, struggling with her coarse hides, her frail bone needle, and her crude stone needle-pusher. I wonder if she cursed very much?

Why Collect Thimbles?

"I believe thimbles are an excellent example of the need our forebearers had to decorate, and so cherish even their most humble of possessions.

Thimbles can be intricately beautiful, miniature works of art. They have challenged the skills of master craftsmen for centuries. Every known art technique and medium has been touched upon in thimble making.

Their remarkable variety is as endless as God's snowflakes. And lastly, I believe these tiny collectibles stand in mute testament to the awesome creativity of the human mind."*

---

*Except from the program "Thimbles as an Art Form"
given at the T.C.I. convention in Dearborn, Mich.
August 1982 by author

1 2 3 4

A

Abalone Shell — The irridescent inner layer of the abalone shell, found in the warm waters off the coast of California, Mexico, and in the South Pacific. Abalone shell has been used to overlay metal thimbles, primarily from Mexico and the Philippines. See illustration #1.

Abbasid-Levantine Thimbles — An early Islamic-type thimble found in Asia Minor. They date from the 8th to the 13th century. Many have a distinctive rim and domed top. The top and sides usually have interesting "chevron" motifs separating the hand-punched indentations.

They are not "bulbous" like their cousins, the Turko-Slavic thimbles, nor pointed at the top like the Hispano-Moresque thimbles. The unique "chevron" patterns are not found on the other two main Islamic thimble styles. See page 29.

Acanthus — An ancient Greek-Roman leaf motif used as a decoration on many late 19th century American thimbles. See illustration # 2

Acutrudium — A Latinized word for a group of prehistoric pressure tools. They evolved from stone to bronze by the Roman era. They were used until the 17th century with little change. The modern version is the sailor's palm. See pages 20 and 82.

Adams — Old English pottery firm, dating back to 1657 when John Adams built his first kiln in Burlem. The firm became William Adams & Son in 1818 and remains one of the finest "ironstone" ware manufacturers. They are now a member of the Wedgwood Group.

Adams, Maud — An American actress of the 1890s who gave to friends and fans base metal and silver thimbles stamped with the words: A THIMBLE FROM MAUD ADAMS; made by Simons Bros. She played the original Peter Pan on the New York stage! See Thimble # 4.

Addis, Joseph — English silversmith known to have made thimbles in Birmingham from 1828-1865. His mark is IA.

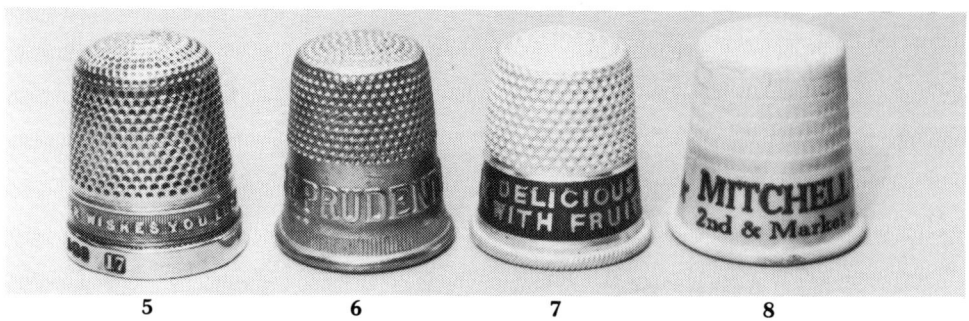

     5   6   7   8

Advertising Thimbles — Any thimble advertising a service or product falls into this category. Originally given away free or as a premium, they are now regarded as a "special field" within thimble collecting. It is estimated there are more than 5,000 different types of thimbles in this category. Most advertising thimbles are plastic, aluminum or brass, but more than 100 are known in silver. One prolific London jeweler advertised on his silver thimbles: "James Walker-Wishes You Well," in the 1920s. The Prudential Life Insurance Company once ordered a million brass thimbles, just before the First World War, from Charles Iles & Co. Later, several million more were ordered from Scovill Manufacturing in Connecticut. Many advertising thimbles are the only trace left of old firms now out of business. See above and below.

Agate — A very hard semi-precious stone of the quartz family, usually formed in streaks or layers of different colors. It is translucent. Many English and German thimblemakers set agate into the top of a thimble to better take the wear of steel needles.

Aiken-Lambert & Co. — American manufacturing jeweler from New York City. Late 19th and early 20th century. These silver thimbles are marked on the band: AL & Co.

Alabaster — A semi-translucent mineral of the gypsum family. It can be carved and delicately shaded. Alabaster thimbles have a soft pearly luster when not tinted. See illustrations 13 and 14.

Foreign Advertising Thimbles

     9   10   11   12

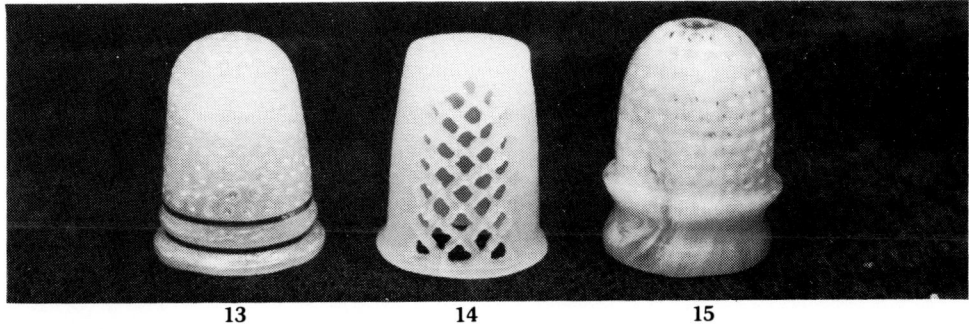

13   14   15

Alaska Silver — Another name for the nickel-silver alloy. Advertised by Sears-Roebuck circa 1900.

Alden Collection — A fine collection of early porcelain thimbles given to the Boston Museum of Fine Arts by Louise D. Alden in 1962. It includes twenty-three 18th century Meissens and a large number of early English porcelains. See collection on page 246.

Aldridge, Elizabeth — English collector and author of *Thoughts on Thimbles,* published by Thimble Collectors International, 1984-86 in serial form.

d'Allemagne, Henry R. — French author of the book *Les Accessories du Costume et du Mobilier.* Illustrates some of the famed Albert Figdor collection. Contains some excellent history of thimbles in early France. Printed in Paris 1928.

Alpacca — A metal alloy of copper, nickel and zinc. Also called German silver or nickel-silver. The term "alpacca" is a Spanish term found on many Mexican thimbles. Aplacca does not tarnish and looks like silver. Thimbles have been made of this material since the mid-19th century.

Aluminum — A metal used chiefly in the manufacture of advertising, political and inexpensive thimbles found in sewing kits. Its low cost and light weight make aluminum an ideal medium for this type of thimble.

Alurine — Brand name of aluminum thimbles made by Charles Iles & Co., Birmingham, England, circa 1920.

Ambiguous Mark — A symbol, initials or touchmark on a thimble whose meaning is unknown to experienced collectors.

Amber — A clear brownish stone-like material of petrified resin used to decorate German thimbles. Some collectors' thimbles have been carved completely from amber. See example #15.

Thimbles of Aluminum

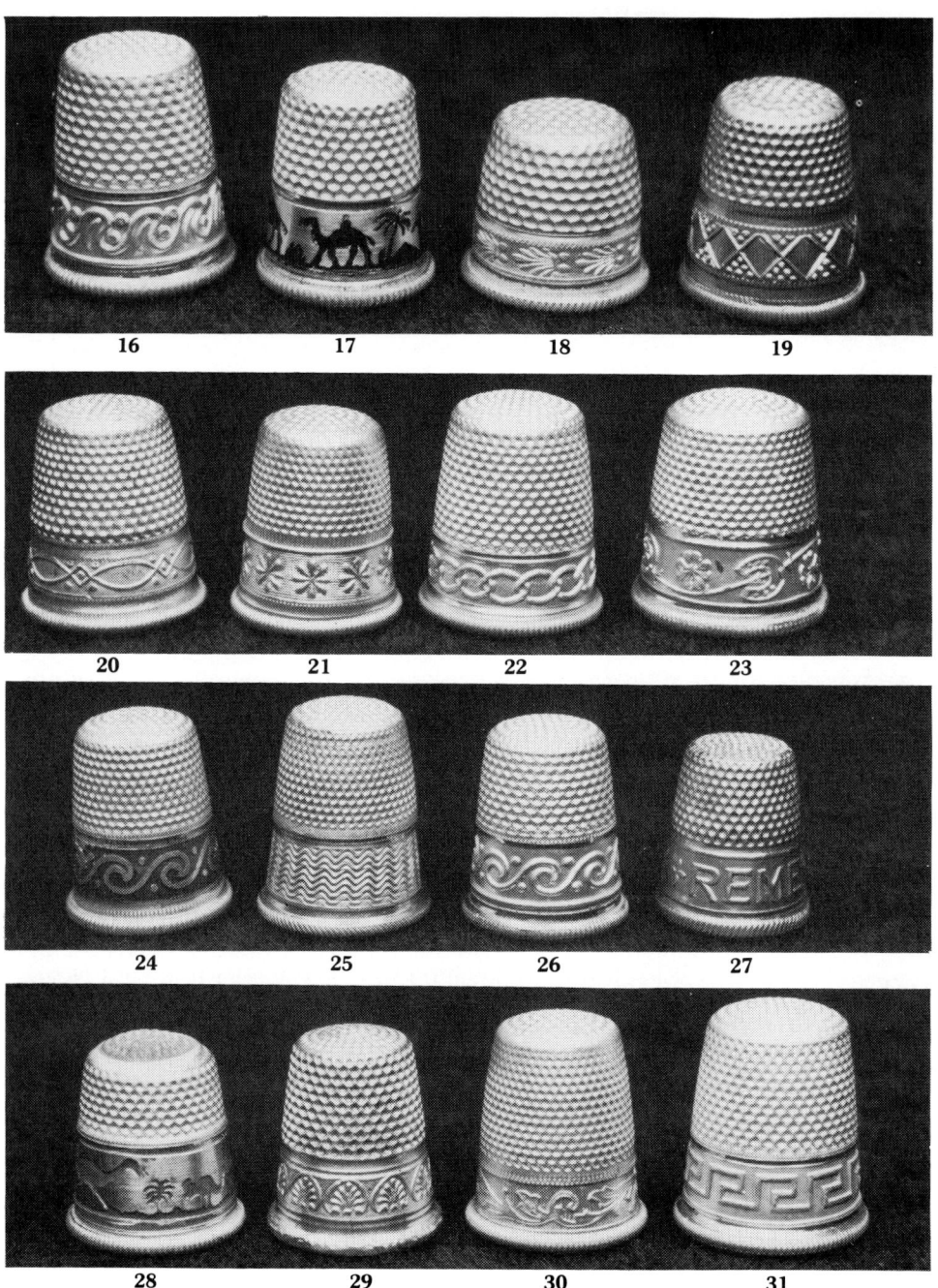

The Thimbles of Colonial America

    32   33   34   35

American Thimbles — Most of the early brass and silver thimbles used in the American colonies were imported from Holland and Germany until the late seventeenth century. American-made silver thimbles of this period are very rare, but several examples do exist. In the collection of the Rhode Island Historical Society there is a topless silver thimble with the name "ESTHER WILLITT" inscribed about the band. Two rather crudely executed motifs of a heart and a flower are cut amidst the indentations. It is believed this thimble dates between 1662-1672. Esther's father was the first English mayor of New York. See illustration # 32.

Other 17th century silver thimbles, excavated in colonial sites from Virginia to Massachusetts, reveal a strong Dutch influence. These thimbles usually have motifs such as two cherubs holding a double heart or a pack of dogs running about the band. These thimbles, of Dutch origin, were imported to the colonies; many examples have also been found in Europe. For examples see illustrations # 34 and 35.

The 18th century found the American silversmith, with his simple thimble stamps, producing many custom-made gold and silver thimbles on demand for those who could afford such luxuries. An example of one of these early gold thimbles is on exhibit in the Yale University Art Museum. Created by Jacob Hurd of Boston, about 1735, this ¾-inch-high thimble is decorated with a chased acanthus leaf design and hand-punched indentations. See illustration # 33.

However, most of the ornate silver and practically all the brass thimbles, by this time, were being imported from England. This change was due to the British conquest of the Swedish, Dutch, and German settlements along the North Atlantic coast. The British prohibited the newly conquered colonist from trading with their mother countries, although smuggled goods often were slipped past British customs officials.

Thus, the English thimble factories in Birmingham became the chief source of American working thimbles during most of the 18th century. This English monopoly was not broken until the American victory in the War for Independence. The opportunity now existed for a home-based thimble industry to get established.

In 1794, Benjamin Halstead, an enterprising New York silversmith of Dutch descent, founded the first American thimble factory. His bold ad below states his aim very clearly. For an example of one of his silver topless thimbles see illustration # 498.

Benjamin Halsted Thimble Manufactory

Benjamin Halsted Respectfully informs his Friends and the Public in general, that he still continues carrying on the Gold and Silversmith business No. 67 Broad Street; he has brought the manufacture of Gold, Silver and Pinchbeck Thimbles with steel top to great perfection and thinks he could make a sufficient quantity to supply the United States. Citizens consider your interest and encourage American Manufactures. Those imported are of the Slightest kind, I will engage that one of mine, will do more service than 3 of them, and I know by experience, that imported ones of the quality of mine cost 18 shillings per doz. and could not be sold by 25 percent, as low as mine. Every dealer in this article will soon find the advantage of keeping **Halsted**'s Thimbles, and have the satisfaction of knowing that he does his customers justice.

Within forty years, protected by high tariffs placed on British goods, American thimble factories had taken root in New York, Providence, Long Meadow, Huntington, Springfield, Newark, and Philadelphia.

These early manufacturers produced millions of thimbles in gold, silver, brass, and steel for a fast-growing nation just beginning to feel its great potential. These factories were founded by men of vision and ingenuity, with names like: Ezra Prime, Jacob Colton, William Coomes, Jabez Gorham, Dimond Chandler, James Peters, Hugh McDougall, Edward Ketcham and George Simons.

The second half of the 19th century became a "Golden Age" for American thimble manufacturers. Skilled designers working in precious metals, rare gems and brilliant enamels, created a range of exquisite pieces never to be surpassed.

The demand for thimbles by the late 19th century continued to grow as many manufacturing jewelers added thimbles to their lines.

Companies such as H. Muhr & Sons, Stern Brothers & Co., Unger Brothers, Webster & Co., Waithe-Thresher, Barker Mfg. Co., Burbank Mfg. Co., Thomas Brogan Co., A.T. Gunner Mfg. Co., LaPierre Mfg. Co., S. Cottle Co., Carter Sloan & Co., Aiken-Lambert Co., and Smith Lesquereux & Co., added a host of new patterns and materials for the thimble-buying public.

American thimblemakers, by 1900, had reached their high-water mark. Thimbles of all the traditional metals were in full production, plus many new materials had been introduced. Goodyear was selling hard-rubber thimbles and Ketcham & McDougall introduced the new metal, "aluminum," to thimble making. See page # 289.

Other companies made thimbles from oriede, celluloid, bakelite, gutta percha and shell. Several manufacturers even began to produce fine porcelain thimbles with hand-painted borders like their English cousins.

But just as the gray stillness of winter follows autumn's final burst of colorful splendor, so it was with the American thimblers. The turn of the century was their magnificent swan song. Within thirty years, the thimble, as an object of art and utility, was becoming a quaint little tool of yesteryear. By the late 1950s only one small company, Simons Brothers, and its owner, Katherine Simons, still tried to keep the traditional skills alive. Read *The Family Simons* for more information.

Today, with the new interest in thimble collecting, many companies manufacture thimbles. Also, a host of artisans have created a wide range of new styles and materials, and once again, unique thimbles are being designed by American thimblers.

American Indian Thimbles

36   37   38   39

American Indian Thimbles — The American Indians of the southwest have a tradition of fine silversmithing and about 90 years ago began to make thimbles for trade and later as souvenirs. The Navajo, Hopi, Taos, Suni and other tribes have created exquisite designs in collector thimbles. Most of their thimbles are made in two pieces, hand chased with Indian motifs and sometimes bejeweled with stones, usually turquoise. Many have the silversmith's sign and his initials plus a "Masa Mark", the Indian equivalent to a British hallmark, stamped inside the bands of their thimbles. See above

Amethyst — A hard semi-precious stone of the quartz family. Colors vary from pale violet to a deep wine purple. Found inset on many German stone top thimbles and as jewels around base.

Anchor Mark — On American gold and silver thimbles, this mark usually means Stern Bros., or Goldsmith Stern Co., circa 1890-1930. See listing on Thimble Marks.

Barker Manufacturing Co. used it to mark their gold-filled thimbles. On English thimbles, the anchor is the assay mark for Birmingham gold & silver.

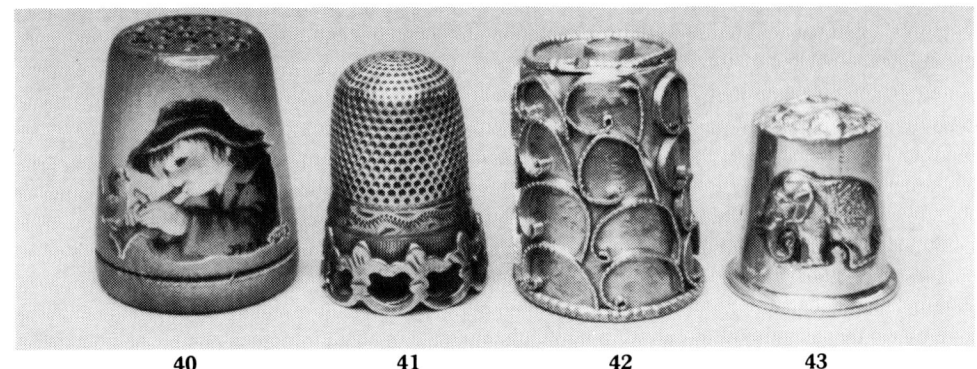

40　　　　　　41　　　　　　42　　　　　　43

Andere, Mary — English author of *Old Needlework Boxes and Tools*. Drake Publishers Ltd., New York 1971. A book on the history of sewing tools, with chapter on thimbles.

Andersen, David — Norwegian maker of brilliantly hand enameled sterling silver and vermeil thimbles. The firm has been in business in Oslo since 1876. Their trademark is a scale inside a circle with a crown on top. See # 238.

Anodized — A process where the upper part of the knurling on a silver thimble has been "blanched" to prevent oxidation or tarnish. Thus the thimble has a "blanch" or whitish color.

Anri — A woodcarving company founded by Anton Riffeser in 1912. The name ANRI is the first two letters of Anton's first and last name. The carving is done in the village of St. Christina in the Dolomite Mountains of Italy. They have produced a series of "Tyrolean-style" wooden thimbles. One current series, by the Spanish artist Juan Ferrandiz Castells, depicts children. Anri thimbles also have colorful alpine flowers, birds and animal motifs. See #40

Ansonia Novelty Co. — American thimble manufacturer in Ansonia, Conn. They made a line of nickel-silver, brass, goldine, enameled-band aluminum and steel thimbles during the first quarter of the 20th century. Ansonian thimbles are not marked and many of the nickel-silver with decorated bands are sold today as silver to the uneducated collector.

Advertising on display cards show Ansonia thimbles were sold under "Sewing Girl," "Blue Bell," "Leading Lady" and "America" brand names. They also made a full line of open-top tailors' thimbles in sizes 9-16.

Antique and Unusual Thimbles — A book written by Jo Anne Rath, and published by A. S. Barnes Co. in 1979. An early book on thimbles which gives a reader an introduction into the wonderful world of collector's thimbles. Lots of pictures in color and black and white; also contains rare photos of thimbles in the Simons Family Collection. 172 pages. Now out of print.

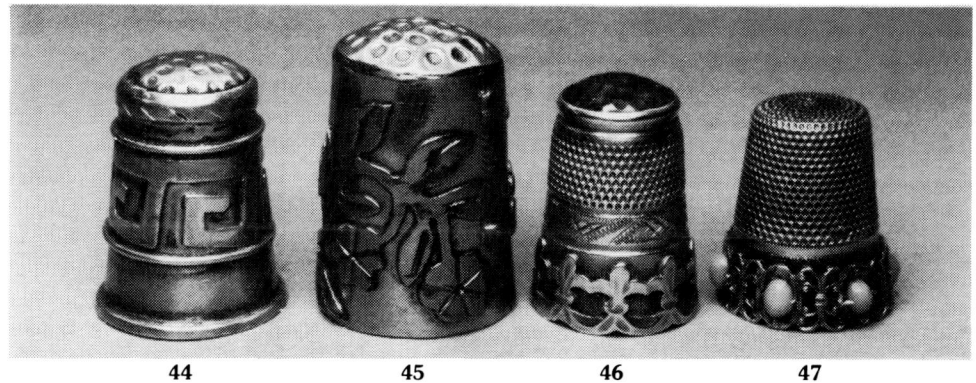

44   45   46   47

Apex — A term used for over a century to describe the "top" of a thimble. The term "under the apex" means: inside, under the top. Many American thimbles are stamped with the maker's mark "under the apex."

Applied Band — A process in which the band is made separately and then soldered to the upper part of the thimble. Thus a gold band can be "applied" to a silver thimble or a detailed decoration can be die cut or stamped and applied to the top part of a thimble. See chapter on "How Thimbles Are Made" and illustrations #47.

Applied Motif — Any emblem or design that is glued, soldered or applied to a thimble to form a decoration. See illustration #44.

Applied Wirework — A process of using fine wire to create a design on the side of a thimble; a very popular technique in Nepal and Mexico. See illustrations on page 64.

Appliqued — A process whereby a design or motif is cut from a thin sheet of metal and soldered to a thimble, thus giving the decoration a low relief look. Also called "cut cardwork." See thimble 45.

Aquamarine — A hard semi-precious stone, pale green to blue-green. It is found on some German stone top thimbles and is sometimes used as jewels about the band on a thimble. See thimble 47.

Arizona Thimblers — A regional group founded at the home of Emily Capin on Feb. 28, 1982. The club provides "an informal exchange of thimble information among friends." They meet every three months.

Ashleydale — English china company in Stoke-on-Trent, Staffordshire; a small firm which is currently making bone china thimbles. Thimbles are marked inside with their name.

Asphaltum Thimbles — Souvenir thimbles were made from this "tar-like" material and sold to tourists visiting the Holy Land around the turn of the century. Asphaltum is abundant around the Dead Sea area.

The Thimbles of Austria

48 49
19th Century

50
18th Century

51 52 53 54

55

The Nadelburg factory outside Vienna, Austria

Atlantic Cable Thimble — An historic silver thimble belonging to Miss Emily Fitzgerald, the daughter of the Knight of Kerry, now on display in the Science Museum in London, England. See thimble # 41.

This tiny thimble borrowed from Miss Fitzgerald was used during the testing of the first Trans-Atlantic Cable in 1856. After several failed attempts, Mr. Latimer Clark borrowed the thimble and, by adding a small amount of acid and zinc, created a miniature electric cell. This thimble cell generated enough current to send a signal across the 3,700 mile-long Atlantic Cable in a second!

The maker of the original Atlantic Cable thimble is unknown, but several variations made by James Fenton are known. The rarest has the applied scallops pierced as seen in illustration # 289.

Austrian Thimbles — Austria has a long tradition of fine gold and silver thimbles. The 18th and 19th century pieces are ornate and very distinctive. See opposite page. In 1757, the Empress Maria Theresa encouraged the promotion of many new industries; one was the manufacturing of thimbles. German thimblemakers came to Austria and began the factory complex which came to be called "Nadelburg." Over the next two centuries, millions of gold, silver and base-metal thimbles were made. Many of the Arabic inscribed silver thimbles found in Turkey and the Near East bazaars today are from this famous factory near Vienna.

Today Austria exports a wide range of collector's thimbles. Brass thimbles with applied petit point or counted cross stitch work on the bands; thimbles with scenes or flowers as below, and thimbles with brilliant, colored enamels, decorated in folk art motifs. See thimbles # 51 to 54.

Aynsley — Modern English china manufacturer known to have made bone china thimbles. Their name is well marked inside.

The Thimbles of Austria

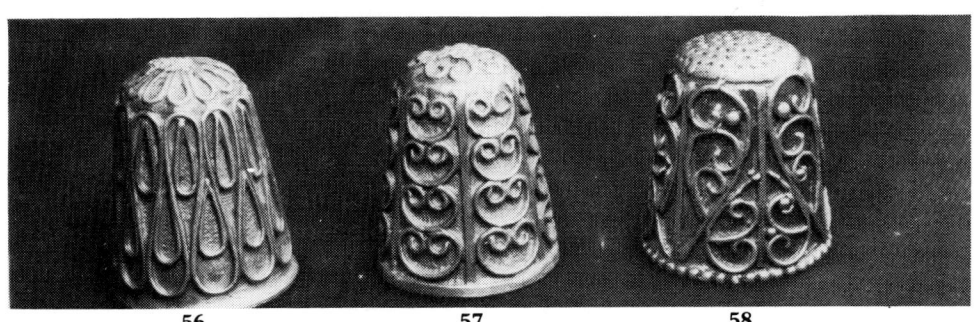

56   57   58

An Old Persian Silver "Angushtahne"
Courtesy, Pat Bordi, Photo by Walt Arrufat

59

60   61   62   63

ℬ

Baird-North Co. — American catalog house from Providence, Rhode Island. They listed thimbles from several American thimblemakers in their early 20th century catalogs.

Bakelite — The tradename of the General Bakelite Company for a cast resin plastic developed in 1909 by L. H. Baekeland; used in the making of thimbles from 1914 to the 1950s. When a hot needle is placed on a bakelite thimble, a "phenol" smell is produced and the needle should penetrate the material. Some Bakelite thimbles look like polished ebony or Irish bog oak thimbles; however, they would not pass the hot needle test. The company was merged into the Union Carbide Corp. in 1939.

Bamboo — A wood used in the Far East to carve or lathe into souvenir thimbles. Many are then painted with birds, flowers or animals. See illustration: # 60.

Band — The area usually just below the indentations and above the rim of a thimble; also known as the "border."

Bareuther-Waldsassen — West German porcelain firm known to have made thimbles. Their name is usually marked inside. For example see thimble # 805.

Bare Crown — A term meaning no indentations were made on top of the thimble. Many older thimbles, pre-1500, have bare crowns due to the practice of using the side only. See page 33.

Barker Mfg. Co. — American company founded in 1860 in Providence, Rhode Island, known to have made thimbles in the late 19th century. The company sold out to Waite-Thresher, who sold the dies to Simons Brothers in the late 1920s. Their trademark was a five-pointed star, later adopted by Waite-Thresher who added a thimble motif.

Basalt — A black, unglazed vitreous fine stoneware developed by Josiah Wedgwood in 1766. Four basalt thimbles were made by the Wedgwood Company in 1980 with gilt cameos applied. See illustration # 62.

Bas-Relief — A decoration in which the main design stands out slightly from the background. See illustration # 63.

Bass, E. & J. — American thimble manufacturer from New York who made thimbles from 1890 till 1920. They used a "B" inside a diamond as their trademark. See "Thimble Marks."

Bateman, Hester — English silversmith known to have made thimbles in the late 18th century. She was from a celebrated family of silversmiths.

Battersea Pewter Ltd. — American pewter company in Colorado which began in 1978 to make a unique line of thimbles in high relief. Their name is pressed into the bottom edge of their thimbles. See thimble # 63.

Battersea Thimbles — The enameling of thimbles began in England during the latter half of the 18th century in South Staffordshire and in the Birmingham areas. One firm, founded by Steven Jensen in Battersea, London, produced works of such high quality that the whole industry is now often erroneously referred to as "Battersea Enamel Ware." See page 225.

Baum, Ruth — English entrepreneur and publisher of the "Shopping Service," a mail order catalog with thimbles a speciality; now out of business.

Bay Area Thimble Society — A San Francisco area thimble group founded in 1978, conceived by Barbara Lockwood, and named by Grace Blackburn. Virginia Weaver was the first president. The group hosted a mini-convention in the fall of 1985.

Beading — A basic design with a row, or rows, of half-round "beads" around bands and/or rims of thimbles. See illustration # 1008.

Beehive — A shape common on older thimbles. See page 28.

Belford, Rozsi R. — Romanian-American entrepreneur who started "The Sewing Corner" mail order catalog in 1970. This was one of the earliest catalogs in the country offering quality and hard-to-find European and American thimbles to collectors.

In 1975, *Collector's Circle* continued this practice and added the *Gazette* in 1976. The *Gazette,* published by Mrs. Belford, is a "member only" thimble magazine for collectors. The business closed in 1983.

Belleek Thimbles — An Irish porcelain manufacturing company founded in 1857 near the village of Belleek. Their thimbles are made of a unique porcelain known as Parian and are now available to collectors. See thimble 877.

Bernardaud & Cie. — One of France's largest porcelain makers in Limoges. Bernardaud bought out the Delinerer Co. in 1910. Delinerer dates back to 1863. The Bernardaud porcelain is fired very high to produce the hardest possible glaze, which is thin, translucent and pure white. Its thimbles are marked: B&C°LIMOGES, FRANCE.

Bertrand, Christine — Dutch-American collector and author of *Brass Thimbles*, a 72-page booklet which covers, in depth, the world of brass thimbles.

Betensley, Bertha — Author of the booklet *52 Thimble Patents*. The book features unusual patents on attempts to improve the thimble for the home sewer. Some must be read with humor, such as the thimble to help cure rheumatism, and some try to overcome basic shortcomings in thimble design. One interesting section is on thimbles with cutters, pullers, and other gadgets. Booklet is self published by Ms. Betensley, Westville, Indiana.

Bilston & Battersea — A tradename now being used by Halcyon Days, a British firm making hand-painted enameled copper thimbles; also a generic term for English thimbles made in the same way during the 18th and early 19th centuries. See "South Staffordshire" Thimbles. See thimble #1067.

Bing & Grondahl — A Danish porcelain thimble manufacturer in Copenhagen, famous for its shaded blue underglaze. Thimbles are marked inside with a B&G. See thimble 808.

Biscuit — A British term meaning a cream or ivory colored background on porcelain. "Biscuit Worcester" are the "blush ivory" or "stained ivory" thimbles made by Royal Worcester from about 1890 to 1910.

Biske, Bernadine — American thimble collector and founder of the "Great Lakes Thimblers" in 1982. She is also a thimble artist and operates the mail order firm of "Biske's Bisque." Her hand-painted porcelain thimbles are signed BB. Her fired-decal pieces are marked with two script B's back to back.

Bisque — A porcelain or ceramic thimble that has been fired and decorated without a glaze to create a dull eggshell surface.

Blackburn, Grace — American thimble collector, keynote speaker at thimble meetings and author of many articles on thimbles and scissors; editor of the "Thimble Collector's Directory."

Blomsterwall, Johann — Swedish goldsmith known to have made thimbles with cornelian tops in the first half of the 19th century.

Blush Ivory — A Royal Worcester term for "biscuit," an ivory stained porcelain used to make thimbles in the late 19th century.

Boar's Head — A French hallmark, usually stamped between the indentations and the border area of the thimble. The boar's head means it was made in Paris of .925 sterling silver or better.

Thimbles of Bone

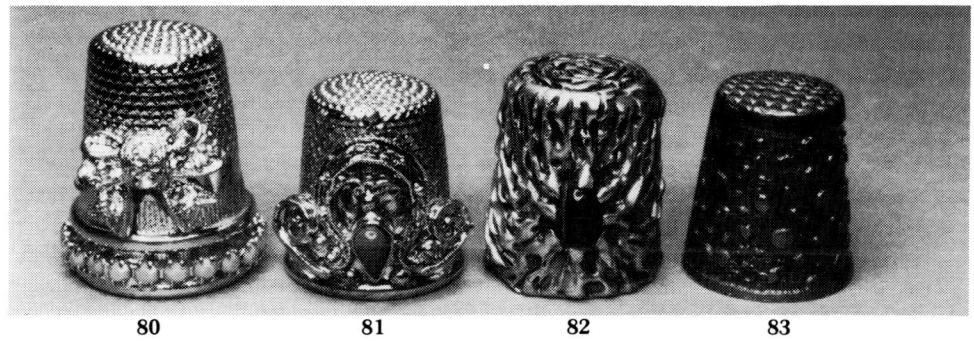

80　　　　　　81　　　　　　82　　　　　　83

Bog Oak — A black, semi-petrified wood found in the Irish bogs; a very hard and strong wood often mistaken for ebony. It may be carved or turned. Old 19th century ones are rare. Bog oak thimbles are still being made. See thimble # 1447.

Bone China — A ceramic paste developed by Josiah Spode in the 1790s. It is a combination of fine stoneware and earthenware, made translucent by the addition of calcined bone. Bone china is usually 6 parts bone ash, 4 parts china stone and $3\frac{1}{2}$ parts china clay. This paste is the most common one used in the British Isles.

Bone Thimbles — Thimbles of bone date back to ancient times. Old bone thimbles are rarer than ivory thimbles. Bone is hard to distinguish from ivory; ivory is more closely grained while bone has tiny tubes throughout its structure. When cut crossways, the tubes are exposed allowing dirt to fill in, creating the illusion of tiny dots in the surface.

Bone splits easily and sometimes a metal disc is fitted into the top to take the wear of the needle. See page 58.

Bonewell, Roger — American artisan in Leadville, Colorado who has designed a line of elegant brass thimbles from cartridge cases. Many have semi-precious stone or dinosaur bone tops. Using fine brass wire applied with gold solder, he has achieved some beautiful motifs. See thimble # 101.

Book of a Thousand Thimbles — Written by Myrtle Lundquist, an avid collector, teacher and writer, the first book ever published (1970) entirely about thimbles. The book is now into its 8th printing by Wallace-Homestead Co., Des Moines, Iowa.

Border — A term used by thimble collectors to indicate the band; the area above the rim and below the indentations.

Boutique Thimbles — A term for describing inexpensive gold or silver colored thimbles, usually with fake stones or applied motifs. Many are made in Spain. See thimbles # 80 and 81.

Bowen, Wendy — Gifted china painter whose work graces both Hurley and Royal Worcester thimbles. In England, her maiden name was Clarke.

Thimbles of Brass

Braatz Thimbles — A series of hand-carved and hand-painted artisan thimbles made by Gary and Trish Braatz. Each thimble is made in birchwood and is signed and dated.

Brand, Eleanor & David — American craftsmen of gold, silver, and metal thimbles. They use many techniques to make thimbles having unique designs. Their thimbles are marked inside the rim ECB and DB. See illustration #82.

Brass — A metal used in making thimbles since the late Middle Ages. Brass has been the basic "workhorse" material for thimbles since the 16th century. Many old ones have ornate, decorated borders and may be stamped with endearing words such as "Friendship," "Remember" and "Farewell." Brass is a generic term for a group of alloys made of copper and zinc. The more zinc, the yellower the color; the more copper, the redder. See page 60.

Brass Thimbles — A 72-page booklet, written by Christine Bertrand and published by T.C.I. in 1986. The work is a good in-depth study of brass thimbles with photographs.

Brittania Silver — A British term for silver which is .9584 pure. This has less alloy than sterling, which is 925/1000 pure silver.

Bright-Cut — A method of engraving with a special beveled tool, leaving a wider cut in the metal to better reflect the light.

Brogan, Thomas F. — American silversmith company doing business from 1896 to 1930 in New York City. They marked their silver thimbles with a five-pointed star under the apex. Gold thimbles are marked with a star + 14kt.

Bronze — An alloy of copper and tin used by our earliest thimblemakers; usually cast in molds using the lost wax method. See page 26.

Brown & Bigelow — An advertising company in St. Paul, Minnesota which sold millions of plastic advertising thimbles in the first half of the 20th century. Many were marked B&B under the apex.

Bulletin — The first official publication of Thimble Collectors International. It was first edited by Lahoma Goldsmith of Oklahoma. The first Bulletin was published after the formation of T.C.I. in 1978, and remains their official publication. The second editor was Joan Geertz of Texas. The Bulletin is presently edited by Debbie Fuller of Kentucky.

Burbank Mfg. Co. — American firm in Springfield, Massachusetts. They advertised in the 1883 *Jewelers Circular,* "manufacturers of thimbles, gold, silver, steel, rubber and shell."

Byzantine Thimbles — The earliest known thimbles found in Europe are attributed to the Byzantine cities of Corinth, Ephesus, and Antioch and date from the 9th to 12th century. See pages 24 and 26.

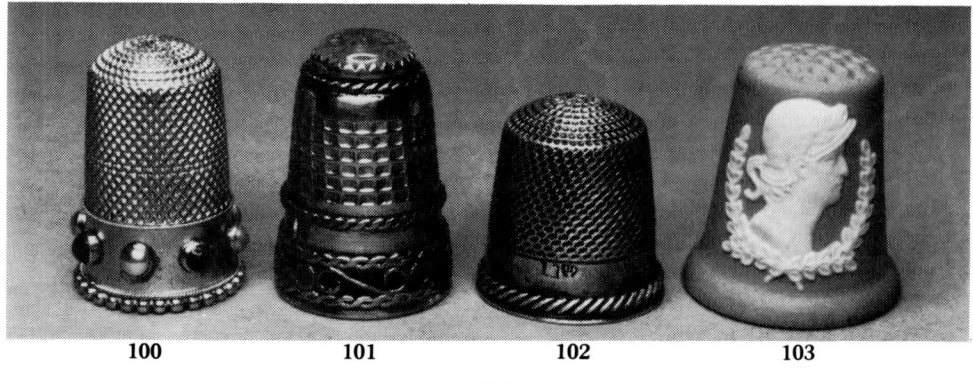

100   101   102   103

C

Cabachon — A term describing a gemstone which is smooth, without facets; usually found in the lower band of a thimble. See illustration #100.

Cabin Fever Creations — An artisan workshop in Leadville, Colorado. They are making high quality ornate brass thimbles with gem stone tops. See "Thimble Sources" and illustration #101.

Cable — A term describing a rope-like motif usually around the rim of a thimble. See illustration: #102.

Calhouns Collector's Society — A sales organization which sold a limited edition set of thimbles designed by Wedgwood depicting the Kings and Queens of England. The thimbles were made of blue jasperware with a white cameo of the monarch on its side. They were issued one per month. See illustration #103.

Cameo Thimbles — The art of carving cameos began in Italy during the Renaissance. The most common are carved from shells which consist of a dark and a light layer. The cameo in most thimbles is carved and then applied to the side. Cameo thimbles have been made for over 200 years in Torre del Greco, near Naples. Old cameo thimbles are rare. See illustration #104.

Campaign Thimbles — A special category of advertising thimbles which promote a political candidate running for public office. Would-be Presidents, Senators, Mayors, down to dog catcher have used these thimbles to try to get elected. They are usually plastic, but older ones are sometimes found in aluminum.

104   105   106   107

Capital Area Thimbles — A Washington, D.C. area thimble group formed in 1984 by Eva Walker to promote an interest in thimbles.

Capo de Monte — Italian ceramic firm which has a long history of fine designs in porcelain and earthenware. During the 1970s they made a series of thimbles, hand-painted in a baroque style.

Carradus Thimbles — A beautiful series of wooden thimble shapes, lathed by LeRoy Carradus, hand-painted by Donna, and carved by Mary Ann, his daughters.

Using rare woods and unique motifs, the Carradus family has created a wide array of beautiful thimbles for collectors.

Carter-Sloan & Co. — An American manufacturing jeweler in New York and Newark, New Jersey. Their trademark was an arrow head with the letter C within. They made only gold thimbles during the late 19th century. See ad on page 283.

Cartouche — A design, shield-like motif to frame initials, dates or inscriptions on the side of a thimble. See illustration # 106.

Cathedral Thimbles — A pair of silver thimbles designed in the shapes of the domes of St. Peter's in Rome and St. Paul's in London, and made by M.I. Dormon — Brailsford. The first commemorates the visit of Pope John Paul in May 1982 to England and the latter, the wedding of Prince Charles and Lady Diana in July 1981. See illustration # 107.

Caverswall — Modern British porcelain firm currently making a line of fine bone china thimbles, both hand-painted and with fired decals. Thimbles have scenes of hunting, royalty and other typical English panoramas.

Central American Thimbles — This large group of inexpensive thimbles are usually made in Mexico or Guatemala. They are hand-made in many metals: gold, silver, silver-plate, alpacca and copper. They incorporate a wide range of styles and decorative patterns. The use of applied wire to create designs is very common. For illustrations, see pages 64 and 65.

Thimbles of Central America

Thimbles of Central America

The Thimbles of Caverswall

148   149   150   151

Ceramic — A generic word for any item made of baked clay. Porcelain is considered the elite of ceramics; bone china, Parian ware, basalt, ironstone, terra cotta and earthenware are also in the family.

Ceramic Art Co. — Original name of the Lenox China Co. founded by Walter Lenox in 1889. Thimbles were listed among items manufactured. They were not marked.

Ceramic Artistica — A Mexican company making religious themes on bisque porcelain thimbles in bas-relief with hand tinting. Thimbles are marked with two R's, one above the other.

Celluloid — The first of the plastic materials used in thimblemaking. John Hyatt was looking for a substitute for ivory. In 1869, he found that by dissolving cotton in nitric acid and adding camphor oil, he had a plastic material he could mold into almost any shape. It could be tinted to look like ivory, bone or even mother-of-pearl. When touched by a hot needle it has a camphor smell.

Chalmer's Pearl Thimbles — A sterling silver advertising thimble sent to any customer who would send to the Chalmer's Pearl Button Co. five empty button cards and a nickel; the offer was stated on the backs of their carded buttons. Made by Webster. Early 20th century.

Chamberlain, G. S. — American author of "Hand Wrought Silver Thimbles of Guatemala." *Hobbies Magazine,* 1947.

Chamfered — A term for the chipped corners of a rectangle as used around the hallmarks of many English thimbles.

Champleve — A method of enameling metals where the area to be enameled is chiseled out or etched by acid. These created hollow spaces are then filled in with enamel. For example see thimble 168.

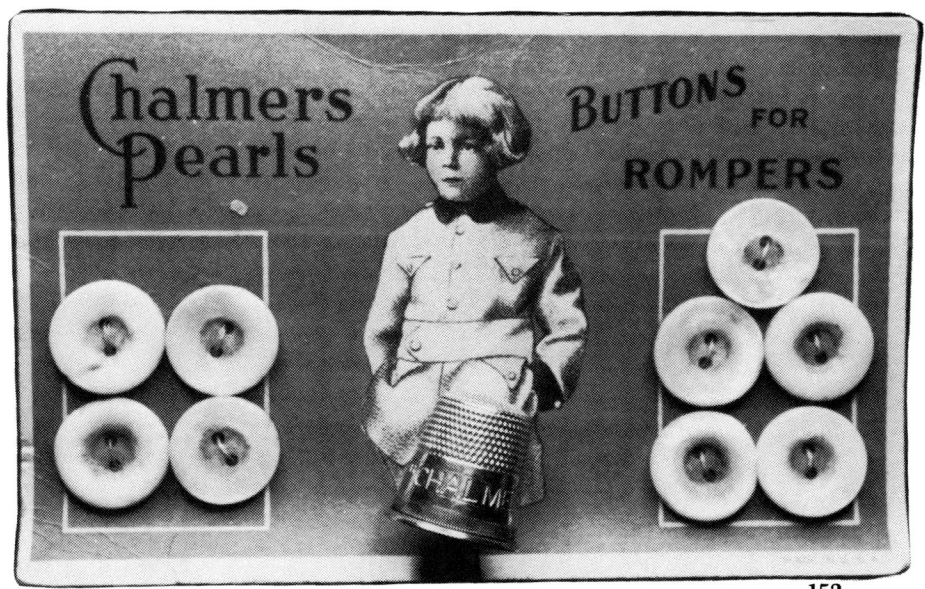

Early Chalmer's button card and thimble

Chandler, Dimond — American silversmith in Longmeadow, Massachusetts. He was known to have made thimbles from 1838 till 1847. He learned his trade in New York. His thimble factory was one of the earliest in New England. There are no known thimble marks. He sold his business to his nephew Jacob Colton in 1847.

Chased — A process in which the craftsman used punches and a hammer to indent the design into the thimble without removing any of the metal.

Cherub Motif — A popular motif used for centuries by many leading thimblemakers. A design using plump children with wings, or like little angels. Also known as putti. Simons, Webster, Stern Bros., Ketcham-McDougall and Goldsmith-Stern all made cherub thimbles. See thimble 170.

Children's Thimbles — Any small thimble which was made for a child's finger. Thimbles ⅜" wide or smaller fall into the area of doll's thimbles.

Chinaware — A generic term for porcelain, bone china, and fine quality stoneware.

Chinese Needle Rings — Ancient term for a tailors'-type sewing ring. This version is not soldered and is adjustable. It usually has some decoration where the two ends meet. See page 22.

Chinoiserie — A style of ornamentation used by artists and craftsmen during the 18th and early 19th centuries; influenced by oriental porcelain and artwork. See thimble # 1429.

Chrysanthemum — A design used as decoration on bands and as the indentation on many English and Dorcas thimbles. See # 172.

Chinese Cinnabar Thimbles

153 154 155

Chinese Cloisonne Thimbles

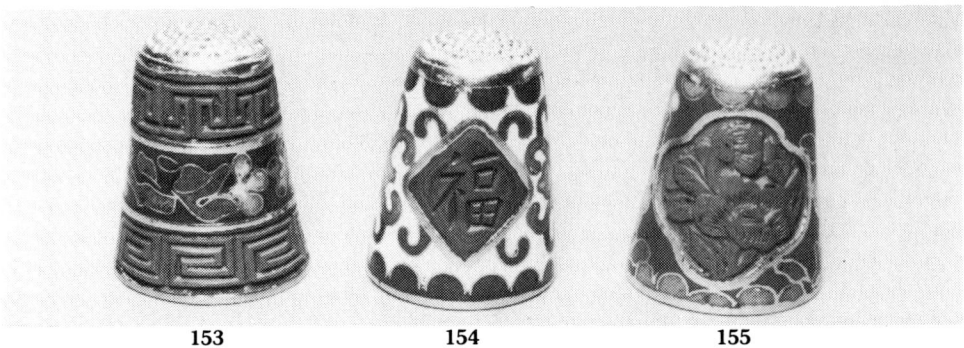

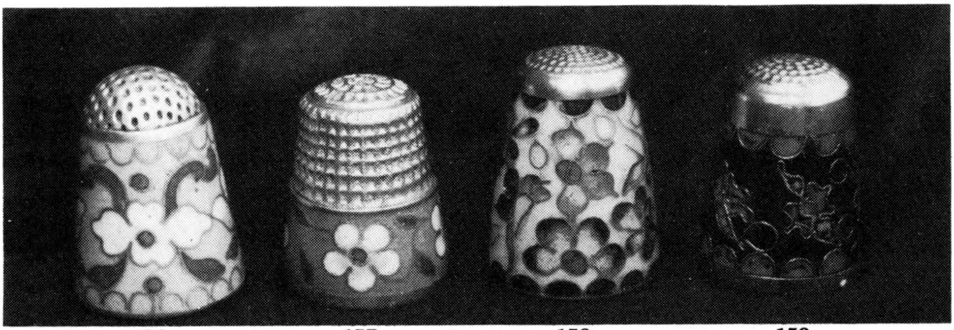

156 157 158 159

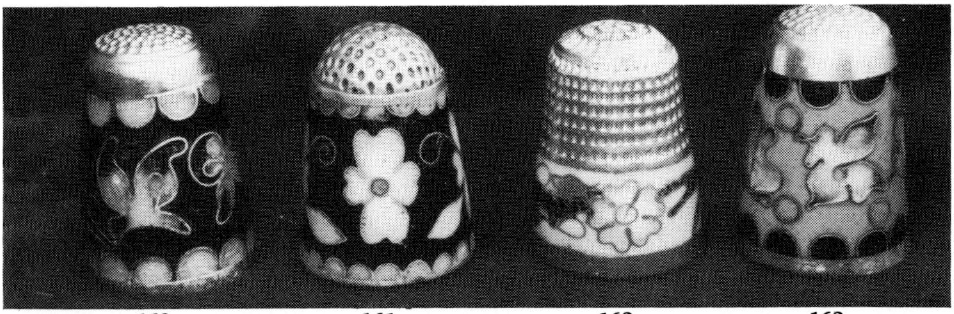

160 161 162 163

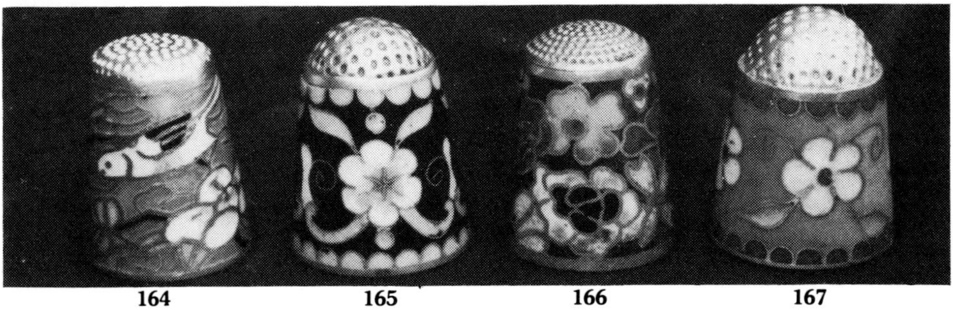

164 165 166 167

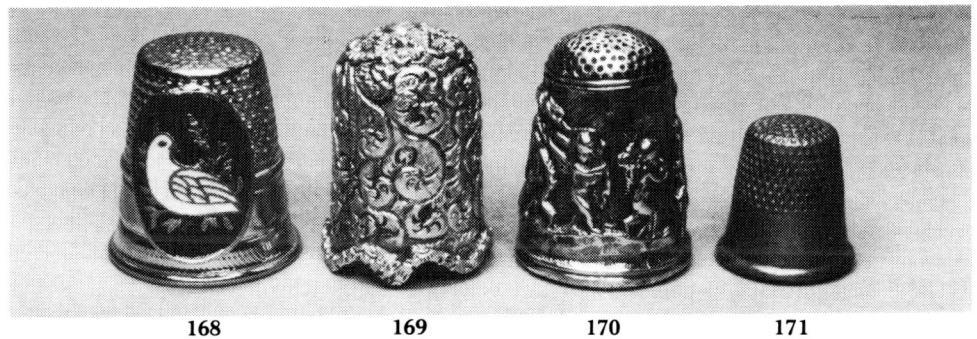

168   169   170   171

Chrysophrase — A light mint-green gem stone sometimes found on many "Italian-style" German thimbles. See # 173.

Cinnabar Thimbles — An Oriental medium made of layers of red satin lacquer. Cinnabar thimbles are often carved with Chinese motifs and symbols. In the past decade, this art form has been incorporated in the cloisonne thimbles of China. For examples see thimbles # 153 to 155.

Cloisonne — An art form introduced to China from Persia in the late 13th century. Cloisonne is created by soldering thin metal strips to a thimble shell in intricate patterns, then hand-enameling the encased areas with bright colors. The brass strips prevent the enamels from melting into each other. Most cloisonne thimbles date from the later half of the 20th century.

Coal — A very hard coal from the deepest layers in the mines, also called jet, sometimes used to decorate thimbles. Like black diamonds, coal jet can be set about the band. In the coal fields of eastern United States, craftsmen carve items from the jet. Illustration # 174 is an example of an entire thimble carved from this medium.

Coalport — British ceramic firm founded by John Rose in 1795 in Coalport. The firm is known to have made thimbles during the 19th century; these were unmarked. Modern Coalport thimbles are fine examples of English bone china and are so marked. See illustration # 814.

172   173   174   175

176 177 178 179

Coin — A word found on old American silver thimbles denoting that the thimble was made of silver melted down from coins or equal to "coin silver"; usually .850 to .900 parts fine silver.

Collector's Circle Gazette — A thimble collector's magazine published by Roz Belford four times a year. It was available to members of the Collector's Circle, a mail order firm now out of business.

Collins, James — English silversmith known to have made thimbles from 1828-1870. His mark, JC, can sometimes be found on thimbles.

Colonial Williamsburg Collection — A unique collection owned by the Colonial Williamsburg Foundation, Williamsburg, Virginia. Many fine old thimbles show the great variety of style and media used in making thimbles. Williamsburg, Virginia. Seen by appointment only.

Colton Co., Jacob — Manufacturing jewelers, successors to Dimond Chandler of Longmeadow, Massachusetts. Founded by Jacob Colton in 1830, they are known to have made "fine thimbles." The company was sold to William W. Coomes about 1864. There are no known thimble marks.

Columbian Exposition Thimble — Two thimbles were made to commemorate this major exposition in Chicago in 1893. One thimble has a scene with beautiful buildings, canals, boats and trees and the words "World's Columbian Exposition 1492-1892." The other has just the words "World's Columbian Exposition 1492-1892" in a gothic style about the band. Made by Simons, the originals do not have Simons' mark inside. Restrikes have the large Simons mark inside the apex. See thimble 175.

Commemorative — Any thimble which was issued for a specific event, and having that event stated or illustrated on the thimble. The Paris Exposition of 1889 is an example. See thimble # 176.

Connecticut Nutmeg Thimblers — A social and educational thimble club founded in 1978 by Natalie Borg, Lois Fisher, Dickey Everson, and Eileen Schwall for collectors in the New England area.

      180   181   182   183

Connemara Marble — A greenish marble found in Ireland used to inset in the tops of thimbles.

Conner, Jeannine — An American thimble collector and founding member of the Philadelphia Thimble Society in 1979; co-author of "Thimble Language," a glossary of thimble terms.

Continental Silver — A general term referring to .800 silver. This is less silver than the .925 sterling, but many continental thimblemakers believe the .800 silver thimbles are more durable.

Coomes Co. W.W. — American thimble manufacturer, successors to Jacob Colton Co. of Longmeadow, Massachusetts in early 1860's. Advertised in the *Jeweler Circular and Horological Review* July, 1888 as "Manufacturers of gold & silver thimbles in every style." No known thimble marks. Out of business due to death of William Coomes in 1893. Company employed 14 men and women. See page 289.

Copper — A basic metal sometimes used in its pure form as a material for thimbles. Old copper thimbles are rare due to the softness of the metal. Copper thimbles were also worn as cure-alls for medical ailments.

Coral — The colorful, rock hard, remains of ancient sea creatures. Pink and red coral have been used in thimbles as decorative stones about the base and sometimes an entire thimble has been carved from it. In the Orient, black coral is inlaid in strips on a metal thimble base and scrimshawed with flowers. See illustration # 997.

Cornelian — A reddish, semi-precious gem stone used on some German stone top thimbles.

Corning Glass Thimble — A prototype thimble was developed by the Corning Glass Works in Corning, New York, due to the shortage of metal needed for defense during the Second World War. The thimbles were made in light blue and clear pyrex. Some were marked PYREX or Corning Glass. The thimbles are rare and were never sold commercially. See illustration #180.

English Commemorative Thimbles

184   185   186

Elizabeth II's Coronation Thimbles, 1953
Center: Victoria and Albert's Wedding Commemorative

187

Queen Victoria's 60th Jubilee, 1837-1897 — 3 views

188   189

George V's Coronation, 1911

Corozo Nut Thimbles and Cases

Coronation Thimbles — A special souvenir commemorative thimble made to record the coronation of a King or Queen. There are many English and European thimbles in this category. See thimble # 189.

Corozo Nut Thimbles — A South American nut also known as Vegetable Ivory. Thimbles carved out of this material are often believed to be ivory. A great many were carved in England in the late 19th century with matching holders. They are still being made today, but not with the skill of the older ones. See Vegetable Ivory.

S. Cottle Co. — An American manufacturing company based in New York 1865-1915. They marked their thimbles with an "S" intersected with a "C." See "Thimble Marks."

Crab Hallmark — A tiny French mark indicating sterling silver made in the Provinces; usually found where the indentations meet the band of the thimble.

Creamware — Another loose term for biscuit Worcester or "stained ivory" thimbles made by Royal Worcester in porcelain.

Crenellated — A term referring to a type rim which has been cut away, giving the thimble the appearance of standing on short square legs.

Crosby, Lorraine — American thimble collector and editor of the "Thimbleletter," an informal newsletter on thimbles which she started in Oct. 1973 with 15 paid subscribers. Today it is nationwide with over 600 readers. Published bi-monthly, it was the first thimble letter open to all thimble collectors.

Crown — A term for the top or apex of a thimble.

Crown Alloy — A Joseph Muhr brand name for an "oreide type" copper alloy metal used in making thimbles. Three crowns in a line underneath the word were registered as a trademark on July 3, 1888, by Joseph Muhr.

Cut Glass Thimbles

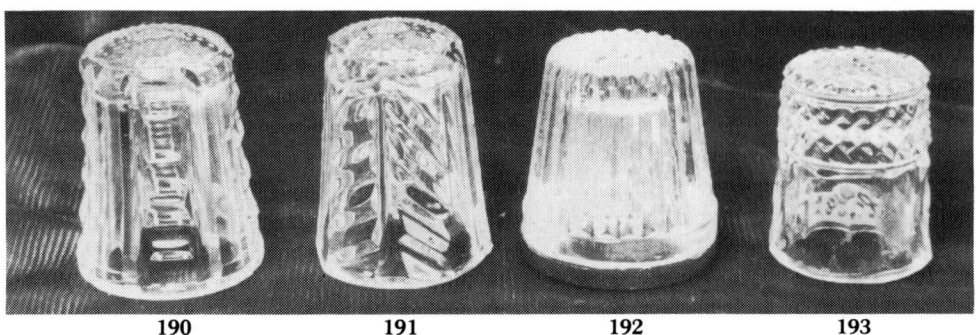

190   191   192   193

Crown Staffordshire — A British pottery firm which traces back to the Churchyard Works in Burslem, Staffordshire, before 1790. The firm underwent several name changes until 1903 when the above name was adopted. In 1973 it became part of the Wedgwood group.

Crummles & Co. — British enameled thimble manufacturer, founded in 1974 in Poole, Dorset. Crummles thimbles are a high quality gilt copper with enameled scenes within cameos, flowers and geometric designs. Their 1981 Royal Wedding commemorative has the feathers and crown of Prince Charles. See thimble 248.

Cuming, Syer — English author of "On Thimbles," *Journal of the British Archaeological Society,* March 1879; an interesting early work on thimbles but one having errors, especially when noting the existence of "Roman" thimbles found at Herculaneum. See page 305.

Cupid — A true cupid should have a bow and arrow as made by Stern Brothers in silver. Most cupid thimbles are really cherub thimbles.

Cupro-Nickel — A generic term for many alloys of copper and nickel; first used in the mid-19th century for making thimbles. Cupro-nickel thimbles look like silver, and some late Victorian ones are marked "Corozo Silver". The British thimble manufacturer, Iles & Co., is known to have made cupro-nickel thimbles as early as the late 19th century. Other firms such as Simons Brothers, Ketchum & McDougall, and Gabler Brothers advertised thimbles in this medium.

Cut Glass Thimbles — Most modern cut glass thimbles are from Germany. The thimbles are pressed against a diamond wheel and the design is intricately etched in. Fine examples of old cut glass thimbles are in the Williamsburg Collection and in the British Museum. See above illustration.

  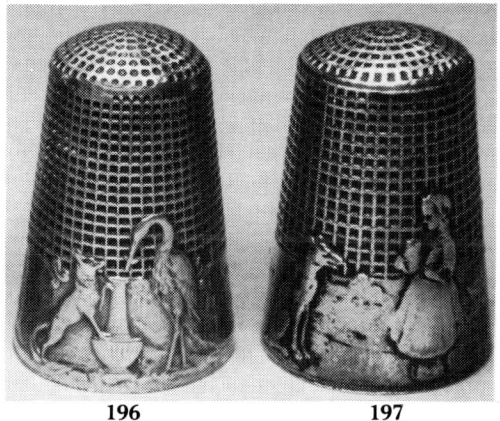

194   195   196   197

D

D'Allemagne, H. R. — French author of *Les Accessories du Coutume et du Mobilier,* which contains a history of thimbles in early France and is illustrated with photos of the famed Albert Figdor Collection.

Damascene — A technique where one metal (silver) is inlayed into another (brass) to form a decoration; an ancient art practiced in China and Egypt. The name comes from the city of Damascus where it spread to Europe in the middle ages. Old Damascene thimbles are rare. Gabler's beautiful gold inlaid thimbles were Damascened in Spain. Modern ones are being made by Reed-Barton. See illustration # 194.

Dames' Thimble — A large heavy thimble used in "thimble-knocking," tapping naughty school children on the head by their teachers.

Damron, Ernest — American craftsman and designer of engraved glass thimbles. Each thimble is hand-blown and signed in limited editions.

David-Andersen Thimble — The Norwegian firm of David-Andersen was founded in Oslo in 1876 by its namesake. They have been making beautiful guilloched thimbles with hand-applied, transparent enamel since the late 19th century. Many of their early pieces have moon-stone tops, while the newer pieces have cross-hatched metal tops. Their mark, a crown above a scale within a circle, may be found in the apex of most of their 20th century thimbles. See thimble # 689.

deBry, Johann Theodor — Famous 16th century German engraver and goldsmith from Frankfort-on-the-Main. His beautiful designs captured classical and religious themes as decorations on thimbles. No examples of his thimbles are known to exist. His designs are illustrated on pages 16 to 18 in Helmut Greif's book *Talks About Thimbles*.

The Five "Dee Sisters" of England

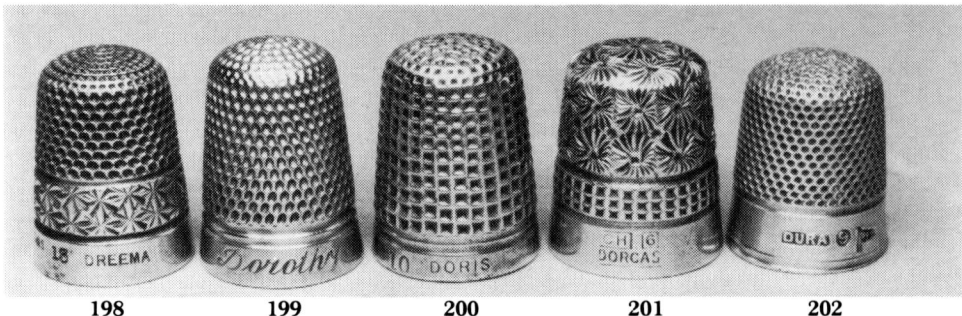

198   199   200   201   202

"**Dee Sisters," The Five** — A nickname given to the five brands of sterling silver-clad, base metal thimbles made in England during the late 19th and early 20th centuries. The first was the "Dorcas," patented by Charles Horner in 1889. Later came the "Dreema," by H. Griffith; the "Dura," by Walker & Hall; "Dorothy," by Charles Iles, and the "Doris," made by Abel Morrell.

de la Fontaine Thimbles — A series of 14 silver thimbles made in France in the late 19th century. Each thimble depicts in bas-relief one of the French poet Jean de la Fontaines' fables. Thimbles were made in .950 silver, lined in 14K gold by the famed French thimblemaker, P. Lenain. The series was reminted in the 1970s from the original dies. See illustration # 195.

Delfi — An Italian firm which makes brass thimbles for the mail order house of Lillian Vernon.

Delft — True delft is a Flemish pottery, popular since the early 17th century. Delft thimbles are usually off-white with blue designs, hand-painted or stenciled on the sides. They run the gamut from coarse, cheap souvenirs to lovely Dutch scenes in brilliant color under a clear glaze.

Demirjian, James (Hagop) — An Armenian silversmith who worked in Israel for many years, now living in California. His beautiful thimbles have been collector's items for a decade. See "Thimble Sources" and the following illustrations.

The Thimbles of James Demirjian

203   204   205   206

Derby — British porcelain company established in 1755 by William Duesbury and Andre Planche, a Dresden-trained porcelain artist. Derby thimbles are rarer than Worcester and most are not marked. Those that are marked, sometimes have a S.H. (Stevenson-Hancock) mark inside. These were made after 1862. Derby thimbles feature insects, birds and flowers hand-painted on white glaze in its celebrated brilliant colors.

DerMarderosian, Evelyn — American thimble collector and chairman of the Philadelphia Thimble Society from 1979 to 1984; chairman of the Philadelphia T.C.I. Convention 1984.

De Vingerhoed — A Dutch mail order and antique firm founded in 1980 by Kay Sullivan. They publish a quarterly catalog on thimbles and related sewing items. They are sponsors of the "Thimble Friends," a social and educational group for European collectors.

Die Stamped — A process invented in the 1780s in England, in which a skilled engraver cuts into a steel slab, a motif or design which can be stamped into a gold or silver band. The band was then applied to a knurled top, thus making fancy thimbles available on a grand scale at greatly reduced cost.

Digitabulum — A Latin name for the thimble. A digitabulist would be a scholar of thimble lore, or a high-brow name for a thimble collector.

Dine-American — An American advertising, publishing and manufacturing company founded by John von Hoelle. The company specializes in publications for the home sewing and art-needlework industry. In 1981, due to the interest of its president, the company began to publish a series of literature for thimble collectors.

The brochure, *Thimble Language*, was published in 1982; using this format, they published the first edition of *Thimble Collector's Encyclopedia* (156 pages) in 1983. The following year they printed the stories of *John Lofting* and *Charles Iles* for Thimble Collector's International. That fall they re-issued an expanded second edition of *Thimble Collector's Encyclopedia* (247 pages).

They also commissioned the translating of Helmut Greif's book, *Talks About Thimbles*, from German into the English language for exclusive distribution worldwide.

In 1985 the company continued to publish three more 24-page booklets in their series on the histories of thimble manufacturers; *The Family Simons: Thimblers to America for 130 years; The Story of Stern Brothers: The American Thimblers Who Added Integrity to our Golden Dreams*, and *Benjamin Halstead: America's First Thimble Manufacturer*.

The company also manufacturers original designed 14K to 18K gold and sterling silver thimbles, many set with precious jewels. They also reproduce classic masterpieces from famous collections for major mail order catalog companies, thimble clubs, and museums around the world. Their thimbles are marked JVH, SU or BFS inside rim.

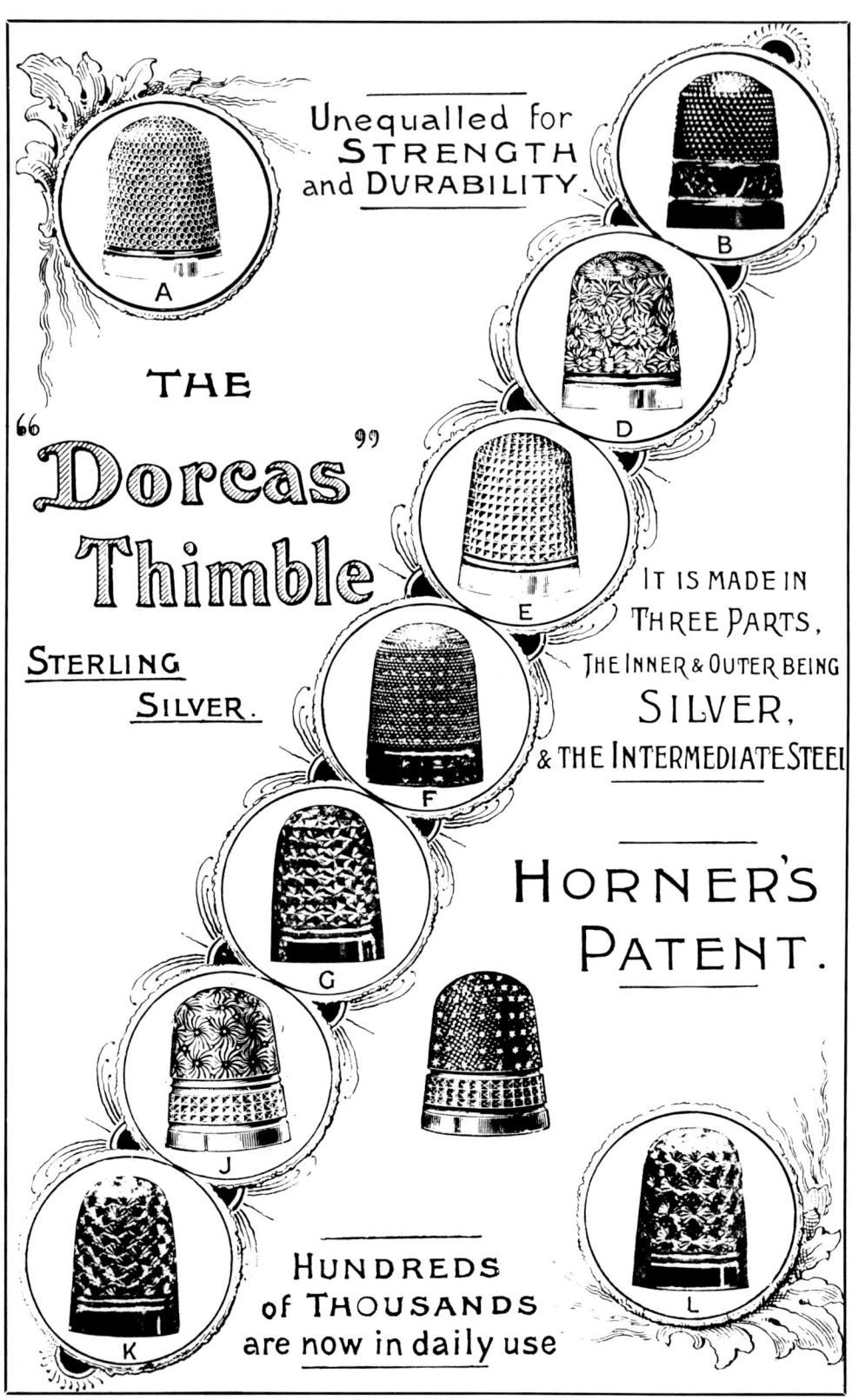

Steel design dies from Ketcham & McDougall

Diri Gold — An alloy of 90% copper and 10% gold, also called Scandinavian gold. Thimbles marked Diri Gold are very hard and take a high shine.

Doll's Thimble — Tiny thimbles usually less than ⅜" in diameter at base. If a loop is on the thimble it would be a charm.

Donohue — American company in Denver, Colorado which makes silver looking pewter thimbles in many bas-relief designs. See thimbles 414-415

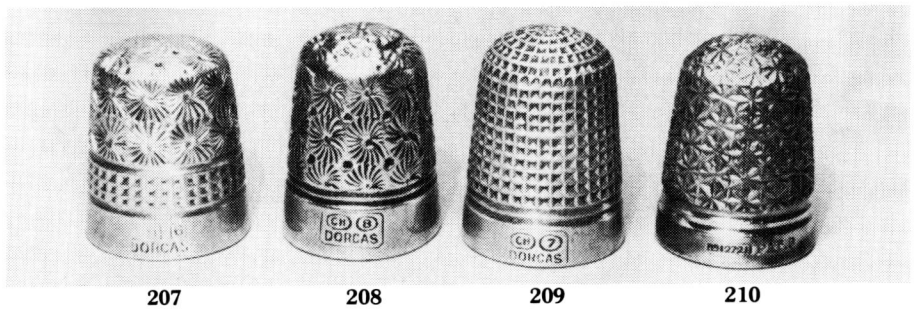

    207   **208**   **209**   **210**

Dorcas — The Dorcas thimble was hailed as the greatest improvement in thimbles since its invention! Patented in 1884 by Charles Horner, this thimble was sold with a life-time guarantee: "Free exchange if rendered useless from any cause whatsoever!" A Dorcas thimble was really three thimbles inside one another. The outer and the inner were made of sterling silver and the middle one of steel. Early Dorcas thimbles were marked PAT., but later ones were marked with C. H. in a circle, the size and the word DORCAS on the band. The Dorcas thimble comes in many designs, some of which were also produced in solid sterling silver and hallmarked. The Dorcas was last made in the 1940s. See Dorcas advertisement and above illustration

English Silver-Clad Steel Thimbles

Dorcas Thimblers — A Florida-based collectors group founded by Gladys Zabriskie to promote interest in thimbles. In 1985 they hosted a mini convention in Sarasota.

Doris Thimbles — A sterling-cased, steel thimble made in England by Iles for the Abel Morrell Company. The Doris is the rarest of the Dorcas copies, which are: Dorcas, Dreema, Dura, and the Dorothy. These five brands are known as the "Five Dee Sisters." See thimbles #219 and 220.

"Dorothy" Thimble — A brand name of the Charles Iles & Co. of Birmingham, England. Dorothy was the name of Charles Iles' daughter. The thimble was made with 4 different designs. A 1921 company catalog states they were "silver cased." See thimble #199.

Dorset Thimble Society — Founded in England by Elaine Gaussen, publisher of an international newsletter called "At Your Fingertips," to promote interest in thimble collecting.

Doskow, Lenore — American silversmith company founded in 1934 by Lenore and David Doskow in New York City, moved to Montrose, N.Y. in 1942. Their thimbles are marked on the band with a Greek ʻΔʼ superimposed over an L. See Thimble #795.

Dreema — Tradename for a steel core thimble made by the British firm of Henry Griffith of Leamington. Steel core, silver thimbles made famous by the DORCAS were the best sellers of their day. See #218.

Dreesmann, Cecile — Dutch-American collector and author of *A Thimble Full,* an 80-page book with many interesting photographs of her unique collection.

Duchess Bone China — A British firm which is making a fine line of fired-decal bone china thimbles. All thimbles are marked inside.

Dumeny, Sieur — French silversmith from Saint Julien-der-Sault; maker of fine steel thimbles of great beauty and style. His name is often found in auction catalogs. Praised by D'Allemagne for his skill.

Dupes — Thimble slang for duplicates, used for trading by thimble collectors.

Dura — Tradename for a steel core sterling thimble like a Dorcas, made by Walker & Hill of Sheffield, England. See thimble #213.

Durand & Co. — American manufacturing jewelers founded by James M. Durant in 1838 in Newark, New Jersey. James retired in 1880 and his son Wallace became president of the 150-employee firm. Wallace designed a unique ball-shaped thimble, Pat. 188,110 in 1877. Their trademark was a D formed from a horseshoe and a nail. The firm was still in business in 1920.

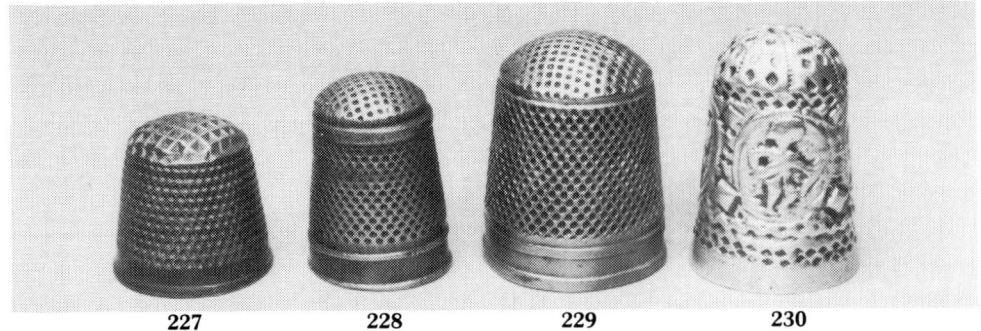

227 228 229 230

Dutch Thimblers — The decline of the city of Nuremberg as Europe's major brass thimble exporter in the mid-17th century gave birth to the golden age of Dutch brass thimbles.

The cities of Schoonhoven, Urtecht, Vianen, and Amsterdam hosted thimble mills operated by close-knit families known as "Vingerhoeds." Each mill was identified by its own marks.

In 1687, the four leading "Vingerhoeds," Willem and Albert van Rijssel, of Amsterdam and Vianen; Cornelis van de Wetering, of De Weerd; and Hendrik Schot-Berent van Bekum, of De Bilt, formed a cartel which produced over three and a half million thimbles a year.

This monopoly set prices, quotas and styles. They discontinued all makers' marks among themselves. It lasted until the 1730s, when English and German production methods once again took over world markets. By the 1770s, Dutch brass thimble supremacy was over, but their silversmiths turned out unique silver thimbles until the early 20th century. See above illustration

Sailor's Palm

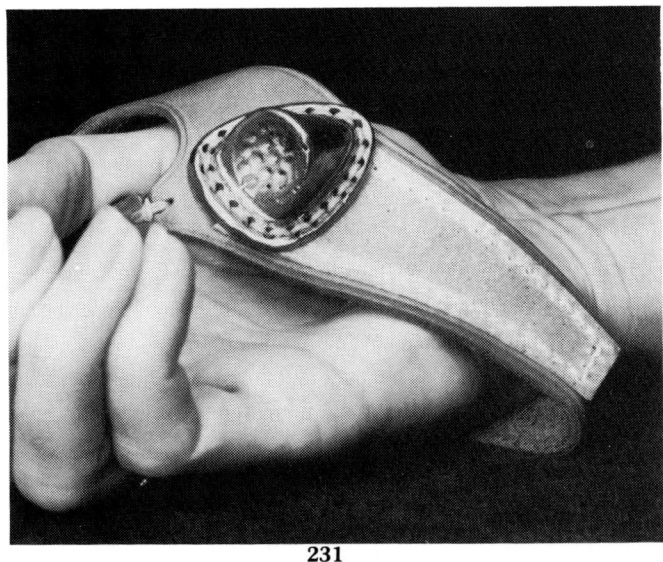

231
Modern form of the ancient Acutrudium

232   233   234   235

E

Eber, Frederich — German thimble manufacturer; last owner of the Lotthammer-Stutzel-Eber line of fine thimblemakers. The firm closed in 1980, the machines were sold to Thorvald Greif.

Ebony — A tropical wood, cut from the center core of the tree; a heavy, deep black wood of great durability. It turns well on lathe and takes a high polish. Ebony thimbles or "Widows Thimbles" were made from Victorian times to the present.

Elfin — An Australian brand name on thimbles made by Price & Jardine Ltd. in Sydney, Australia; early 20th century.

Embossed — A process in which a design or motif is hammered on one side of a metal thimble so as to give it a raised or bas-relief look on the other side and may be done by hand or machine.

Embroidery Thimbles — A term usually describing a thimble with ornately designed indentations going down to the rim. See thimbles # 233 and 234.

Empire State Thimble Collectors — A New York State thimble group founded by Joann Ryan and Marcia Holmes in 1984 to promote research and interest in thimble collecting. Joann Ryan was elected their first president.

Enameled Thimbles — Enamel is ground silica, mixed with mineral colors to form a powder. This powder or frit, when mixed with water, can be painted on a thimble and fired in a kiln. Enamel can be opaque or transparent, depending on the craftsman's end effect. Some of the most beautiful thimbles in the world fall into this category. Russian, Norwegian and Chinese cloisonne thimbles show different enameling techniques. See thimbles on page 84.

Encyclopedia of American Silver Manufacturers — One of the most complete books on American silversmiths and their marks, written by Dorothy Rainwater in 1975.

The Beauty of Enameled Thimbles

The Beauty of Enameled Thimbles

252 253 254 255
256 257 258 259
260 261 262 263
264 265 266 267

The Thimbles of Great Britain

268   269   270

271   272   273   274

275   276   277   278

279   280   281   282

Engelen, Marihelen — Talented American artist and china painter, well known for her nature scenes and flowers on bisque porcelain thimbles. Her works are signed.

Engine Turned — A process in which a repetitive motif or design is created on a thimble by being turned on a lathe. The design may be seen under the clear enamel on many older thimbles.

English Thimbles — The earliest metal thimbles used in England were imported from Europe during the 14th century. These pieces looked very much like the pre-Renaissance thimbles of Germany. Before this, it is believed the English used mostly "themels of leather." By the 16th century, a distinct style of English-made thimble came on the scene. It was tall, made in two pieces; it was rolled up into a cylinder and capped. Decoration was limited to hand-chased, chevron motifs, and sometimes mottoes engraved about the rim. The work appeared to be a bit crude, but had a certain Elizabethan charm. See thimbles 268, 339, 340, and 341.

Until the late 17th century most of the brass thimbles used in England were still imported. In 1693, a Dutchman named John Lofting established the first thimble mill at Islington and later at Great Marlow. This was the first large-scale thimble production in Great Britain. By the mid-18th century, English thimble production centered in Birmingham, with over a dozen manufacturers making gold, silver, pinchbeck, steel, brass, and steel-topped thimbles.

By the 1770s enameled brass thimbles, so-called "Bilston-Battersea," were being made in South Staffordshire. These rare pieces with their elegant raised enameled cartouches, painted with exquisite landscapes and sprays of flowers are among the most beautiful thimbles ever made. See thimble 1333 and page 225.

The late 18th century witnessed the first manufacturing of porcelain thimbles by firms in Worcester, Derby, and Chelsea. From these humble beginnings a great industry arose and by the 19th century, British thimble manufacturers were producing millions of thimbles in a wide array of materials and styles. See pages 88 to 90.

John Lofting Style Thimbles

283

284   285

The Thimbles of Great Britain

The Thimbles of Great Britain

302   303   304   305

306   307   308   309

310   311   312   313

314   315   316   317

Nineteenth Century English Porcelain

| 334 | 335 | 336 | 337 | 338 |

Engraving — The art of cutting lines into a thimble to create a design or words. Engraving differs from "chased." In the former, metal is removed by cutting; whereas in "chased-work," punches are used to "dent" the material. Most of the engraving found on thimbles is names, initials and dates.

Eskimo Thimbles — Thimbles of ivory, bone, horn and stone have been carved by Eskimos to sell as souvenirs for over a hundred years. The thimbles are works of art in the form of seal heads, scrimshaw and scenes carved around ivory, horn and stone. Popular motifs are the little hand-carved igloo thimbles and animal heads of the Canadian Eskimos. See thimbles 335-336

Etching — A process of forming a picture or design on metal thimbles with acid. A protective coat made up of a thick mixture of wax, gums and sometimes asphaltum, is applied to a flat piece of metal. After the coating hardens the artist scratches lines though the coating down into the metal, and the exposed metal is seen as bright shiny cuts against the dull background. The metal is then etched by placing it in a tray of acid and water. The acid "eats" or etches the metal where the coating was removed.

English 16th & 17th Century Chevron Thimbles

339

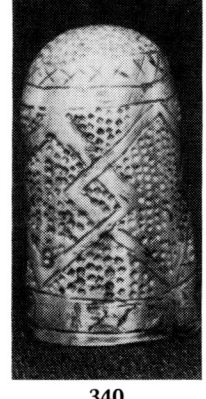
340

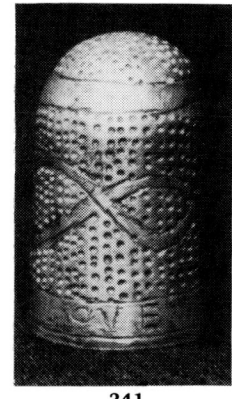
341

The Thimbles of James Fenton

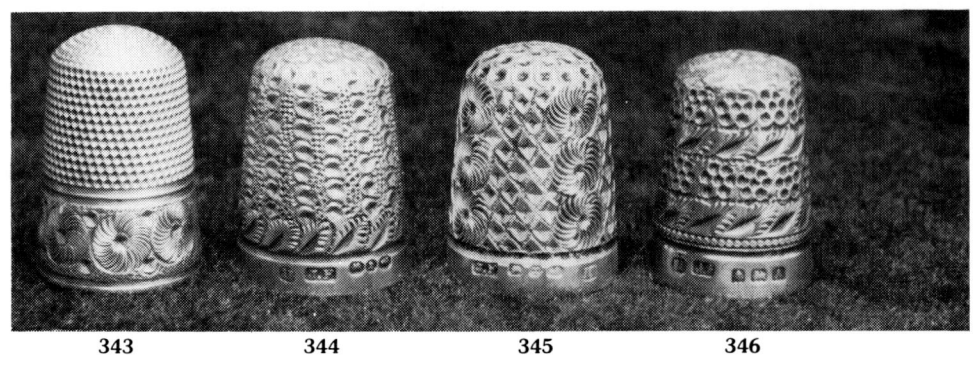

343   344   345   346

F

Faberge, Peter Carl — The famed master jeweler of the Russian Czars who was known to have made thimbles, six of which are known to be in private collections. One was sold at Christie's in Geneva, on Nov. 13, 1985, for $4,500.00. It was two-toned gold with guilloched enamel on the side, signed with the initials of Michael Perchin, a workmaster of Faberge, and dated about 1880.

Faceted — A design using a series of flat surfaces, each at a slight angle to create its effect. See page 150.

Family Simons, The — A 24-page booklet, written by John von Hoelle, published by Dine-American in 1985; detailing the history of the family who founded the famous thimblemakers, Simons Brothers Company of Philadelphia.

Fenton, James — One of the oldest thimblemaking firms in Birmingham, England. As silversmiths, they made both gold and silver thimbles from the early 19th century to the early 20th century. Some of their thimbles are marked J.F. on the band near the hallmark. See above illustration

Ferrandiz, Juan — Spanish artist whose loveable paintings of children grace the wooden Anri thimbles of Italy.

Ferro, Nick — American craftsman and glass engraver whose hand-blown thimbles are graced with his intricate "on the blind" designs.

Figdor, Albert — European thimble collector whose thimbles were used to illustrate H. R. d'Allemagne's books. See bibliography.

The Fingerhut Museum

Fingerhut Museum — A thimble museum founded by Thorvald & Brigitte Greif in August, 1982. The museum is on the lowest floor of an old mill known as Kohlesmuehle (Kohl's Mill) in the town of Creglingen, West Germany.

On May 29, 1983, a thimble society, "Friends of the Thimble Museum," was formed to help support the goals of the museum. Each year, Thorvald designs a special thimble available only to members. They meet each May and hold a "Thimble Fest."

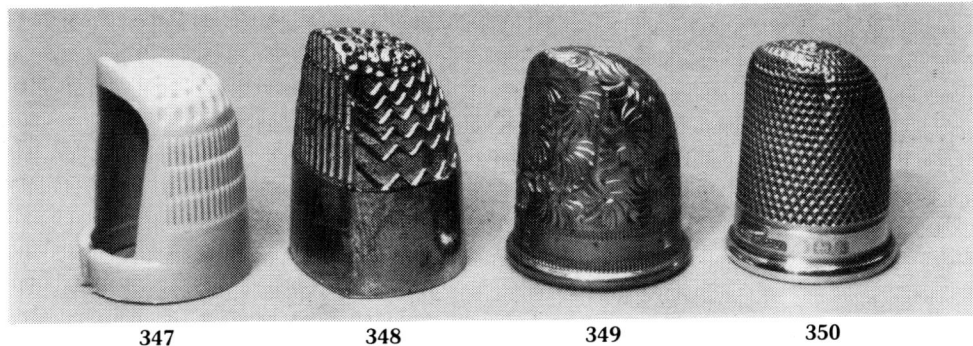

347   348   349   350

Finger-Shaped Thimbles — Thimbles made in the shape of a finger came in vogue during the latter half of the 19th century. They were made in gold, silver, base metal, bone china, and porcelain. See above illustration

Filigree Thimbles of the World

351

352   353
18th century English

354   355   356   357

358   359   360   361

362   363   364   365

366 367 368 369

Filigree — An art form over 4000 years old. It is a method of using delicate wire to create intricate designs like lace. In England, fine filigree thimbles were made from the early 18th to the early 19th century by a group of Italians who settled near Birmingham. Today, filigree thimbles are a fine art in Portugal, Peru, the Near East and the Philippines, with many distinct styles for collectors.

Fired Decal — A design printed with china paint on a thin cellophane film. The decal is mounted on the side of a thimble and fired in a kiln. After firing, the design is permanent.

Fisher, Conan — American craftsman and designer of beautiful wooden and horn thimbles. See thimble 367.

Florentine — A technique of engraving where a craftsman "textures" the surface of a thimble so as to give it a "satin look." See thimble # 368.

Forker, Idabelle — American thimble collector, author of articles on thimbles and keynote convention speaker; twice elected President of Thimble Collectors International, 1980 and 1982.

Foskett, Samuel and Henry — English silversmiths known to have made thimbles from 1865 to 1912 in London. Their maker's mark SF or HF can be found on hallmarked thimbles.

The Thimbles of Samuel and Henry Foskett

370 371 372 373

95

The Thimbles of the Franklin Mint

Fossilized Thimbles — A series of thimbles made in China from fossilized bone. They have a mottled look with hand-made indentations on top. See illustration 369

Foster & Bailey — American silversmith company in Providence, Rhode Island, from 1878 to 1951. Their thimbles have a waving flag with the initials F & B stamped inside. See "Thimble Marks."

Franciscan — An American firm organized in 1875 in Lincoln, California. Its first line, a translucent light ivory china, was developed in 1942. The Franciscan artisans are admired for their imaginative and unusual free-hand decorative styles. The company is now a member of the British Wedgwood Group.

Frank, Beryl — American thimble collector, speaker and author of many articles on thimbles. See bibliography.

Franklin Mint — American company near Philadelphia, PA, specializing in making fine collectors items and thimbles. Their "13 Colonies" series is considered to be one of the finest examples of bas-relief in American sterling thimbles. Each thimble represents one of the original colonies. By 1978, three thousand, four hundred and thirty-five sets were sold at $390.00 each! See thimble #410.

Next they designed and issued a set of fine bone china thimbles called the "First Ladies" series. These consisted of 42 thimbles with fired decals of the first ladies of America. This series sold 10,700 sets at $399.00 each by 1979. These were followed by the "Flowers of Holland" (12) and "Garden Birds" series (25) in porcelain. In 1981, The Franklin Mint issued "The Greatest Porcelain Houses of the World" series. These were made by 25 world famous porcelain makers, many of whom had never made a thimble before, such as Lladro and Noritake. Next came the porcelain "Country Store" series (25), the "Baby Animals of the World" (25) and the sterling gilt Victorian jewelled set (12). See thimble #374.

All these series were available by subscription only, one thimble per month. They also made a pewter series (25), depicting in bas-relief, scenes from Grimms' fairy tales. See thimbles 386 to 389.

Other thimbles offered by F. M. are their Alphabet line, their "4 Seasons with Cupid" thimbles, and the sterling Christmas issues. These are not by subscription.

The Franklin Mint is the largest manufacturer of collector's thimbles in the United States. They were the first major firm to recognize the potential of this new collector's market. They were the first to sell thimbles via nationwide television commercials, and other advanced advertising techniques.

The Thimbles of France

410 411 410 411
Two thimbles from the Franklin Mint's "13 Colonies" series

French Thimbles — France has a long history in thimbles. Her thimble guilds can be traced back to the 13th century. Old French thimbles have a special look: taller, more elegant than their other European counterparts. Their unique mother-of-pearl thimbles are much sought after. See page 98.

Fret Work — A design made of a repetitive pattern of straight lines intersecting at right angles, derived from classical Greek motifs. Most commonly found on thimbles in the "Greek Key" pattern; also called "The Walls of Troy". See thimbles #412 and 413.

Fried, Paula — American designer of the Donohue pewter thimbles on different modes of transportation. Her initials PF are on each thimble.

Friia, Lucien — American designer of the "Hail to the Chiefs" series of thimbles, decorated with blue enameled cameos of the American Presidents on gold-plates brass thimbles.

Frosted Glass Thimbles — Glass thimbles which have been etched with acid to give them a "a frosted" look. See thimble #417.

Fueter, Daniel Christian — Colonial American silversmith who arrived in New York from London in 1754. He retired to Switzerland in 1770. Silver thimbles are known with his mark, D.C.F./N. York, on the band.

412 413 414 415

Frosted Glass Thimbles

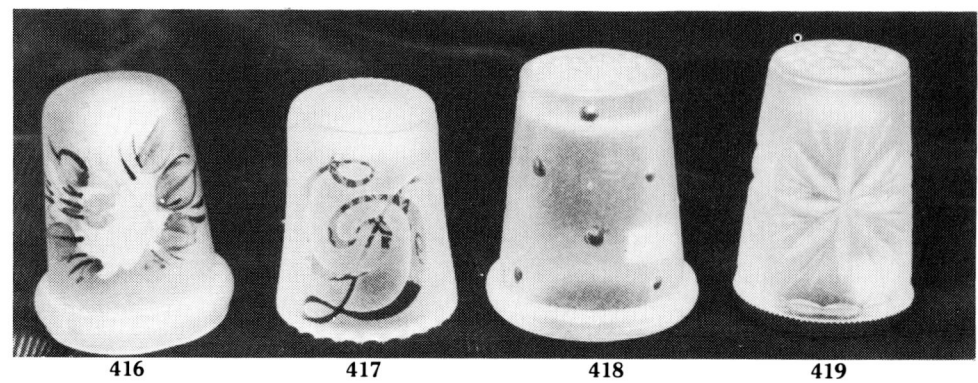

416 417 418 419

Fukagawa Thimbles — Japanese porcelain manufacturer, founded in 1650, who first began to make thimbles for collectors in 1985. Fukagawa porcelain is made only from the clays of the Arita area. See thimble # 823.

Fuller, Debbie — Thimble collector, speaker, researcher and editor of the *T.C.I. Bulletin;* founder of the Ohio Valley Thimblers, a study and social group for collectors in Ohio, Indiana and Kentucky.

Furstenburg Porcelain Co. — An early German porcelain factory known to have made thimbles in the late 18th century.

"Thimble Servants," three ceramic thimble holders

Thimble Classics

Did you ever meet a thimble bear?

"Love is . . . lots of thimbles!"

The Thimbles of Gabler Brothers

The Old Gabler Mill, 1850

G

Gabler Brothers — German thimble manufacturer founded in 1824 by Johann Ferdinand Gabler, a Swabian silversmith in Schorndorf. Johann had been making thimbles by hand since 1807. Unable to keep up with the demand, he began to build a machine to increase his output. By 1824, after six years of modifying, he opened his thimble factory. The outstanding quality and beautiful designs soon created a great demand.

Around 1850, the grist mill was converted to a water-wheel powered plant. In 1853, Johann's sons established Gabler Brothers, and by the late 19th century they were exporting thimbles to every part of the world.

Gabler made thimbles in gold, silver, brass, plastic, steel and aluminum. They can be found topped with stones and beautifully hand-painted on enamel. The Gabler Brothers Co. discontinued making thimbles in 1962.

Helmut Greif bought the precious metal inventory and equipment, and moved it to his Winterbach factory. His goal was to continue in the Gabler tradition. See page 111

The Wizardry of Gadget Thimbles

453 455 456

Gadget Thimbles — A category of thimbles which have the ability to do some other feat besides protecting one's finger. Over the last 150 years, many patents have been issued to people who have tried to "improve" and expand the uses of the thimble. These thimbles are sub-divided into at least 7 types. **CUTTERS:** A thimble with a thread cutting device attached. **MAGNETICS:** A thimble with a magnet set into the top or upper sides to pick up pins and needles. **GRIPPERS:** Thimbles which have some type of clamp attached, so as to grip a needle and help pull thread through a heavy fabric or leather. Some gadget thimbles have several of these items on them. **HEMMERS:** Thimbles with a built in hem roller on the side. **FOLDERS:** Thimbles which can be telescoped or folded down to a third of actual size. **THREADERS:** Thimbles which have some device to help thread a needle. **RIPPERS:** Thimbles which have a cutting tool attached large enough to be used as a seam ripper. See page 104.

Gadroon — A classic design usually found on thimbles near, or on, the rim. The basic design is made up of a series of convex curves vertically or slanting to one side or the other.

Gagiana Thimbles — A group of 40 brass thimbles found in the wreckage of an Italian merchant ship which sank in a storm in 1583. They were among cargo which was shipped out of Venice, bound for eastern markets. They are now on display at the Zavicajni Muzej, Biograd Na Morv, Yugoslavia. See Thimble # 453.

Garden State Thimblers — A New Jersey based thimble collector's club founded by JoAnne Rath in 1978 to promote interest and research on thimbles.

Geertz, Joan — American thimble collector, keynote speaker and editor of the *T.C.I. Bulletin* 1982 to 1984.

German Silver — An alloy of copper, nickel and zinc; also known as nickel silver and in Spanish speaking countries, Alpacca; used for making thimbles as far back as the mid-19th century. When polished, it looks very much like silver, but does not have the oxidation smell of old silver.

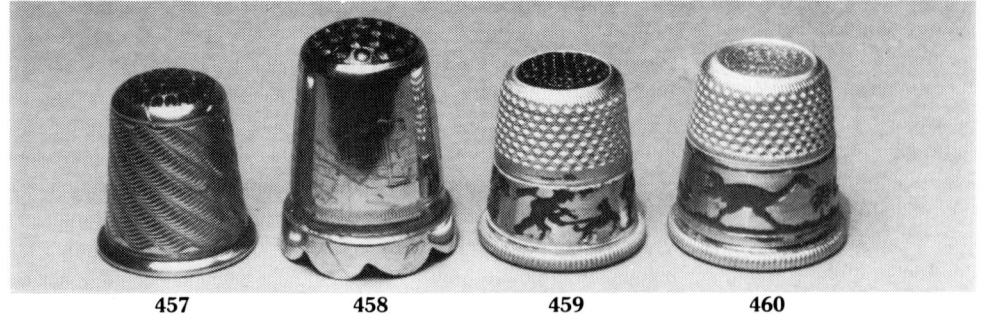

457   458   459   460

Ginori — An Italian porcelain manufacturer which has made some fine contributions to thimble design. See thimble # 824.

Gish, Nicholas — Modern American designer of novelty thimbles in pewter. His name GISH is seen stamped into parts of his thimbles. See page 146.

Glass Thimbles — Glass, as a medium for making thimbles, is rare in older thimbles. The British Museum and the Colonial Williamsburg collection have some fine examples. Within the last 20 years, Germany has been making "collectors" glass thimbles. Italy has some very ornate styles, and several American craftsmen have etched many designs on hand-blown glass thimbles. They are unsuitable for sewing. This is a category within thimble collecting and is a specialty to some collectors who collect nothing else. See pages 74 and 100.

Glass Top Thimbles — The substitution of glass to replace semi-precious stones in the tops of thimbles became a common practice just after the First World War. Nadleburg in Austria, Gabler in Germany, and Charles Iles of Great Britain were the three largest producers. Glass-top thimbles may be found in silver, brass tombac, and aluminum. See above illustration

Goebel — Famous German porcelain manufacturer. Goebel thimbles have a unique style which is easily recognized. Most are marked inside.

Gold Coast Thimblers — A Florida regional group of thimble collectors based in Miami. The winter meetings, which are usually in February are very popular with visiting collectors

Gold-Filled — A jeweler's term meaning a thimble has a layer of at least 10K gold bonded to the base metal and this layer is at least 5% of the total weight of the thimble. A mark such as 1/20 14K GF would mean 14K gold filled, and this layer is 5% or 1/20th the total weight of the thimble.

Gold Plated — A jeweler's term meaning a thimble has been electroplated with a thin coat of gold. A mark such as 1/50 14K GP would mean a layer of 14K gold was plated and is 1/50th the weight of the thimble.

Masterpieces in Gold

461   462   463

Gold Thimbles — Once the proud province of noble women, this metal became so plentiful that by the turn of the century 14K gold thimbles, hand-chased with scenes, were selling at $4.00 each in Montgomery Ward's Catalog. Sears Roebuck sold 10K plain gold thimbles for $1.90. Still, Grandmom's gold thimbles are treasured in many households and collectors the world over seek them out. When buying older American gold thimbles, one should be very cautious. America, without a hallmark system, as established in Great Britain, is a "Buyer Beware" situation.

Gold plated lead, brass, copper and silver is very common and many a new collector has been burned. "Gold-filled" and "gold-overlay" are also very common and some of the more honest makers did mark their "filled" thimbles. Unfortunately, many of these early "gold-filled" symbols are unidentifiable to us now.

The Simons Bros. Co. of Philadelphia used a trefoil symbol (see "Thimble Marks") inside the top to indicate gold-filled. Muhr used three crowns side by side to identify his "pinchbeck" type of metal alloy that looks very much like gold. On his gold overlay, he used a crown, a number and a lion symbol, which looks like a rough English hallmark series. Percival of Boston stamped a star into his gothic P to show gold-filled. Barker Co. in Providence used stars, anchors, crescents, keystones and crosses to mark his gold-filled thimbles. But gold thimbles made in the 18th, 19th and 20th centuries remain the most beautiful examples of the thimblemakers craft. See pages 226 to 230.

Gold Band Thimbles — A decorative technique created by applying a gold band to a silver thimble. Usually the band is made separate and applied. American thimblers were the most prolific in the style. See thimble # 465.

Golden Crown — A British company which is making modern bone china thimbles with fired decals.

American Gold-Band Thimbles

464   465   466   467

Golden Spike Thimble — A rare commemorative thimble designed by Simons Brothers for the St. Louis Exposition in 1904. About the band is a panoramic scene of the opening of the American West: a sunset, buffalo, Indians and riders, covered wagon, and a locomotive! Originals are marked "Official 1904" on band; restrikes have large Simons trademark inside apex. See illustration #455.

Goldsmith, Lahoma — An American collector and author of numerous articles on thimbles and related items. She has done extensive research on silversmithing and designs on thimbles made by the American Indians. She also edited a detailed account of the campaign thimble. She was first editor of *T.C.I. BULLETIN*.

Goldsmith-Stern — American thimble manufacturer in New York City, circa 1913-1932. The company was a continuation of the older firm of Stern Brothers, founded in 1869, in Philadelphia. There are many variations of their anchor and G S C trademark. See "Thimble Marks" and thimbles below

The Thimbles of Goldsmith-Stern

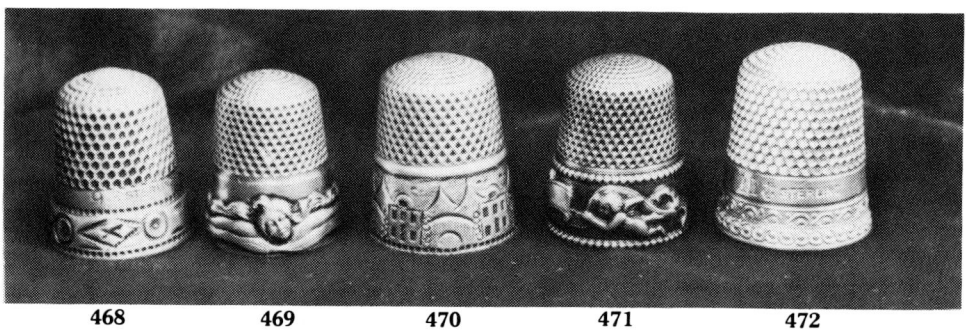

468   469   470   471   472

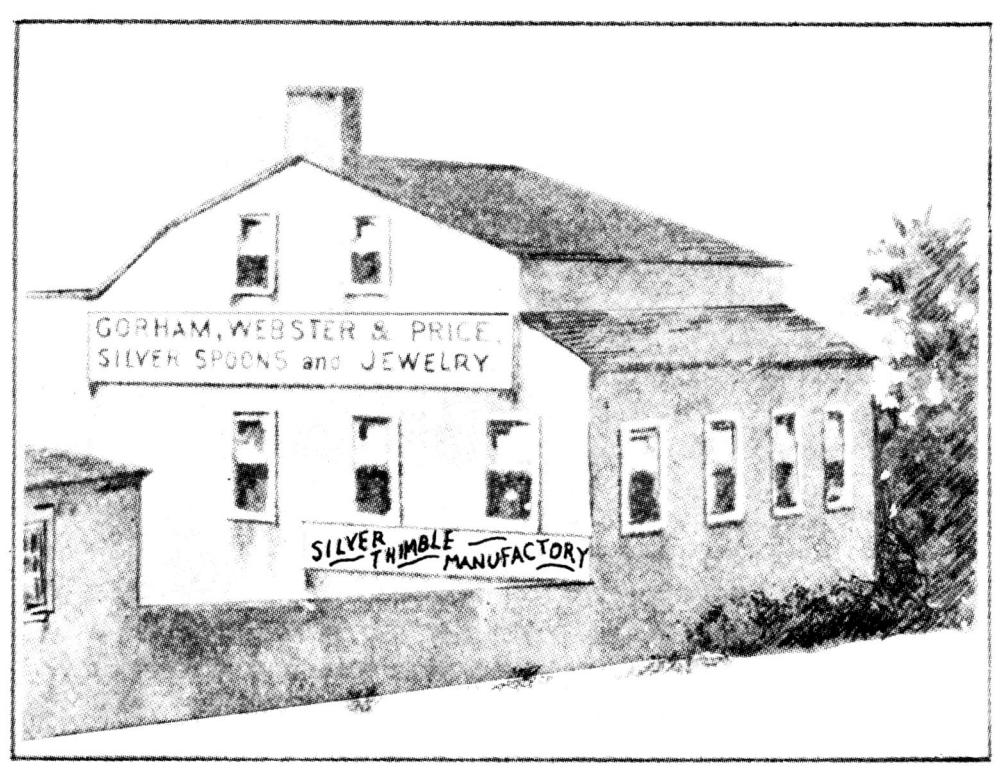

Jewelers' Circular - Weekly   Feb. 5, 1919

Gorham — An American company which is currently making a line of thimbles with fired-decal scenes taken from the works of Norman Rockwell, as depicted on the covers of *Saturday Evening Post Magazine*. Their Christmas series depicts Rockwell's painting of Charles Dickens classic "A Christmas Carol."

Gorham, Jabez — American silversmith apprenticed to Nehemiah Dodge of Providence, Rhode Island in 1807; joined in partnership with Christopher Burr, William Hadwen, George Clark, and Henry Mumford for five years. Gorham formed Gorham & Breebe in 1825, Gorham & Webster in 1831, and Gorham, Webster & Price in 1835. In 1841 Jabez's son John joined the firm which then became Gorham & Son. John was one of the first to introduce machinery, much of which he built himself, to speed up their craftsmanship. This company became the foundation of the massive Gorham Corp. of today, one of the world's largest manufacturers of silver merchandise. One of their early specialities was "silver thimbles." Note lower sign on their 1835 factory in old print above.

Grainger thimbles — A line of hand-painted porcelain thimbles made by the British firm of Grainger & Co. in Worcester during the last quarter of the 19th century. The firm merged with the Royal Porcelain Works in 1889, which became Royal Worcester.

The Thimbles of Greece

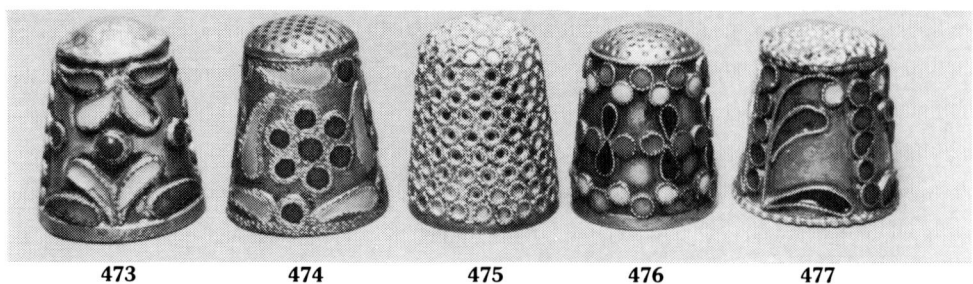

473   474   475   476   477

Great Lakes Thimblers — A Michigan-area thimble collector's club founded by Bernadine Biske in 1982. They issue a semi-annual newsletter for members only.

Grate — Another word for the indentations or knurlings. This term was used in the 1921 catalog of Charles Iles & Co. describing their thimbles with fine grate, medium grate, or coarse grate.

Greek Thimbles — Greek sewing-rings found in Byzantine Corinth are among the oldest known metal thimbles in Europe. See page 24. Modern Greek thimbles have a unique style all their own. Colorful enamels are fired within geometric shaped silver wires which have been applied to the side of the thimbles. See above illustration.

Greek Key — An ancient Greek motif also known as "Fret-Work" and "Walls of Troy"; a design made up of repetitive patterns of straight lines intersecting at right angles. See thimbles: #412 and 413.

Gregory, Mary — In the art world of glass, few women have surpassed the beauty and charm of the work of Mary Gregory. This young artist worked for the Boston and Sandwich Co. of Boston in the 1870s and 1880s. She developed a style using white enamel on colored glass depicting scenes of children catching butterflies, tending sheep, climbing trees, and running in fields. She captured the romantic innocence associated with the Victorian era. The modern glass thimble pictured here is in the Mary Gregory tradition. See thimble 456.

The Thimbles of Helmut and Thorvald Greif

478   479   480   481

Helmut Greif at the 1984 TCI Convention in Philadelphia

Greif, Helmut — German goldsmith and author of *Gesprache uber Fingerhute* (Talks About Thimbles) printed in Klagenfurt, Austria in 1984 for Dine-American in English.

Herr Greif took over the precious metal division of the famed Gabler Brothers thimble factory in Schorndorf in 1964. He moved the equipment and dies to Winterbach. There he modernized production methods, and published a color catalog of his thimbles. Within weeks an arsonist set fire to the factory and the entire plant was burned down. Destroyed were all the original Gabler machines, records and Helmut's inventory.

His dream of continuing the Gabler tradition was destroyed.

Several years later he helped his son Thorvald get out of East Germany. They purchased the thimblemaking equipment from Frederich Eber, the last owner of the famed Lotthammer-Stutzel thimble factory in Pforzheim. This equipment was set up in Creglingen.

Helmut then began to write his book on the history of European thimblemakers. This book inspired Thorvald's wife Brigitte to create a "Fingerhutmuseum" (thimble museum) in an old mill in Creglingen, West Germany. Helmut Greif's dream to continue the traditions of the "Fingerhuters" lives on in the works of his son Thorvald.

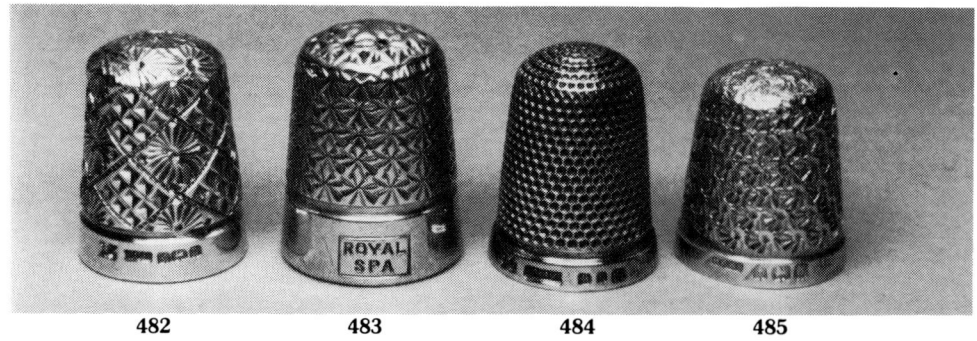

482　　　　　483　　　　　484　　　　　485

Griffith, Henry & Sons — British silversmiths and manufacturers of the "SPA" thimbles. The "SPA" thimbles comprise a series of sterling souvenir thimbles in traditional English styles with the words "THE SPA" on rim, and above it, stamped on a ribbed background, "Stratford-on-Avon" or any of some 50 or so historical towns or beach resorts. See thimble #483.

Henry Griffith established a factory in Leamington, near Birmingham, in 1856 and became one of England's leading thimblemakers. The company marked its thimbles with an HG&S or HG&S LTD inside a rectangle on the outside rim. They stopped making thimbles in 1956.

Guilloche — An ornamental design using series of paired lines and curves flowing and sometimes interlacing around series of circular motifs. Often seen through the translucent enamel on German and Norwegian thimbles, it was a technique used to better hold the enamel onto the surface of the thimble.

Gunner, A. T. Mfg. Co. — An American thimblemaker in Attleboro, Massachusetts, during the early 20th century. Some of their silver thimbles are marked with a G inside a five pointed star. The company sold the molds and dies to Simons' Bros. Co.

Gutta Percha — A milky latex fluid found in several types of Brazilian and Oriental trees. When dried, it can be molded into any shape. It looks like hard rubber and old thimbles made of gutta percha are almost black. See #490.

The Thimbles of Henry Griffith

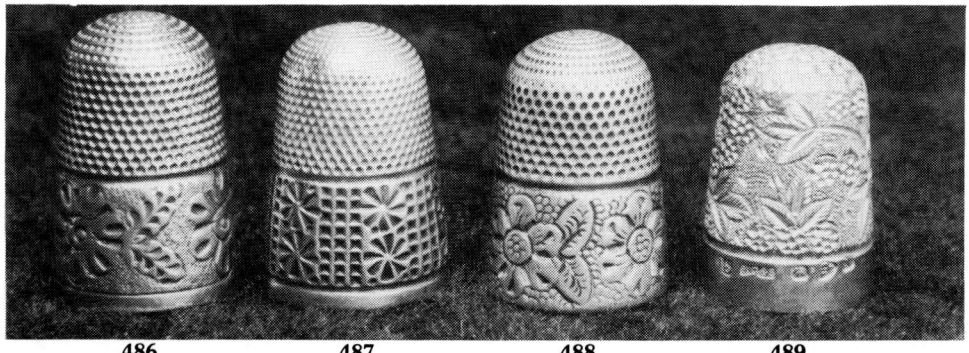

486　　　　　487　　　　　488　　　　　489

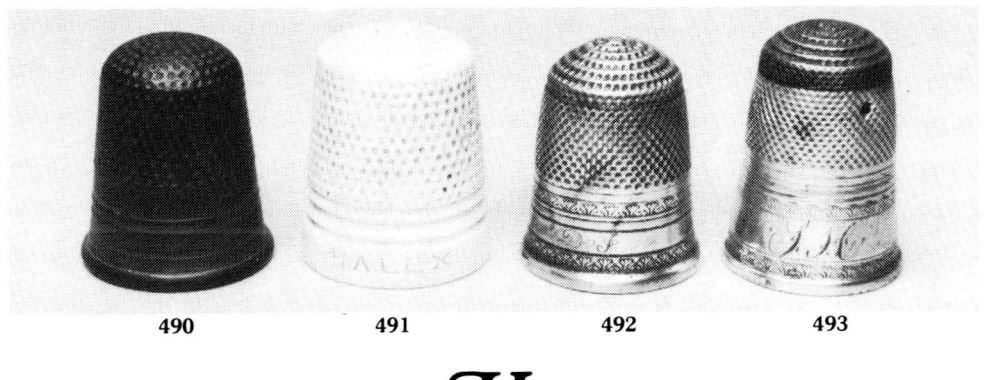

490   491   492   493

H

Hale, David R. — American silversmith from Lowell, Mass. known to have made silver thimbles in the mid-19th century. His thimbles have D HALE on the band.

Halex — A brand name for plastic thimbles with hand painted flowers about the band; circa 1920-30s.

Hallmark — The origin of the "hallmark" comes to us today from the Middle Ages when skilled craftsmen formed their guilds to set prices, establish rules on quality and customs, etc. These guilds, or trade unions as we call them today, met in the "Guild Hall." Here, the Masters would examine articles of gold, silver, etc., and strike their "Hall Mark", should it prove to be the workmanship and quality of material required by that guild.

In England, a system of hallmark has existed since A.D. 1300. Over the centuries, the British hallmark system has become an elaborate and accurate method of indicating not only the quality of material, but when the item was made, who made it, and where it was made!

A complete British hallmark has four parts. On a modern silver thimble, for example, the first mark would usually be the marker's or sponsor's mark, (usually several initials, i.e., JJ&R).

Second is the "lion symbol," meaning .925 sterling silver. This is the quality or standard mark.

Third is the assay office mark which identifies the office which tested and marked the piece. There are now four British Assay Offices: London (head of lion symbol), Birmingham (an anchor), Sheffield (a rose), and Edinburgh (a castle). The other main assay offices in Chester, Newcastle, Dublin, Glasgow and Exeter are now closed.

The last symbol of a complete British hallmark is the date letter. This shows in which year the thimble was hallmarked, and each year is given a letter with its own style.

Books on British and European hallmarks are available at many larger libraries and need to be used to translate these tiny symbols.

Hand Punched Indentations

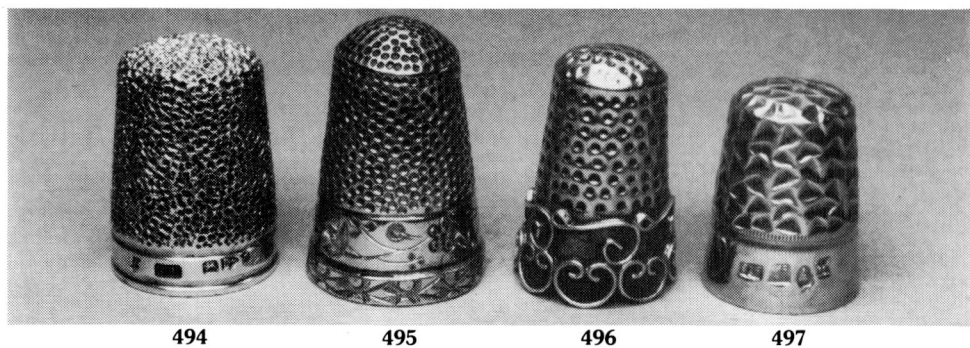

494 495 496 497

Halsted, Benjamin — American silversmith born in 1734 in Elizabeth, N.J. Opened a shop in New York City about 1760. Became the first American to manufacture thimbles on a large scale in 1794. For a detailed account on the life of this remarkable man read the booklet *Benjamin Halsted, America's First Thimble Manufacturer,* by John von Hoelle, published by Dine-American in 1985. Halsted made thimbles in gold, silver and pinchbeck, some are marked B H or his name spelled out on the band. See thimbles 493 and 498.

498

French Thimbles by Haviland

499   500   501   502

Hammersley — A British fine china manufacturer at Stoke-on-Trent. The name of Hammersley can be found listed among English potters as far back as 1697, when Cornelius Hammersley was accused of a patent infringement. The firm went through a list of name changes until 1874 when the present name was established. Hammersley bone china is of the highest quality and reputation. An example of their design in thimbles is # 830.

Hand Punched — A term to describe hand-made indentations, not made by a knurling wheel. See illustration # 495.

Hard Rubber — Natural hard rubber thimbles were made by Goodyear in the mid-19th century, but were discontinued because they wore out quickly and cracked.

Harmer, Chris — English artist who painted the portrait of Queen Elizabeth II on the 1977 Jubilee thimbles. The thimble was a hard enamel on sterling silver. See illustration # 241.

Haviland — The family name made famous by David and Daniel Haviland. These two American brothers revolutionized the French porcelain industry at Limoges in the mid-19th century by introducing mechanical methods instead of the long, hand labor to process the clays before molding and firing. They also perfected the firing kilns and introduced lithography techniques. The Haviland name still stands for fine French china. For examples of Haviland thimbles, See above illustration.

Hawkeye Thimblers — An Iowa regional collector's club founded in 1981 by Idabelle Forker. Wanda Kauffman was the first President. The club hosted the 1986 T.C.I. Convention in Des Moines.

Hayes, Herman — American craftsman and parson who carved a series of thimbles called "Earthly Characters." These hand-whittled thimbles were carved in wood and soapstone to represent the humorous faces of men such as Gramps, Uncle Chester, Brother Jim and Pa.

Thimbles by Herend

503   504   505   506

Healacraft — British china firm now making a line of beautiful hand painted thimbles. See illustration # 832.

Heirloom Editions Ltd. — One of the largest manufacturers, importers, and wholesale distributors of collectors' thimbles in the world. This California firm, founded by Barbara Ringer in 1978, commissions talented artists to create many of their own exclusive designs. The company's line includes thimbles made of silver, brass, semi-precious stone, horn, wood, pewter, glass, ceramic, papier mache, as well as bone china and porcelain.

Hem Roller — A thimble novelty with a device to roll a hem attached to the side. Sometimes the rollers were made of ivory. See above illustration.

Her Majesty Thimbles — A brand name found on brass thimbles made in Great Britain. See thimble # 89.

Herend — Hungarian porcelain factory founded in 1826 near Budapest. Like several British firms, Herend made artistic imitations of rare old Meissen thimbles, even to the point of copying the original blue "crossed swords," maker's mark! Now these forgeries are collector's items in their own right.

Today, Herend makes a beautiful series of thimbles with hand-painted flowers on a brilliant white ground with a gold band at the rim. See above.

Highland China — A Scottish bone china manufacturer who makes fired-decal thimbles for modern collectors. Their name is on inside of thimble.

Hispano-Moresque Thimbles — An early Islamic thimble style, cast in bronze with a pointed top. Circa 10th to 15th century, they are found usually in North Africa, Spain, and sometimes France. See page 28.

Hobnail — A technique in glass design where little blobs of glass are added to the sides of a glass thimble to create a hobnail effect.

Holes — A British term for thimble indentations or knurlings. They were referred to as fine, medium or large holes.

Thimbles of Horn

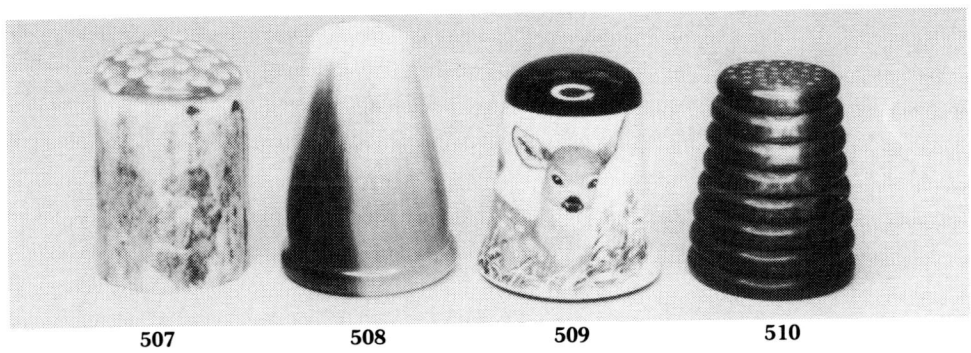

507   508   509   510

Hollis, Lynn — An American artisan who works primarily in bronze and brass. His collector thimbles are machined from solid metal bars into many interesting designs. They are marked L.HOLLIS. Some have been beautifully engraved by Richard Perkins and are marked R.P. See Thimble Sources and thimble #1518.

Hollohaza — A Hungarian fine china manufacturer. Their thimbles are tall, brilliantly white with hand-painted flowers on two sides. See thimble #835.

Holmes, William James — British silversmith (1882 to 1938) from Birmingham. His initials, W.J.H., can be found on hallmarked English thimbles.

Holmes, Edwin — British collector and author of two books on thimbles. The first, *Thimbles,* was published in 1976, and the second, *A History of Thimbles,* was published in 1985. These works are the first attempts to trace the history of thimbles.

Holthuizen, Henny — Dutch thimble collector and researcher of early Dutch thimblemakers. He was a keynote speaker at the 1984 T.C.I. Convention in Philadelphia and is the husband of Kay Sullivan, of de Vingerhoed, in Amsterdam.

Hopi — A tribe of American Indians in the southwest United States known for fine silversmithing. Their silver thimbles, made for tourists, are distinctive with Indian designs and many are embellished with turquoise.

Hoppins, Mary Gallatin — American thimble collector whose superb collection is now on display in the Smithsonian Institute, Hall of Textiles. Mrs. Hoppins collected all types of thimbles, from rare Meissen and old French gold to common plastic politicals and souvenir brass. She believed a thimble was a thimble, all were "important."

Horn — Cattle, elk and buffalo horn have been used for ages in making thimbles. Although not really suitable for hard wear, this was sometimes the only material available. See above illustration

Thimbles of Charles Horner

511 512 513

Horner, Charles — British thimble manufacturer and inventor of the "Dorcas" thimble. Charles Horner was a silversmith who conceived the idea of an armor-plated silver thimble. This thimble was to be made in three parts: an inside and outside shell of sterling silver, and an in-between shell of steel. This thimble, which he patented in June of 1884 was called a "DORCAS" thimble. Mr. Horner built a plant in Halifax and a sales office in Birmingham. His Dorcas thimbles were sold world wide. See "DORCAS."

Horoldt, J.G. — Johann Gregorious Horoldt, German artist and chemist. He joined the Royal Saxon Porcelain works at Meissen in 1720 and for over a decade he dominated the Meissen artistic scene. His experiments with metallic oxide colors gave to western porcelain the brilliant color range known then only to oriental china. Meissen porcelain thimbles, hand-painted in the "Horoldt" style, are among the most valuable to collectors. One sold at auction on December 3, 1979 at Christie's for $18,000.00!

Houston Thimble Group — A regional thimble collector's club founded by Leona Coad. The club issues a new thimble each year to its members.

Howard & Cockshaw Co. — American silversmiths in New York, late 19th century till 1915. Their silver thimbles have H&C on the band.

Howell, Dorothy — British collector of an extraordinary collection of rare thimbles, author of "Thimble Love" printed in an English magazine in 1973. In her collection was a thimble made by Faberge and one owned by Queen Elizabeth I of England.

Hum, Robert — American thimble collector and elected treasurer of Thimble Collectors International for two terms.

Hunt, Emily — American collector whose fine collection is on display at the Historical Museum of the Gunn Memorial Library in Washington, Connecticut.

Hurd, Jacob — (1702-1758) Colonial American goldsmith in Boston who was known to have made thimbles. One example of his work is on display at the Yale University Art Gallery. See illustration # 33.

Hurley — American porcelain manufacturer who made a fine line of hand-painted porcelain thimbles. Each thimble was hand-poured and hand-painted. Hurley thimbles are thin, translucent and each a work of art. Their "Heroines of the World," "Christmas around the World," "Historic Trust Houses," and "Holiday" thimbles are prized collector's items. See Thimble # 836.

Hutschenreuther — German porcelain manufacturer, who makes a line of small inexpensive thimbles with popular designs. See thimble 837.

Hyde, Louise F. — American thimble collector who assembled an outstanding collection of early silver, porcelain and gold thimbles, which are now on display at the Hyde House in Glens Falls, New York.

The Thimble Fleet

Souvenir Thimble Holders

The Thimbles of Charles Iles

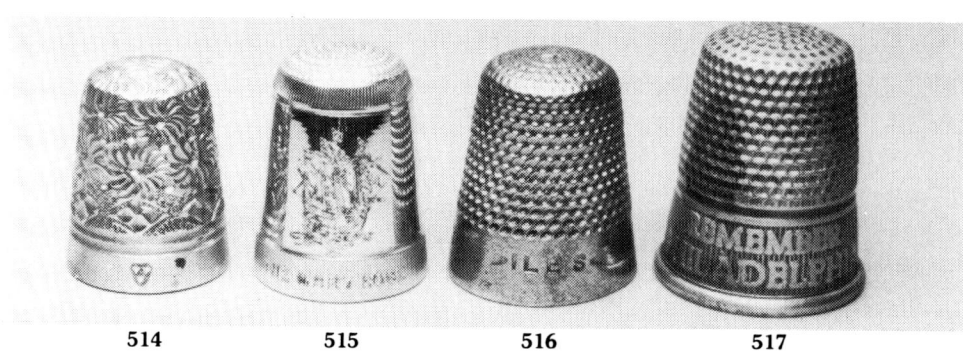

| 514 | 515 | 516 | 517 |

| 518 | 519 | 520 | 521 |

Charles Iles' advertising thimbles, 1920-1950s

See chapter on "A Visit to Charles Iles," page 271.

I

Iles & Gomms Ltd. — British thimble manufacturer in Birmingham, England. Founded in the 1840s by Charles Iles, Sr. as Peyton & Iles, they are makers of buttons, hook and eyes, and thimbles. Charles Iles won prizes in the "Great Exhibition" in 1851 at the Crystal Palace and at the International Exhibition in London in 1862.

These early thimbles were stamped from brass sheet with turned-over rims. His son Charles Iles, Jr. took over the business in 1870 and ran it successfully till his death in 1927. Thimbles of aluminum, celluloid, nickel-silver, and steel were being made by the millions.

In 1927, Alfred Cox, Charles' son-in-law, took over the firm and bought the firm of Gomms, a souvenir manufacturer. Thus glass-headed electroplated thimbles were sold at holiday resorts and exported around the world by Iles & Gomms Ltd.

After 1965, the firm improved its quality industrial thimbles by nickel and chromium plating the steel. Some early 20th century Iles thimbles are marked with three small thimbles within a large one. The firm is still making thimbles and is owned by Richard Mealings, who acquired it in 1971. Recently they issued the beautiful "Mary Rose" thimble in sterling. They also custom make brass, steel and silver thimbles for clubs and companies all over the world. See "Thimble Sources" and page 271.

Imari Thimbles — A Japanese art style famous for its bold color and geometric patterns.

Incised — A design which is drawn by hand.

Indentations — The pits on the top and sides of a thimble, designed to prevent the slipping of the needle. They may be hand punched or knurled by machine. Indentations come in many designs; round, hexagonal, square and diamond shapes are the most common, but many floral motifs, basket weaves and other combinations abound. In some thimbles the overall design itself is the needle-gripper. In England indentations 50 per inch are called lower case fine and those large 10 per inch are the dreadnoughts! Some thimbles have lathe grooves or rings cut around the sides to prevent the needle from slipping.

Indian Thimbles (British Colonial India) — The silver and goldsmiths of India created an ornate style of thimble which is very distinctive. Most are hand-chased in beautiful elaborate floral patterns, some with elegant scalloped rims. Most date from the last half of the 19th century. See page 122.

Inlay — A process in which one material is set into the body of another so the surface is level. See thimble # 1374.

Irish Dresden Thimbles — An Irish porcelain company which uses the old Dresden lace technique to capture a very distinctive look about their thimbles. See illustration # 838.

The Thimbles of British Colonial India

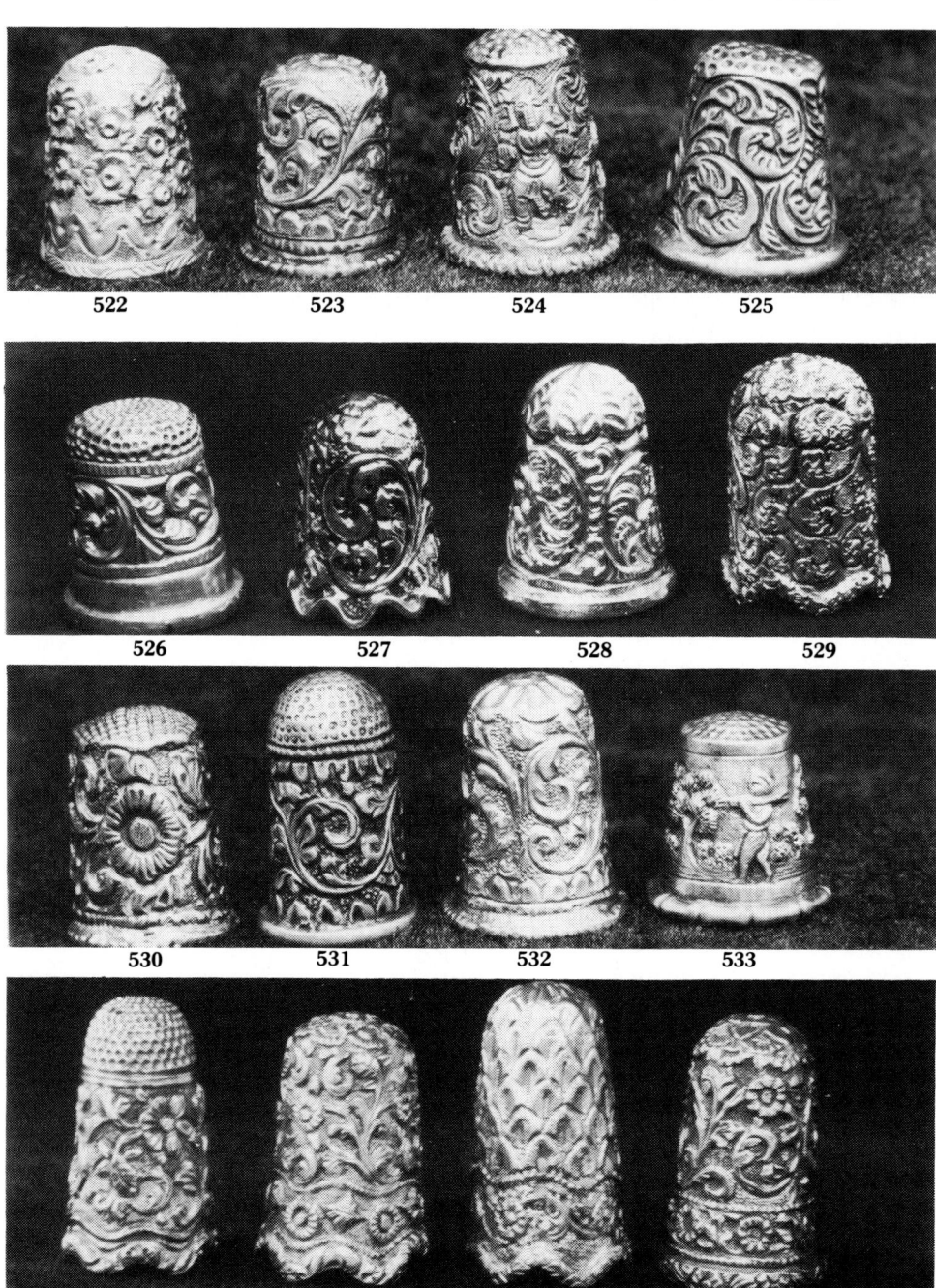

522   523   524   525

526   527   528   529

530   531   532   533

534   535   536   537

538
Ivory thimble and acorn holder

Irish Thimbles — Thimbles carved from bog oak by craftsmen were sold to tourists in Ireland during the late 19th and early 20th centuries. Irish hallmarked silver thimbles are scarce, and the tiny harp motif within the hallmark is much sought after by collectors. See thimble #936.

Ironstone — A hard, durable ceramic body developed by Miles and Charles Mason in 1813, and used by that company and others to make thimbles. See pages 127-128.

Ivorine — Brand name of the Charles Iles & Co. for a casein and celluloid thimble sold during the first quarter of the 20th century. Several shapes are known.

Ivory — The tusk of elephants and the teeth of whales have been the main source of ivory since ancient times. Ivory thimbles have been advertised as early as 1767 by Charles Shipman of New York.

The smooth and pleasant feel of ivory made them popular with sewers of the 18th and 19th centuries. Many came with other sewing tools such as ivory clamps, reels, birds, needles and bodkins in beautiful carved work boxes. Most of the elaborate thimbles were carved in the Orient for the Western market. Smooth ivory thimbles without indentations were used as finger guards.

Ivory scrimshaw thimbles are highly collected in the United States and are an American folk art form. Whalers out of ports such as New Bedford were at sea two to three years. Many hours were spent carving useful articles and thimbles from whale teeth. After carving, the item was scrimshawed or etched to produce delicate scenes from the sea. These were sold upon return to port. Since 1978, ornate ivory thimbles inlaid with precious and semi-precious jewels, and often banded with gold or silver rims, have been carved by John von Hoelle. To date about 100 of these thimbles have been created for friends and collectors. See examples on page 126 and 231.

Hand Carved Thimbles in Ivory

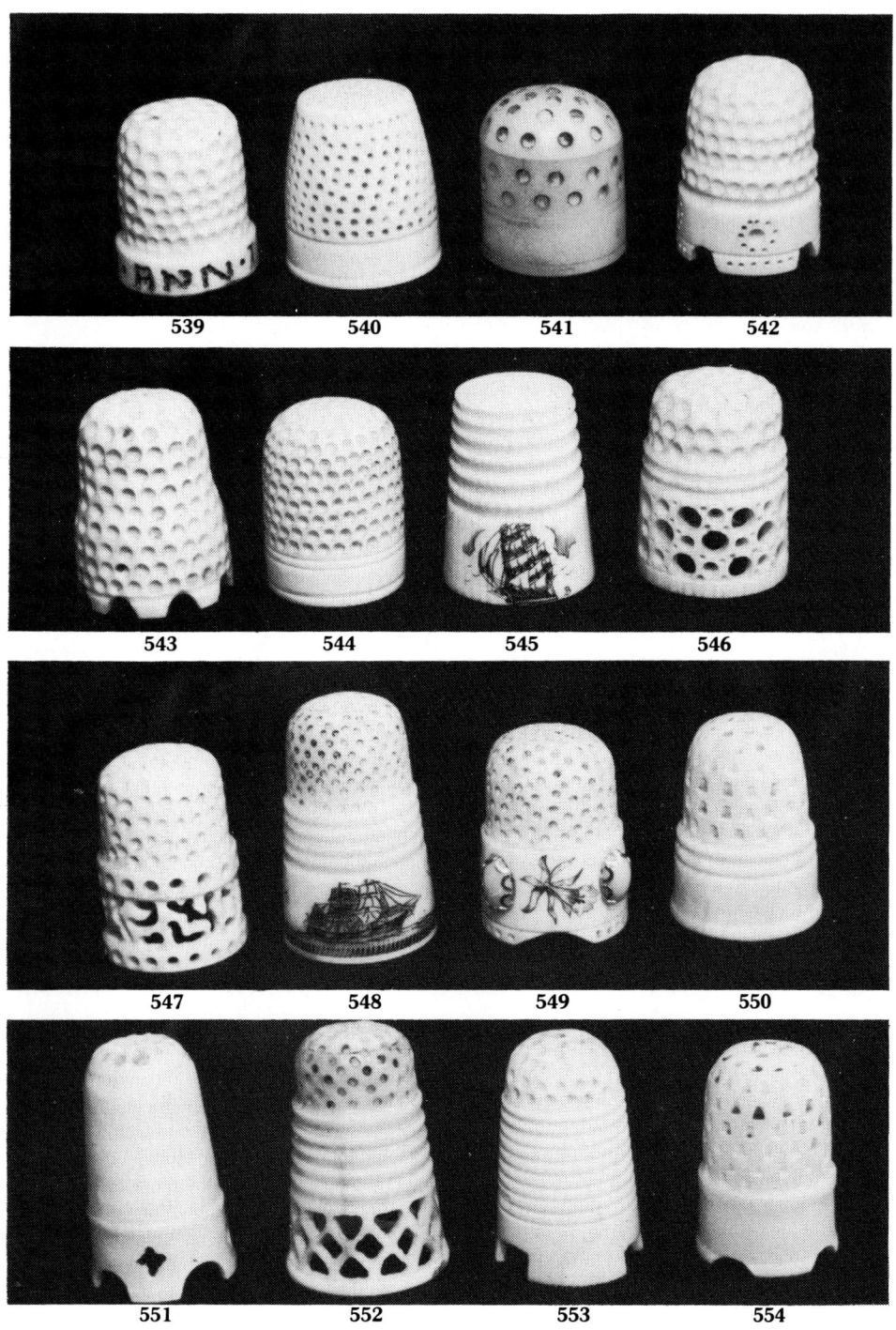

Hand Carved Thimbles in Ivory

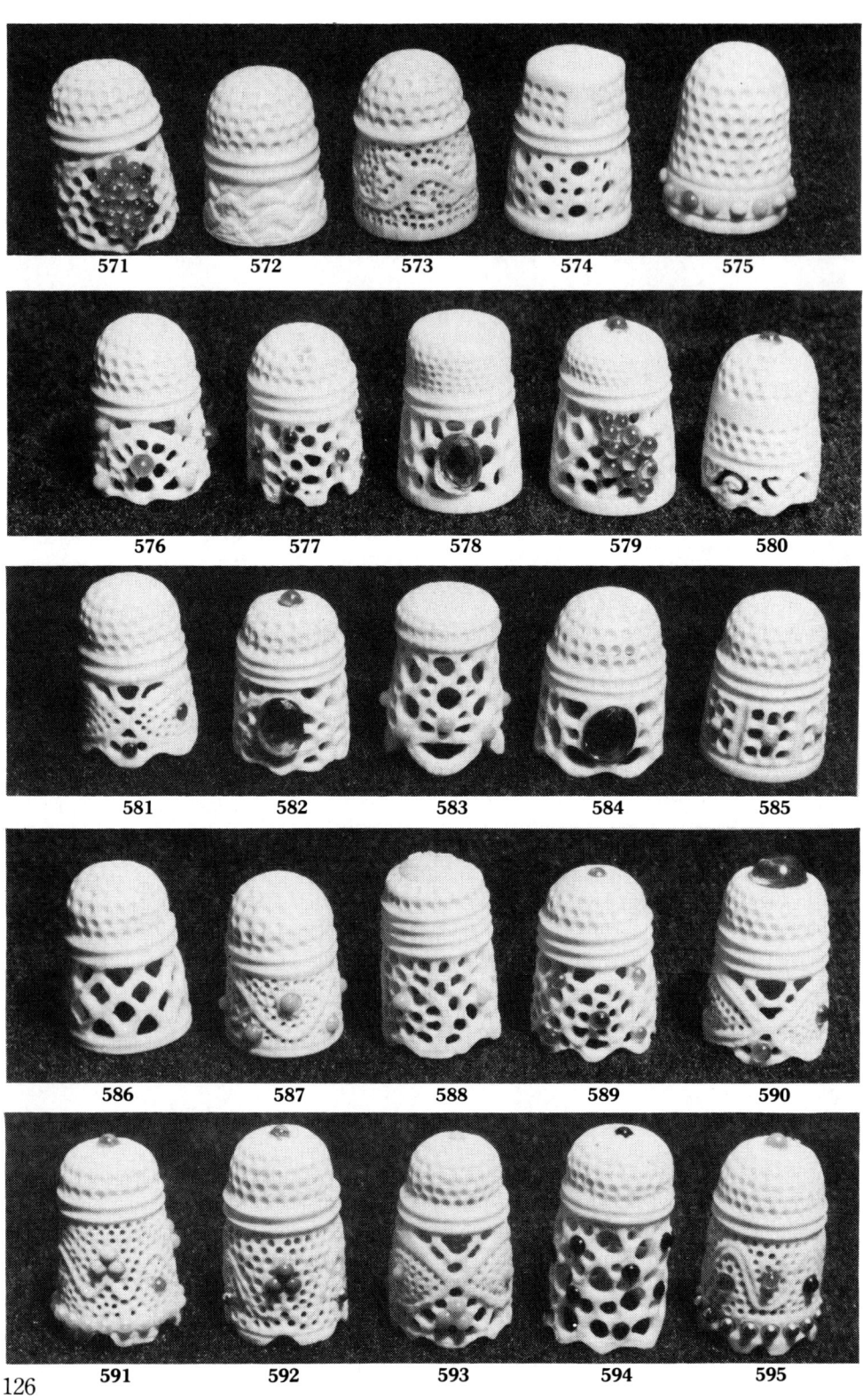

Thimbles of Ironstone and Earthenware

Thimbles of Ironstone and Earthenware

Jeweled-Top Thimbles

628 629 630

J

Jade — A semi-precious gemstone which ranges in color from white to dark green. The Chinese consider jade the symbol of justice, courage, wisdom and good fortune. Jade thimbles with these Chinese characters cut into them have been made for the Western market. For example, see thimble # 1097.

Jasperware — An unglazed vitreous fine stoneware which may be stained black, lilac, blue, yellow, maroon or green. Jasperware is the most famous of Josiah Wedgwood's ceramic inventions which he developed in 1774. It made an excellent ground to which bas-relief motifs were applied, usually in white of the same body. Jasperware thimbles were in limited production from 1791 to 1800. They again started to make thimbles in 1979. See thimble on page 215.

Jeffords, Mignon — American thimble collector and author of *Sharing Sewing Sets,* a unique booklet about her collection and collecting techniques; President of T.C.I. 1984-86.

Jeweled Top — Any thimble with a semi-precious gem set into the top of the thimble to take the wear of the needle; also called "stone top."

Johnson Brothers — British porcelain house founded in 1883 by Henry, Fred, Robert and Alfred Johnson, who established their factory in Hanley. Johnson Brothers have been a division of Wedgewood since 1968. They operate six plants in Stoke-on-Trent. Thimble # 839 is an example of their work.

Jones, Shreve & Brown — An American silversmith company of Boston, Mass., known to have made silver thimbles in the mid-19th century. Their initials, JSB&CO., can be found on the outside band.

The Thimbles of Ketcham & McDougall

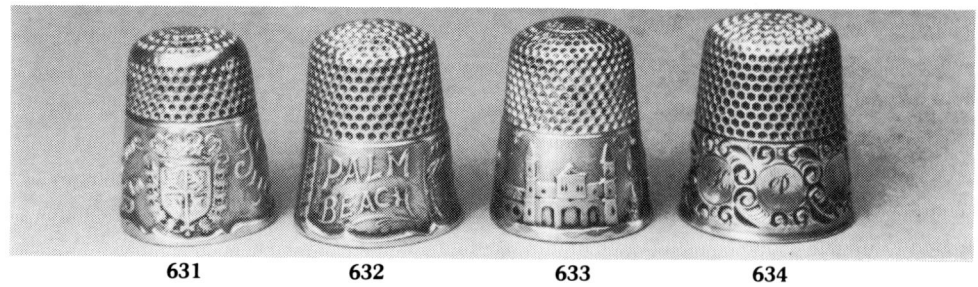

631   632   633   634

𝒦

Kaiser Porcelain — German porcelain firm founded by August Alboth in 1872 in Coburg. In 1922 his daughter Erna married George Kaiser, who became a partner, and the trademark "ALKA-KUNST" was adapted. The "ALKA" was the first two letters of Alboth and Kaiser. "Kunst" means art in German. In 1970, the tradename was changed to Kaiser Porcelain. The company now produces a line of well-designed porcelain thimbles. Their annual Christmas edition is highly collectible.

Kaolin — A special clay, and the main ingredient in the making of fine, hard paste porcelain. Many famous porcelain manufacturers were founded near large deposits of kaolin such as Limoges, France and Meissen, Germany.

Keene, Charles A. — American silversmith of the early 20th century from New York. The name KEENE can be found on the outside band of his silver thimbles.

Ketcham & McDougall — American thimble manufacturer for a hundred years, beginning with John Roshore, a silversmith who opened a small shop in New York in 1832. Several years later, he took in an orphan boy named Edward Ketcham and taught him the trade. Ketcham became a partner and the business became "Roshore & Ketcham."

In the 1850s, Edward took his brother into the business and it became "Ketcham & Brother." In 1875, Hugh McDougall became a partner and the firm became "Ketcham & McDougall," by which it is known today.

Ketcham & McDougall were prolific makers of gold, silver, aluminum, nickel-silver and steel thimbles. Their advertising campaigns were bold, sometimes humorous, and always to the point. Their designs were clever and are much sought after by collectors the world over.

Their now famous MKD trademark can be found inside the top of their thimbles. They discontinued the thimblemaking division of their business in 1932.

Ketcham & McDougall Thimble Factory
York and Washington St., Brooklyn, N.Y. 1883

Edward Ketcham 1834-1901    Hugh McDougall 1820-1894

Kohls, Mildred — American thimble designer and china painter. Her hand-painted thimbles are in the best tradition of fine miniature art.

Koronis Area Thimble Society — A Minnesota thimble study group founded in 1984 by Ellen Guenther.

Knurling — A term to describe the indentations on the top and sides of a thimble when made by a knurling wheel or tool.

Kuebler, Gertrude — A German-American researcher and collector, who translated Helmut Greif's work, *Nuremberg Thimblemakers*, for T.C.I. She also helped translate, from German into English, Mr. Greif's book, *Talks About Thimbles*, for Dine-American. Mrs. Kuebler has given key programs at T.C.I. conventions and regional thimble clubs.

The Thimbles of Ketcham & McDougall

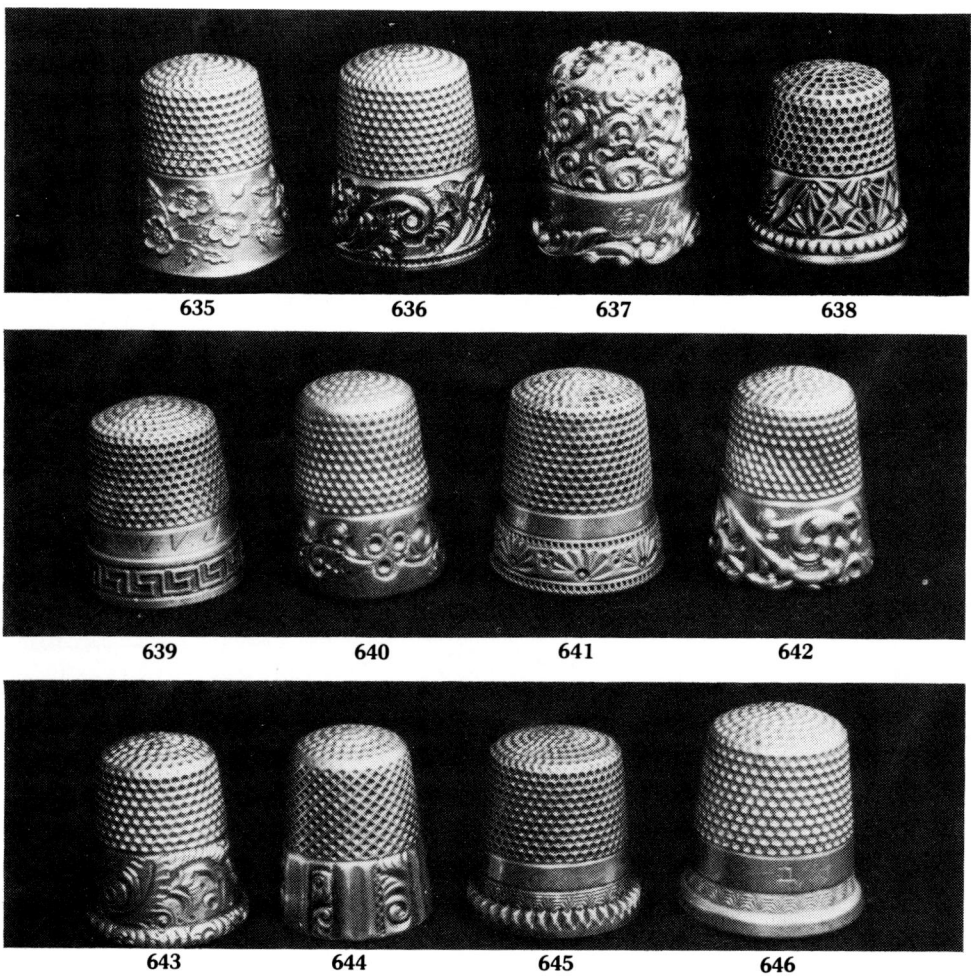

635   636   637   638

639   640   641   642

643   644   645   646

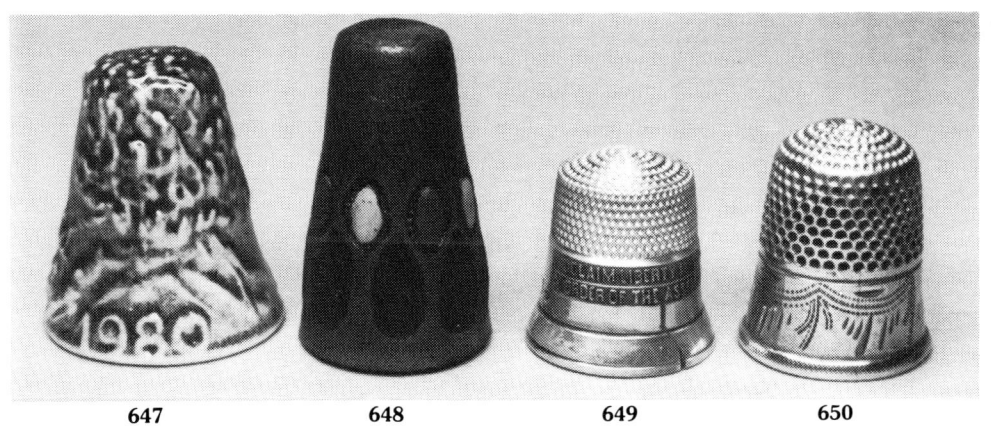

647 648 649 650

L

Laboute, Michaud — French silversmith who displayed thimbles of silver lined with platinum at the Palais du Louve in 1819.

La Pierre Mfg. Co. — American silversmiths in Buffalo, who made thimbles from 1885 to 1929. Founded by Fran H. La Pierre, they are known to have marked silver and gold thimbles with a script ℒ on the band.

Larkin — An American mail order house in Buffalo, NY, which issued a silver thimble to its secretaries at a convention in June 1916. The thimble is considered in the advertising category with the word LARKIN on the band. It was made by the Waite-Thresher Co. of Providence, R.I.

Latten — An alloy of copper and unrefined zinc, similar to brass, which replaced bronze for making thimbles from the 11th to the 16th century.

Lattice Work — Thimbles which have been pierced to create an open design or motif; may also be referred to as being thimbles with pierced work. See example # 1049

Lava — Souvenir thimbles of porcelain with glaze made from the ash of famous volcanoes, such as Vesuvius and St. Helens, have been sold for over 100 years. The lava ash gives white porcelain thimbles a mottled look. See example # 647.

Leather — It is widely believed that most thimbles were made of leather in Europe until the 1300s. These were known as "fingerlings," and have been used in one form or another from Europe to Asia. Hard leather rings and leather sailor's palms for sewing heavy canvas are used to this day. The development of low-cost latten thimbles for the working class replaced the need for homemade leather thimbles See thimble #648

The French Thimbles of Lenain

651   652   653   654

Lenain P. — Famous French thimble manufacturer of tall beautiful thimbles; makers of the de LaFontaine series and other fine silver thimbles. Their touchmark is a diamond with an L and an F separated by a large X with the diamond. A tiny mercury head denoting .950 silver is usually on their thimbles.

Levi & Salaman — British silversmith from Birmingham, late 19th Century, known to have made silver thimbles. Their maker's mark, L & S, can be found on some hallmarked thimbles.

Liberty Bell Thimble — A series of bell-shaped thimbles made by Simons Brothers in silver, gold, and pewter. The first design patent was issued in 1892. The thimble was made in 1917 as part of the Liberty Bond campaign, and again in 1925 as a souvenir of the Philadelphia Sesquicentennial. It was last issued in 1976 for the nation's bicentennial. It has the same words and crack as does the original Liberty Bell. It is the official club thimble of the Philadelphia Thimble Society. See thimble # 649.

Limoges — A district in Haute-Vienne, France where large deposits of kaolin (the key element in the making of fine hard porcelain) gave rise to many porcelain firms as early as 1783. The name is synonymous with fine French porcelain and is the home of Bernardaud, Haviland and other famous firms which have produced many beautiful porcelain thimbles.

Lincoln Drape — A design about the band of a thimble resembling a swag or drape, usually hand-chased. See thimble #650.

Linwood, Matthew — British silversmith working in Birmingham in the early 19th century. His mark, ML, is sometimes found on thimbles.

Lion Passant — A British symbol on silver denoting it is sterling, or 925/1000 percent pure. See page 300, bottom left corner.

Lladro — Famed Spanish porcelain house established in 1951 in Almacera by the Lladro brothers. Only one thimble has been made by this company. See illustration # 843.

655   656   657

Lofting, John — A Dutchman who received a patent from England's William and Mary for a thimble knurling machine in 1693. His thimbles were sand cast in brass, and he was the first to manufacture them on a large scale in Great Britain. It is the Dutch-style Lofting thimble which is found in many American colonial site excavations. See illustration on page 87.

For more detailed information, read the T.C.I. booklet, *John Lofting*, researched by Elizabeth Aldridge, written by Edwin Holmes, and printed by Dine-American.

Lost Wax Method — An ancient process of precise casting. A wax model is made and then invested in a clay or plaster mold. When the mold dries, the wax is removed by heating and vaporized. A cavity is then created. Into this cavity is poured gold, silver, etc. When this is solid, the mold is broken and the object is removed for finishing. See page 257.

Loth — A standard unit of purity in Central Europe until the mid-19th century. An old silver thimble with the hallmark stamped with the numbers 13 or 12 would have probably been made somewhere in the domain of the Austro-Hungarian Empire. One loth represented $6¼\%$ pure silver. Thus 12 lothige equaled .750 silver and 13 lothige was .8125 silver.

Lotthammer-Stutzel — German thimble manufacturer from Pforzheim who sometimes used a six-pointed motif on top of their thimbles. The company became Lotthammer-Eber when Frederich Eber took over. They went out of business in 1979 and the equipment sold to Thorvald Greif.

Louis XV Edge — An ornamental, rococo-style edge used by the Ketcham & McDougall Company on some of their thimbles. See example #657.

Low & Co., Daniel — Founded in 1867 by Daniel Low in Salem, Mass. The mail order firm began a reputation for unusual gifts. One such was the "Salem Witch" thimble designed by his son Seth in 1891. There are several styles of the famous thimble. See thimble #655.

Lundquist, Myrtle — American thimble collector, and author of three books on thimbles: *The Book of a Thousand Thimbles,* 1970; *Thimble Treasury,* 1975, and *Thimbles Americana,* 1981. It is said Miss Lundquist lit a candle in the darkness that was our knowledge of thimbles by her books. Many pictures and interesting stories make these three books a thimble triology to collectors around the world. All were published by Wallace-Homestead Co. of Des Moines, Iowa. Myrtle was working on her fourth book when she passed away in late 1985.

Lupp, Henry, 1760-1800 — Early American silversmith from New Brunswick, New Jersey, known to have made thimbles which he advertised for sale in the local paper on Oct. 14, 1783. His maker's mark consisted of H. LUPP or H.L. in a rectangle.

Lutz & Weiss — German thimble wholesalers from Pforzheim. Their thimbles are marked with a monogram of an L and a W.

Lysander — A British bone china manufacturer which is now making thimbles. Their unicorn thimble with a scalloped rim is their most unusual design.

Mager, Milton — American collector and authority on advertising thimbles. He was Vice President of T.C.I. and has written several articles on his specialty.

Mahoney, D. J. — American silversmith from New York City made thimbles about the turn of the century. His thimbles are marked with an "M" on the band.

Maker's Mark — Any mark (initials or symbol) on or inside a thimble which conveys the identity of the person or company which made the thimble; also known as the sponsor's mark in England.

Mann, Ruth — American thimble collector, first President of Thimble Collectors International, author and guest speaker on thimbles and publisher of the early newsletter "Thimble Collecting."

Marble — A rock which can be carved into thimbles, it is tough and able to give a high polish, and is available in many colors. Many beautiful artisan thimbles have been made from this versatile mineral. In Ireland, the famous olive green Connemara marble is used to inset into the tops of thimbles.

Maruri — A Taiwan porcelain manufacturer who is now making a line of thimbles with porcelain flowers in deep relief, fired onto the side of the thimble; also a line of novelty thimbles in the shape of hats.

Masa Mark — A symbol used by American Indians of the southwest to identify their tribe location. It can be found on the inside band, usually next to the silversmith's initials on better hand-made Indian thimbles.

Masons — A British ceramic manufacturer founded by Miles Mason. In 1813, Miles and his son, Charles, developed their famous "ironstone" ceramic body which they patented. The company underwent a series of name changes until 1968 when the name Mason was resumed. The Mason Company has made ironstone thimbles. See example # 847.

Massey, Samuel — A late 18th century English steel-top thimble manufacturer.

Masta — A private-label name found on thimbles made by Gabler for an American importer.

Matted Ground — A technique where a silversmith produces a dull background surface by chasing with repeated hammering, creating a contrast to a raised or shiny design. This can also be done by a die stamp.

May, Charles — English goldsmith in London who made exquisite gold thimbles during the second half of the 19th century. His mark was CM.

Miniature Masterpieces in Meissen Porcelain

658

659

660

661

662

663

138

| 664 | 665 | 666 | 667 |

Meerschaum — A light, creamy-white magnesium silicate material which is easily carved. Meerschaum thimbles, some with silver tops, are made in Turkey and several African nations for sale to tourists. See thimble #665.

Meissen Thimbles — The western world's first porcelain manufacturing company. Established in 1710, as a result of the experiments of Johann Bottger, who discovered the secret of making hard paste porcelain, then known only in the Orient. This discovery was to create an entirely new industry, as its secret leaked out all over Europe. Meissen was a small German town on the river Elbe, near large deposits of kaolin, the chief ingredient for porcelain. Here the Royal Saxon Porcelain Works were built with the backing of King Augustus of Saxony.

Meissen was to lead the western world in fine porcelain articles including thimbles. Their famous blue "crossed swords" symbol, marks it as a collector's masterpiece. In 1979 a dentil-shaped Meissen thimble in lemon yellow ground, made circa 1740, was auctioned at $18,000.00! Meissen made thimbles from the 1730s to approximately 1910. In 1981, Meissen produced the first of their annual limited edition thimbles. Once again Meissen thimbles are available to collectors. For 18th and 19th century Meissen thimbles see pages 138, 237, 238, and 239.

Mennecy-Villeroy — French porcelain manufacturer who was known to have made thimbles during the mid-18th Century. An example is in the Musee National de Ceramique in Paris.

Michigan-Indiana Thimble Society — A regional thimble study group founded in 1982. Lois Erdman was elected president.

Miller, Betty Jo — California thimble collector and designer of many unique collector's porcelain thimbles; keynote speaker at many thimble meetings.

Milne, Alexander — American manufacturer of gold and silver thimbles in Newark, New Jersey. He advertised in the *Jewelers' Circular*, 1883, and was listed in city directories 1871 to 1892.

Meissen Porcelain 18th century

668   669   670

The miniature panoramas painted by the skilled artists of the Royal Saxon Porcelain Works at Meissen during the 18th and 19th centuries make these thimbles one of the foremost collectibles in the world. Although these exquisite pieces bring bids in the thousands of dollars at the famous auction houses, a good friend of mine recently purchased one at a Wilmington antique fair for $27.00! The thrill of the hunt is alive and well.

671   672   673

These are the reverse side of above thimbles.

The Thimbles of Muhr

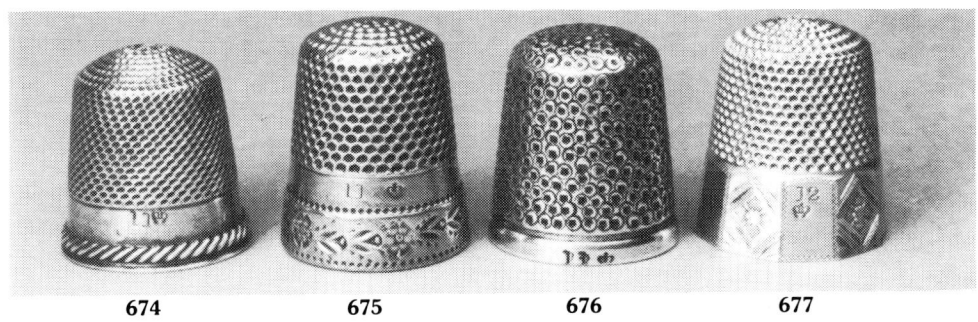

674   675   676   677

Mix, James — An American father and son silversmithing firm in Albany, New York. They are known to have made gold and silver thimbles from the early 19th century until about 1890. At this time, they discontinued making thimbles and purchased them from Ketcham & McDougall until about 1930. Their mark, J. MIX, is on both series. See page 286.

Moir, William — American silversmith from New York City during mid-19th century, 1844 to about 1870. His thimbles are marked "Wm MOIR" on the band.

Morral, Abel — British brand name found on iron and steel thimbles. Some are steel, lined with white metal. The name Abel Morral is stamped on the band near the rim. They were made by Charles Iles.

Moss Agate — A member of the agate family of very hard semi-precious stones. The moss agate has mossy, cloudy layers with different colors streaking through it, and is translucent. Many can be found on English "stone top" thimbles.

Mother-of-Pearl Thimbles — Mother of pearl thimbles became popular in France during the first half of the 19th century. Tall, dome-top thimbles with gold rings and sometimes enameled gold pansy medallion were made in little shops around the Palais Royal in Paris. Jacob Schwarz made flat-top mother-of-pearl thimbles in Austria during the mid-19th century. Today Mexico, Japan and the Philippines make metal thimbles overlayed with mother-of-pearl. See thimbles #55 and 1380.

Mt. St. Helen Thimbles — After the eruption of the volcano Mt. St. Helen in 1980, several porcelain firms began to use the ash as a glaze over their thimbles. The thimbles were hand-painted or had fired decals for decoration. The mottled look of this ash glaze gives the thimbles an unusual old look.

Muhr, Joseph — Son of Henry Muhr, founder of H. Muhr & Sons. He learned thimblemaking in his father's company. In 1888 he left the firm and made thimbles on his own until 1892, the year he died of mental illness. He registered a trademark (3 crowns in a row) in 1888 for his "crown alloy" thimbles. These look very much like gold. See thimble #182.

SIMON MUHR

Muhr, H. & Sons — A Philadelphia jewelry firm founded by Henry Muhr in 1854. Henry was destined by his parents to be a Rabbi, but he apprenticed himself to a watchmaker in Cologne, Germany. He migrated to America in 1853 and set up shop on Vine St. above Front in Philadelphia in 1854.

In 1863, Simon Muhr joined his father as a salesman and the firm soon became one of the foremost jewelry and silver manufacturers in Philadelphia. They opened offices in New York, Chicago and Antwerp, Belgium. By 1892, their seven-story factory at Broad & Race Sts. grew to 94,000 square feet with over 400 employees. Simon took over the company following his father's death in 1892. His younger brothers, Jacob, Philip, and Joseph were also partners in the firm.

The company assets were sold in 1898 owing to the death of several brothers. Their trademark was a crown with a Maltese cross atop, usually on the outside rim of their thimbles. Joseph Muhr made thimbles on his own for 4 years after leaving the company in 1888. For more detailed information, see the excellent 24 page booklet on firm by the Philadelphia Thimble Society.

678

Mrs. Sarah Anne Weisbrot

National Thimble Collectors — A thimble study group formed by Sarah Anne Weisbrot of New Jersey in 1955. This group sent a round robin newsletter to its members who each contributed information and mailed it to the next member. NTC is considered the first American thimble collector's group. Its membership was the "who's who" of thimble collectors: Elizabeth Sickels, Emily Hunt, Alta Thompson, Aline le Mire, Wilna Lane, Margret Parshall, Doris Ramstead, Ann Blakeslee, Kitty Simons, Nellie Price, Lucy Earle, Edna Butterfield, Nell Anderson, Kate Searl, Isabel Murray, Wellene Dernehl, Hinda Nathan, Leasa Jennish, and Bessie Arnold. The group is no longer active, but its members wrote countless articles in magazines and newspapers, and some members donated their collections to museums for all to enjoy. They were also the first club to commission a sterling thimble from Simons with the letters NTC on the band and the date 1955.

Navajo — An American Indian tribe in the Southwest United States known for their exquisite hand-crafted silver work. Navajo thimbles inset with petrified wood, turquoise, and other stones of the region are made for collectors. Most have Indian maker's marks inside.

Needle-Pusher — The common name for a group of pressure tools which were used to force large needles through heavy hides or canvas; also known by the Latin name "Acutrudium." Needle-pushers date back to neolithic times. See page 18.

| 679 | 680 | 681 | 682 |

Newhall — British bone china manufacturer who is now making a line of fine bone china thimbles. See illustration # 850.

Niello — An ancient art form process where a silversmith makes a black, lustrous metal alloy of sulphides of silver, copper and lead and fuses the "enamel-like" mixture into an engraved area on the band of a thimble, thus highlighting the contrast between the bright silver design and the black background. Russian, American Indian, Iraqi and Spanish thimblemakers often use this technique. See above illustration.

Nifty — An Australian brand name found on the boxes containing silver thimbles; early 20th century.

Noritake — This world famous Japanese porcelain firm was founded in 1876. Noritake artists take great effort to achieve a uniqueness by unusual shapes rather than decoration. Noritake has made only one thimble to date. See illustration # 851.

Norrkoping Thimbles — The town of Norrkoping was the site of the first thimble mill in Sweden. Founded in 1757 by Sven Rinman and Jean Henrich Lefebure, the mill turned out up to 70,000 brass and silver thimbles a year. Due to fire, and war-interrupted commerce, the factory fell into insolvency in 1796.

Norwegian Thimbles — The silversmiths of Norway have created two distinct styles which are unique to their country. The first style uses delicate cloissoned-enamel motifs to capture the geometric patterns of Norway. The second style used multi-colored enamels to create a "Northern Lights" background. Against this, Norwegian artists paint, in black silhouette, breathtaking scenes of wildlife and young children at play. Many older thimbles are set with moonstone tops, while newer ones have cross-hatched metal tops. The firm of David-Andersen, founded in 1876, still makes these exquisite thimbles. See thimbles 683 to 691.

The Thimbles of Norway

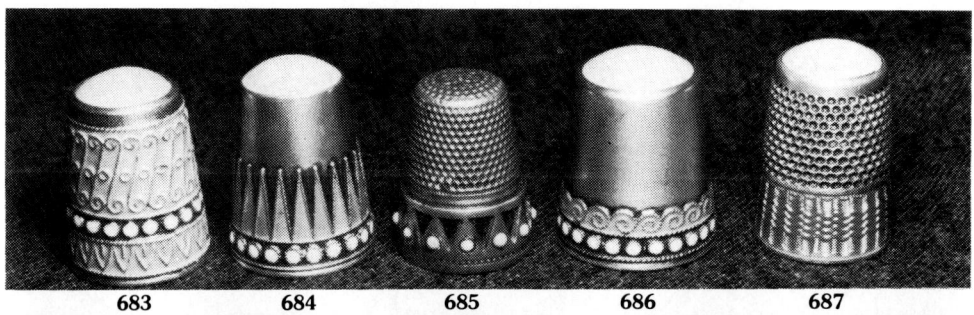

683   684   685   686   687

688   689   690   691

Novelty Thimbles — During Victorian times, and up to our own days, many novelty thimbles were sold as souvenirs and gimmicks. Stanhope (peep show type), telescoping thimbles, thimbles with rattles and whistles, thimbles with secret compartments, and thimbles that glow in the dark were the delight of our ancestors.

Today, we have novelty thimbles that change color, have little doors which open and show a scene, or a moving train or a merry-go-round which revolves around the band. We see beer steins, animals, houses, castles and hats, all in the shape of a thimble. There are porcelain thimbles with so many flowers and lace applied as to be useless as a real thimble, or shaped like the bust of famous men and women.

All these are novelty or pseudo thimbles. They have become a collectible in their own right and perhaps one day will command the prices old Victorian novelty thimbles do now. See page 146.

Nun's Thimbles — Nickname given to some ebony and bog oak thimbles due to their black satin finish.

The Wacky World of Novelty Thimbles

692   693   694

695   696   697   698

699   700   701   702

699   701   700

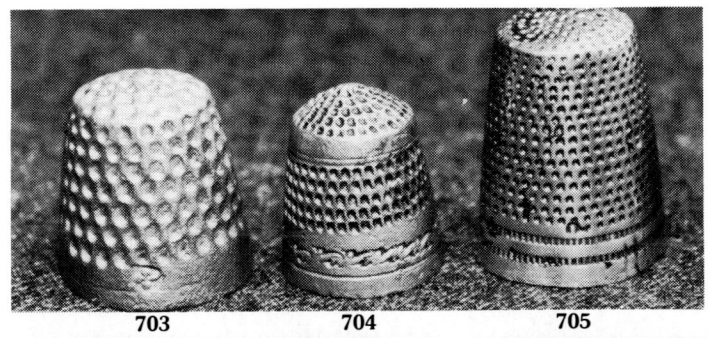

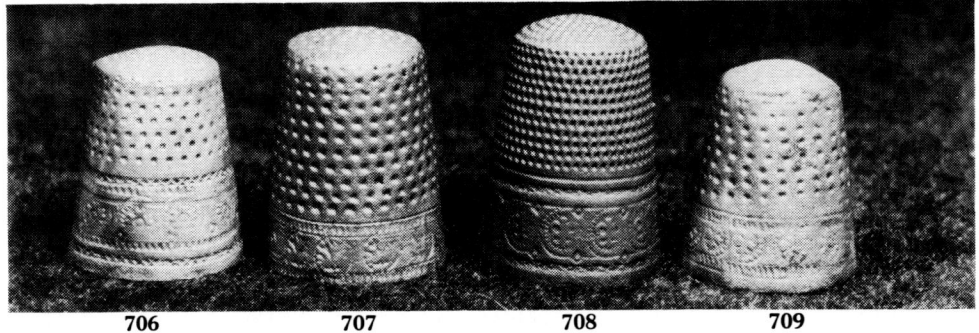

Nuremberg Thimbles — The medieval German city of Nuremberg developed an early preeminence in thimble making. An old drawing of a monk drilling indentations into a cast latten thimble is our earliest known documented evidence of this craft. The drawing, in the Nuremberg city archives, dates about 1390. The Nuremberg thimblers had their thimbles cast by the coppersmith guild. The thimblers had only to indent and finish them, as was done in most of western Europe at the time. See page 37.

Early in the sixteenth century the city's celebrated craftsmen discovered the secret of refining zinc from calamine. The discovery gave the thimblemakers a new, non-brittle brass alloy, which could be hammered (deep-drawn) from a thin coin-like disc into a thimble shape quickly, without cracking. This new method was much faster and produced a better quality thimble. See thimbles above.

With its strong tradition of guilds, Nuremberg soon became the leading producer of brass thimbles, exporting them via Spain, Venice, and Holland to the world.

War, siege, and narrow-minded aristocratic rulers crippled the city and her guilds. By the mid-17th century Holland had taken the lead from the renowned German "fingerhuters" in the production of working brass thimbles.

Many Nuremberg brass thimbles have maker's marks, usually found where the indentations begin near the rim. The Nuremberg thimble illustrated (top center) was part of the cargo of the ill-fated ship Gagiana which sank in 1583. For a more detailed history on Nuremberg, I recommend Greif's *Talks About Thimbles,* published in English for Dine-American.

      710   711   712   713

Oakley China — A small British china company which made a bone china thimble commemorating the wedding of Prince Charles and Lady Diana. Their mark is inside.

Objects of Virtu — The name of the category in which major auction houses, such as Christie's and Sotheby's, list thimbles in their preview catalogs.

Ohio Thimble Seekers — A regional group of collectors formed in 1983 by Evelyn Eubanks to study thimbles.

Ohio Valley Thimblers — A regional club for collectors in Kentucky, Indiana, and Ohio. The first meeting was coordinated by Debbie Fuller in June 1983.

Olney, Amsdan & Son — British manufacturer company known to have made thimbles about the turn of the century. Their mark was OA&S.

Onyx — A stone from the chalcedony family available in many colors. Onyx thimbles are being made today for tourists in Mexico and South America.

Opal — A semi-precious gemstone of translucent silica of various colors which reflects a rainbow of colors. Opals have been used to decorate thimbles around the base.

Open-end — Any thimble made without a top, or the so-called "Tailor's Thimble." These are used from the side leaving the fingertip free. These are the oldest known style of sewing thimble.

Openwork — An ornamental design formed by piercing the body of a thimble and creating a perforated area, also known as latticework. See thimble 712.

Oreide (o-re-ide) oroide — An alloy of copper, zinc, and tin which looks like gold when shined. Some Simons' SBC designs were made of this material.

Ottignons Thimbles — A British porcelain firm in Norfolk which is producing a line of exceptionally beautiful hand-painted thimbles.

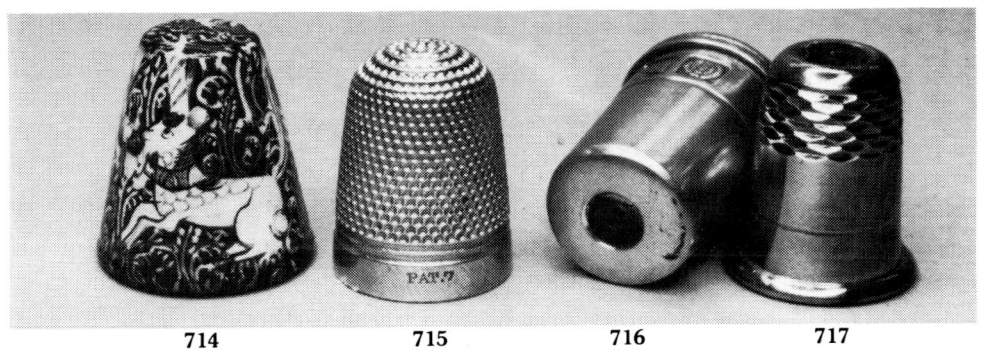

714　　　　　　715　　　　　　716　　　　　　717

𝒫

Palais Royal — A term used for a unique style of mother-of-pearl thimbles made in Paris in the first half of the 19th century. The name came from the location around the Palais Royal of the artisan shops engaged in making them. The thimbles usually had one or two gold rings about their lower half. Some are inset with an enameled medallion of a pansy. See thimble # 1380.

Palmate — An ancient design with a central dot or circle with radiant lines flowing from it.

Papier Mache — A material made of paper, salt, flour and water. It becomes like a clay and can be formed into many objects. Once dry, it can be painted. Papier Mache thimbles in bright colored grounds and hand-painted native designs have been made in India and other Oriental countries in recent years and sold as folk art thimbles. See # 714.

Paneled Thimbles — A very different design that became popular in the late Victorian era and came to be called "paneled." The design was created by a series of flat angled surfaces or facets on what was usually a smooth round band. The edges of the facets were "fluted" with vertical grooves in parallel rows. By changing the cadence of the fluting and the sizes of the facets, a multitude of paneled designs came forth from American thimble-makers. See page 150.

Parian Ware — A highly vitrified and translucent frit porcelain invented by the British firm of W.T. Copeland in 1842. Most Royal Worcester thimbles were made of this slightly off-white porcelain from 1860 to 1939.

Paris Exposition Thimbles — A series of silver thimbles made by the French firm of Lenain to commemorate the Expositions held in Paris in 1889 and 1900. See thimble # 176.

Pat. — Abbreviation for the word patent found on early Dorcas and many other British and American thimbles. Many times a date will follow the word Pat.

American Paneled Thimbles

734

JAMES PETERS,

GOLD AND SILVER THIMBLE AND PENCIL CASE MANUFACTURER,

No. 65, ARCH-STREET,

Between Second & Third streets,

Has constantly on hand the above articles of as good quality and on as low terms as can be obtained. Also, Silver Spoons, Spectacles, Jewellery, &c. wholesale and retail.

Orders will be thankfully received and punctually attended to.

Peters, James — Early American silversmith, 1790-1872; advertised in De Silvers Philadelphia Directory as a gold and silver thimble manufacturer. He marked some of his thimbles: J. Peters, 65 Arch St., Phila., Pa. Records show him at this location from 1820 to 1824. See band on above thimbles.

Thimbles of Pewter

Collector's Personal Thimbles

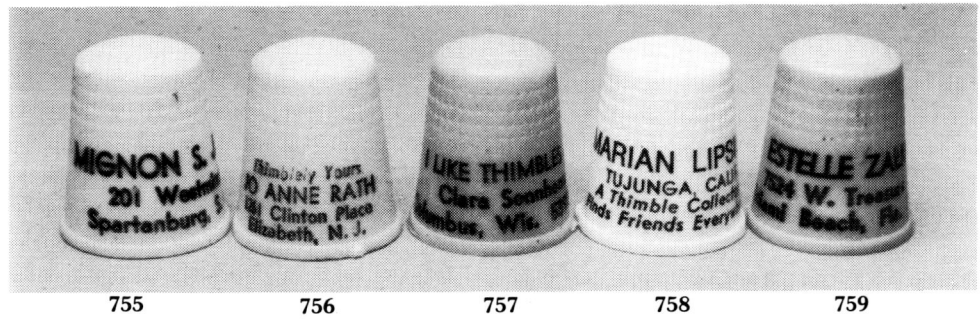

755　　　　　　756　　　　　　757　　　　　　758　　　　　　759

Paye & Baker Mfg. Co. — American silversmiths from North Attleboro, Mass., from 1898 to 1935 known to have made thimbles. Their mark is three hearts in a row with a "P" in the first, the "and" symbol ("&") in the second and "B" in the third.

Peephole Thimbles — A type of Victorian novelty through which, when held up to a light and to the eye, the viewer could see a magnified scene. Peepholes, also referred to as a "STANHOPE," can also be found in needle cases and other items which were often sold as tourist souvenirs. Modern versions are now available. See thimble 444.

Pemberton, Samuel — English silversmith from Birmingham who made gold and silver thimbles in the late 18th century. His marker's mark was SP.

Percival, D.C. & Co. — A Boston jeweler, circa 1892, who sold thimbles of gold and silver with an old English P in the top. The thimbles were made by Waite-Thresher Co. Percival gold-filled thimbles have a star stamped into their old English "P" trademark.

Perkins, Marjorie — American thimble collector, founding member of the Philadelphia Thimble Society and co-author of "Thimble Language", a glossary of thimble terms.

Personals — A thimble collector's slang word for a thimble with a personal message and/or his name and address printed on the outside band. See above illustration

Petit Point Thimbles — A very small needlepoint design applied around the side of a thimble for decoration. Austria is a leading exporter of this type of collector's thimbles. See illustrations: # 780 and 781.

Pewter Thimbles — The lead-alloy metal called pewter was widely used during the 16th, 17th and early 18th centuries. Few early thimbles were made from this metal due to its softness. Antique pewter thimbles are very rare.

Within the last decade a great many lead-free pewter thimbles have been made for collectors. Some have the dull finish one usually associates with pewter, while others look almost like silver. Today's collectors have a bewildering array from which to choose. See pages 152 and 154.

Thimbles of Pewter

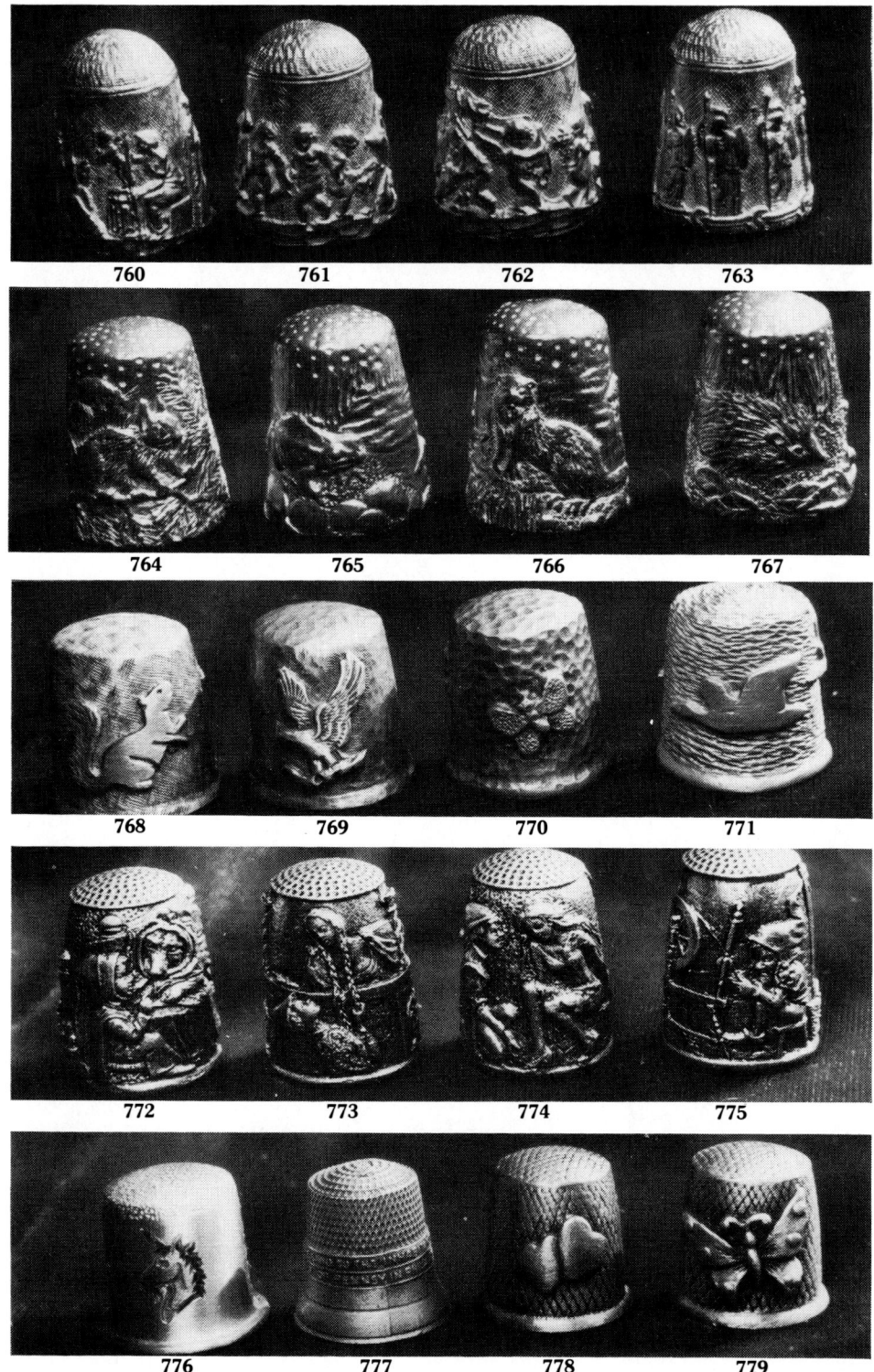

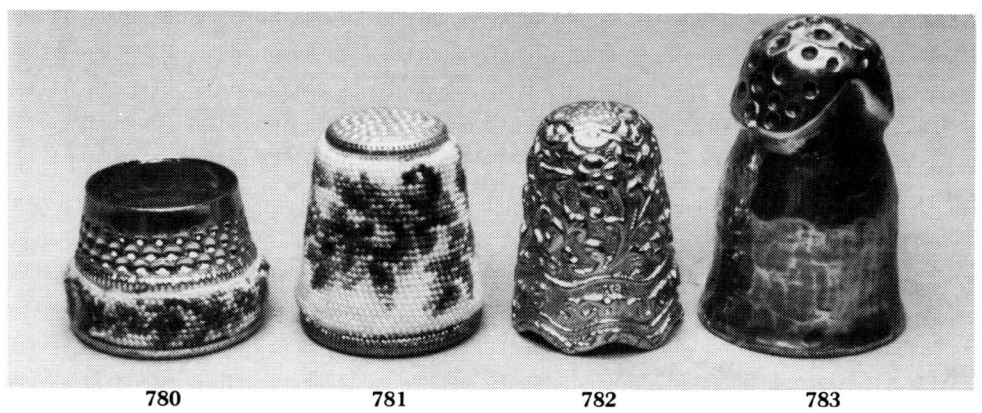

780   781   782   783

Pforzheim — A city in Germany with a long history of thimblemaking. In 1978, there was a special "Exhibition of Thimble and Historical Sewing Items" in the Pforzheim Jewelry Museum. The exhibition was the inspiration of Mr. Helmut Greif, and featured some of the rarest thimbles in the world from many museums and private individuals. A special silver thimble was designed in a rococo style, with a scalloped rim and the words Schmuckmusem Pforzheim 1978 on the band to commemorate the events. See thimble # 782.

Phallic Motif Thimbles — A curious, if not odd, motif for a thimble which seems to have its origin in the Victorian era.

Over a half dozen styles are known to exist in silver and ivory. In her book, *A Thimble Full,* Cecile Dreesmann illustrates an ivory one on pages 75 and 76. It is hand-carved and inscribed "Love Russ." One in sterling silver is illustration # 783.

Philadelphia Thimble Society — Founded in 1979, Evelyn Der Marderosian was chosen as chairman. The society hosted the 1984 T.C.I. Convention in Philadelphia. The group sponsored the H. Muhr booklet as a club project.

Pierce-Work Thimbles — A decorative effect created by cutting through the side walls of a thimble. Also called lattice-work. The pattern of the piercing usually creates a design or motif. See thimbles 784 to 791.

784   785   786   787

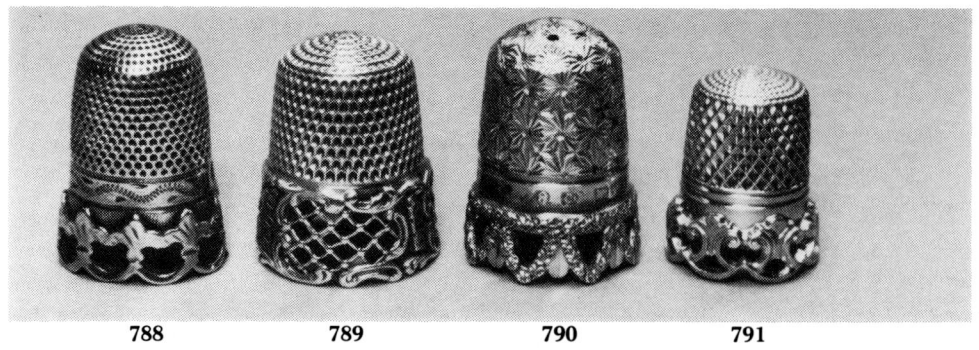

| 788 | 789 | 790 | 791 |

Piercy's Patent Thimble — John Piercy, an Englishman, patented a process for making tortoise shell thimbles in 1816. These thimbles were lined and tipped with steel, silver or gold. One example has a coat of arms piqued into the side with the words PIERCY'S PATENT on a ribbon below. These are rare collector's items. One is on display at the Colonial Williamsburg Collection. For example, see thimble #1377.

Pinchbeck — An alloy of five parts copper and one part zinc which was invented by Christopher Pinchbeck (1670-1732). The gold-colored metal was used as a substitute for gold. One American silversmith, Benjamin Halsted, advertised pinchbeck thimbles in 1766.

Pique — A technique of inlaying a metal, usually gold, into tortoise shell. The shell is heated until it becomes soft enough to press in the gold motifs. It was very popular in the 19th Century and is the process used on the Piercy's Patent Thimble. See thimble # 792.

Plastic Thimbles — In the United States plastic thimbles became popular as an advertising give a way after the First World War. The firm of Brown & Bigelow of St. Paul, Minnesota made millions. Soon the plastic political thimble was being used by every office holder from Dog Catcher to President. The plastic thimbles of today are descendants of the early celluloids and come in a bewildering variety of shapes, sizes and colors.

Platinoid — An alloy of copper, zinc and nickel. This "silvery" material was used by several British thimble manufacturers late in the 19th century.

Platinum — A silvery-white metal which does not tarnish. Platinum lined thimbles were made in France as early as the 18th century. Also known are Russian enameled thimbles made of platinum.

Platt, George W. (1798-1881) — American silversmith who, with Nathaniel Potter, opened a shop in Huntington, Long Island, circa 1819. In 1828 he bought out Potter's interest, and worked alone. Later he taught his younger brother, Nathan, the art of silversmithing and thimblemaking. The shop was listed as GW & NC Platt Jewelers. The firm's name was changed several times over the years and was in business until 1915. See page 284

792   793   794   795

Political Thimbles — Any thimble which expresses a political point of view, has a political party's motif, or requests you to vote for a candidate is considered a political thimble. These are also referred to as campaign thimbles, and may one day be of historical importance.

During the first World War, the Axis powers issued a series of unusual thimbles declaring a distinct point of view. One stated about its band: Gott Strafe Italien (God Damn Italy) or Gott Strafe England (God Damn England)!

The Nazis, during the second World War, issued silver and base metal thimbles with their swastika applied to the bands.

It seems a bit sad that this little benign tool, a symbol of quiet domestic industry, should have been used to carry messages of such hate and fear. The above iron thimble, with its applied red-enameled swastika, was given to loyal party supporters, who had donated their gold or silver thimbles to the Third Reich.

War Time Political Thimbles

796   797   798   799

157

Porcelain Thimbles — Johann Bottger's accidental discovery of the secret of making porcelain was a major achievement of the early 18th century.

For centuries, the Chinese held a total monopoly on the precious translucent ceramic. Some of the earliest items made in this new material, were the exquisite Meissen thimbles with meticulous hand-painted scenes about their borders. One sold recently at Christie's auction for over $18,000.00! Other 18th century Meissen thimbles have sold for $3,500 to $7,500.

By the late 18th century, porcelain thimbles were being made by many other noted manufacturers, such as Sevres, Mennecy, Chelsea, Derby, Nymphenburg, Royal Copenhagen, Worcester and Wedgwood, to name a few.

The porcelain thimble continued its popularity throughout the 19th century. The English introduction of bone china (porcelain made with bone) gave rise to another generation of thimble-making firms such as Grainger, Royal Worcester, Royal Crown Derby, Sampson Hancock and others. These companies created a vast array of beautifully hand-painted thimbles for the gift-giving public.

In the 20th century, both hand-painted and fired-decal porcelain thimbles continue to be offered by over a hundred manufacturers. Many enthusiasts try to collect one thimble from each company. The following pages illustrate some of the varieties available to collectors, plus a list of most of the known manufacturers and their country of origin.

There is also another group of porcelain thimbles which invites the attention of collectors. They are the creations of local artisans. These thimbles are usually hand-made and hand-painted. Some are beautiful miniature works of art, while others capture simple folk arts. Many are worthy of a place in any collection, and are modestly priced.

Talented artists have worked painstakingly to bring us these unique collectibles. In tribute to their skills and imagination, I have begun a list of their names, before only the memory of their thimbles is left.

Ann Armentor	Joann Hall	Graham Payne
Bernadine Biske	Reba Hast	Shirley Rains
Gail Boekel	Mildred Kohls	Rayma Robertson
Wendy Bowen	Betty Jo Miller	Stines Family
Marihelen Engelen	Carol Mossey	Peter Swingler
Joan Geertz	C. Nunn	W. R. Tipton
Mary Grant	Rae Nuttall	Judith Viges

A List of Known
Porcelain Thimble Manufacturers

*ADAMS — ENGLAND
*AGOSTINELLI — ITALY
 ARCADIAN CHINA — ENGLAND
 ARISTOCRAT — ENGLAND
*ASHLEYDALE — ENGLAND
 AUDRE CHINA — U.S.A.
 AYNSLEY — ENGLAND
*B.C. HIGHLAND — SCOTLAND
*BAREUTHER WALDSASSEN — GERMANY
 BELEEK — IRELAND
*BELMAR EDITION (Bel) — U.S.A.
*BERNARDAUD & CIE (B&C) — FRANCE
*BING & GRONDAHL — DENMARK
*BIRCHCRAFT — ENGLAND
 BRYLIAN PORCELAIN — U.S.A.
*CANADIAN CLASSIC — CANADA
*CANADIAN SUPERIOR — CANADA
 CAPO de MONTE — ITALY
 CARSON MINT — U.S.A.
*CAVERSWALL — ENGLAND
 CERAMIC ART CO. — U.S.A.
*CERAMIC ARTISTICA — MEXICO
 CHELSEA — ENGLAND
*COALPORT — ENGLAND
*CORAL — U.S.A.
*COUNTESS — ENGLAND
*CROWN STAFFORDSHIRE — ENGLAND
 DERBY — ENGLAND
*DELOREA — U.S.A.
 ELLARD — U.S.A.
*FENTON — ENGLAND
*FINSBURY — ENGLAND
 FRANCESCA — ENGLAND
*FRANCISCAN — U.S.A.
*FRANKLIN PORCELAIN — U.S.A.
*FUKAGAWA — JAPAN
 FURSTENBURG — GERMANY
 G S M — WALES
 G J K — U.S.A.
*GINORI — ITALY
*GOLDEN CROWN — ENGLAND
*GORHAM — U.S.A.
*GRIDLEY, FREDERICK (FG) — U.S.A.
*HAMMERSLEY — ENGLAND
*HAVILAND — FRANCE
*HEALACRAFT — ENGLAND
*HEIRLOOM EDITIONS — U.S.A.
*HEREND — HUNGARY
 HEXAGON STUDIOS — ENGLAND
*HOLLOHAZA — HUNGARY
 HUNTER PORCELAIN — U.S.A.
*HURLEY PORCELAIN — U.S.A.
*HUTSCHENREUTHER — GERMANY

*IRISH DRESDEN — IRELAND
*JOHNSON BROTHERS — ENGLAND
*KAISER PORCELAIN — GERMANY
*KUBA — GERMANY
 LADY ELEANOR — ENGLAND
*LINDNER — GERMANY
*LLADRO — SPAIN
*LORD NELSON — ENGLAND
 LUCKENBOOTH — SCOTLAND
*LYSANDER — ENGLAND
*MARURI MASTERPIECE — TAIWAN
 MARY JANE — ENGLAND
*MASONS — ENGLAND
*MEISSEN — GERMANY
 MENNECY-VILLEROY — FRANCE
 MINTON — ENGLAND
*MOSA — HOLLAND
 MOUNT ROYAL — ENGLAND
*NEWHALL — ENGLAND
 HOHENSTRAUSS — GERMANY
*NORITAKE — JAPAN
 OAKLEY — ENGLAND
*OKURA — JAPAN
*OTTIGNUNS — ENGLAND
*PALISSY — ENGLAND
*PORSGRUND — NORWAY
*QUEENS — ENGLAND
 QUEENSWAY — ENGLAND
 RADNOR — ENGLAND
*REUTTER — GERMANY
*ROMAN — MEXICO
*ROSTRAND — SWEDEN
*ROYAL ADDERLEY — ENGLAND
*ROYAL ALBERT — ENGLAND
*ROYAL COPENHAGEN — DENMARK
*ROYAL DOULTON — ENGLAND
 ROYAL GRAFTON — ENGLAND
*ROYAL TARA — IRELAND
 ROYAL WINDSOR — ENGLAND
*ROYAL WORCESTER — ENGLAND
 ST. ANDREWS — SCOTLAND
*ST. GEORGE — ENGLAND
 SANFORD — ENGLAND
*STAFFORDSHIRE — ENGLAND
 SCHOOREN — SWITZERLAND
 SCHULZ PORCELAIN — U.S.A.
 SHEER ELEGANCE — ENGLAND
*SOUTHERLAND — ENGLAND
*SPODE — ENGLAND
*THEODORE PAUL — ENGLAND
*VISTA ALEGRE — PORTUGAL
*WEDGWOOD — ENGLAND
*WHITE HERON (Hereford) — NEW ZEALAND

*Company's thimbles illustrated on following pages.

Thimbles of Porcelain and Bone China

Thimbles of Porcelain and Bone China

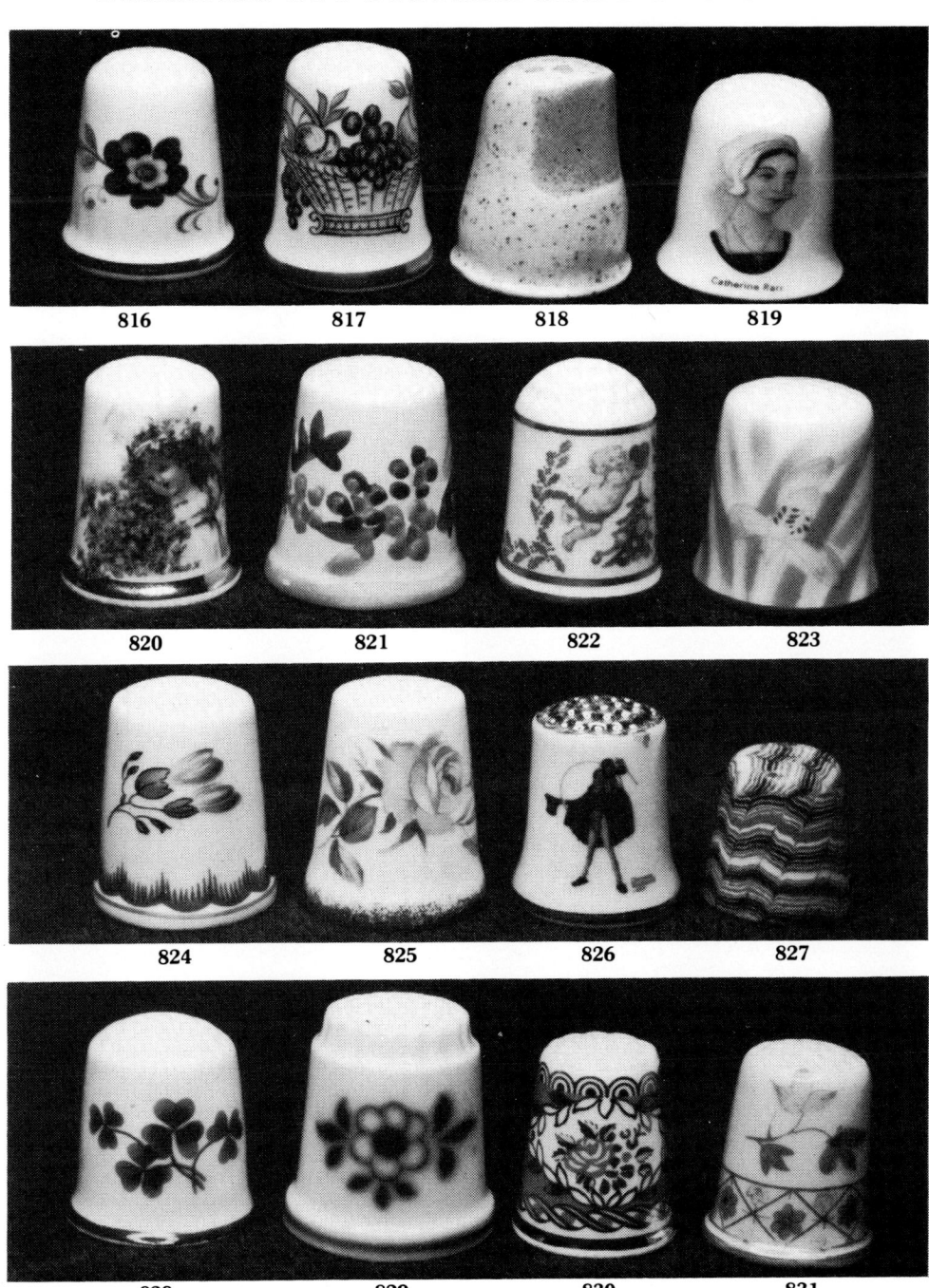

816 817 818 819
820 821 822 823
824 825 826 827
828 829 830 831

Thimbles of Porcelain and Bone China

832 833 834 835

836 837 838 839

840 841 842 843

844 845 846 847

Thimbles of Porcelain and Bone China

848	849	850	851
852	853	854	855
856	857	858	859
860	861	862	863

Thimbles of Porcelain and Bone China

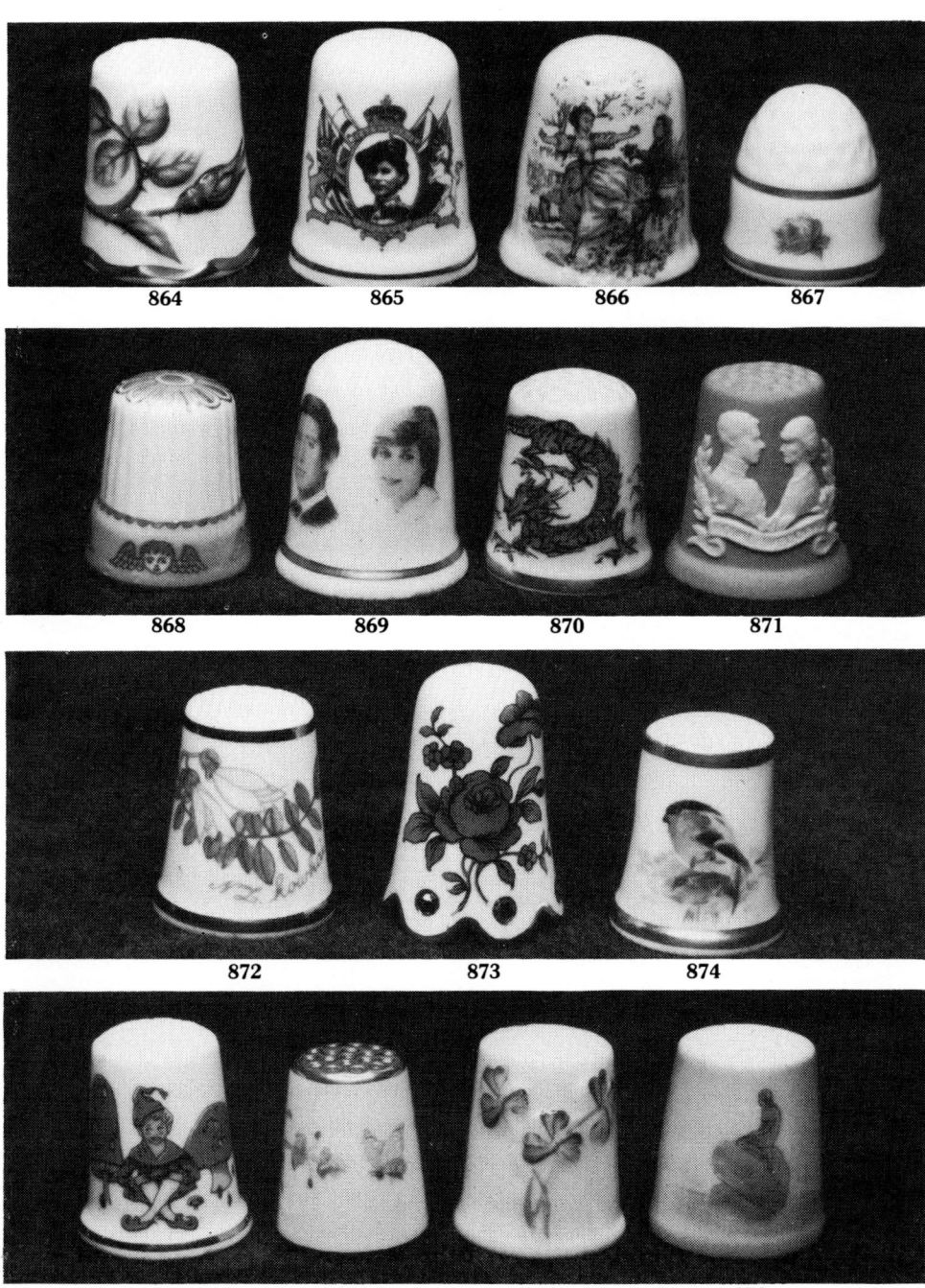

Artisan Thimbles in Porcelain

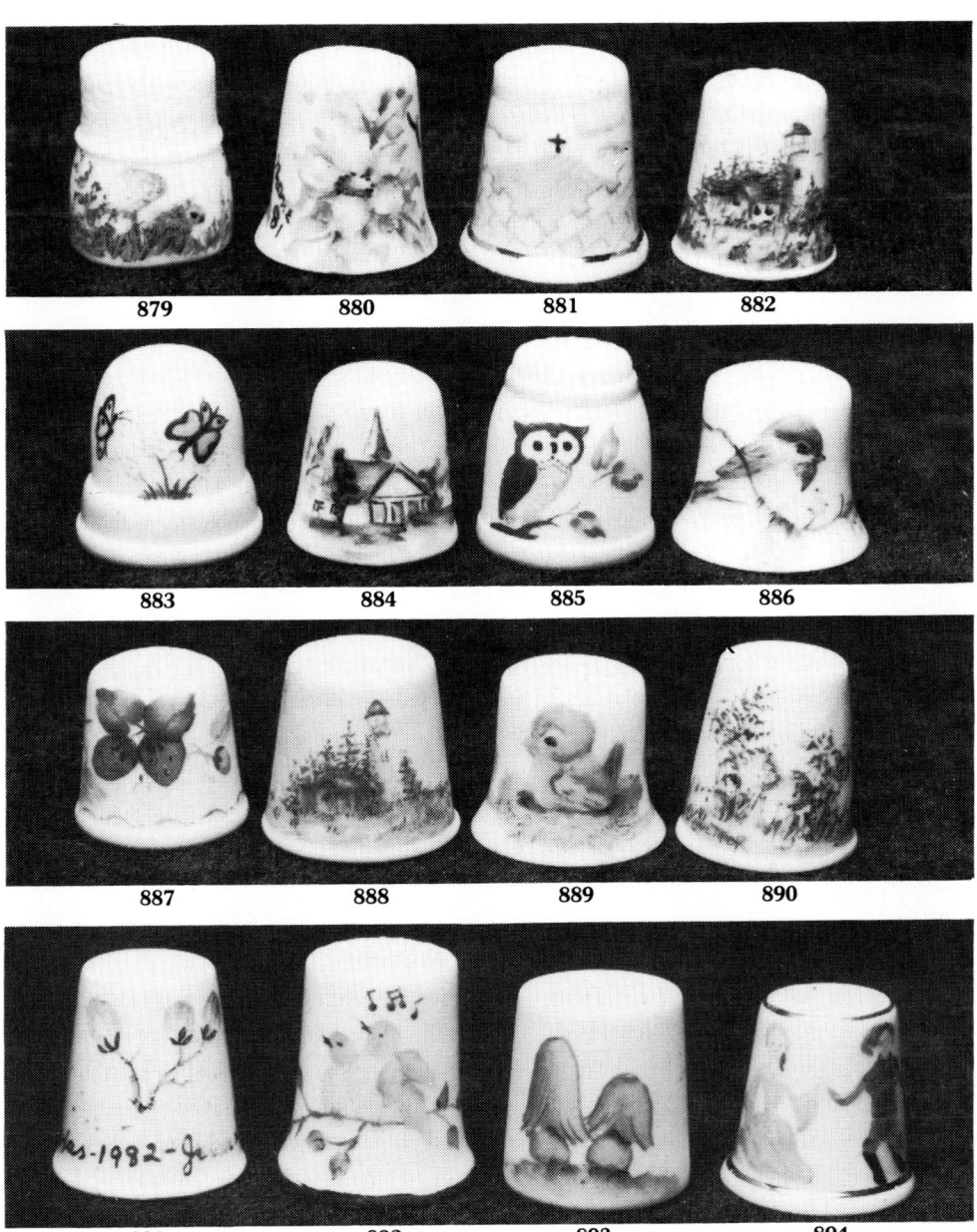

879	880	881	882
883	884	885	886
887	888	889	890
891	892	893	894

Thimbles of Portugal

895	896	897	898
899	900	901	902
903	904	905	906

907 908 909

Porsgrund — Norwegian manufacturer of fine hand-painted porcelain thimbles. See example #854.

Portrait Thimbles — Any thimble which has a picture of a person as its main decorative motif. Portrait thimbles of great beauty have been hand-painted by Peter Swingler for about $125.00 per thimble. The work is done on an enameled silver thimble.

Portuguese Thimbles — There is a series of thin, silver-plated embossed thimbles made in Topazio, Portugal with hand-painted flowers, animals and scenes on them. These inexpensive thimbles are very similar to the sterling silver ones from the same factory. The sterling ones have a tiny 925 stamped into the side or on some, the top.

Powell, William — "Little Willy," as his fellow painters at the Royal Worcester Porcelain Works called him, was one of that company's most charming artists in the painting of native English birds. He loved feeding them with crumbs from his meals and this close observation and admiration was translated into his work. William painted thimbles from 1900 to 1950. He was a badly deformed hunchback, but this handicap never prevented him from loving to talk to any visitor about his work. Powell's thimbles today bring $150-$250 at auctions.

Priscilla — A tradename stamped under the apex of one design of silver thimbles made by Simons Brothers during the late 19th and early 20th century. See thimble #910.

Priscillas, The — A Massachusetts regional thimble group founded in May, 1981, at the Massachusetts mini convention by Lorraine Crosby and Dorothy Mager.

Prime, Ezra Conklin — (1810-1898) Early American silversmith, who served his apprenticeship under George Platt. In 1832 he formed a partnership with John Roshore. He later established a thimble factory in Huntington, Long Island. Three of his five brothers were also silversmiths specializing in the making of thimbles. By the mid 1800s, E.C. Prime & Co. was the largest thimble manufacturer in America, and considered the "Father of the Thimble Industry." Ezra Prime taught Hugh Mc Dougall, George R. Rogers, and Miles Griffith the thimble business. Each was to make his mark on the industry. The Prime thimbles have no touchmark.

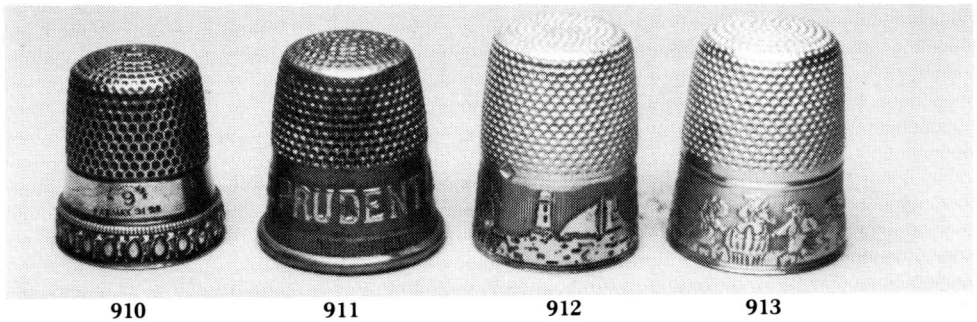

910　　　　911　　　　912　　　　913

Proctor Collection — A fine collection of diverse and rare thimbles on display in the Munson-Williams-Proctor Institute in Utica, New York. The collection was the labor of love of two sisters: Mrs. Frederick Proctor and Mrs. Thomas Proctor.

Prudential Thimbles — An American life insurance company which distributed millions of brass and aluminum thimbles during the early part of the 20th century. These were part of advertising campaigns. There are three versions of the Prudential thimble. See thimble # 911.

Prudhomme, O. — French silver manufacturer founded in 1887 in Paris. They make a line of shorter, flat-top thimbles. See "Thimble Marks" for their symbol and illustrations # 912 and 913.

Pseudo Thimbles — Any thimble shaped object which purports to be a thimble, but could not easily be used to sew with. See below illustration.

Punchmark — An identifying mark, initials or symbol stamped into a metal thimble with a hand-made die by the maker.

Pseudo Thimbles

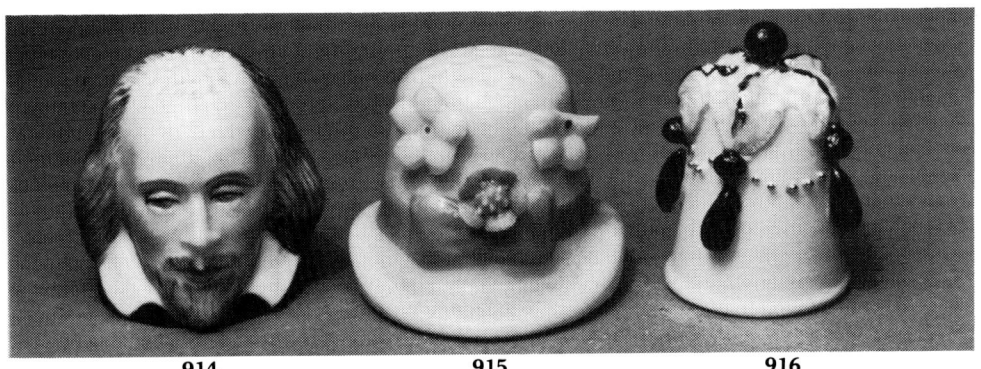

914　　　　　　　915　　　　　　　916

Quaker — A tradename stamped under the apex of a specially designed silver thimble, made by Simons Brothers Company of Philadelphia.

Quaker Style — A plain band thimble without a rim or any form of decorations.

Queens China — A small British china manufacturer who is now making a line of bone china thimbles. Their name is stamped on the inside. See illustration #855.

Quincy Brothers — American silversmiths in Portland, Maine, known to have made thimbles, circa 1823-1878. Their thimbles are marked on the band with "Q. Bros."

917   918   919   920

Thimbles with something to say

921

A thimble with something to hide!

Thimble Classics

OK, all ready! So beauty ain't my strong set, but I got feeling!

"I jus wov phimbles!"

Thimbles With Religious Themes

The Thimbles of Ludwig Redl

938   939   940   941   942

Rae, William T. Co. — American silversmith company in Newark, New Jersey, 1856 to 1908. Their thimbles are marked with "Rae & Co." on the band.

Rains, Shirley — American china painter best known for her renditions of small birds on porcelain thimbles.

Rainwater, Dorothy — American author of *Encyclopedia of American Silver Manufacturers*, a history of 1400 American silversmiths with more than 2200 illustrated marks.

Red Top Thimbles — A series of plastic advertising and political thimbles painted red to "catch the eye." The lower half was usually in white or ivory and carried a message printed about the band. Red top thimbles were popular from the late 1920s to the 1950s. See thimble #943.

Redl, Ludwig — An Austrian sculptor who designed in 1984 a series of Britannia silver thimbles commemorating the American Revolution. Using famous paintings of critical points during the war, Redl created in bas-relief twelve historic thimbles in thin silver. Later he created a series of "Shakespearian" and "Wagnerian Ring" theme thimbles highlighted in 24K gold. The thimbles are hallmarked in England. See above thimbles.

Reed & Barton — American manufacturer and silversmith company which is making silver thimbles with a damascene medallion attached to the side. See thimble 945.

Religious Theme Thimbles — Thimbles with religious motifs have been sold in many church gift shops and pilgrimage sites for more than a hundred years. The German firm of Soergel & Stollmeyer was especially active in the "devotional thimble trade." Religious thimbles have been made in silver, brass, aluminum, alpacca, silver gilt, gold, and plastic. See opposite page.

Courtesy Museum of Fine Arts, Boston

943   944   945   946

Replaceable Top Thimbles — Otto Weber designed a thimble with a removable crown which unscrewed from the base. He reasoned, in the patent of Nov. 30, 1886, waste not, want not. If all you need is a new top half of a thimble, why have to buy the whole thing? The Weber thimble had eight panels about the base.

Repousse — A process or technique where the design on a thimble is stamped or hammered from the back of the metal so as to raise it on the show side; a French word for embossing.

Revere, Paul 1835-1818 — American patriot and silversmith known to have made gold and silver thimbles in the tall, slender "French Style." It is documented that he made two gold thimbles for his daughters. The one he made for Maria is available for viewing by collectors in the Boston Museum of Fine Arts. The other's location is unknown, and remains one of the lost treasures haunting thimble collectors in America. Its value is estimated to be over $25,000! See # 946.

Rhodochrosite — An attractive rose-pink stone with wavy light and dark layers through it. In Argentina, beautiful veined translucent thimbles are cut from Rhodochrosite.

Ribbed Ground — A design created by uniform vertical ridges or "ribs" about the band or edge of a thimble. Some other design could be created within these ribs, leaving them as the background.

Ring Thimbles — The ring thimble has a history dating back to the ancient Chinese era. When most sewing was done with the side of the thimble, this design was perfect. Ring thimbles are still used in the Orient and are the forerunner of today's tailor's thimbles. See page # 22.

Risdon — An American manufacturer in Connecticut who has made brass thimbles for more than 100 years. No mark is on these thimbles.

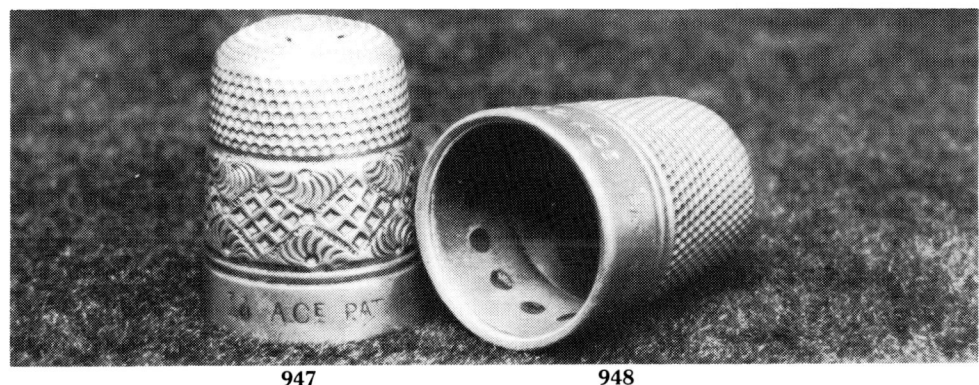

947   948

Rheumatism Thimble — Alfred Constantine of Birmingham, England, designed a remarkable thimble. To note the description on the patent #6253, dated 3-16-1909: "The reason for this patent is that it (thimble) is designed to have a curative effect on ailments such as rheumatism." The patent goes on to say the outer layer could be made of silver, but the secret is a lining of magnetic steel forming a horse shoe and a band of zinc with holes in it. "Directly behind this is a circle of copper with studs that protrude from the holes. These protruding studs make contact with the finger and when the finger is moist, a galvanic action is set up, which is supposed to have curative powers."

These rare thimbles are known in at least two patterns, both with the words "ACE PAT 6253" on outside band, next to the size number. See above.

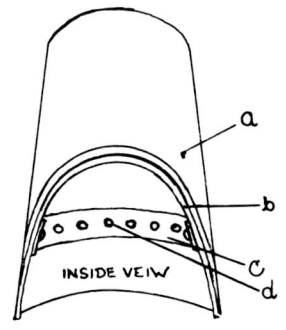

Rheumatism Thimble

A. Outer casting may be made of silver or brass.

B. Steel Lining which has been magnetized.

C. A band of zinc on the inside with holes in it.

D. Behind the zinc band is a circle of copper with studs protruding through.

NOTE: These protruding copper studs form a ring about the finger. When the thimble is being used, the perspiration sets up a galvantic action which is said to have wonderful curative powers.

Robertson, Rayma — American china painter and artist known for her exquisite baby birds on thimbles. Her work is signed "Rayma."

Rock Crystal — A mineral of colorless quartz, long believed to be glass from heaven. Rock crystal has been carved into many objects, including thimbles. The work in this medium of the famous jeweler to the Imperial Russian Court, Peter Carl Faberge (1846-1920) is celebrated. Old rock crystal thimbles are rare, but new ones are available to collectors by craftsmen skilled in working with stone.

Rococo — An elaborate style of decoration found on some "embroidery" thimbles. It was popular during the 19th century and made by English American thimble firms up to the 1930s. The rococo design creates foliage, scrollwork, and elaborate shell motifs in an ornate overall style. See #971.

Rogers, Gay Ann — Thimble collector, speaker and author of *An Illustrated History of Needlework Tools,"* a 244-page volume with excellent photographs on many antique sewing tools and a full chapter on thimbles. The book was published by John Murry of London, England in 1983.

Roman Thimbles — The question of whether or not the ancient Romans used metal thimbles was given official sanction in 1879 when H. Syer Cuming, vice president of the prestigious British Archaeological Association, wrote the erroneous article, "On Thimbles." In this so-called "authoritative" work, he stated that bronze ring-type thimbles were found in the ruins of Herculaneum, a Roman city buried in the eruption of Mt. Vesuvius in A.D. 79, and were in the "Genevieve cabinet." To date no such thimbles have ever been found. However, the legend of "Roman" thimbles was created and kept alive by other noted writers until the late 1970s when this tradition was first questioned. These doubts sparked a great deal of backtracking by other writers, including me.

Today, it is believed the metal thimble originated in China during the 2nd century and reached Europe around the 9th century, over four hundred years after the fall of Rome. For more information read "In Search of the Origin of the Thimble," page 13.

Rope Design — A decorative technique where two wires are twisted together and applied to the rim of a thimble; or a design which has been made to look like a rope or cable. See gadroon for a similar motif.

Rorstrand — A Swedish ceramic manufacturer founded in 1726 in Stockholm. By 1820, when fine English clays became available, they began to produce their superb porcelain items.

Rose, S. J. & Son — British silversmith company in Birmingham. Their maker's mark is SJR&S in rectangle.

Rouy et Berthier — Early 19th Century French silversmiths who displayed steel thimbles at the 1819 exhibition in the Palais du Louvre. They were judged as "perfectly executed and of a pleasing shape, beautifully finished, and without any of the faults of thimbles in copper, gold, ivory, mother-of-pearl and wood."

Rousseau, Gloria — American thimble collector, guest speaker, and chairman of the 1982 T.C.I. Convention in Dearborn, Michigan.

Royal Adderley — English bone china manufacturer in Longton; once a division of Ridgway Potteries, as of 1971 a part of Royal Doulton. Their thimbles are marked with their name inside.

Royal Albert — A British ceramic firm founded by Thomas Wild in Longton. In 1898 the enterprise changed its name from Thomas Wild & Co. to Royal Albert Crown China Works. The company has made thimbles and is now part of Royal Doulton. See thimble # 860.

Royal Brierly — A British glass manufacturer which made a pair of frosted glass thimbles to commemorate the wedding of Prince Charles and Princess Diana in 1981. See thimble # 417.

Royal Copenhagen Porcelain — Founded in 1775, the Danish company has made, off and on, fine porcelain thimbles for over one hundred and fifty years. Their trademark is three wavy blue lines representing Denmark's three main waterways. See thimble # 861.

Royal Delft Thimbles — The Royal Delft Ware Manufactory or "De Porceleyne Fles" was established in 1653. Recently they have created a line of hand painted delft-ware thimbles for collectors.

Royal Doulton — A famed British porcelain and crystal house founded in 1818 by John Doulton in Vauxhall, but moved to Lambeth in the 1820s. The firm has made handcut crystal thimbles which are not marked. Their other division, Royal Adderley, has made many bone china thimbles. See illustrations # 862.

Royal Tara — An Irish porcelain manufacturer established in 1953 by Kerry O'Sullivan. Their thimbles are marked inside and many have a green shamrock as part of the the decoration. See example # 863.

Royal Windsor — British bone china manufacturer who is making a line of thimbles. Their name is stamped inside each thimble.

Four Treasures from Royal Worcester

Courtesy Smithsonian Institute

949 950

Two rare Royal Worcester landscapes

951 952

Two beautiful Royal Worcester enameled jewels

The Thimbles of Royal Worcester

953   954   955   956   957

958   959   960   961   962

Royal Worcester — A British porcelain manufacturing company founded in 1751. Over the years, the company went through many owners, name changes, and mergers, but always maintained a tradition of fine artistry in the highest quality porcelain. Worcester's records from as early as 1785 show the company was making thimbles. Actual orders during 1790s were: "Thomas Emery of Bristol—6 dozen thimbles, pattern 55;" "John Richardson of Cirencester—24 thimbles, assorted patterns;" and Miss Bowen of Bath—6 dozen thimbles, Royal Lily Pattern." These early thimbles were not marked and must be recognized by body glaze or style of painting. Artists signing thimbles were not common until the early 1900s. Most Worcester thimbles made from 1860 to 1939 were in a glazed Parian body, which is creamier than bone china and not translucent.

Worcester's thimbles went through many phases: oriental motifs from 1800-10; rare and fancy birds, 1810-1815; flowers and landscapes, 1815-1850; Continental and French designs, 1850-1870; stained ivory and Japanesque, 1870-1890; and the rare blush ivory with fruit and flowers, 1890 to 1914. All during this time, thimbles were also painted with crests, monograms, birds, fruit, insects, and flowers; some with mottoes such as "Remember Me."

Today Royal Worcester still makes hand-painted thimbles and fired-decal ones. A list of their painters is available at the back of this book. Many collectors try to find Worcester thimbles with as many different signatures as possible. One painted, William Powell, is especially looked for. His superb painting of birds shows the love he felt for these winged creatures. See above thimbles and the ones on opposite page.

List of Royal Worcester Artists

Although Royal Worcester first painted thimbles as early as 1785, it was not common for their artists to sign their work until about the turn of the century. Today collectors are paying up to $400.00 for early signed Worcester thimbles. The company hand-painted some of their thimbles until 1985, and these newer ones sell for under $25.00.

The following is a list of known Worcester artists who painted thimbles:

Austin, Reginald,
Austin, Walter
Ayrton, Timothy
Badham, Arthur
Bagnall, William
Bakewell, Fiona
Barker, Earnest
Bee, William
Blake, Kitty
Cameron, C.
Collins, J.
Cox, Clair
Clarke, Wendy
Dajda, A.
Davies, T.
Davis, L.
Delaney, Gerald
Duffield, S.
Dunkley, Pat
Erdman, Christine
Evans, Yvonne
Footman, A.
Garcia, Gioran
Gegg, S.
Gibson, M.
Griffiths, Freda
Griffiths, Lybbe

Hardy, T.
Henshaw, Gioran
Herd, F.
Higgins, Frank
Holloway, G.
Holloway, Melvyn
Hinitt, A.
Hemming, H.J.
Hughes, Carole
Igoe, M.
Johnson, George
Lewis, Arthur
Lightheart, H.
Lockyer, Thomas
Lot, C.
Love, Peter
Meredith, S.
Milward, Marie
Moody, Gilian
Mosely, George
Munslow, Mundy
Park, C.
Parker, Christine
Perry, D.
Phillips, Ernest
Post, L.
Powell, William

Platt, Peter
Price, Horace
Rea, Daisy
Rigby, Pat
Roberts, Susane
Rob, S.
Round, Fiona
Sands, S.
Sedgely, Eveline
Selby, S.
Shuch, Albert
Smith, Lorraine
Sparks, Dorothy
Stanley, Jack
Stevens, Fay
Sutton, H.
Taylor, Angela
Taylor, L.
Townsand, Ted
Twilton, Charles
Twinberrow (Twin)
Vass, I.
Vickers, Judy
Waldron, Susane
Well, F.B.
Walter, B.
Wilson, M.

List, courtesy Mrs. Kay Gardner

Rumpe, Johann Caspar — German founder of a brass and iron thimble mill in the Lenne Valley of Westphalia. By the early 19th century the mill employed 50 thimblemakers and produced about a million and a half thimbles a year. Records show that the Emperor Napoleon visited the factory and the Empress ordered some thimbles, but never paid the bill.

The Thimbles of Imperial Russia

963   964   965   966

Russian Thimbles — The thimblemakers of Imperial Russia had a tradition of producing beautiful cloisonned enameled thimbles on gold, silver, and platinum. Using the brilliant enameling techniques learned from the ancient Byzantines, Russian craftsmen created several distinct styles now much sought after by collectors. Most Russian thimbles fall into two groups. The first and most beautiful are the delicate cloisonne pieces with their brilliant enameled floral motifs. Most of these pieces have the maker's initials, city mark and solothnik grade stamped on the outside rim. These thimbles are rare and command prices in excess of six hundred dollars. See # 964.

The second group of Russian thimbles are the niello-souvenir types. This style is decorated with black niello leaf-vine motifs on the sides with indentations on the top. Sometimes, on the band in Cyrillic letters, are the names of Russian holiday areas such as the Caucasus. See thimble 965. Very rare is this type of thimble, inset with tiny turquoise gem stones.

Rarest among the Russian thimbles are the ones produced in the workshops of Faberge during the late 19th and early 20th centuries. These objects of art created in gold & silver, inlaid with semi-precious gems and usually enameled, bring prices in excess of five thousand dollars at auction. There are only seven known examples among private collectors.

A crude attempt to copy the Russian enameled thimbles came to light in 1983. These cast copies marked with 84 and initialed, feel a bit heavy and clunky. Five different bands had surfaced before warnings were printed in the T.C.I. Bulletin. For example see thimble # 1608.

Imperial Russian Thimbles

967   968   969

The Marks of Faberge's Workmasters

Erik August Kollin	E.K.
Michael Evlampievich Perchin	M.П.
Henrik Wigström	H.W.
Julius Alexandrovitch Rappoport	I.P.
August Wilhelm Holmström	A.H.
Alfred Thielemann	A.T.
August Fredrik Hollming	A.H.
Johan Viktor Aarne	B.A.
Karl Gustav Hjalmar Armfelt	Я.A.
Anders Johan Nevalainen	A.N.
Gabriel Niukkanen	G.N.
Philip Theodore Ringe	T.R.
Vladimir Soloviev	B.C.
Anders Michelsson	A.M.
G. Lundell	Г.Л.
Fedor Afanassiev	Ф.А.
Edward Wilhelm Schramm	E.S.
Wilhelm Reimer	W.R.
Andrej Gorianov	А.Г.
Stephan Wäkevä	S.W.
Knut Oskar Pihl	O.P.
Fedor Rückert	Ф.Р.

Scalloped Rims in Silver

970   971   972   973

Saint Eligius — The medieval patron saint of thimblemakers, adopted patron saint of thimble collectors.

Sailor's Palm — A heavy leather hand strap with a brass needle-pushing device, which sets in the palm of the hand. Used by seamen to sew sail cloth. A modern version of the ancient bronze acutrudiums. See page 82.

Salem Witch — Commemorative sterling silver thimbles made by Webster and Ketcham & McDougall. The band has in bas-relief a witch on a broom, a cat, and a new moon. See # 1241 and 1242.

Sandalwood — An aromatic-smelling soft wood from certain oriental trees. Sandalwood thimbles have been hand-carved to place into sewing baskets. They are believed to discourage moths. See thimble 1168.

SBC — A trademark of the Simons Brothers Co. of Philadelphia. These were industrial thimbles made from nickel-silver, oreide and other base metals. They come in a complete size range and many patterns. The SBC thimbles were made from 1919 to 1952. The initials SBC are stamped within a Thimble/Keystone design inside the top of the thimble. See thimble # 992.

Scalloped — A term to describe an ornamental rim found on many thimbles; a series of curves made by cutting away part of the rim of a thimble. See above illustration.

Scenic — Any thimble with a scene chased or engraved into its band. Scenic thimbles were very popular in the United States from 1870 to the 1920s. See page 184.

Schmid — An international marketing firm which has been active in the thimble market by importing to the United States the Anri, Meissen and other collector thimbles.

American Scenic Thimbles

| 974 | 975 | 976 | 977 |

| 978 | 979 | 980 | 981 |

| 982 | 983 | 984 | 985 | 986 |

English Steel-Top Silver Thimbles

| 987 | 988 | 989 | 990 |

Simons' "SBC" Thimbles

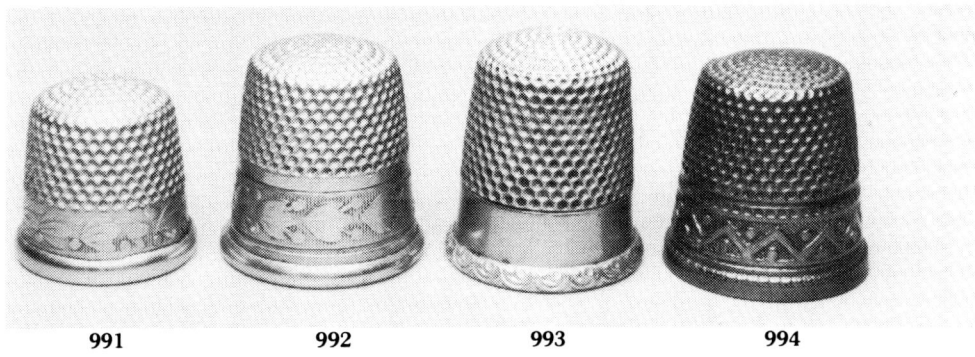

991   992   993   994

Schuetz & Sons, Charles — American jewelry manufacturers, est. 1876 in Newark, New Jersey. The firm Charles Keller & Co. took over the Schuetz plant about 1898. They list gold thimbles among items made. Their factory at 213 Mulberry St. "is a fine four-story structure, and is the only one in the city operated completely by gas." There is no known mark on their thimbles.

Schwarz, Jacob — Austrian manufacturer who made in the mid-19th century flat-top mother-of-pearl thimbles very similar to the French Palais Royal type, except they did not have domed top nor inset enameled pansy.

Scovill Mfg. Co. — America's largest producer of base metal thimbles. The company bought out the "Curtis" Thimble Works of Woodbury, Connecticut, in the early 1860s. They "made steel, brass, nickel silver, and aluminum thimbles in a basic design best suited to mass production." They were the manufacturers of the 'Prudential' thimble, of which over a million were produced. "Scovill reached its peak of production in 1918 when 8,388,552 thimbles were made at its Waterbury plant." They now make about 4 million a year.

Scrimshaw — An American art form made popular by whalers during their 2-to-3-year voyages. The teeth, tusks and bones of whales were carved and etched, like fine line engraving with scenes of the sea. Among items so made and decorated were thimbles. See example # 548.

Scroll Edge — An ornamental edge developed during the golden age of the rococo style. It was used by several American thimblemakers, including Ketcham & McDougall, who called it their Louis XV edge. See # 637.

Sea Shell Thimbles — In the past decade, craftsmen in the Orient have been using rare and unusual sea shells to create thimbles of great natural beauty. Sometimes the entire thimble is formed from the shells; other times, they are inlaid on a base metal core. See page 186.

Sea Shell Thimbles

995 996 997 998

Seilliere, Baron Jean — French thimble collector whose magnificent collection was featured in *Realities Magazine* Oct. 1956. His collection sold for over $125,000.00 at Christie's in Geneva, Switzerland in 1979.

999

Courtesy, Ketcham-McDougall

Seybold, Lorentz M. — A designer for the Ketcham & McDougall Company who created the "hanging rim" thimbles. These unique thimbles were patented on Sept. 3, 1912. They were made in four patterns, with the KMD mark inside the apex. Sometimes birthstones were inset in the center of the flower motif. See above illustration.

Sgraffito — A ceramic technique where a thimble is cast in a mold with two contrasting colors of slip. One color slip is poured in the mold and almost at once poured out, leaving a thin wall of clay. Then the second slip is poured in and allowed a little more time to set, and then poured out. When the thimble is released from the mold and dried to a leather-hard state, an artist can create an ornamental design by cutting away some of the top layer of clay, exposing the other color beneath.

Shepard Mfg. Co. — An American silversmith company from Attleboro, Massachusetts, which made thimbles from 1918 to 1960. They were marked with "S" on the band.

Shield Motif — A small shield design applied to the side of a thimble for an inscription or initial; usually found on French and German thimbles'; called "cartouche." See # 1289.

Shipman, Charles — American wood and ivory turner who served his apprenticeship in Birmingham, England. He advertised in the *New York Journal* Aug. 6, 1767 his ability to make at "reasonable terms," ivory thimbles among other articles.

Shoup, Jean — American thimble collector and founder of the thimble mail order firm of "Thimbles Only" in La Crescenta, California. Her catalogs are noted for beautiful, detailed pictures with some history.

Sickels, Elizabeth G. — American thimble collector and author of "New York Thimble Makers from Huntington, Long Island," published in the *Antique Journal*, Sept., Oct. and Nov., 1964. She was a tireless researcher and remarkable woman. See her story on page 302.

Silk — In the Far East, thimbles made from brightly colored silk are used. In Korea, they are called "Kolmi." They often have beautiful gold brocades and embroidered designs. See illustration below.

Korean Silk "Kolmi" Thimbles

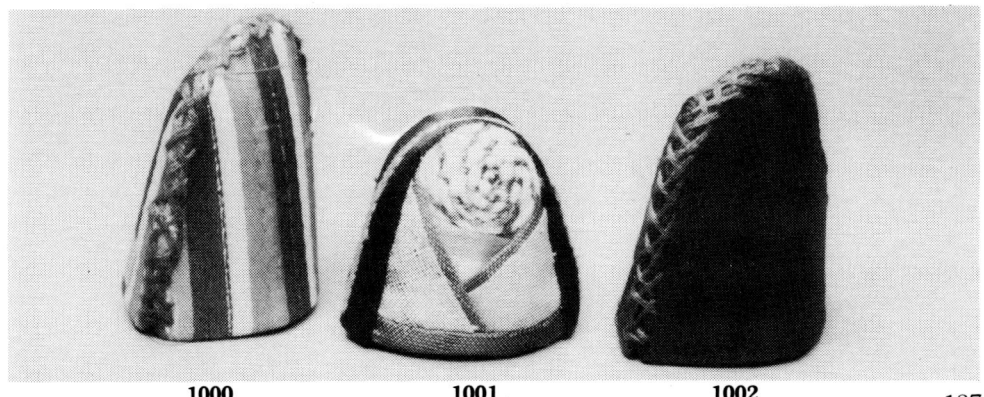

1000   1001   1002

Silver — A metal of great intrinsic beauty and remarkable versatility. Silver has been a favored metal of jewelers and craftsmen since the dawn of civilization. Silver thimbles have been mentioned as early as the 12th Century in manuscripts. Several from the 16th century are on display in museums in Europe and the United States. It was the 18th century when silver thimbles were made in quantity and during the 19th century, tens of millions were produced. Fine or pure silver, being too soft to take the wear of a steel needle, was mixed with other metals, usually copper, for more strength. But some dishonest silversmiths during the Middle Ages debased their silver by as much as 70% and tried to sell their wares as "solid silver." This led to a hallmark system in England as early as A.D. 1300. To avoid the unethical methods of some silversmiths, each piece was stamped with dies by the master silversmiths of the Guild. Over hundreds of years the laws changed, but always quality was assured.

One early decision on what made a good alloy was a mixture of 92½% silver with 7½% base metal. This came to be known as "Sterling" and was so marked on silver articles by a symbol of a "lion passant" in England. The number .925 is also seen on sterling thimbles. It means: 925/1000 pure silver.

A higher grade than sterling is sometimes used in England. This is called Britannia silver, and is 95.8% pure. A symbol of the head of Britannia marks this grade (.959). In colonial America, coins were melted down for making many silver items, including thimbles. These were sometimes marked "coin" silver. This is usually about 90% silver or .900. In Europe a grade of 80% silver was used for centuries and the number .800 is stamped on some thimbles. This grade is referred to as continental silver. In France, one will find thimbles marked .950 which is 95% pure. Other varieties of silver alloys are: .835, .930, .916, and .833. In Russia, a system based on the solothniks is used and in Central Europe, the standard unit of purity was the Loth until 1860.

Silver Cased — A term used by Charles Iles & Co. meaning extra heavy silver plate over brass.

Silver Gilt — A process where a thin coat of gold is electroplated onto silver. The French term is "vermeil." This is more a finish and prevents the silver from tarnishing.

Silver Thimble Fund — In Britain, during the first World War, a drive to raise money was completed in 1917. The sum of $75,000 was received for hospital equipment. All donations were in the form of silver thimbles, "from people who thought they had nothing to give." This sum of money was the approximate value of 350,000-400,000 thimbles melted down!

Three Treasures from Simons

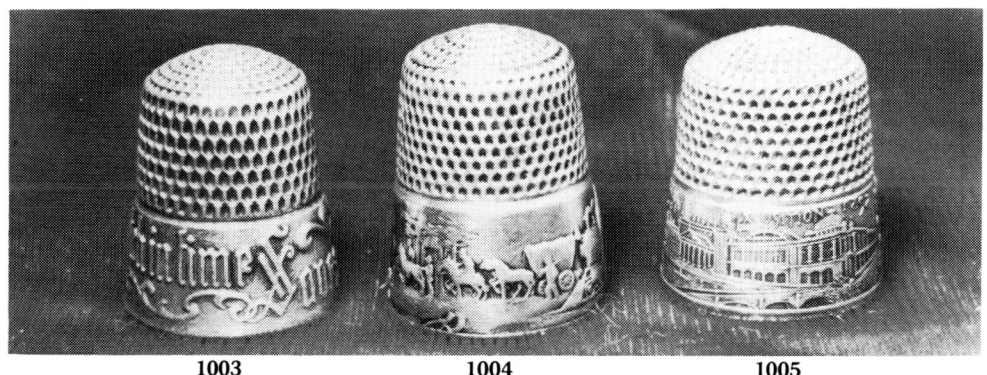

1003	1004	1005
Stitch-In-Time	St. Louis Expo, 1904	Chicago Expo, 1893

Simons Brothers Co. — American manufacturing jewelers founded in 1839 by George Washington Simons in Philadelphia. George had learned the skills of silversmithing from Jacob Stockman of the same city. Peter, his younger brother, joined him in 1853. He left to set up a sales branch in San Francisco in 1863.

The firm went through several name changes until 1881 when the name Simons Bros. & Co. was adopted. George's four sons, George, Jr., John, Edwin, and Frederick were all destined to work for the growing company.

Simons reached its greatest era of prosperity during the late 19th century. Over 150 employees worked in its factory and retail stores. Their Chestnut street store was "one of the most elegant establishments in the city. No expense has been spared to create a tasteful simplicity."

By 1900 Simons had over-extended itself and mounting financial problems forced Frederick and his brothers to sell off its retail operations and cut back on its manufactured lines.

The next decade found the embarrassed company in considerable debt. By 1912, the courts found the firm bankrupt.

Frederick and his brother Edwin formed a new corporation in 1913. The new firm once again began the manufacturing of gold and silver merchandise.

About 1890 Simons, with a joint licensing agreement with Charles Horner, tried to manufacture the Dorcas silver and steel thimble, which had proved to be so popular in England. The venture proved to be less than successful and American-made Dorcas thimbles are rare. The high cost, two and a half times the cost of a regular silver thimble, and the fact that they would not even be "solid silver," may have made them unpopular. The words DORCAS, size number and pat. 6-11-89 are inside the apex. Several patterns exist, including the Greek key.

Simons' Factory "Artisans Hall" circa 1885

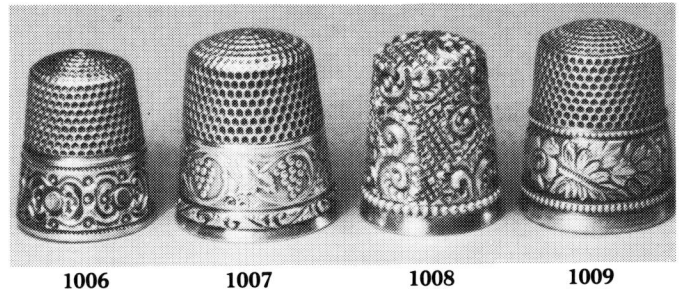

1006   1007   1008   1009

Lillian Simons took over the management of the company upon her father's death in 1935. Her sister, Katherine W. Simons ("Kitty" to her thimble collecting friends) took over in 1944. Her death in 1968 turned Simons over to its third woman owner, Elizabeth Bassett, Katherine's niece. The firm is now operated by Nelson Keyser.

Simons Bros. registered a simplified Old English S within a shield as their trademark in 1907, although they believed they had used it off and on since the 1880s. Their gold-filled thimbles were marked with a trefoil symbol inside the top. The names "Priscilla" and "Quaker" are Simons' tradenames. Besides gold, silver, and filled thimbles, they made a line of basic nickel-silver, and oreide thimbles from 1919 to 1952. These are marked with the initials SBC inside a thimble/keystone motif under the apex.

An "A" over their trademark indicates the exact karat weight in their gold thimbles. Simons Brothers has been one of America's most prolific thimble makers. Their commemoratives, such as the "Golden Spike" made for the St. Louis World's Fair, and the 1893 World Columbian Exposition in Chicago, are prized acquisitions to any collector. Their most novel is the "Liberty Bell" thimble in the shape of the Liberty Bell.

By 1927 Simons Brothers had sales offices in New York, Chicago, San Francisco, and Toronto, Canada. Many of their beautiful designs were re-made for collectors around the world, till the early 1950s.

Slip — The liquid state, about the consistency of heavy cream, of porcelain, stoneware, earthenware, etc., which is poured into molds.

Smith & Smith — American silversmith company from Attleboro, Massachusetts, who made thimbles from 1918 to 1930. They were marked with S&S.

Soergel & Stollmeyer — A German silversmith company founded in 1863 by George Soergel and Friedrich Stollmeyer in Schwabisch Gmund. Their mark was an S inside a triangle. The company went out of business in 1969.

Solothniks — A Russian unit of purity. Until 1925 there were 96 solothniks to a Russian pound. Pure silver was then 96 solothniks. The numbers 84, 88 and 91 are found on the rim of older Russian thimbles. The silver content of .84 equals .875 on a sterling grade; the number 88 would be almost sterling, and 91 would be higher than sterling.

Thimbles of Simons Brothers

Thimbles of Simons Brothers

The Thimbles of South America

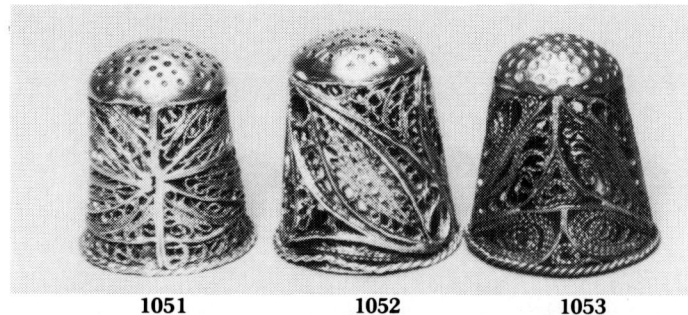

1051   1052   1053

1054   1055   1056   1057

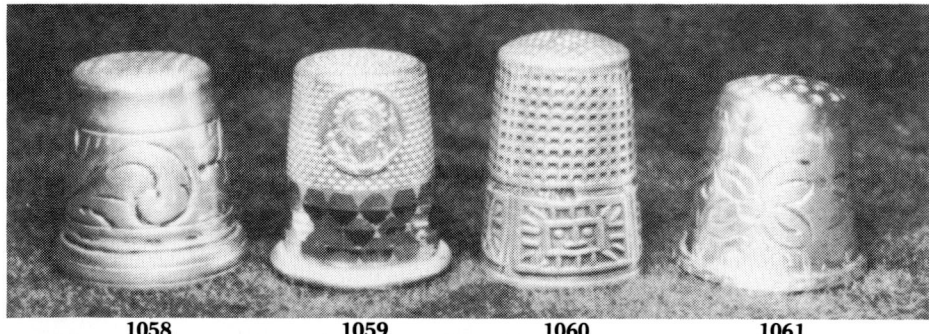

1058   1059   1060   1061

1062   1063   1064   1065

Courtesy: L. S. de Viana

Bicho-Canasto Thimbles

1066
Bicho-Canasto thimbles of Paraguay

South African Thimbles — Although there are no known major firms mass producing thimbles in South Africa, a large number of artisans have turned their hand to creating some unique collectibles.

Many exotic woods from the Kruger National Park have been used along with serpentine and phyrophylite stone from the Namib Desert. Native artisans scrimshaw wild game horn and ivory thimbles to create unusual effects. Zulu custom-made, silver-bead thimbles in tribal patterns are also available, along with gold and sterling silver pieces made by South African silversmiths.

South American Thimbles — The thimbles made in this great Latin American continent are often unique in design and creative in concept. Most are the work of Indian artisans. In Argentina, many silver thimbles are made with waffle tops and geometric bands. They tend to be made "on the flat," and then rolled up and topped. For examples see thimbles # 1060 to 1063.

In Peru, the Indians create exotic silver-filigree thimbles, some with golden llamas applied. See thimbles # 1051 to 1053.

In Brazil, wooden thimbles are carved from the black coquilla with ornate gold studs and rim applied. See thimble # 1134.

Most thimbles made by the skilled non-Indian silversmiths have a "Spanish air" about them. Many set with stones are distinctive pieces and would be welcomed in any collection.

Long before the Spanish conquest of South America, it is known the Indians used leather "thimble" protectors on their fingers while sewing leather. Two enterprising tribes in Paraguay, the Tupi and Guarani, had the local insects make their "thimbles."

The insect, called the "bicho-canasto," creates a long finger-size nest from a silky fiber secretion, which is very strong. Inside this tough-woven cocoon, the insect's larva is nurtured. After the larva exits, the Indians cut the cocoon into "sewing-rings" and finger protectors, which they still use when sewing shoes, saddles, and other heavy leather items. See above photo.

South Staffordshire (Bilston) Thimbles

1067	1068	1069
1070	1071	1072
1073	1074	1075

South Staffordshire Enameled Thimbles — A term given to a group of beautifully hand-painted, enameled brass thimbles popular in late 18th century England. Some early pieces were made in Battersea for a short time; however, by the 1760s the trade had centered in Bilston, South Staffordshire. The term "Bilston-Battersea" is sometimes used to describe these types of enameled thimbles, but the name South Staffordshire is more correct.

The Bilston thimbles came in a variety of shapes and styles. Some are enameled on the top and sides, while others have a brass cap with

Souvenir Thimbles

| 1076 | 1077 | 1078 | 1079 | 1080 |

indentations. All are hand-painted, some with simple flowers, while others are decorated with elegant, raised enamel cartouches with exquisite landscapes, sprays of flowers, or portraits.

The tall style, with raised cartouche and landscape is the most rare. See thimble 1333 and page 225.

Southern California Thimble Collectors — A regional thimble collectors group for the Greater Los Angeles area. Roberta Kenney was elected their first president. The group hosted the outstanding T.C.I. "Pasadena Convention" in 1982. Marian Lipsius is editor of their newsletter, *Thimble Line*.

Souvenir Thimbles — Any thimble which bears the name or a scene from a geological location falls into this category. See above illustration.

SPA — A series of silver thimbles made by the British firm of Henry Griffith & Son during the 1930s. Some thimbles have just the word SPA on the band, others have the names of English towns and beach resorts. At least 50 name places are known to have been made. See "Royal Spa" 483.

Spode — British porcelain company founded by Josiah Spode (1733-1797—). Spode, while looking for a stronger, whiter and more translucent body, found by replacing the frit in standard porcelain with bone ash, he had his new "bone china." This discovery became the foundation of the English bone china industry. The Spode company underwent several name changes until William Copeland's son (Josiah's partner) took over the company in 1833. The name "Copeland" had been the name of the company since 1847. In 1970, the name was again changed to Spode Limited. See thimble #868.

Spun Porcelain Thimbles — A process, developed by Frederick Gridley in 1975, which creates unique "one-of-a-kind" multi-colored porcelain thimbles. These hand-made thimbles in ever changing styles represent the newest concept in utility and contemporary design. Each thimble is now being stamped with "FG" under the apex. See thimble 1082.

      1081   1082   1083   1084

"Steel Clad" Thimbles — These Dorcas-type, silver-steel-silver-clad thimbles were made by Henry Griffith for the London jewelry firm of James Walker. The words, "STEEL CLAD," are incised on band along with J.W.Ltd. See thimbles #221 and 222.

Steel-Top Thimbles — In an effort to prolong the life of their thimbles, British manufacturers began to use steel and iron to cap their thimbles as early as 1740. Steel-top gold, silver and pinchbeck thimbles were widely advertised from the 1740s to the 1830s. Benjamin Halstead was the first American to manufacture this type of thimble on a large scale, circa 1794 to about 1816. American steel-top thimbles are usually marked on the outside band with a size number. The English did not start this practice until the late 19th century. The steel top phased out as the steel core "Dorcas" type thimble was introduced in the 1880s. See thimbles #1083 and 987.

Steinbock Studio Thimbles — These beautifully enameled thimbles of silver and copper are created by the renowned Steinbock Studio of Vienna, Austria. Most have stylized birds, flowers and other wildlife motifs. Their mark is a stag with an urn. See "Thimble Markings" and thimble #249.

Sterling — An English word meaning an article of silver is $92\frac{1}{2}\%$ pure silver and $7\frac{1}{2}\%$ alloy. On many thimbles its decimal equivalent is stamped .925.

Stern Brothers & Co. — American manufacturing jeweler founded by Nathan Stern in 1868 in Philadelphia, moved to new York City in 1871. The firm made its first thimbles in 1890. From 1890 to 1908 their thimbles were marked with a fouled anchor. In 1908 a trademark using the letter "S" enclosing a "B" and "C" was adopted. The firm re-organized in 1913 and became Goldsmith Stern Co. See "Thimble Marks." For a more detailed history of this unique company, read *Stern Brothers* by John von Hoelle, Dine-American, 1985.

Stitch-in-time — A much sought silver thimble made by Simons Brothers of Philadelphia and the Ketcham McDougall Co. of New York. See #1081.

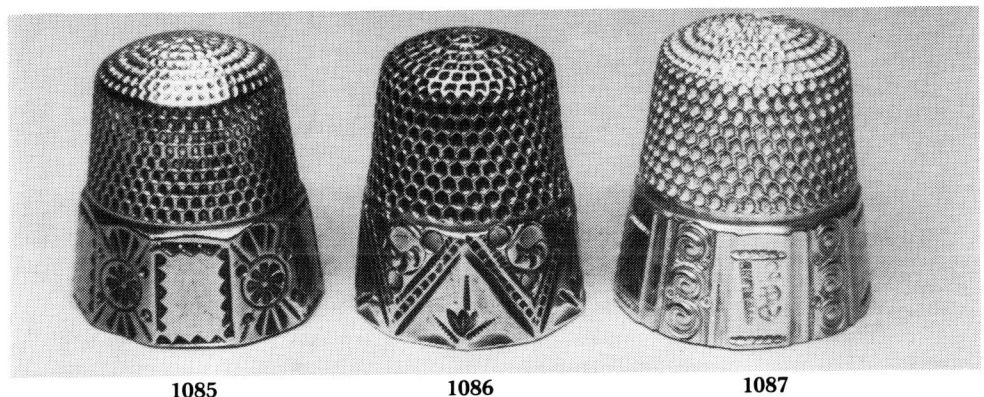

1085   1086   1087

Stone Thimbles — Many thimbles have been cut from stone, such as jade, marble, rhodochrosite, soapstone, alabaster, onyx, rock crystal and jet, by craftsmen the world over. Some are beautiful, elegant works of art and others, crude but workable, thimbles. Many are very interesting, if rather odd. See thimbles 1088 and 1089, and page 200.

Stone Top Thimbles — The custom of fitting semi-precious stones in the top of thimbles is believed to have started in northern Europe sometime during the latter half of the 18th century. High grade silver and gold wore too quickly and the hard stone top could take the wear of the steel needles better. Thimbles with moonstone and cornelian tops were popular in Scandinavian countries. Moss agate, bloodstone, coral and other colorful stones graced the thimbles of Germany and England. Connemara marble topped thimbles with Irish motifs were popular and, although made in England, were widely sold in Ireland. Recently, cheap simulated stones made of glass and plastic have come onto the market, but these look to be poor imitations of the beautiful capped thimbles well known to collectors. See #1110.

Strap Work — An ornamental design which gives an open basketweave effect to the band of a thimble. See example # 1090.

Stratnoid — A brand name of the Laughton & Sons Company of Great Britain. Stratnoid thimbles are made from an aluminum alloy. See # 1091.

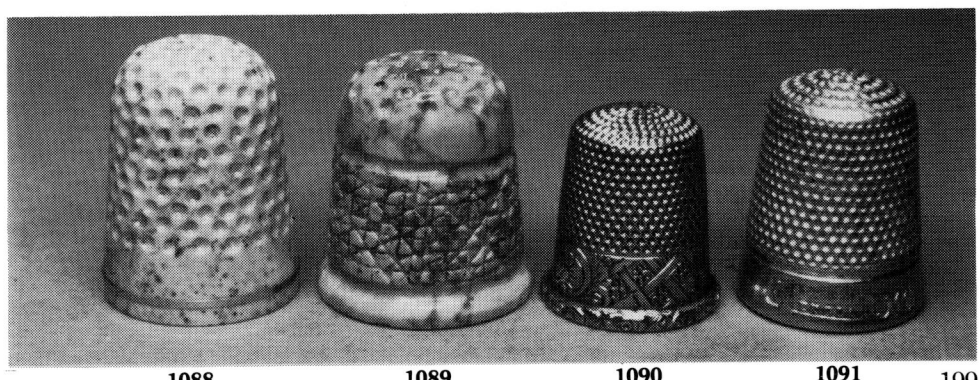

1088   1089   1090   1091

Thimbles in Semi-Precious Stone

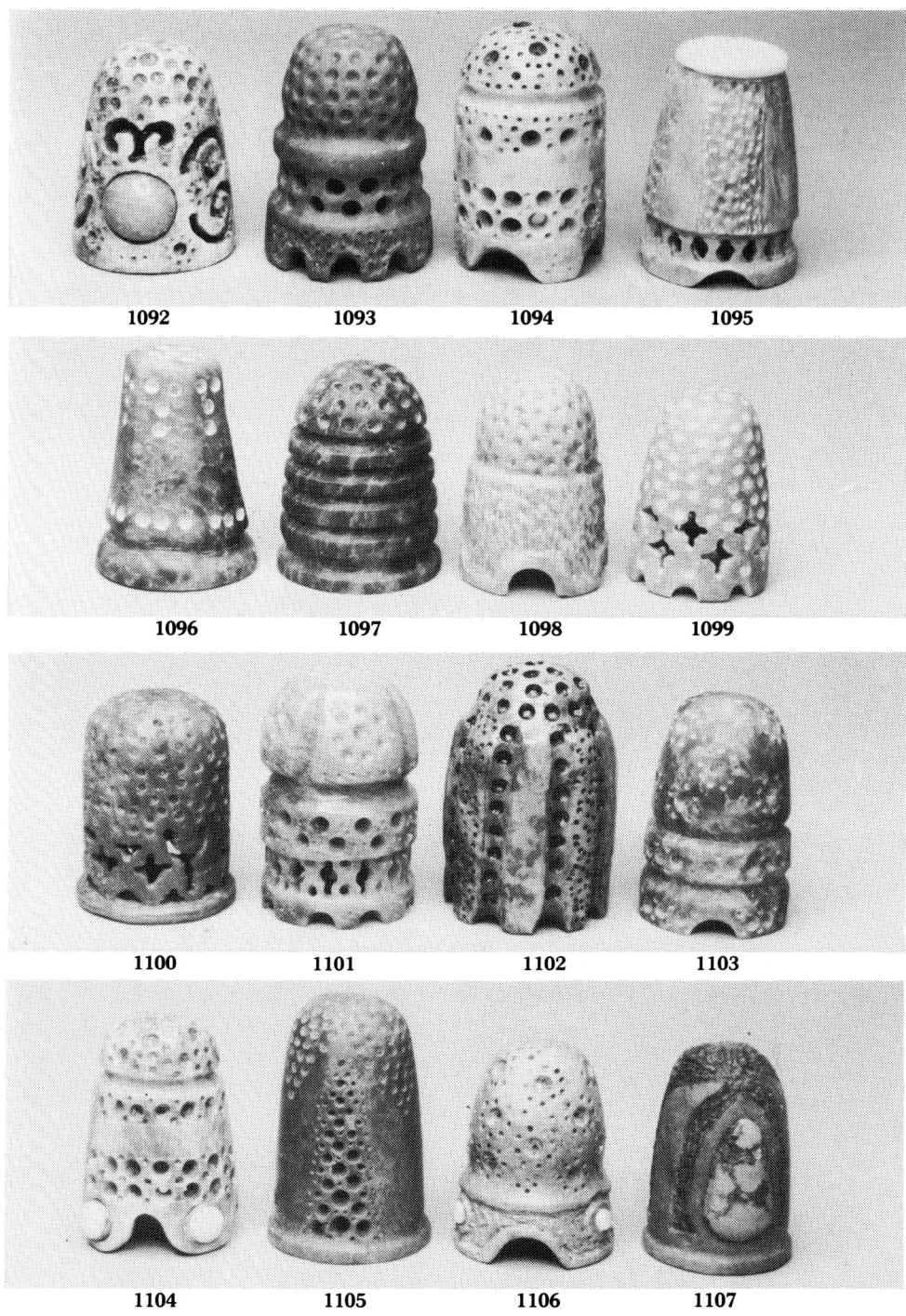

    1108   1109   1110   1111

Strawberry Banke — A 100-acre historic restoration in Portsmouth, New Hampshire. The area displays life in a colonial American seaport. A sterling thimble with a strawberry motif applied to a plain band Simons thimble is sold there. The silver applique work is done at Strawberry Banke.

Sullivan, Kay — Thimble collector and founder of "De Vingerhoed," a Dutch firm which sells antique and modern thimbles via catalog worldwide. See "Thimble Sources."

Sutherland — British porcelain manufacturers currently making hand-painted thimbles, with domed top. Their thimbles are marked SUTHERLAND ENGLAND. See #1113.

Swann & Son, Joseph — An English silversmith firm in Birmingham which has made gold and silver thimbles since 1847. They are still the largest producer of precious metal thimbles in Great Britain. See Thimble Markings, and thimbles 1110 and 1111.

Swingler, Peter — Fine English miniature artist who paints on hand-enameled sterling silver thimbles. He signs his work P.S. See #254.

The Thimbles of Sutherland

    1112   1113   1114   1115

1116
A Tagua nut with thimble

𝒯

Tagua Nut — A palm nut from South America used to carve small objects. From the late 19th century, thimbles were made of this material, also called "vegetable ivory." See illustration above.

Tailor's Thimble — A common term for an open end, or thimble without a top. This type of thimble was popular with tailors. The oldest form of the sewing aid, it dates back to the first century in China. It reached Europe by the 9th century. See illustration below.

Talks About Thimbles — by Helmut Greif, Carinthia, Klagenfurt, 1984. First published in German, the book is now available in English. This 140-page book is an excellent source of information on medieval thimble guilds, Nuremberg thimbles and European thimble manufacturers. It contains many color and black and white illustrations.

Topless Tailor's Thimbles

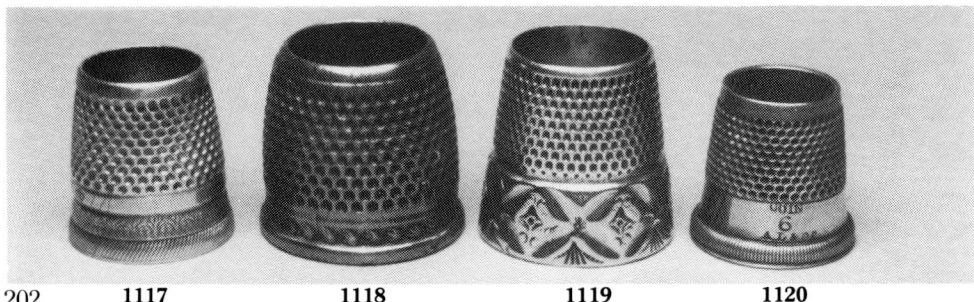

1117   1118   1119   1120

Taos Indian Thimbles — An American Indian tribe located in New Mexico, the Taos tribe has a long history of silversmithing. Their thimbles usually have a flat top and scalloped rim. Chased Indian motifs usually decorate the sides. Often turquoise can be found used in unique settings. Many Taos thimbles have touch-marks. See thimble 36.

Taxco — A city in Mexico famous for its hundreds of silversmiths. The word TAXCO is sometimes found on silver thimbles made in Mexico.

Taylor, Joseph — English silversmith working in Birmington in the early 19th century. His mark, IT, is sometimes found on silver thimbles.

Taylor & Perry — English silversmiths from Birmington believed to have made the "Historical Building" series of silver thimbles in the second quarter of the 19th century. Their mark, T&P, is sometimes found on thimbles and finger guards. See thimble with scene of Dover Castle # 1127.

Telescoping Thimble — A thimble which folds down to a smaller size. Grace Holden patented a unique thimble in 1907 which folded down to 1/3 of its extended size. She reasoned that, this way, a lady could carry it more conveniently in her purse.

Themel — Old English spelling for thimble, circa A.D. 1500.

Thimbilitis — A common term for a serious psychosis which has occurred among avid thimble collectors. Medically known to most psychiatrists as DIGITABULITIS. In severe cases, this condition causes the victim to act in a totally irrational manner; deceiving their spouses by hiding sales slips and new purchases; spending vast sums of money on little sewing tools, which they will never use; falling into deep depression when an out-of-state collector finds a rare Meissen at "their" local flea market.

Another symptom is when the victim adopts the philosophy of HALFGOSIS (telling everybody they paid half of what they really did).

Thimbilitis is known among trial lawyers as excellent grounds for divorce. To date, there is no known cure, but a dedicated group called DIGITABULICS ANONYMOUS has been able to save some marriages, including this author's!

Thimble — A sewing aid; a "cap like" or ring of material to cover a finger to protect it against the wear of a needle. A basic, utilitarian object, the thimble has, over the centuries, challenged the imagination of many gifted craftsmen.

Thimble Collector's Guild — A Scottish commerical and social group founded by Susan and Arthur Bell in 1983. They publish monthly catalogs on new and custom-made thimbles. See "Thimble Sources."

American Club Thimbles

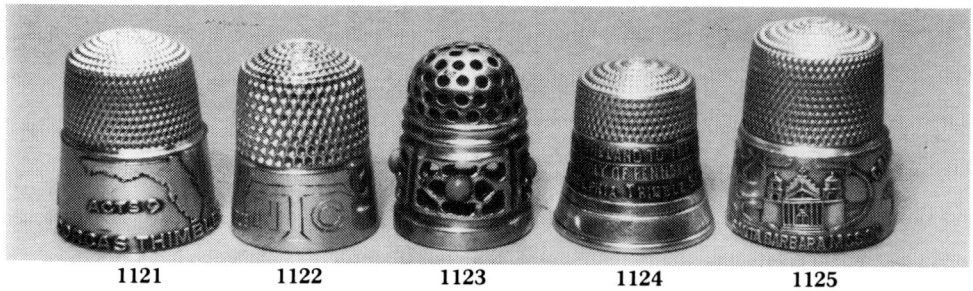

1121　　　1122　　　1123　　　1124　　　1125

Thimble Collectors International — An organization of thimble collectors, by thimble collectors, for thimble collectors. TCI's aim is to promote study and research on all aspects of thimbles, and make it available to all through its newsletter "the Bulletin," its conventions, and its publications. TCI is open to all persons interested in thimbles. TCI was born in concept in 1976 in Toledo, Ohio. After years of "gatherings" by dedicated collectors in different cities, it was recognized that a more formal organization was needed. Thus at the Toledo meeting, which was coordinated by Jerry Baker and Jacquelyn Whetro, a "feasibility" committee was selected to draft bylaws, propose a slate of officers and take care of other countless details.

This committee was headed by Joann Ryan and Rose Marie Kerchner. These two ladies, along with members Xenia Fane, Ruth Mann, Mary Keyser and Shirley Newton, planned the "birthing of TCI" at the 1978 Chicago convention.

At this meeting, TCI was officially organized. The adoption of the TCI constitution and election of its officers and board members were consummated. One hundred and thirteen charter members were registered. Shirley Newton acted as the Chairperson.

Ruth Mann was elected as TCI's first President. Shirley Newton, Evelyn Eubanks, and Pat Rich were elected 1st, 2nd, and 3rd Vice Presidents. Joann Ryan and Marcia Holmes were Corresponding and Recording Secretaries. Robert Hum, Treasurer and Leona Coad as Historian. During this administration, the official newsletter, *TCI Bulletin,* was published by Lahoma Goldsmith.

Velda Skagen won the contest to design the TCI logo. Membership had grown to 302 by August 1980.

The second TCI Convention was held in Pasadena, California in 1980. Idabelle Forker was elected President. Pearl Hazen, Evelyn Eubanks and Fern Hill were elected 1st, 2nd and 3rd Vice Presidents. Marcia Holmes and Natalie Borg became Recording and Corresponding Secretaries. Robert Hum remained Treasurer and Lettie Williams became Historian.

The third TCI Convention was held in Dearborn, Michigan in August 1982. Idabelle Forker was re-elected as President; Milt Mager, Estelle Zalkin, and

Lettie Williams were elected as 1st, 2nd and 3rd Vice Presidents; Kathi Gordon, Treasurer; Dorothy Chambers, Recording Secretary; and Joann Ryan, Historian.

The fourth TCI Convention, hosted by the Philadelpia Thimble Society, elected Mignon Jeffords as President; Leona Coad, Avis Jackson, and Lettie Williams and 1st, 2nd and 3rd Vice Presidents; Joanne Rath as Recording Secretary; Emily Capin as Corresponding Secretary; Kathryn Gordon, Treasurer; and Evelyn Eubanks as Historian.

The Fifth Convention will be hosted by the Hawkeye Thimblers in Des Moines, Iowa.

Thimble Collectors of South Africa — A Johannesburg-area club, founded in 1984 by Jenny Scharff, to promote interest in thimble collecting. With over one hundred members, they are the largest club in South Africa. They meet four times a year and issue a newsletter bi-monthly.

Thimble Collectors of Tampa Bay — A Florida based group founded in 1985 by Xenia Fane and Bertha Kallinick to promote interest in thimbles.

Thimble Collectors San Diego — A regional group of interested thimble collectors founded in 1981 by Betty Kraviecki and Elva Griffis. The idea for the group was conceived at the 1980 T.C.I. Convention in Pasadena.

Thimble Collecting — A national study group of thimble enthusiasts which issued a quarterly newsletter edited by Ruth Mann. This group joined with members of the 'Thimble Guild' group and held one of the first mini conventions in Washington, D.C. in 1970. Ruth Mann and Pat Rich were co-chairpersons.

Thimble Fools of Northern Illinois — A regional thimble collectors group founded by Lina Whiting.

Thimble Guild — An early thimble collector's club founded by Evelyn Eubanks of Ohio in 1970. This study group mailed a newsletter every two months. They helped sponsor the Warren, Ohio "gathering" in 1972 and the Troy, New York meeting in 1974. At this latter convention, exhibits from the Hyde, Hunt, Proctor and Alden collections were featured. In attendance were 55 collectors.

Thimble Language — A short glossary of basic thimble terms written by Jeannine Conner, Marjorie Perkins, and Evelyn DerMarderosian in 1981.

Thimble Rigging — Any alterations, additions or subtractions done to fool a would-be buyer into paying a higher price. Any activity which results in making a less expensive thimble look like a more expensive or rare thimble, such as: gold plating lesser metal thimbles to sell as solid gold; the application of stones, where no stones were originally set; plastic and old celluloid sold as ivory; porcelain filed off to look like aged porcelain. Thimble rigging is cheating.

Thimble Society of London — A commercial organization formed by Betty Huntley-Wright and her daughter, Bridget McConnel, in 1981. They publish a catalog four times a year which offers many antique and rare thimbles to members, plus articles of interest to collectors of sewing implements. The Society also commissions limited editions and commemorative thimbles for members. See Thimble Sources.

Thimble Treasury — The second of three books on thimbles written by Myrtle Lundquist. This volume illustrates the famous Hunt-Proctor collections as well as other rare thimbles; printed 1975 by Wallace-Homestead, Des Moines, Iowa.

Thimbler — An old term for a person who makes thimbles.

Thimbles — An English book written by Edwin F. Holmes on the history and evolution of thimbles. Mr. Holmes, a collector himself, explored the dim past and sheds a great deal of light on the subject. He illustrates his writings with examples from private collections and museums from around the world. Published in 1976 by Gill and MacMillan, Ltd., Dublin, Ireland, this book is now out of print.

Thimbles Are Us — A thimble group in Dallas/Fort Worth area, formed in 1985. Wynneth Mullins was elected as first president.

Thimblers of Oklahoma — A regional thimble collecting group founded by Lora Wilkinson for area collectors.

Thimbles Only — An American mail order firm which specializes in thimbles; founded by Jean Shoup in 1981. See "Thimble Sources."

Thimbles of Time — The name given to a newsletter started in September, 1973 by Sandy Cortese of Colorado. This newsletter was another source of information for collectors in earlier years. A total of 15 newsletters were issued.

Thimbletter — A publication printed bi-monthly on thimbles for collectors; founded in 1973 by Lorraine Crosby. Thimbletter was the first thimble news and information letter in America open to all collectors.

Thimbling — A collector's slang term for "looking for thimbles to add to one's collection."

Thompson, Janet — A Montana artist who has oil painted a beautiful line of elk horn thimbles with portraits of wildlife. Each thimble has a black buffalo horn tip. See thimble # 509.

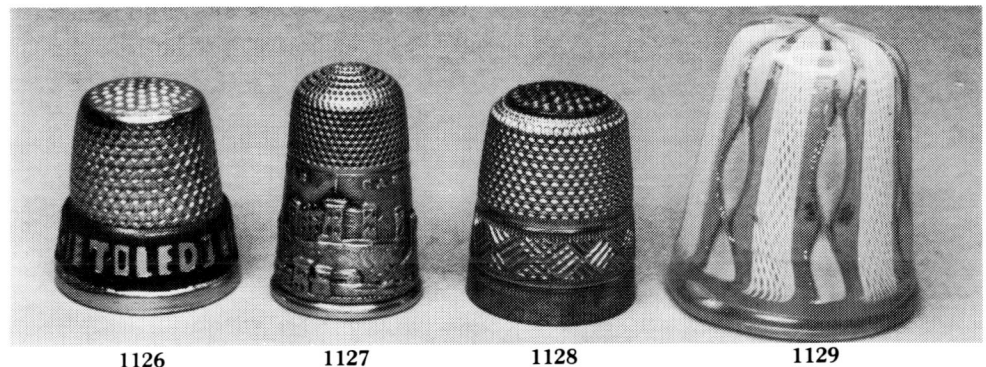

1126 1127 1128 1129

Thoughts on Thimbles — A history of thimbles written by Elizabeth Aldridge, an English collector, it was published in serial by T.C.I. from 1983/86. The manuscript was found among her possessions after her death in 1982. Mr. Edwin Holmes supplied detailed photos to illustrate Mrs. Aldridge's extensive and knowledgeable work. It is still available from T.C.I.

Three Rivers Thimbles — A Western Pennsylvania social and informational group founded by Pearl Hazen for thimble collectors.

Thymel — Old English spelling for thimble, circa A.D. 1000; also spelled: Thymbyl.

Tiffany & Co. — Famous New York Jewelry firm founded by Louis C. Tiffany in 1837. Originally Tiffany & Young, this firm grew to a world famous reputation as offering the best in luxury merchandise. Their first catalog of 30 pages was published in 1845 listing silver thimbles. A later 1880 catalog listed: "Thimbles: Plain, Etruscan, Engraved, Faceted or Enameled Gold; $5.00 to $12.00. Some richly jeweled at higher prices. Silver; plain .30 to .50 cents; ornamental borders, 1.25 all sizes." Most of the thimbles made by Tiffany unfortunately were not marked and the author has seen only two gold ones with the name Tiffany & Co. on their box. See thimble # 1130.

Tiny Thimble Treasures of Iowa — A regional thimble study group founded by Tiny Meyerhoff and Generose Evans in 1980. The club is open to all collectors in their area.

Toevs, Carol — American artist whose hand painted designs grace delicate glass thimbles. Her work is signed.

Toledo — A city in Spain which has produced many silver and brass thimbles. Many brass ones have the word "Toledo" in black niello about the band. These are considered to be souvenir types.

Tombac — A light brass alloy used in making thimbles in Germany and Austria during the 1920s and 30s. See thimble 1128.

1130

A rare Tiffany thimble with holder — 1870-75

Tools and Toys of Stitchery — A book written by Gertrude Whiting in 1928. Published: Columbia University Press in New York. A chapter entitled "Thimble, Thimble, Who Has the Thimble" takes its reader through a quick course on thimbles with excellent illustrations from the author's collections and other rare thimbles. A reprint of the book is called *Old Time Tools and Toys of Stitchery,* Dover Press, New York.

Tortoise Shell Thimbles — In the first quarter of the 19th century, a patent was given to John Piercy for a process which produces thimbles from tortoise shell. These thimbles are usually lined with metal and decorated with gold, silver and sometimes a base material. Many older tortoise shell thimbles have little motifs such as stars, anchors, leaves and crosses in gold pique. See examples # 1131 to 1133.

Touchmark — A design or initials stamped on a thimble to identify the maker.

Trademark — A logo made up of either letters, numbers or symbols to identify the seller. A trademark may or may not be the maker's identification. For example, the Percival thimbles have a gothic "P" inside their top, but were made by Waite-Thresher.

Trefoil Mark — A three-pointed design found under the apex, it was used by Simons Brothers Co. of Philadelphia to mark their gold-filled thimbles. See "Thimble Marks."

1131   1132   1133   1134

Wooden Tunbridge Thimbles

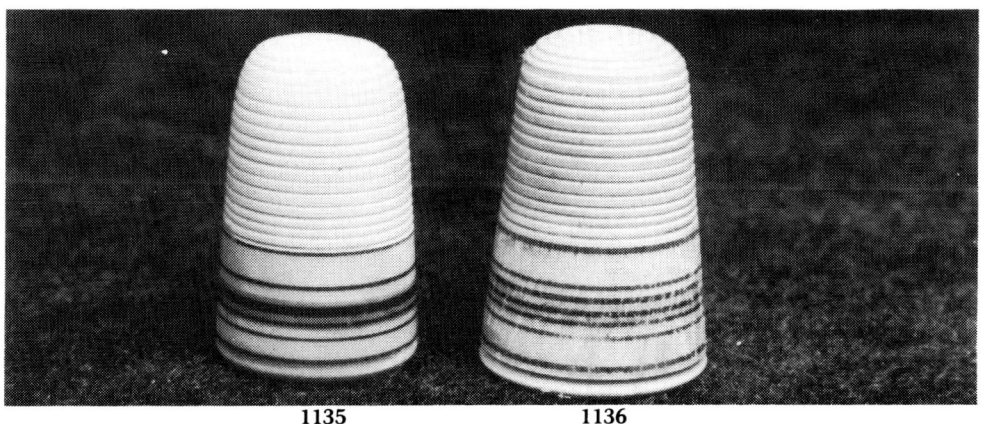

1135   1136

Tunbridge Thimbles — An early style of wooden thimble, created by the artisans of Tunbridge Wells, England, in the late 18th century for sale to the tourist trade. These early souvenir thimbles were lathed from a rod of beechwood with circular rings around the sides of the thimble and the apex. The bands were painted with colorful rings. See thimbles # 1135 and 1136.

About 1830, a second style known as Tunbridge "stickware" was introduced. These "mosaic-looking" thimbles were created by glueing different-colored wooden sticks together, such as beech, sycamore, holly, and cherry; then they were lathed like the earlier pieces. This exposed the multi-hued woods and created the mosaic effect.

These pieces are very rare, although the stickware thimble holders they were sold in are more common. It is believed the stickware thimbles were soon abandoned, and in their place a simple, but more practical brass thimble, was used. A Tunbridge stickware thimble sold recently in England for over seven hundred dollars, making it one of the most expensive wooden antiques in the world for its weight.

Turko Slavic — The name of a group of early Islamic bronze thimbles found in the northeastern Mediterranean countries and Bulgaria, Rumania, and Hungary. They have a distinctive "bulbous" shape. They date from the 13th to the 18th century. See page 26.

Turquoise — A rather soft semi-precious stone which ranges from green to dark blue in color. The pale sky blue is the most popular. Turquoise is used as a decorative stone on many English and Indian thimbles.

Turton, William — English silversmith who made steel-top silver thimbles in the late 18th century. His marker's mark was W.T.

Thimble Classics

Some thimbles have bright ideas!

"Thelma! The Collection or ME!!"

The Thimbles of Sok Ung

1137   1138   1139   1140

U

Unfired Decal — A printed piece of clear "cellophane-like" material which is glued on, to decorate a thimble. Usually used in the low end types of cheap thimbles, the design may peel off and can easily be scratched by the fingernail.

Ung, Sok — Cambodian-American gold and silversmith. Creator of the "Masterpieces in Replica" series of collector's thimbles using the originals in the von Hoelle Collection. The thimbles were cast using the lost wax method. Mr. Ung also cast, in silver and gold, ivory thimbles carved by Mr. von Hoelle. These are set with precious and semi-precious stones. His mark, SU, may be found in the apex. See illustration above.

Unger Brothers — An American firm founded by Herman Unger in 1866, which made silver articles including thimbles and holders. The firm was located in Newark, New Jersey, from 1896 to about 1918. Their thimbles were not marked, but on their thimble cases, a "B" with a superimposed "U" was stamped. See "Thimble Marks."

Unite, George — English silversmith working in Birmingham late 19th century. His maker's mark is GU.

Untermeyer-Robbins Co. — American firm known to have made silver thimbles in New York from 1909 to about 1935. The joined initials UR can be found stamped in the thimble. See "Thimble Marks."

19th Century Vegetable Ivory Thimbles

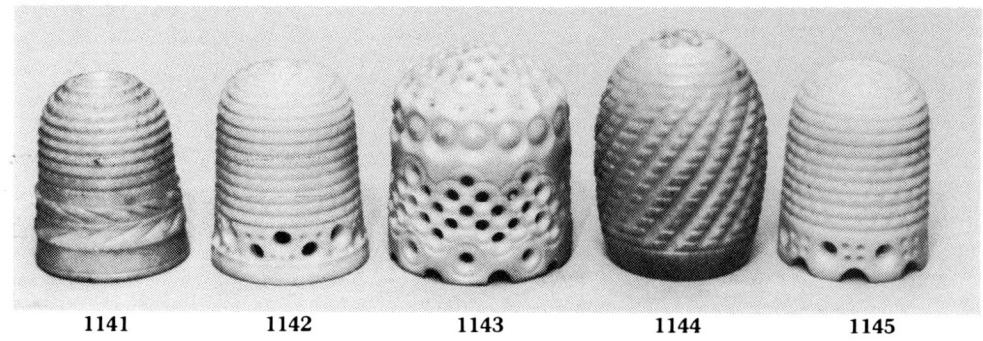

1141   1142   1143   1144   1145

V

Van Benschoten, Nicholas — Legendary Dutch inventor of the thimble. So the old story goes; the first European thimblemaker was a young goldsmith from Amsterdam. In 1684 he designed a metal guard to protect the finger of his girl friend.

Vegetable Ivory Thimbles — In the late 19th century thimbles of the Corozo nut were carved in England. They looked very much like ivory thimbles and came in many interesting holders. Thus "vegetable ivory" as it came to be called, was imported from South America. Old vegetable ivory thimbles are scarce. They are still made and sold today in several countries in South America as souvenirs to tourists. The modern ones may be painted in bright colors and do not have the workmanship of the early ones.

Venetian Latticino Glass Thimbles — Thimbles hand-blown with fine "lace-like" designs embedded within the glass are an old art form in Venice. Called "Latticino," these glass thimbles are beautiful to behold, and rare. See example # 1146.

Ventilated Thimbles — A series of American & British patents were filed from the mid-19th century to the 1970s. These patents were for a thimble in which a sewer's finger would not sweat. All these type of "ventilated" thimbles had a special lining or a space for perspiration to escape between the inner and outer shell. Today they make interesting collectibles of yesteryear's need to improving even the humblest articles. See thimble 445.

Vermeil — A French word for the process of plating silver with gold.

Vista Alegre Thimble — The famed Portuguese porcelain firm of Vista Alegre was founded in 1824 by Jose Basto. Known around the world for its fine objects de art, Vista Alegre made only one thimble. It was of pure white translucent porcelain, with a hand-painted rust-red dragon and a 24K gold fired ring about the rim. See thimble # 1148.

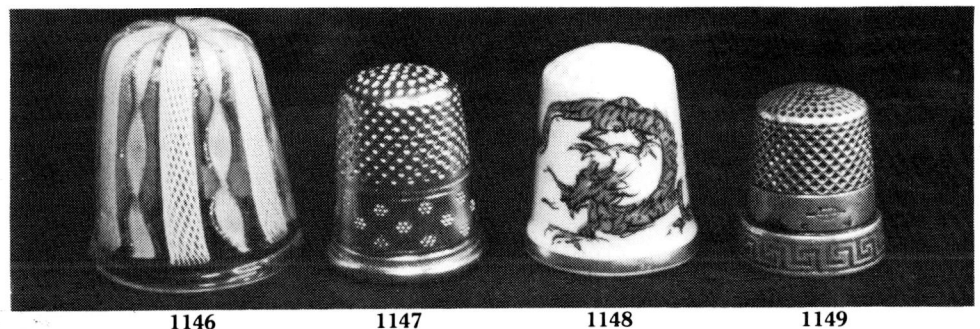

1146　　　1147　　　1148　　　1149

Von der Becke, Johann Bernhard — German thimble manufacturer who sold his factory in Iserlohn when he was ordered to stop producing thimbles by the City Council of Nuremberg. Von der Becke set up a new factory in Sundwig and started production again in 1698. Learning the casting techniques of the Dutch thimblemakers, Von der Becke increased production in 1712. By the end of the 18th century his family operated six thimble mills and helped German manufacturers take over much of the Dutch thimblemakers' Continental business. See below illustration

1150
*Cast Iron — von der Becke Thimble
circa 1740, excavated in Sundwig
Iron Cross motif on top*

The Thimbles of Waite-Thresher

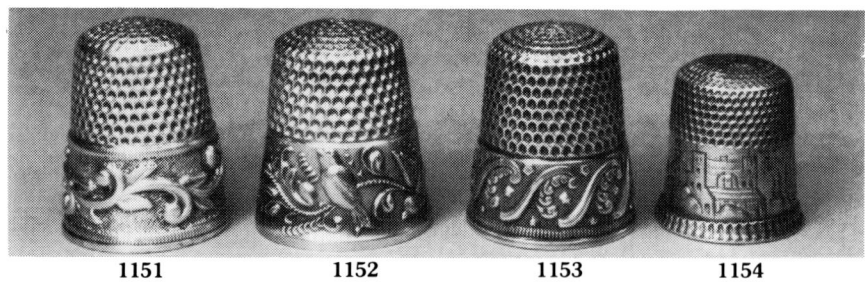

| 1151 | 1152 | 1153 | 1154 |

W

Waite-Thresher — American silversmith firm in Providence, Rhode Island; established by Daniel B. Waite in 1860. After several name changes and a new partner, Henry Thresher in 1884, the name Waite-Thresher was incorporated in 1892. The firm made both gold and silver thimbles. Their early mark was a plain five-pointed star stamped inside the top. Later a star with a thimble within was used as the trademark. The Barker Manufacturing Co. was bought by Waite-Thresher before 1920. The company discontinued the making of thimbles in the late 1920s. Simons Bros. bought their designs. See below.

Walker & Hall — British manufacturer of the "DURA" thimbles late 19th century. A sterling silver cased steel thimble similar to the "DORCAS." Their trademark is a W&H inside a pennant with staff.

Walls of Troy — A merchandising name given to thimbles which have a Greek key pattern going around their band. See #412.

Walter, Peter J. — German antique dealer from Lindau who publishes a full color catalog illustrating hundreds of new and antique thimbles for collectors worldwide. See "Thimble Sources."

Webb, James — English silversmith active in Birmington from 1843 to about 1890. His mark, JW, can be on some of his thimbles.

Webster Co. — American company founded by George K. Webster in 1879 in north Attleboro, Massachusetts. In 1950 the Webster Company became a subsidiary of Reed-Barton. They made a line of sterling thimbles marked with a "W and C superimposed over each other and an arrow running through both." See "Thimble Marks" and 413.

| 1155 | 1156 | 1157 | 1158 | 1159 |

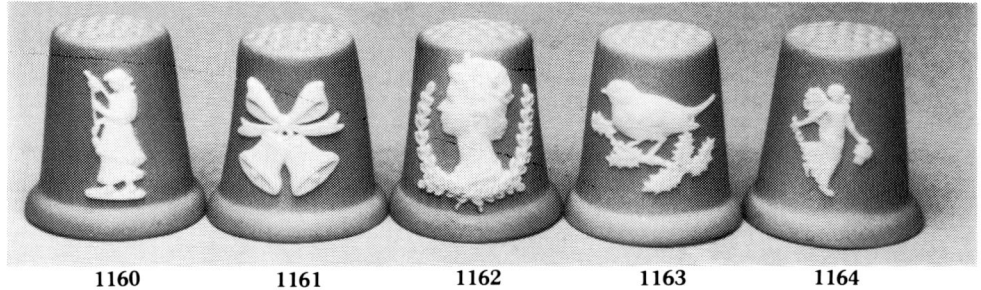

| 1160 | 1161 | 1162 | 1163 | 1164 |

Wedgwood — A major British porcelain manufacturer founded by Josiah Wedgwood in 1759 in Burslem. Wedgwood developed most of his own ceramic paste; best known is his black basalt, and his blue & white jasper. It is believed that Wedgwood never made thimbles until 1979, at which time, a blue jasper thimble was created with a white cameo of Josiah Wedgwood to honor the 250th anniversary of the birth of the company's founder. Today Wedgwood makes a range of thimbles in black basalt, blue, pink, lilac, yellow, green and white grounds. See illustration above.

Weihman, Henry — American thimble designer for the Simons Brothers Co. in Philadelphia. Of his many design patents, the 1893 Washington Souvenir Thimble (White House & Washington Monument, and Capitol Building) and the 1905 "Cherubs with garlands" are much sought after by collectors. In 1889 he received a patent for a beautiful thimble with deep embossing of a variety of flowers, almost in bas relief. Mr. Weihman continued to receive design patents from 1889 to at least 1905. See page 268.

Weingberg, E.M. Co. — American silver plated novelty manufacturer in New York City from 1915 to about 1922. Their thimbles are marked with a W within a diamond. Their base metal is nickel-silver.

Whistle Thimbles — A novelty thimble with a whistle device built into its top. These were primarily made as advertising items with slogans such as "BLOW FOR DODD FOR MAYOR" printed on the band. Most were usually made of aluminum or plastic. See 1165 and page 217.

1165

Thimbles in Wood

1166   1167   1168

1169   1170   1171   1172

1173   1174   1175   1176

1177   1178   1179   1180   1181

Aluminum Whistle Thimbles

Whiting, Gertrude — American author of *Tools and Toys of Stitchery*, a chapter on thimbles. Published in New York, 1928 and reprinted by the Dover Press in 1971.

Woodside Sterling Co. — An American manufacturing firm known to have made silver thimbles in New York from 1896 to about 1920. Their Trademark is a "W" in a circle.

Wooden Thimbles — Thimbles of wood have been carved as souvenirs since the late 18th century. Wood, being not the most durable of materials for making working thimbles, has been used by many artisans to create a remarkable variety of styles as keepsakes. English Tunbridge thimbles of the late 18th and 19th century are very collectible, and are among the most expensive wooden antiques, per weight, in the world. See "Tunbridge Thimbles."

In France at about the same time, beautifully carved and lathed thimbles of sandalwood, camphor, and cedar were sold. Many had ornate gold or steel rims, sometimes studded with tiny cut-iron nails, which looked like faceted jewels about the bands. It is believed these very lovely old wooden thimbles were not used to sew with, but acted to deter moths in sewing baskets. See thimbles # 1167 and 1168.

In Ireland, wooden souvenir thimbles were carved from bog oak, a semi-petrified blackwood, during the latter part of the 19th and early 20th centuries. See thimble # 1447.

Today's collectors have an array of styles to choose from. Many are fine examples of skilled craftsmanship and unique artistic abilities. Contemporary thimblers in wood keep alive the centuries-old traditions of beautiful keepsake thimbles. See opposite page.

Worcester — See article on Royal Worcester.

The Thimbles of Yaacov Yemini

1182　　　　　1183　　　　　1184　　　　　1185

Y

Yemini, Yaacov — A modern Yemenite silversmith working in Jerusalem. His thimbles are sterling silver and are chased with scenes from the Holy Land. He also uses the technique of filigreed medallions to feature famous women of the Bible and other historical motifs. For examples of his work see thimbles #1182 to 1184.

Young, Jennifer — English designer of Queen Elizabeth's 25th Silver Jubilee commemorative thimble. See thimble #283.

Z

Z-Mark — A tiny z can sometimes be found stamped on top of modern thimbles. This means the thimble was imported to the Netherlands. A ZI is for .925 sterling, ZII is for .835 silver, and a plain Z means .800 or continental silver.

Zalkin, Estelle — American thimble collector, keynote speaker, and author of articles on "Dorcas" and other thimble subjects; Vice-President of T.C.I. in 1982-84.

Zen-Huan — Mandarin Chinese word for "needle-ring"; an ancient term for a tailor's style thimble or sewing ring; the oldest known form of metal sewing thimble, circa 2nd century A.D. See page 22.

Zig-Zag Geometric — A "stitch-like" design found on many older thimbles. See illustration #1516.

Zinc Thimbles — The German firm of Gabler Brothers made some rare, pure zinc thimbles during the last years of the Second World War, due to the rationing of most other metals. These can be recognized by their dull pewter-like appearance. For illustration see thimble #1185.

Thimbles of the Near East

1186　　1187　　1188　　1189

1190　　1191　　1192

1193　　1194　　1195

The Thimbles of Spain

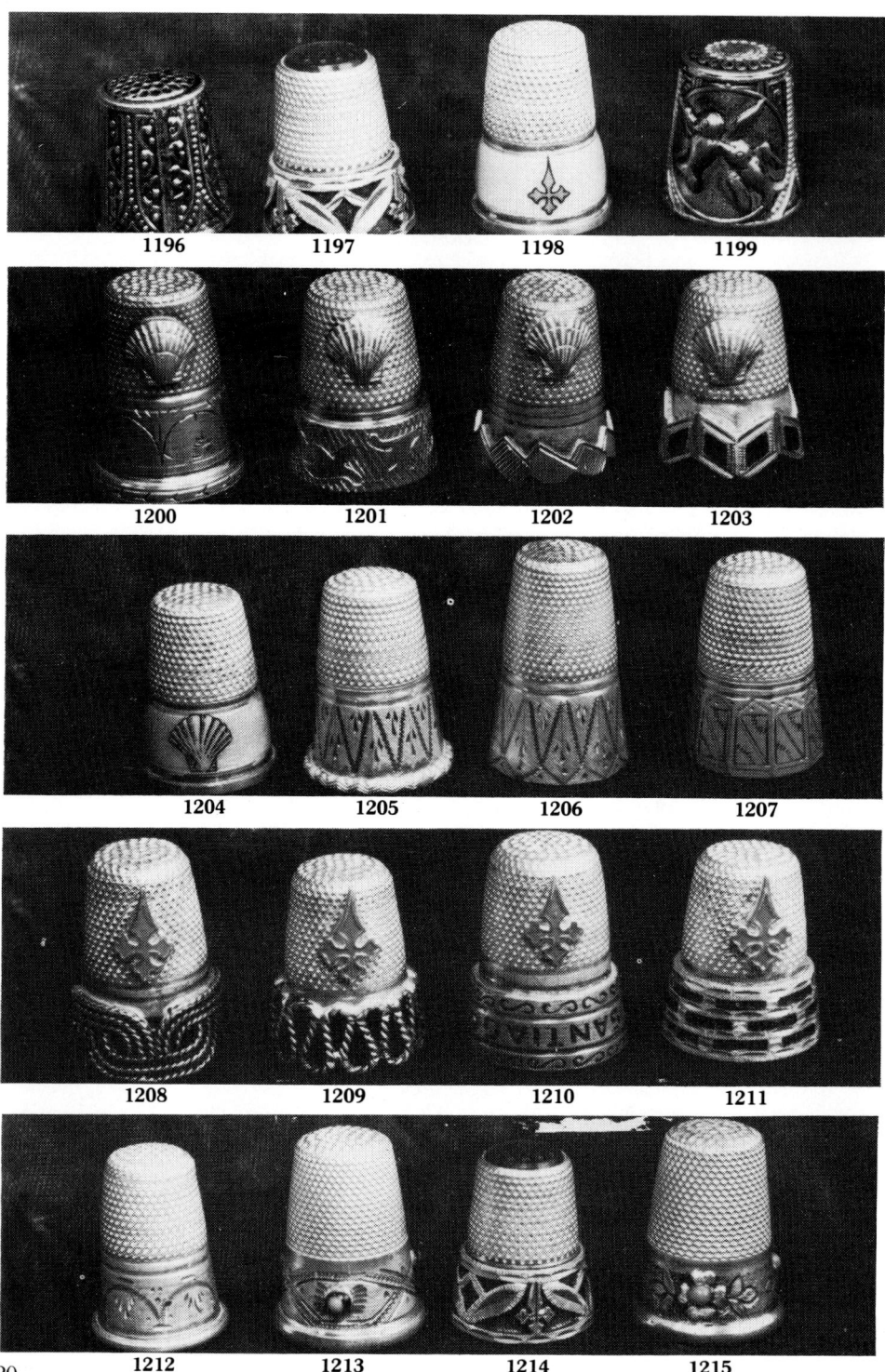

Thimbles of Many Nations

Courtesy: J. A. Rath

Beautiful Thimbles of Many Nations

Courtesy J. A. Rath Collection

1232　　1233　　1234　　1235

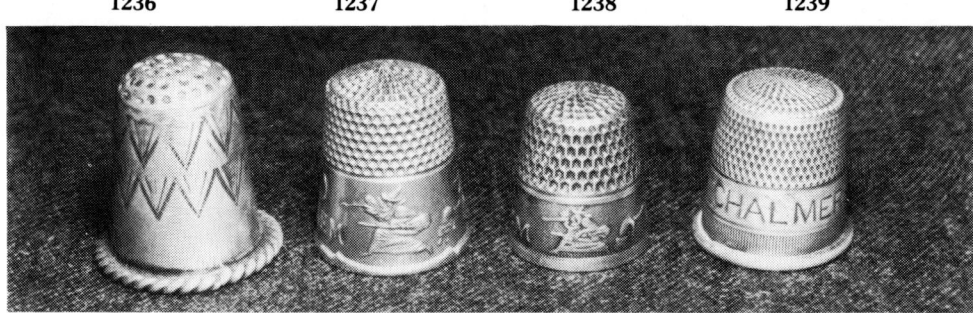

1236　　1237　　1238　　1239

1240　　1241　　1242　　1243

1244　　1245　　1246　　1247

Courtesy M.&D. Regine Collection

1264 1265 1266 1267
1268 1269 1270 1271
1272 1273 1274 1275
1276 1277 1278 1279

Antique Enameled Thimbles
(English, Persian and American)

1280　　　　　　1281　　　　　　1282

1283　　　　　　1284　　　　　　1285

1286　　　　　　1287　　　　　　1288

225

Antique Thimbles of Gold
with Pearls and Precious Jewels

1289　　　　　　　1290　　　　　　　1291

1292　　　　　　　1293　　　　　　　1294

1295　　　　　　　1296　　　　　　　1297

Antique Thimbles of Gold with Pearls and Precious Jewels

Antique Thimbles of Gold

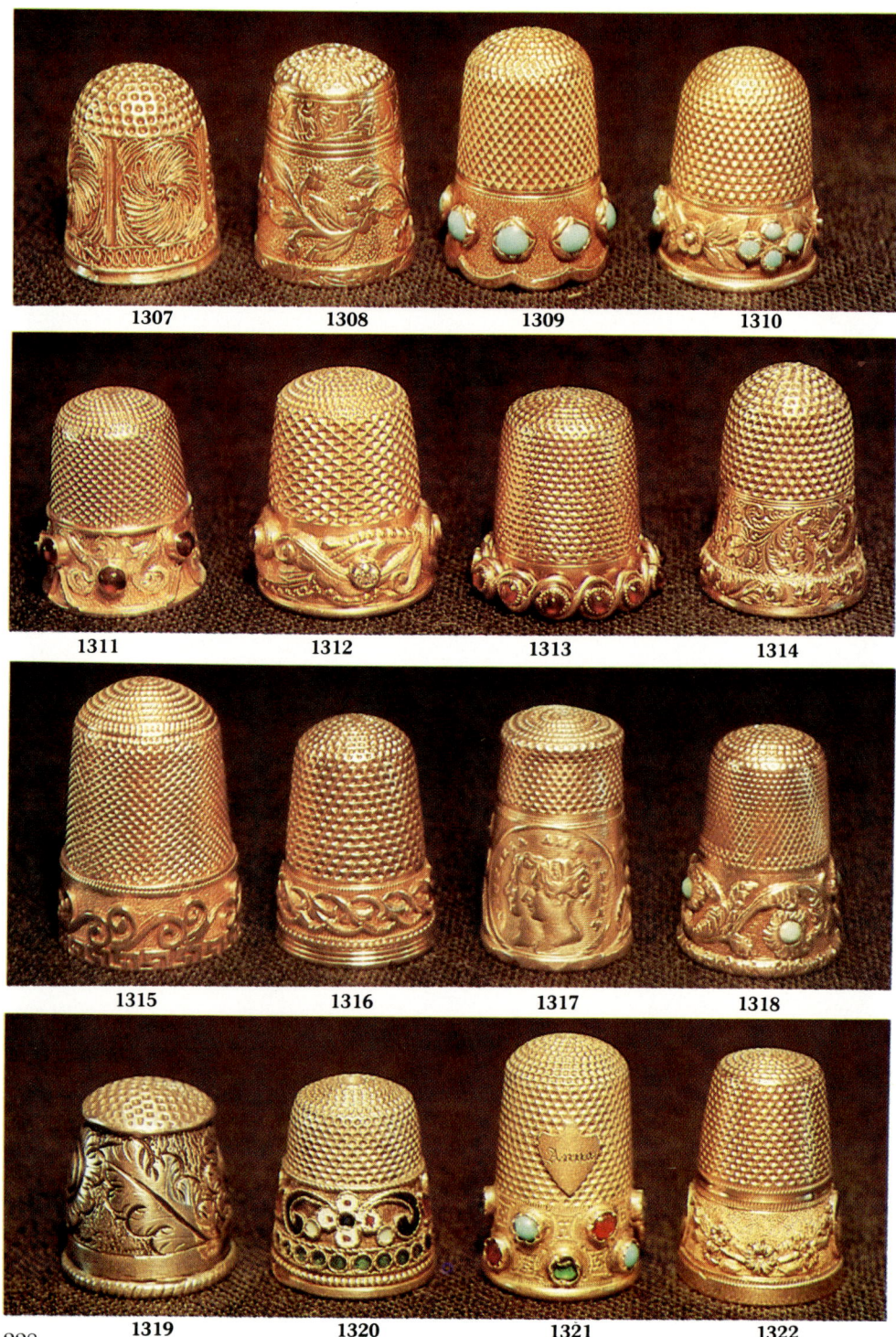

Thimbles of Gold and Enamel

Antique Thimbles of Gold with Pearls and Precious Jewels

1339 1340 1341 1342
1343 1344 1345 1346
1347 1348 1349 1350
1351 1352 1353 1354

Thimbles of Ivory
Inset with Gold, Silver and Jewels

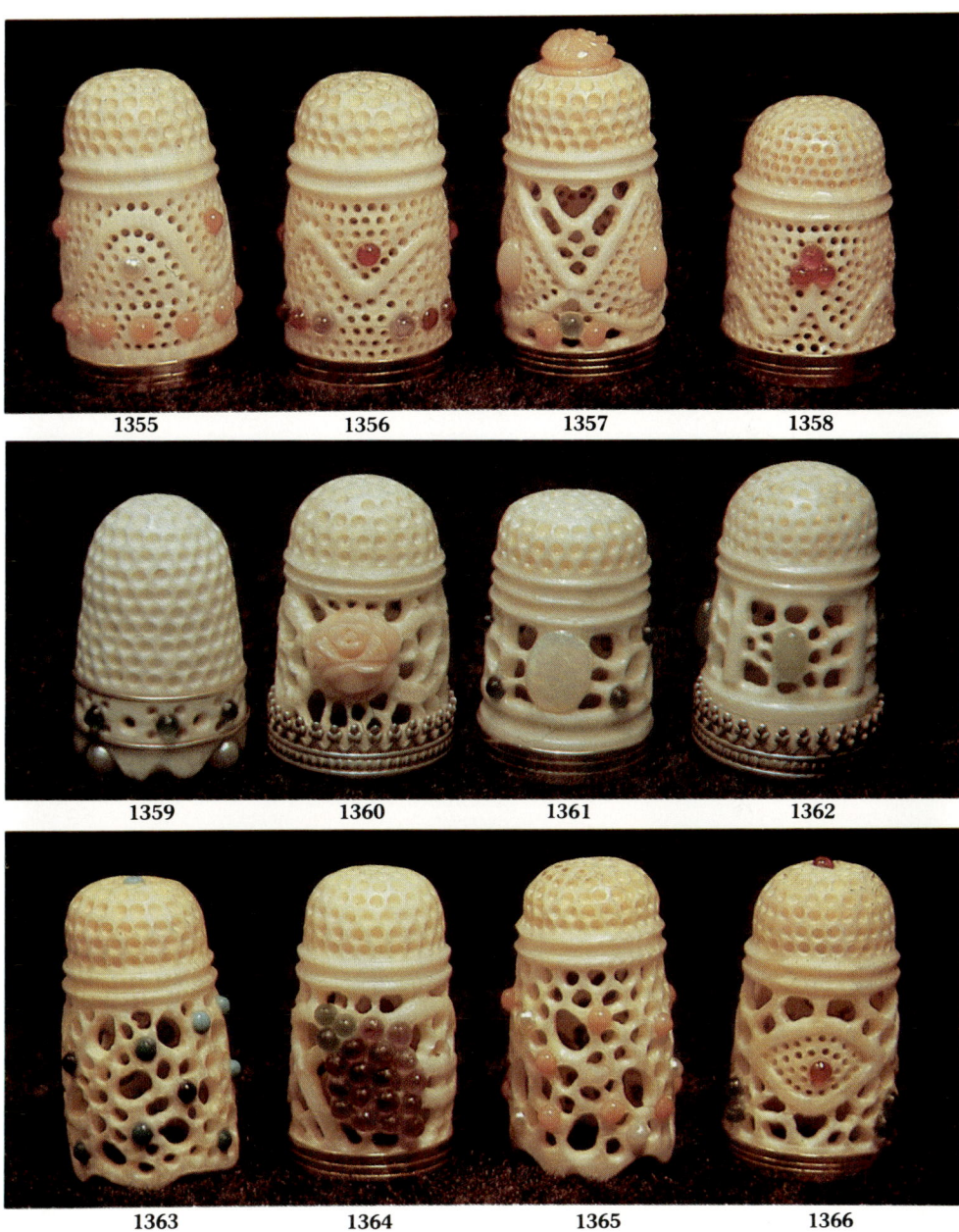

1355 1356 1357 1358
1359 1360 1361 1362
1363 1364 1365 1366

Thimbles of Imperial Russia and German-Spanish Damascene

1367   1368   1369

1370   1371   1372

1373   1374   1375

Antique Thimbles of Tortoise Shell, Filigree, Gold, and Mother-of-Pearl

1376   1377   1378

1379   1380   1381

1382   1383   1384

Antique Thimbles of the World

1385   1386   1387

1388   1389   1390

1391   1392   1393

Antique Thimbles of Gold

1394　　　1395　　　1396

1397　　　1398　　　1399

1400　　　1401　　　1402

Antique Thimbles of Gold and Enamel

1403 1404 1405

1406 1407 1408

1409 1410 1411

The Legendary Thimbles of Meissen

1412   1413   1414

1415   1416   1417

1418   1419   1420

The Thimbles of Meissen

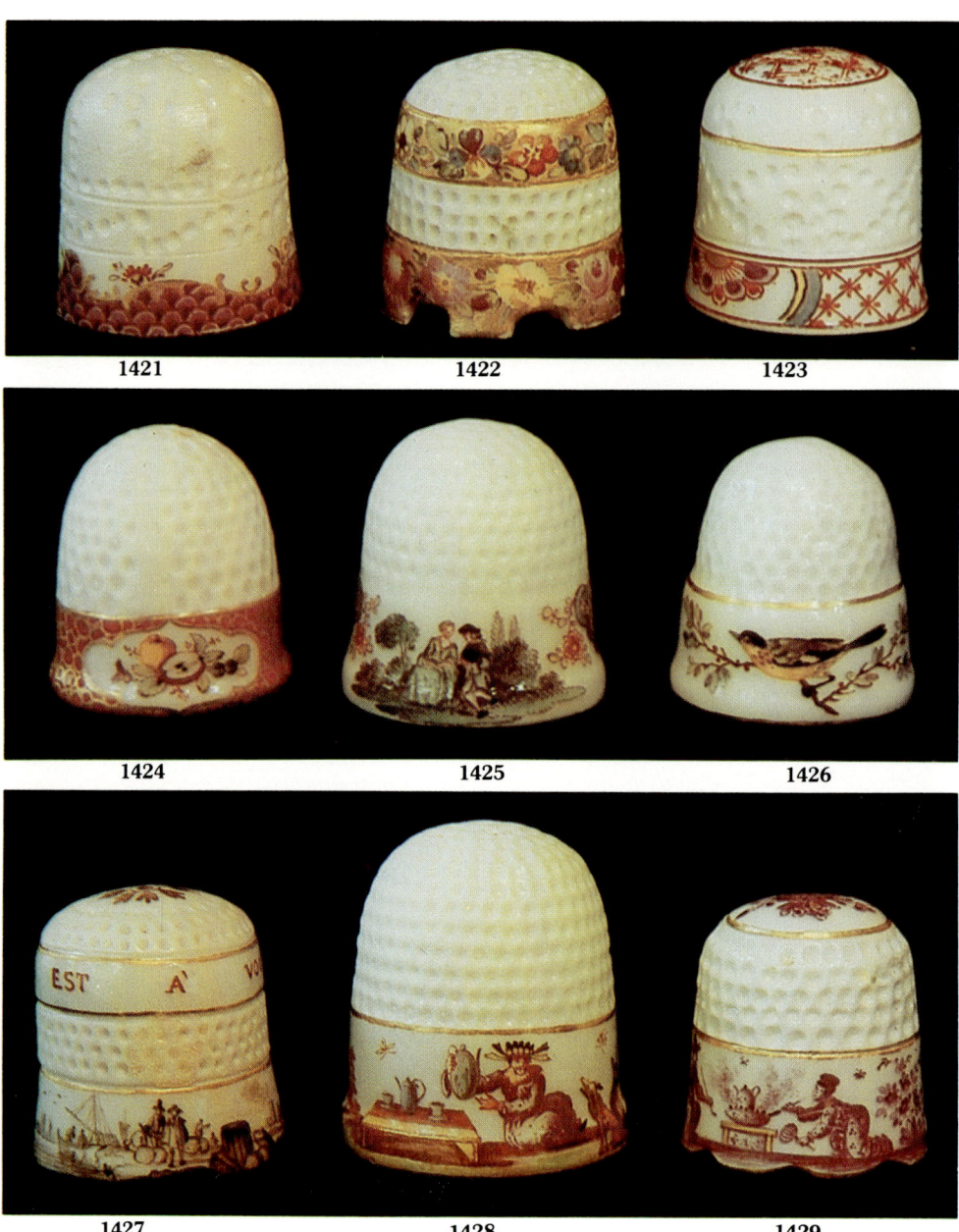

1421   1422   1423

1424   1425   1426

1427   1428   1429

The Thimbles of Meissen

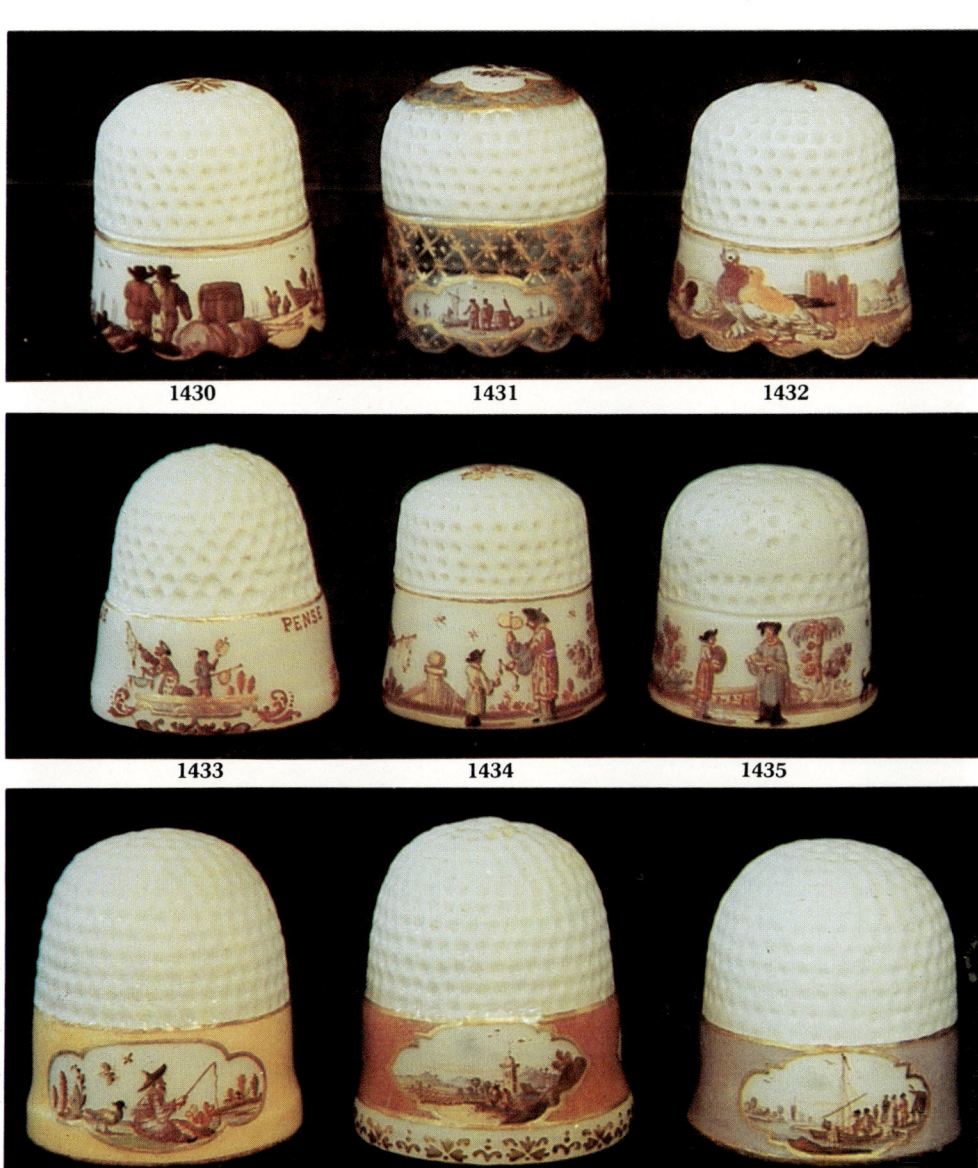

1430 1431 1432
1433 1434 1435
1436 1437 1438

"Victoria's Collection," by John von Hoelle

Courtesy Smithsonian Institute

This still-life photograph captures the haunting nostalgia, which is part of the charm of collecting yesteryear's thimbles.

Courtesy J. A. Rath Collection

Beautiful Thimbles of Many Nations

1471 1472 1473 1474
1475 1476 1477 1478
1479 1480 1481 1482
1483 1484 1485 1486

Beautiful Thimbles of Many Nations

1487　　1488　　1489　　1490

1491　　1492　　1493　　1494

1495　　1496　　1497　　1498

1499　　1500　　1501　　1502

Beautiful Thimbles of Many Nations

The Louise D. Alden Collection
Courtesy, Museum of Fine Arts, Boston

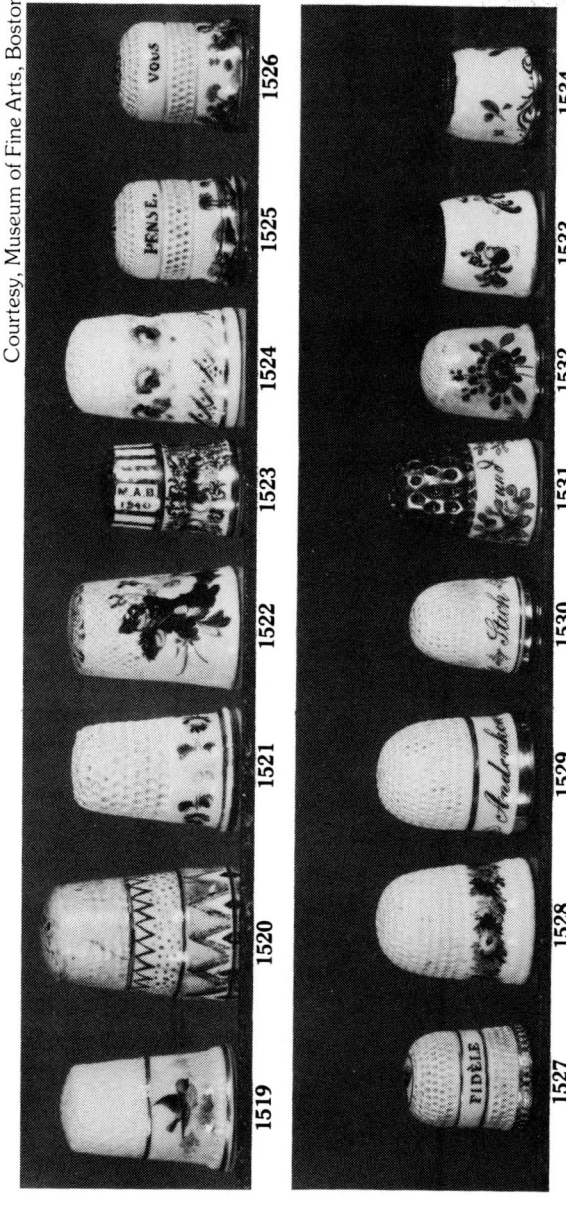

A superb collection of 88 hand painted porcelain, bone china, and enameled copper thimbles, purchased in England during the 1930's by Mrs. Alden.

These thimbles represent some of the finest examples of the 18th and 19th Century works of MEISSEN, SEVRES, WORCESTER, CROWN DERBY, BATTERSEA, BILSTON, COALPORT, and ROCKINGHAM.

The collection was donated to the Museum of Fine Arts, Boston, in 1962 It was available for viewing by appointment only.

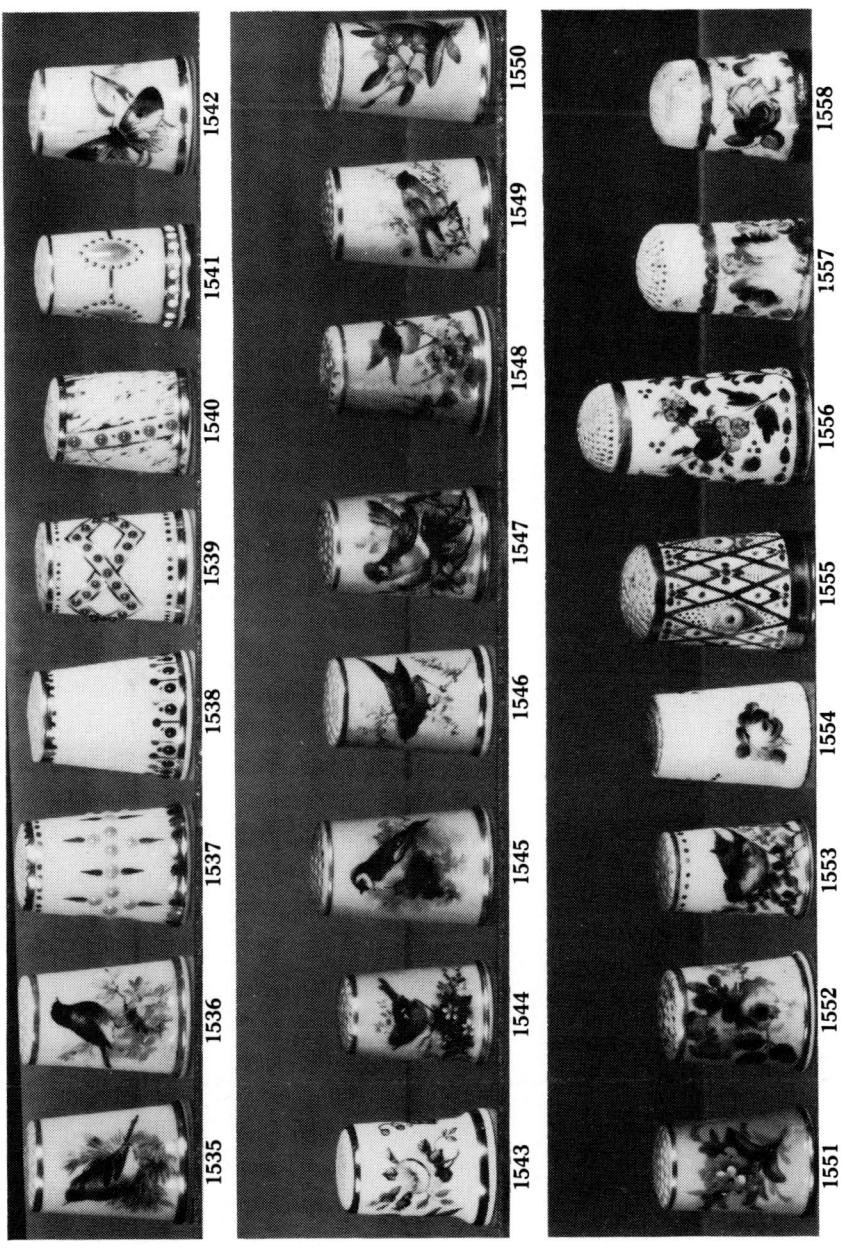

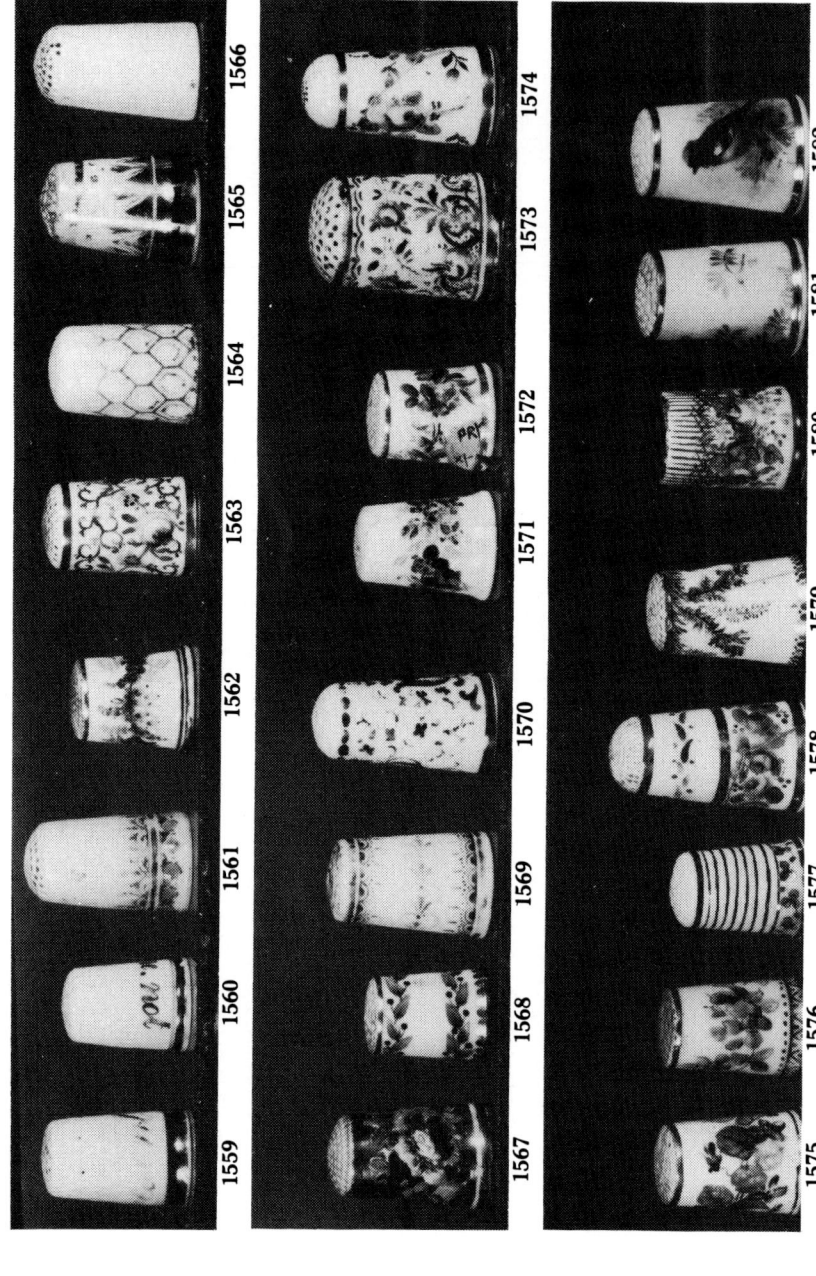

Louise D. Alden Collection

Courtesy, Museum of Fine Arts, Boston

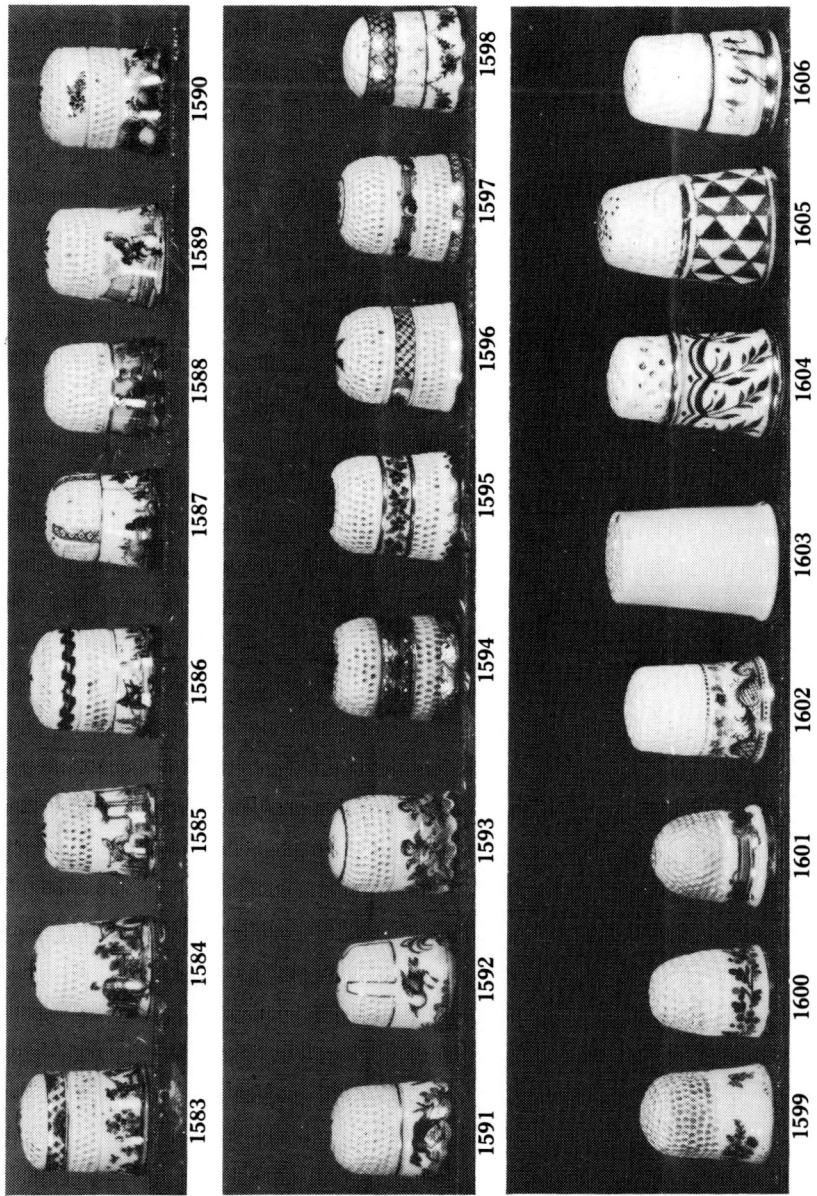

A "Thimble" In Other Lands

The word for thimble is found in over 150 of the world's languages. We have listed some of the most common, just to help you on your next "around the world thimble safari."

ARABIC	KASTIBAN	ICELANDIC	FINGURBJORG
ARMENIAN	MADNOTZ	INDONESIAN	SARUNG DJARI
BENGALI	ANGUSHTHANA	ITALIAN	DITALE
BRAZILIAN	DEDAL	JAPANESE	UBI WA
BULGARIAN	NAPRUSTNIK	JAPANESE	NUIMO UNI WA
CALABRESE	IIRITALE	JAVANESE	BIDAL
CHINESE	SU CHI ING	LATVIAN	FINGERROD
CHINESE (Cantonese)	JUM TING	LEBANESE	OMEH
CZECH	NAPRSTEK	MEXICO	DEDAL
DANISH	FINGERBOL	NORWEGIAN	FINGERFORT
DUTCH	VINGERHOED	PERSIAN	ANGUSHTAHNE
EAST INDIAN	ANGUTI	PHILIPPINES	DIDAL
ESKIMO	TEE KEEK	POLISH	NAPARSTEK
ESTONIAN	SORM KUBER	PORTUGESE	DEDAIS
FINNISH	SORMUSTIN	ROMANIAN	DEGETAR
FLEMISH	VINGERHOOT	RUSSIAN	NAPIONSTOCK
FRENCH	De'	SCOTTISH	THUMMEL
GAELIC IRISH	MEARACAN	SERBIAN	NAPRSTAK
GERMAN	FINGERHUT	SPANISH	DEDAL
GREEK	DAKTILITRA	SWEDISH	FINGERBORG
HINDI	ANGUSHTANA	THAI	POLK SUAM NIEW
HOLLAND	VINGERHOED	TURKISH	YUSUK
HUNGARIAN	GYUSZU	UKRANIAN	NANEPCMIN

A Word About Reproductions, Restrikes and Fakes

In the last twenty years, as thimble collecting has become increasingly popular and prices on rare or hard-to-find pieces have soared into the hundreds or even thousands of dollars, many reproductions have come onto the market.

Most of these pieces are sold by fine organizations such as the Smithsonian Institute, the Metropolitan Museum of Art, the Boston Museum of Fine Art, P.J.W. Thimbles, Thimbles Only, Heirloom Editions, Dine-American's Brandywine Studios, and other reputable companies. The thimbles are sold as reproductions, at a fraction of the cost of the original. Thousands are purchased each year and are welcomed in most collections.

The problem begins when unscrupulous people remake rare thimbles, striking them with phony marks, and sell them as originals. This was the case in 1983 when a flood of "rare" Russian enameled thimbles found their way onto the antique markets of the United States. Before "alerts" could be published in the T.C.I. Bulletin, collectors had paid up to $600.00 for these fakes.

In the coming years, I expect to find many thimbles, now sold in catalogs as repros, with the marks removed, artificially "antiqued," and sold as "originals" in antique and flea markets by naive or unprincipled individuals.

To avoid being taken in thimble collectors must learn the same techniques as used by other collectors of such items as coins, paintings, antique silver and porcelain.

Knowledge is the collector's first line of defense against rip-offs. I recommend you join Thimble Collectors International, and a regional group if there is one in your area. Meet and visit with other advanced collectors. See and touch their original pieces. Read and study about your collectibles. Visit the Smithsonian Institute; call ahead to see their "reserve collection." Ask long-time collectors to lend you old copies of catalogs and newsletters. Read, see, talk, feel, and ask questions. Remember, we all began with a very limited knowledge of thimbles, and knowledge is the only thing that separates the novice beginner from the advanced "digitabulist."

Then, the next time you ask to see a thimble, and the seller tells you "it's very old, probably 18th century," but you see the tiny word "sterling" stamped inside, you can give that "do-you-think-I-just-got-off-the-turnip-wagon" look. Over the years I have seen much thimble-rigging and heard some tall stories, but the one that takes the cake happened at last year's Winter Antique Show in Washington, D.C.

I saw a familiar-looking ivory thimble with a gold band. I asked the dealer if I could look at it more closely. The dealer, with an air of authority, handed me the thimble and said, "Old ivory thimbles are very rare you know. This one has been in one family for at least four generations. It may be by Charles Shipman who advertised ivory thimbles in the 1760s." She went on to tell me she had it "tested" and it was *real* ivory, and the band was at least 14K gold. Inside the thimble was a sticker marked $375.00.

As I returned the thimble I began to laugh, for next to the sticker was my own mark; I had carved the piece just three years earlier!

The following pages will give you some idea of the wide variety of reproductions and restrikes that are now in circulation and are offered for sale by many of the above companies.

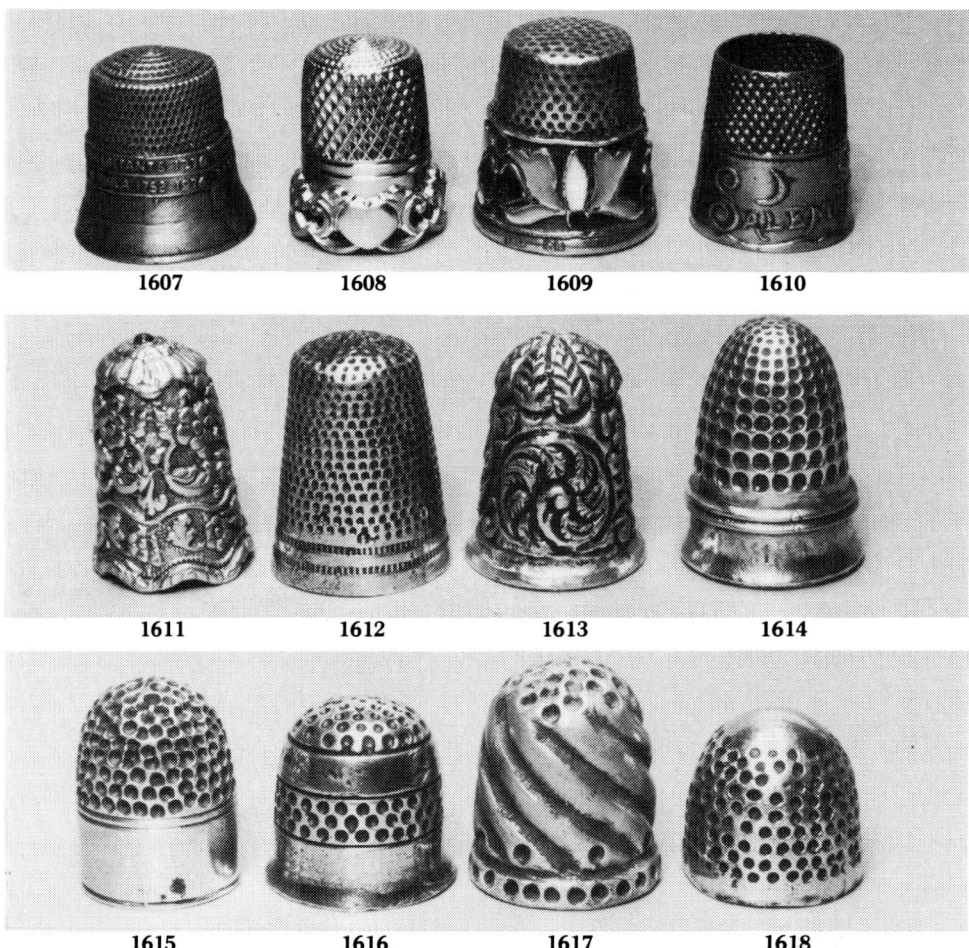

1607   1608   1609   1610

1611   1612   1613   1614

1615   1616   1617   1618

Reproductions, Restrikes, and Fakes

Thimbles That Never Were

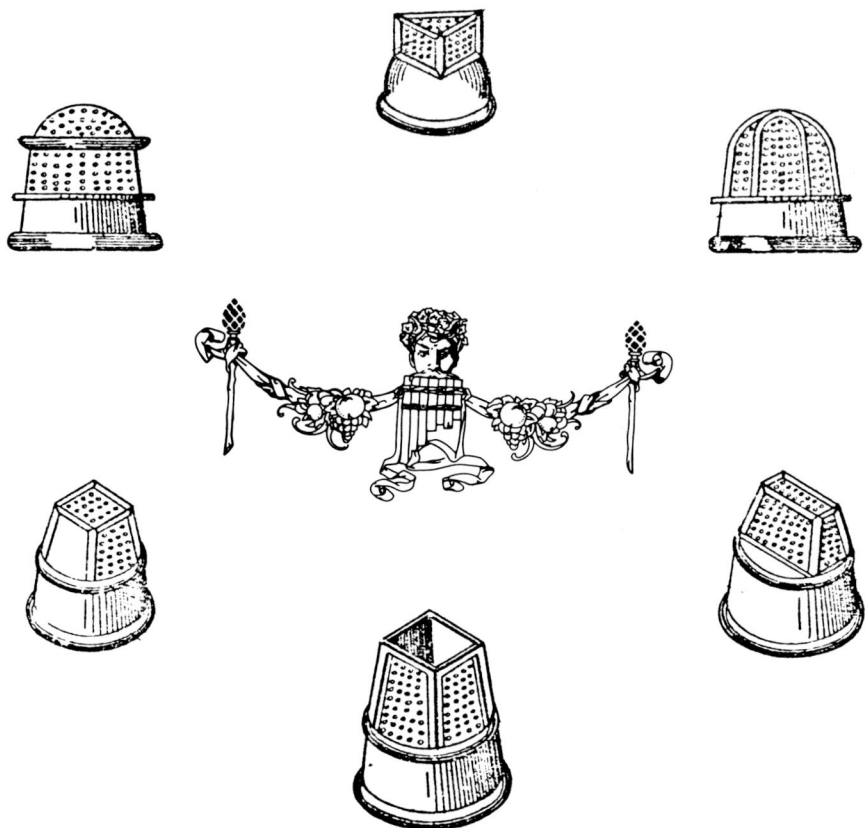

Over the last century and a half, many attempts were made to design the "perfect" thimble. Some of these new and unique thimbles came onto the market and were made by the tens-of-thousands. But many others never got past the drawing board or prototype stage for a host of reasons. Here we see some of the many forgotten thimbles of yesterday.

How Thimbles Are Made

The methods used by thimblemakers to form a thimble are usually dictated by the material used. Most forms of ceramic thimbles are cast in molds, but can also be created on a potter's wheel.

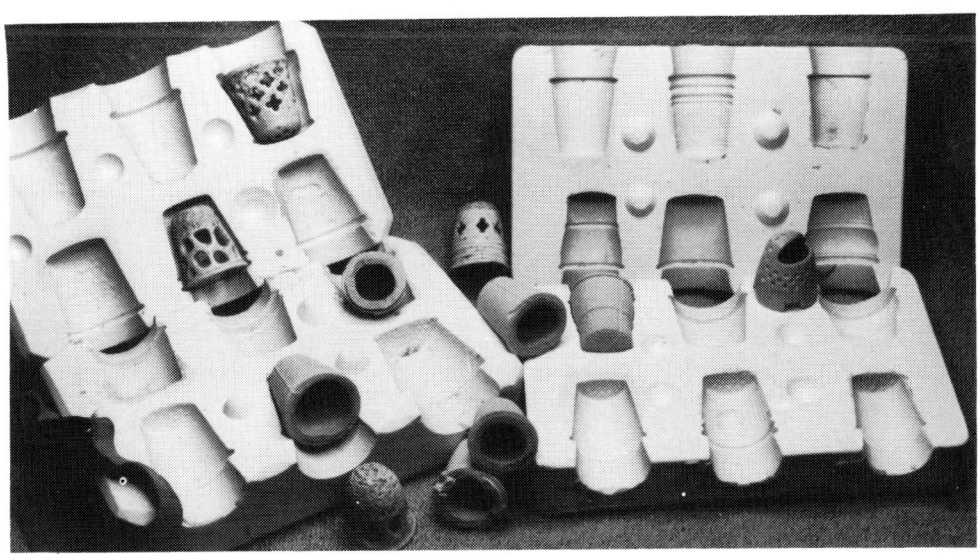

Ceramic thimbles and their molds

Glass thimbles may be hand blown or cast in a mold and etched or hand-cut to beautiful effect. Ivory, wood, bone and stone thimbles are usually hand carved or formed on a lathe. See the following photos, "The Creation of an Ivory Thimble," for illustration of this technique.

Thimbles of metal are made in three distinct ways. First, they may be cast into molds, as were most of the early bronze thimbles and some modern gold, silver and pewter pieces, see following page.

Second, they can be cut from a piece of sheet metal, rolled up and a top soldered on, as in the illustration below. This method is used for many French and Mexican thimbles.

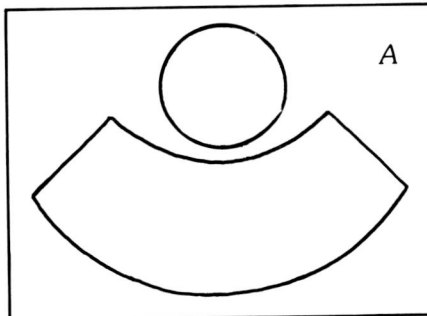
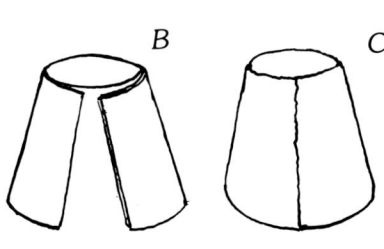

Fig. 1   Two-piece method

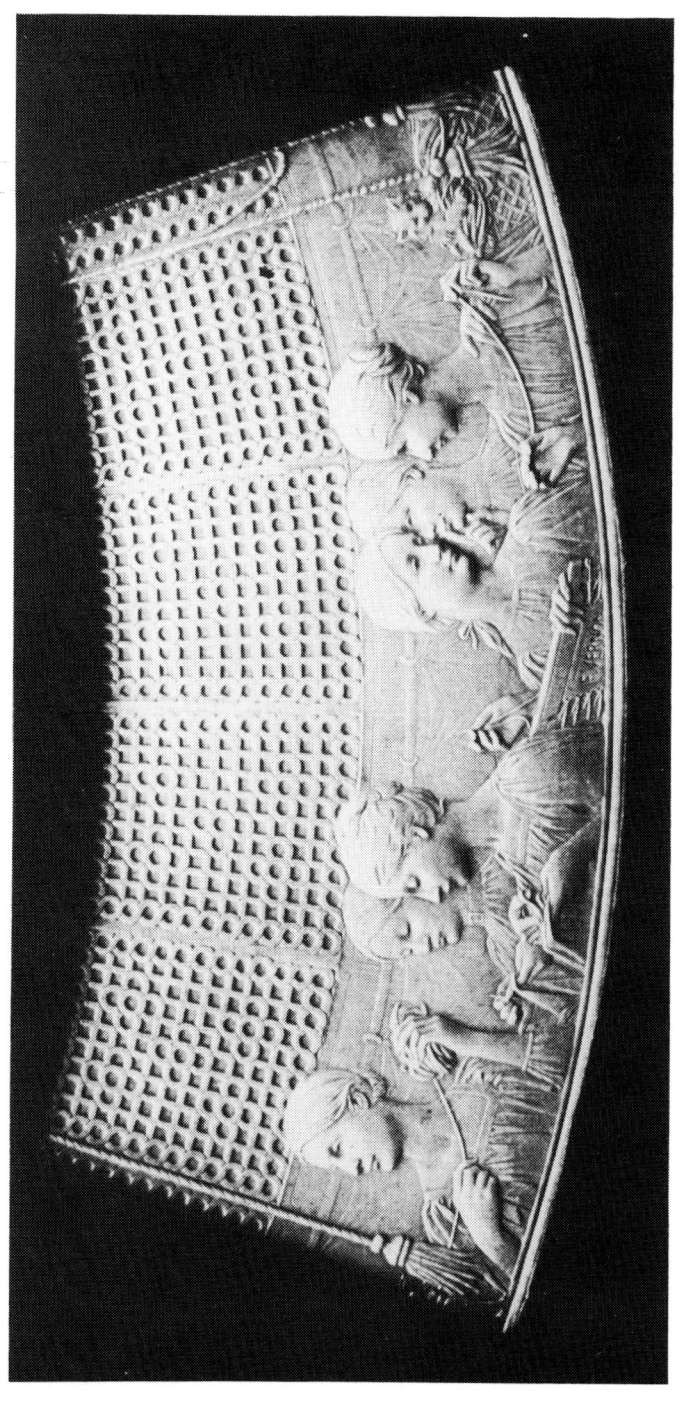

This illustration, from the French magazine "Les Modes," April 1909, shows a die-stamped panorama of a silver thimble. From this stage the thimble is rolled, soldered, and topped. Note: Engraver's name, F. VERNON, stamped on the loom in the young girl's hand. The thimble was made by P. Lenain & Co. of Paris, the manufacturer of the de la Fontaine thimbles.

A "Lost-Wax" Casting in Silver

Silver thimbles being cut from "tree" after casting.

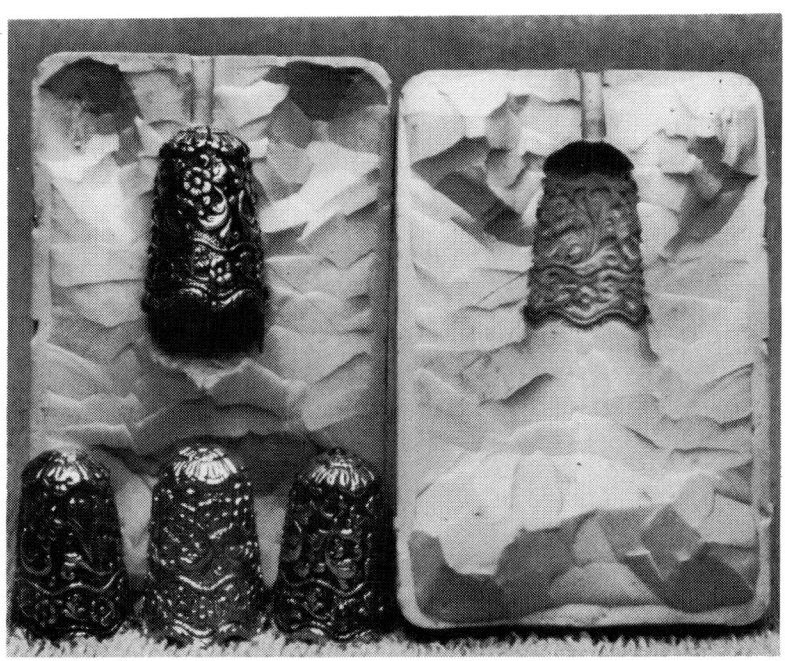

Silver thimbles being released from latex mold.

The third method, known as "deep drawn," stamps a disc of sheet metal over a mandril so as to form a shallow cup which, after several stampings, forms the shape of a thimble. See the following illustration showing the "first nine stages in thimble manufacturing" and page 262 on the "Manufacturing of Sewing Thimbles."

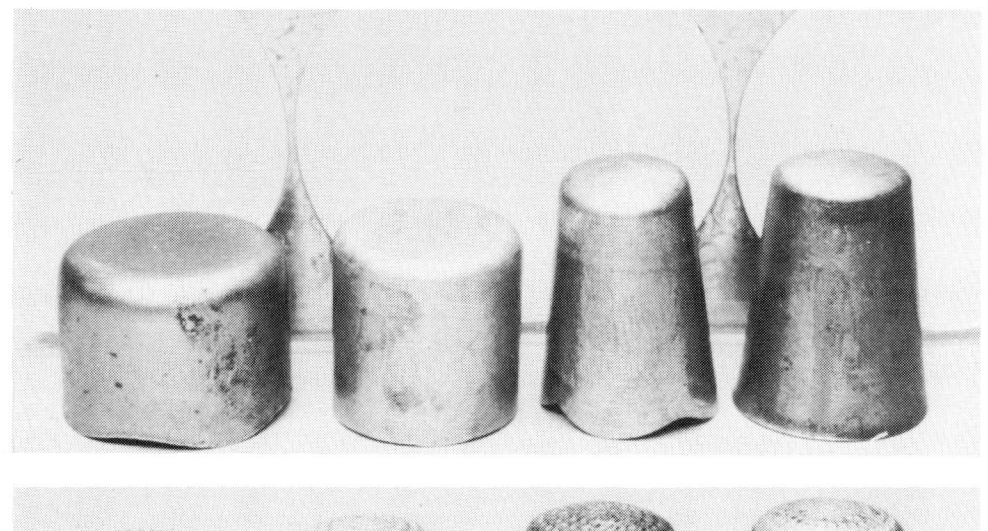

Nine stages of a "deep-drawn" thimble

The birth of a Simons' "Stitch in Time."

There is also a combination technique where the top of a thimble is formed by the "deep drawn" method and the band is die stamped on a flat sheet, cut out and soldered to the top. See illustration "Applied Band Method."

This is one of the techniques used to apply a gold band to a silver thimble. The method of construction of a thimble can help the collector to attribute age, origin, and materials, especially when a knowledge of decorative techniques and styles is also known.

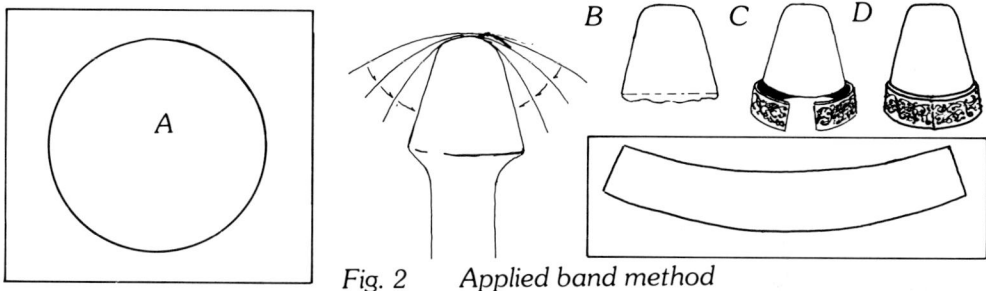

Fig. 2   Applied band method

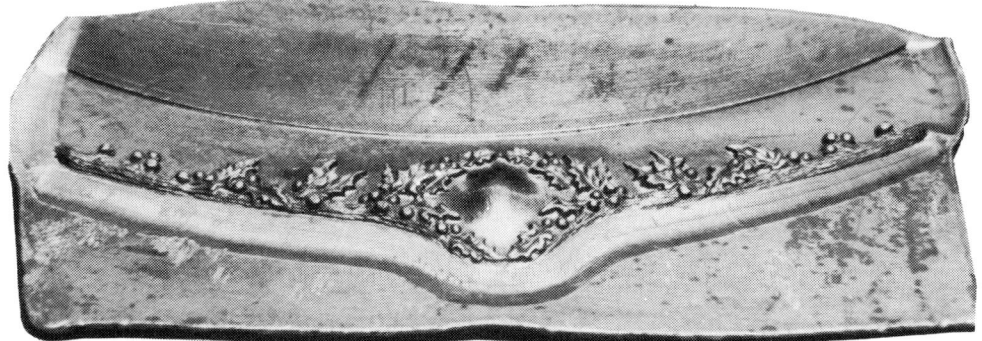

The making of a Ketcham & McDougall "hanging rim" thimble, using the applied band method.

Steel design dies from Ketcham & McDougall. Note top die on right created the pattern on the silver thimble on left.

Tools of 19th Century Thimblemakers

Thimble die stamp and dapping block, Charles Iles.

A Die For A King Who Never Was

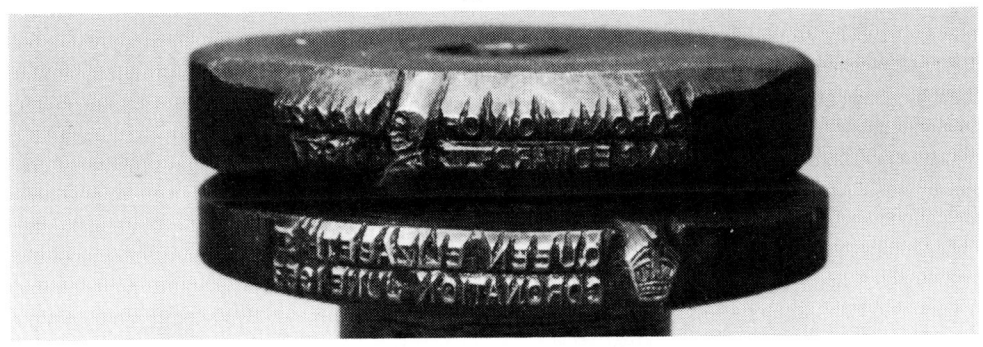

The top die reads: "KING EDWARD VIII CORONATION MAY 12, 1937." Edward abdicated to marry Mrs. Wallace.

Die stamp for the indentations on the top of thimble.

Steel knurling wheel from Charles Iles & Gomms Ltd.

The Manufacture of Sewing Thimbles

It is remarkable that a simple little tool such as a sewing thimble should require so many pieces of heavy equipment. Literally tons of stamping machines, spinning lathes, dies, cutters, and knurling wheels, not to mention a considerable array of special tools and chemicals required to decorate and finish it.

Here we are going to follow the basic stages a round disc of metal goes through as it becomes a sewing thimble. This method is very similar to that used by Scovill, Risdon and Charles Iles.

First step (Fig. A), is the stamping out of a sheet of metal a 1½" round disc about 14/100th of an inch thick.

Second (Fig. B), a heavy stamping press forms the first shallow cup. This cup is "deep drawn" three more times (Figs. C & D) by other stamping presses until it acquires the shape of a thimble.

Figure D shows the stamping press in its up position on the left, and its down position on the right. Thus is the final stage in forming the basic shape. The top indentations are also stamped in at this stage.

Note the thimble has an uneven edge which will be trimmed off on a spinning lathe with cutter (Fig. E).

The sharp edge is now flared or curled out and rolled back into the side of the thimble forming the rim, see Fig. F.

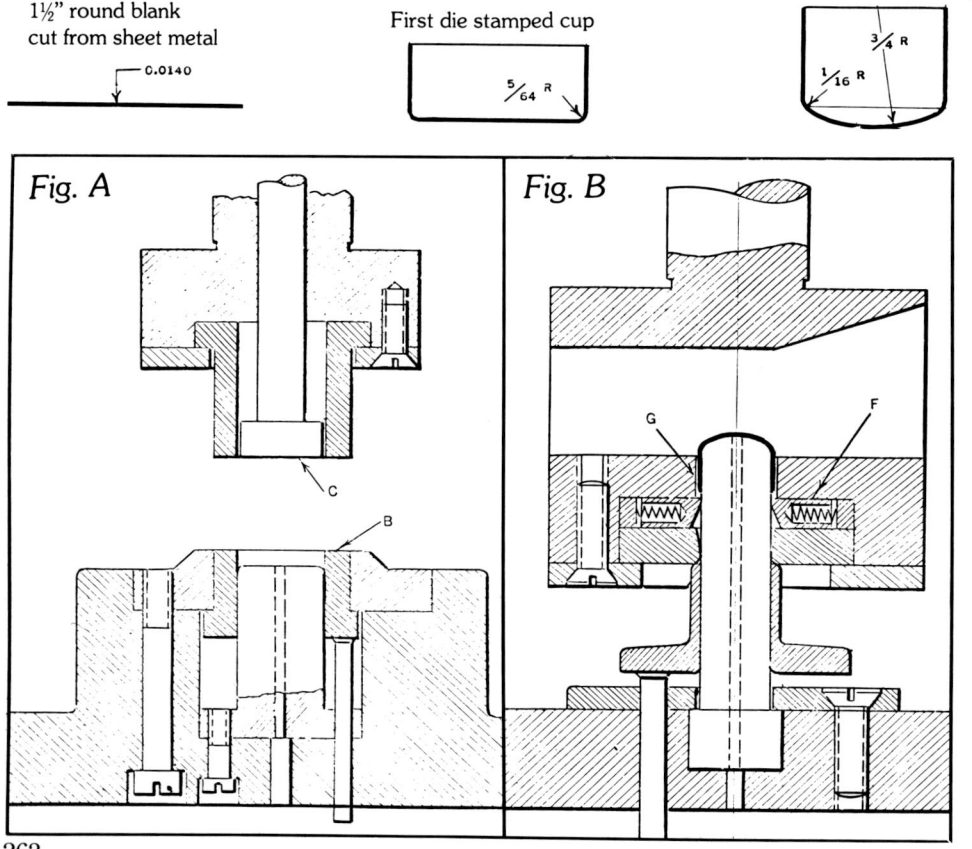

Steps in Thimble Construction

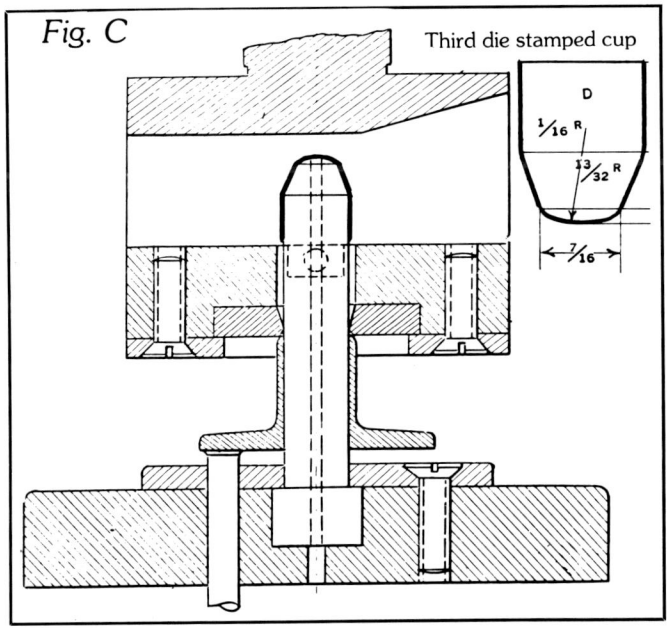

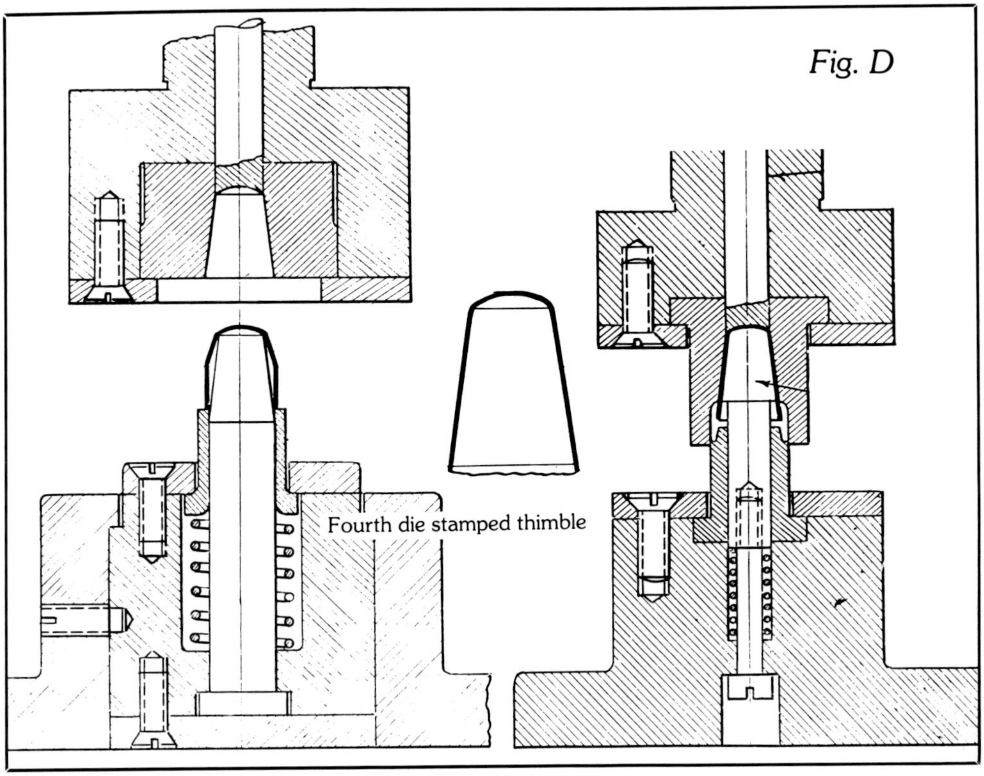

Fig. C
Third die stamped cup
D
1/16 R
13/32 R
7/16

Fig. D
Fourth die stamped thimble

Steps in Thimble Construction

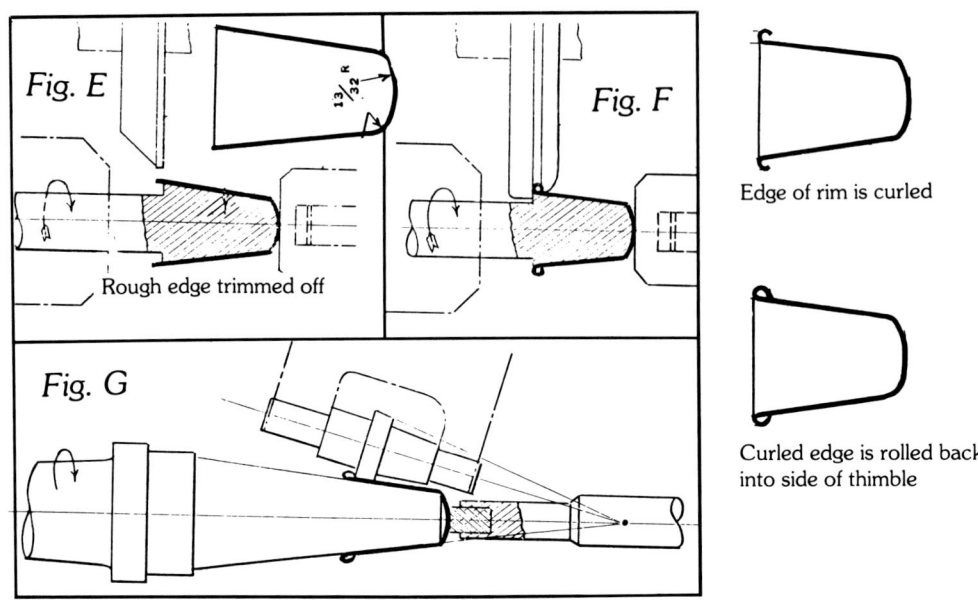

Edge of rim is curled

Curled edge is rolled back into side of thimble

A raised ring is then sometimes pressed into the lower part of the thimble to set off the band from the rim and indentations (Fig. G).

The knurling wheel is now applied to the upper sides of the thimble, rolling on the indentations, see Fig. H. A half cut-away (Fig. I) shows the results of all these stages.

Now a design on the band may be hand chased, engraved or rolled on by machine. The last steps would be the finishing and polishing of the thimble.

This process can make up to 2000 thimbles an hour.

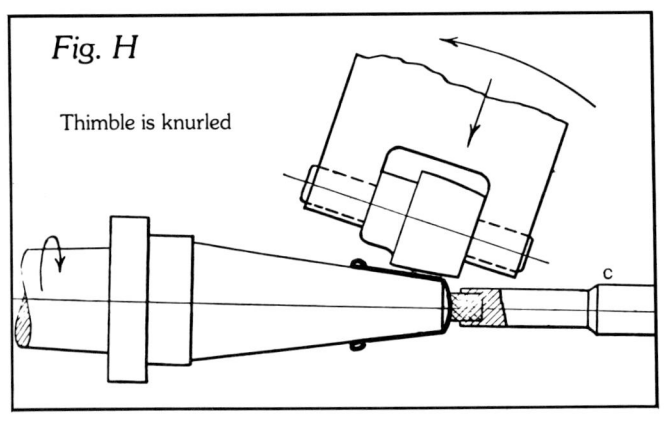

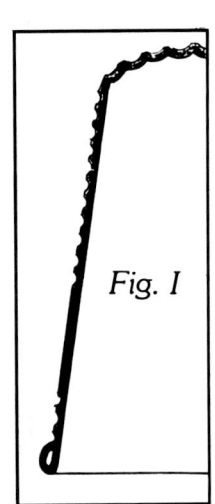

Line art by Fritz Heidinger

The Creation of an Ivory Thimble
(The Grapevine Pattern)

The ivory thimbles illustrated on pages 126 & 231 represent a rare combination of beauty, utility, and comfort. The beauty of style and grace is in the eye of the beholder. The utility is self-evident. The comfort derives from the intricate lattice or piercing work, which promotes air circulation within the thimble. This cuts down on the perspiration moisture which can build up in a more traditional thimble, especially in the warmer climates.

Ivory thimbles were very much a part of the American colonial sewing scene and many were exported by Chinese craftsmen.

This set of photographs shows the transformation of a chunk of ivory into a unique work of art by the author. Beginning with the lathing and hollowing out of the core, to the final sanding and polishing, a skilled artisan requires 6 to 8 hours to complete. One error can ruin hours of work and cannot be repaired.

Fig. #1 Thimble has been sawed and cored

Fig. #2 Domed & grooved

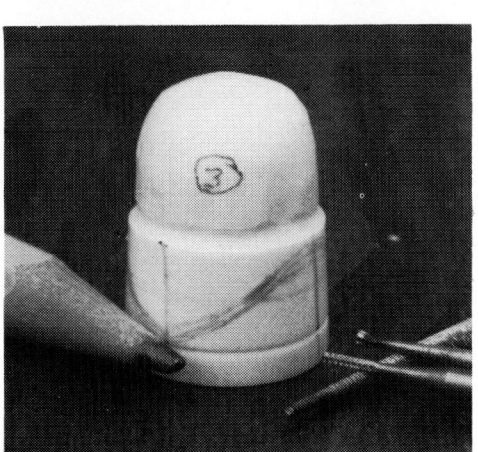

Fig. #3 Designs penciled on

Fig. #4 First piercing

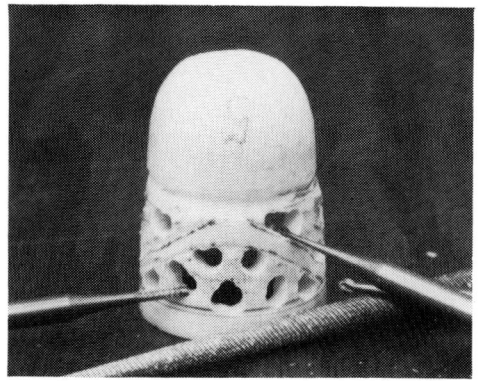
Fig. #5 Creating the lattice work

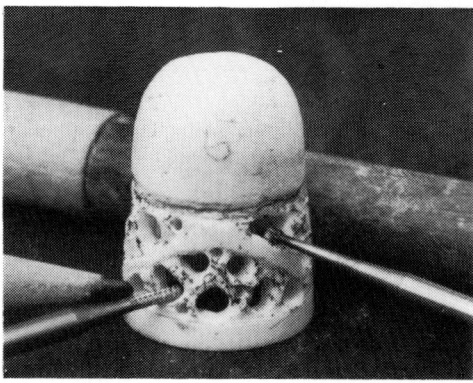
Fig. #6 Detailing the lattice work

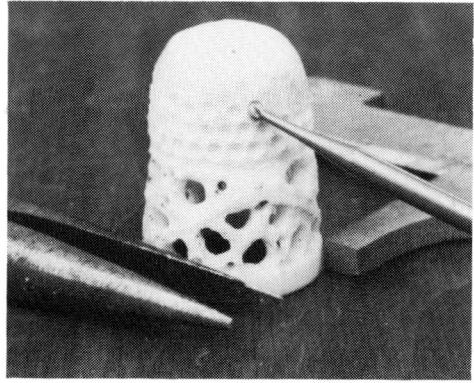
Fig. #7 Drilling in over 100 indentations.

Fig. #8 Removing all sharp edges

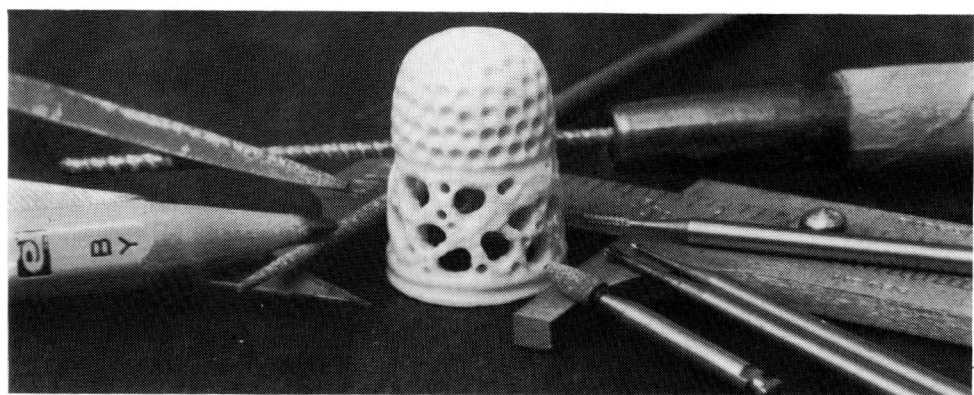
Fig. #9 Sanded and polished, the thimble is ready to use

Thimble Sources

I have found the best source for thimbles to be antique fairs, flea markets, auctions and fellow collectors. The single best source in the United States is the "sales mall" held at the TCI conventions which is open to members only. Other than the above, many craftsmen and catalog houses offer a wide range of contemporary thimbles from plastic to gold. I have listed below some of these which I have used and was satisfied with their service.

Audre China & Gifts
P.O. Box 6685
Burbank, CA 91510

Eleanor & David Brand
5613 Cranberry Place
Dayton, OH 45431

Cabin Fever Creations
1818 Lodestone Drive
Leadville, CO 80461

Cashs
St. Patrick Street
Cork, Ireland

Charterhouse Mint Limited
64 Charlotte Street
London, England

Hagop (James) Demirjian
28719 S. Western Avenue
Rancho Palos Verdes, CA 90732

Down's Collectors Showcase
2778 S. 35th Street
Milwaukee, WI 53215

De Vingerhoed
Bos en Vaartlaan 34
1181 AB Amstelveen
The Netherlands

Dine-American
7 Westbrite Court
Wilmington, DE 19810

Franklin Mint
Franklin Center, PA 19091

Gimbel & Sons
36 Commercial Street
Boothbay Harbor, ME 04538

Frederick Gridley
Manhattan Beach, MN 56463

Charles Iles & Gomms, Ltd.
Tyseley Industrial Estate
Seeleys Road Greet
Birmingham B11 2LF
England (250 Thimble Mim.)

P.J.W. Thimbles
Box 30831
Bethesda, MD 20814

Smithsonian Institute
P.O. Box 2456
Washington, DC 20013

Taylor Gifts
335 E. Conestoga Road
Wayne, PA 19084

Thimble Collector's Guild
Thistle Mill Station Road
Biggar ML 12 6LP
Scotland, U.K.

Thimbles Only
3628 Foothill Boulevard
La Crescenta, CA 91214

Thimblescope
c/o Kit Froebel
10002 Ney Street
Houston, TX 77034

Thimble Society of London
Grays Antique Market
58 Davies Street
London, W1 England

Thimble Collectors Club
47 Richards Ave.
Norwalk, Conn. 06857

Thimble Patents

By the late 19th Century, thimbles were big business and many firms such as Simons, Ketcham & McDougall, Waite-Thresher, and Goldsmith-Stern were producing millions per year.

As competition got sharper, more and more emphasis was put on the designs. Each manufacturer tried to give their thimbles a more unique look. Mass produced thimbles became more ornate, with a greater array of designs then ever before.

To protect their designs from being copied by their competitors, the thimble makers applied for a *design patent* which gave them protection

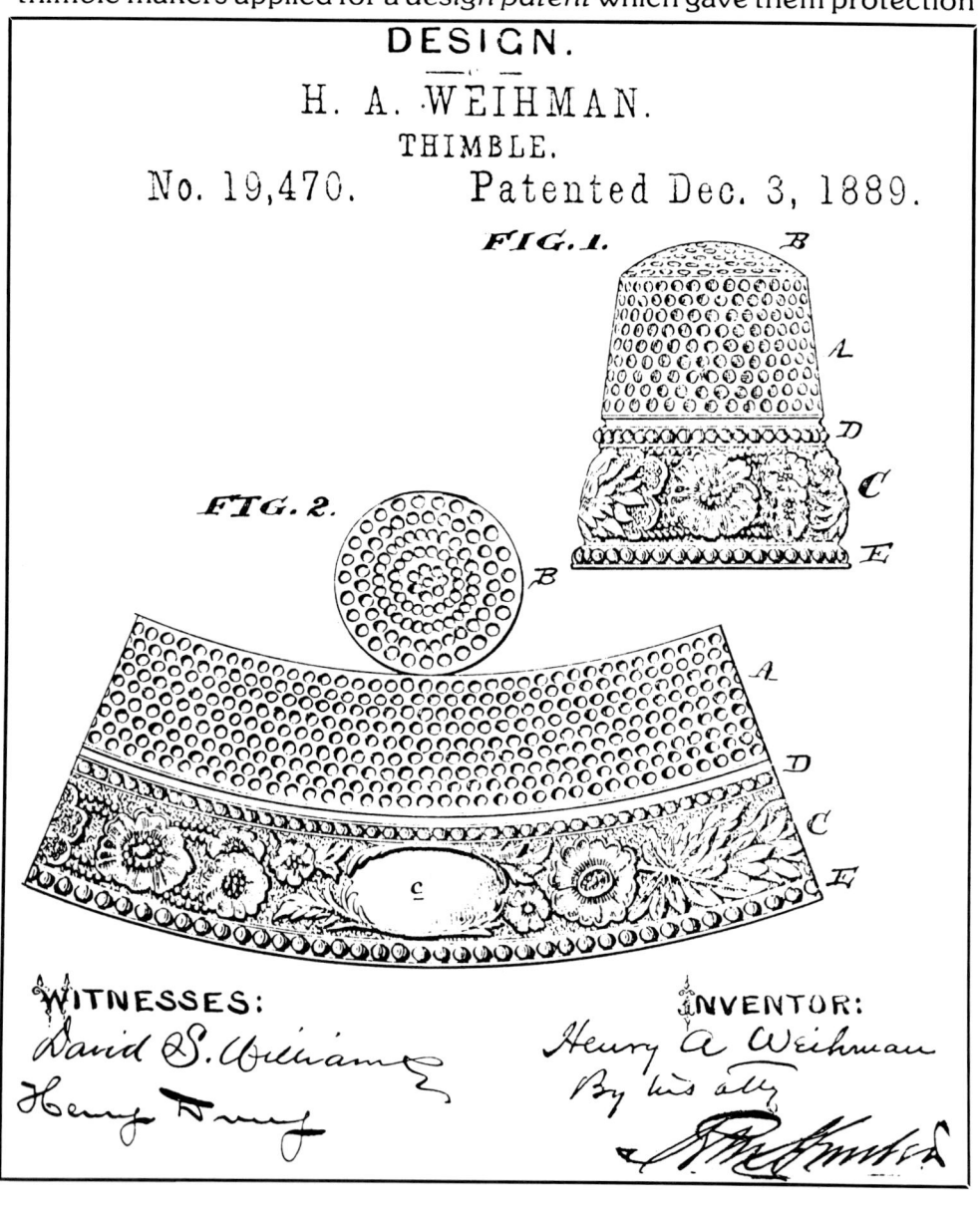

for 14 years. These patents make fascinating reading today, and are available for study at the U.S. Patent Office or at British and European patent offices. Our illustration on the side page is typical of one of these early patents. Henry Weihman was one of Simons most gifted designers with many patents in his name.

United States Patent Office

HENRY A. WEIHMAN, OF PHILADELPHIA, PENNSYLVANIA, ASSIGNOR TO SIMONS BROS. & CO., OF SAME PLACE.
DESIGN FOR A THIMBLE

SPECIFICATION forming part of Design No. 19,470, dated Dec. 3, 1889
Application filed Oct. 30, 1889. Serial No. 328.715. Term of patent 14 years.

To all whom it may concern:

Be it known that I, HENRY A. WEIHMAN, a citizen of the United States, residing at Philadelphia, in the county of Philadelphia and State of Pennsylvania, have invented and produced a new and original Design for Thimbles, of which the following is a specification, reference being had to the accompanying drawings, forming a part thereof.

My design consists, essentially, in a thimble which has a handsome engraved or embossed border, of a floral pattern, raised so as to project outward, and thereby impart an appearance of heaviness and richness to the article.

Cheap thimbles of this design possess an appearance of great richness.

The floral border is bounded above and below by embossed or engraved rings, which more effectively set off the floral pattern included between them.

In the drawings, Figure 1 is an elevation of a thimble embodying my design, and Fig. 2 is a diagramatic view of same.

A is the upper body portion of the thimble, and B the rounded top. The parts A and B are provided with the usual indentation for the needle. C is the border, of a floral pattern, which is formed with a smooth plate C. This floral border is raised so as to swell or curve outward, and has its center projecting beyond the upper and lower edges, as this adds materially to the handsome appearance of the thimble and imparts a massiveness to it.

D and E, are border-lines located at the upper and lower edges of the floral portion C, which materially set off this floral part. These borderlines D and E represent a series of balls of hemispheres arranged in lines, as shown in the drawings.

Having now described the nature and characteristics of my design, what I claim as new, and desire to secure by letters of patent, is—

The design for a thimble, substantially as herein, described, and illustrated in the accompanying drawings.

In testimony of which invention I have hereunto set my hand.

HENRY A. WEIHMAN.

Witnesses:
   Ernest Howard Hunter
   A. J. Dunn

The Thimblers of Charles Iles

A Visit to the Thimble-Works of Charles Iles & Gomms, Ltd., of Birmingham, England

A view of the factory from the supervisor's office

A view of the thimble manufacturing area

Supervisor Bernard Goodman showing worker how to indent quilting thimble

Supervisor checking new knurling machine

Five thousand thimbles, all in a day's work!

Brass thimbles to be polished in tumble barrel

Works Supervisor Cox observing thimble procedure

A lady thimbler "rolling over rims"

Thimbler Doris May Biddle and Richard Mealings

Iles Works-Manager Edward Cox and Gerald Benton
(Mr. Cox is the grandson of Charles Iles)

This Gabler catalog page illustrates thirty of the more than 4000 patterns which were made by the firm during their 138 years of thimblemaking. A complete catalog is on display in the Fingerhutmuseum, Creglingen, West Germany. See page 93.

Catalog Page from Charles Iles, circa 1920s

Real Silver Cased Thimbles.
THE CELEBRATED DOROTHY THIMBLES
IN GLASS TOP CASES OF ONE DOZEN

No. A7. 3/- Per Doz.
Best Plain.

No. 1931. Per Doz.
Chased Border.

No. 1940. Per Doz.
All Chased.

Hand Chased on Velvet Shield.
No. 947 Per Doz.

Glass Top Case used for
Nos. A7. 1931. 1940.

No. 948 Per Doz.

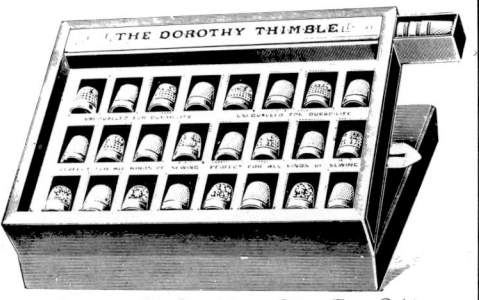

3 Dozen. All Chased in Glass Top Cabinet.
No. 945. Each.

Foreword

IN THE following pages we present a very complete and artistic selection of gold and silver thimbles. Throughout ninety-two years of successful manufacture our original high standard of quality and workmanship has been and always will be maintained, and we are constantly on the alert to keep this line as preeminent in design.

Style in thimbles, as in other things, is another name for good taste. In carrying KETCHAM & McDOUGALL thimbles the retailer not only displays good taste but also good judgment. They will attract to his counter the kind of interested attention that means ready sale to customers who recognize "style."

Order-blanks are inserted in the back of the book for your convenience, and the price list is such that you can resell these thimbles quickly at a liberal profit.

INCORPORATED 1918

14 KT. GREEN GOLD

Catalog pages from Ketcham & McDougall, circa 1920s

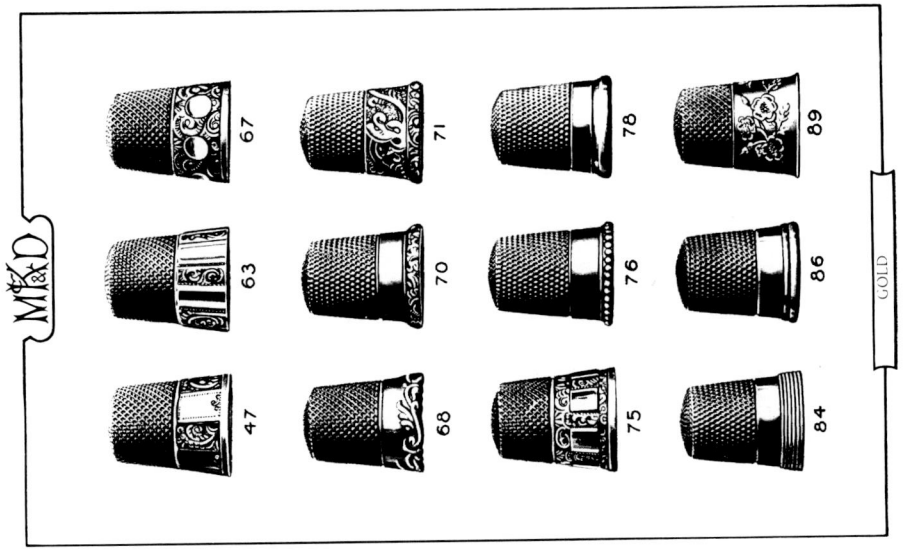
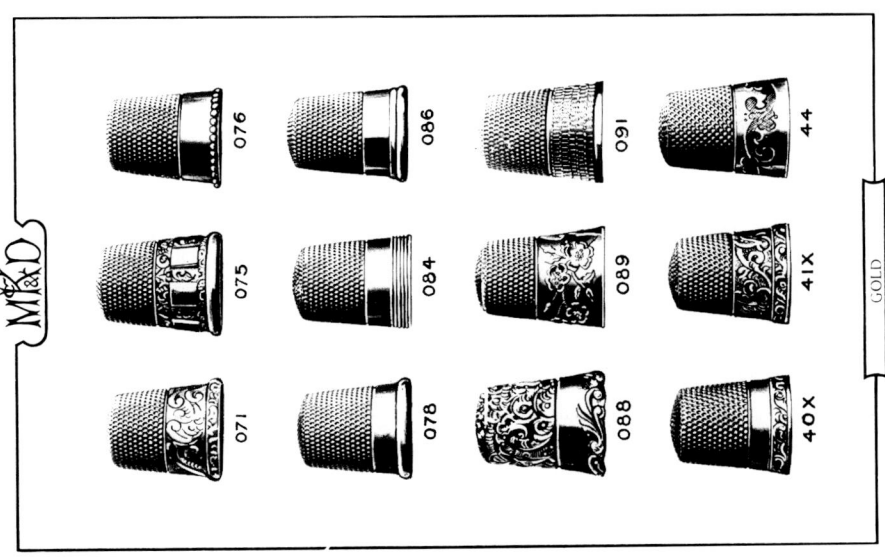

Catalog pages from Ketcham & McDougall, circa 1920s

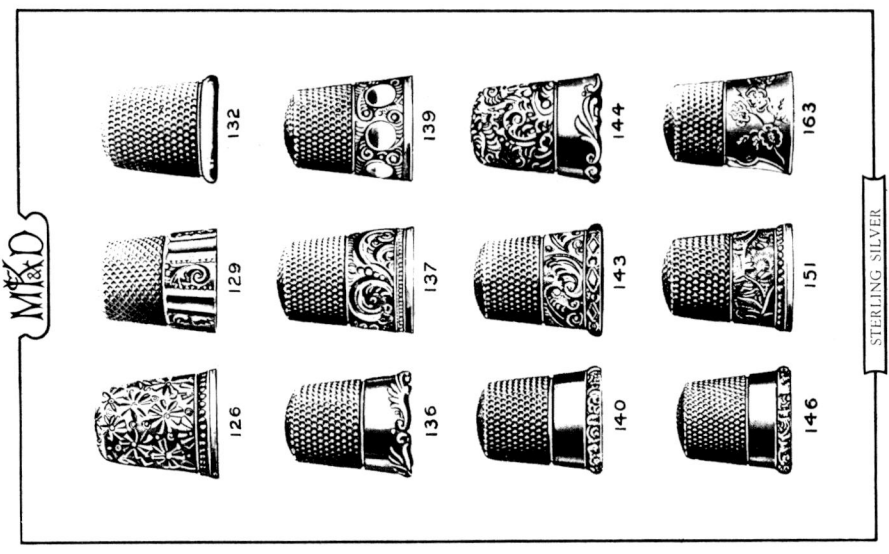

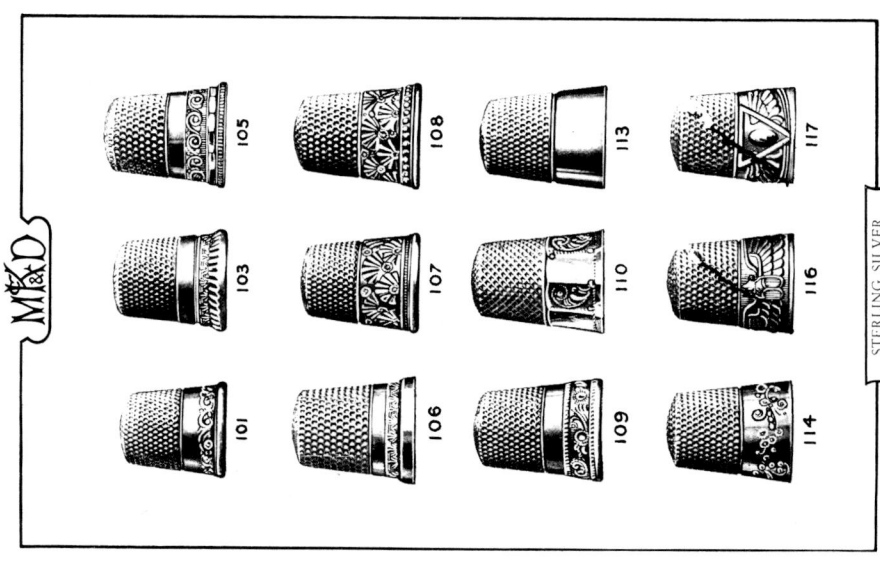

Catalog pages from Ketcham & McDougall, circa 1920s

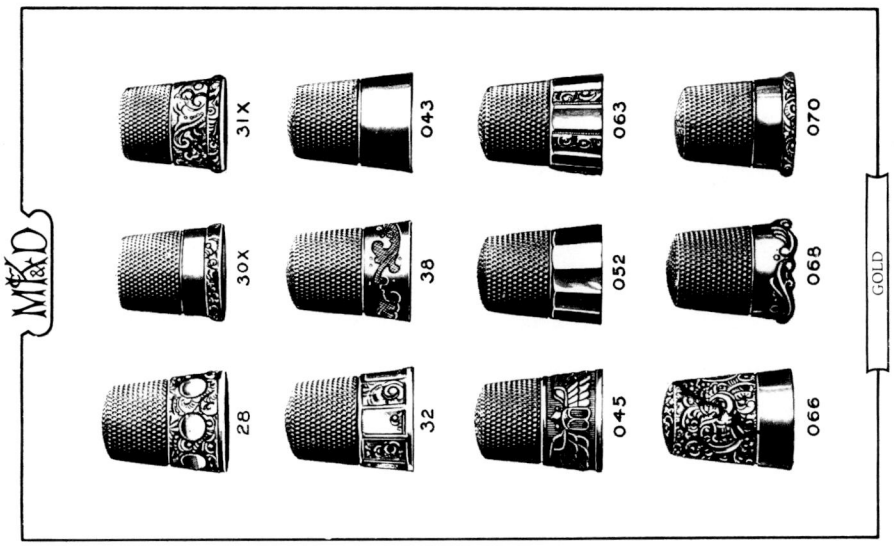

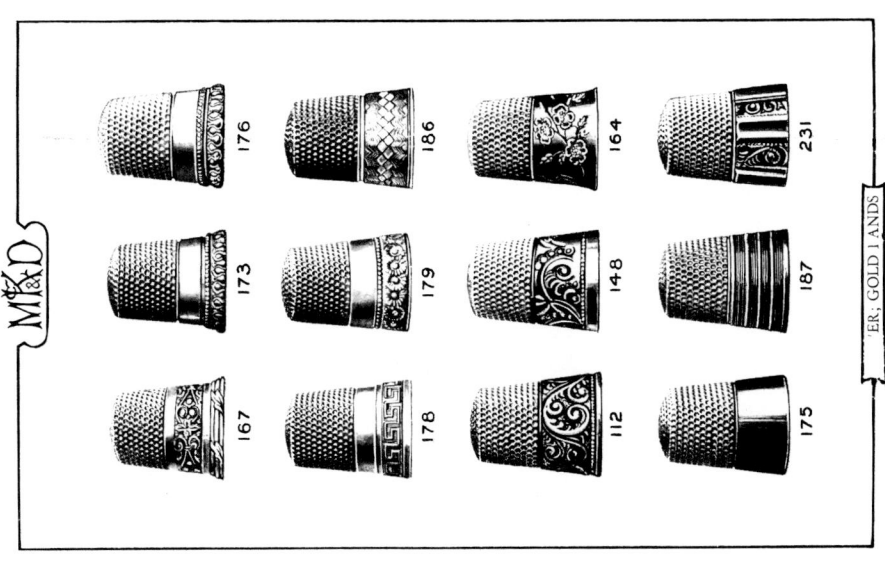

Catalog pages from Ketcham & McDougall, circa 1920s

A Waite-Thresher Catalog Page, circa 1900

Early American Thimble Advertisements

Thimbles had become a basic item in every household. The silver thimble, due to new mass production methods, had become one of life's minor luxuries. The following pages illustrate ads from companies and silversmiths making or selling thimbles from 1823 to 1919.

Carter, Sloan & Co.,
MANUFACTURING JEWELERS
No. 15 Maiden Lane,

A. CARTER, JR.
A. K. SLOAN.
C. E. HASTINGS.
GEO. R. HOWE.
WM. T. CARTER.

NEW YORK.

CARTER, SLOAN & CO. MANUFACTORY, NEWARK, NEW JERSEY.

GOLD BEAD NECKLACES,
HAIR PINS,
GOLD CROCHET NEEDLES,
QUEEN CHAINS,
GOLD AND SILVER GARTERS.

TRADE MARK.

SILVER KEY CHAINS,
SINGLE PIECE COLLAR BUTTONS,
SINGLE PIECE SLEEVE BUTTONS,
(ALL SIZES.)
CHILDREN'S STUDS with CHAINS,
GOLD THIMBLES.

LARGE LINE OF NOVELTIES BEING PRODUCED FOR FALL TRADE.

Jeweler's Circular & Horological Review August, 1888

Jeweler's Circular-Weekly, February 6, 1907

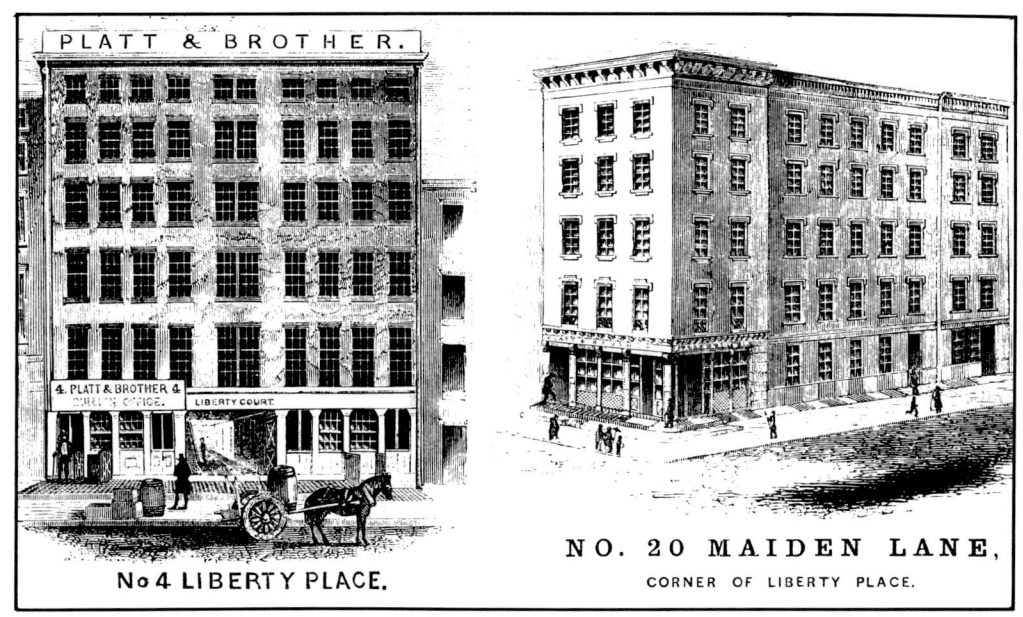

G.W. & N.C. Platt, Jewelers, 1848, New York City

A Convincing Argument

IN FAVOR OF

WAITE, THRESHER COMPANY'S

LINE, IS THAT

Their Goods Sell!

Jeweler's Circular 1895

The Thimble House.

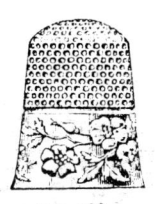

No. 163

Thimbles are not a side line with us—They are our main business. We study Thimbles, our designers study thimbles, our workmen study thimbles— The result is the finest and largest line of Thimbles on the Market.

No. 186.

KETCHAM & McDOUGALL,
Manufacturers,
37 & 39 Maiden Lane, New York.
Send for Catalogue. *Established 1832.*
ALSO MAKERS OF THE NEW AUTOMATIC EYE-GLASS HOLDERS.

Jeweler's Circular 1904

At the request of the Jobbing Trade we have had made the accompanying handsomely lithographed show card for effectively displaying a line of thimbles.

These cards can be obtained by applying to any leading jobber. If unable to obtain them from such as you are dealing with, communicate with us and we will furnish you with the name of one in your neighborhood who can supply your wants.

Stern Bros. & Co.,

Factory: 33-43 Gold St., NEW YORK.

CHICAGO: 149 State St.   Office: 68 Nassau St.

Jeweler's Circular
August 31, 1898

JAMES PETERS,

GOLD AND SILVER THIMBLE AND PENCIL CASE MANUFACTURER,

No. 65, ARCH-STREET,

Between Second & Third streets,

Has constantly on hand the above articles of as good quality and on as low terms as can be obtained. Also, Silver Spoons, Spectacles, Jewellery, &c. wholesale and retail.

Orders will be thankfully received and punctually attended to.

B 2

Philadelphia Directory, 1823

JAMES MIX,

MANUFACTURING JEWELLER,

No. 28 Beaver-street, Sign of the Harp.

Manufactures most kinds of articles in the Jewellery line, and repairs all articles in Silver and Gold, in the neatest manner. Dentists supplied with Gold or Silver Wire at all times. Spectacles made and repaired, and glasses set to suit almost any defect in sight. He has also constantly on hand an assortment of Jewellery, at wholesale or retail, embracing Ear and Finger Rings, Breast Pins, Lockets, Gold and Silver Sleeve and Collar Buttons, Silver Spoons and Sugar Tongs, Silver Ever-pointed Pencil Cases, Silver Thimbles, &c. &c. Cammeos, Agate and Cornelian Stones set in the most fashionable style. Jet and Pearl work made to any pattern. Country dealers are invited to call and examine his articles. They will be sold low at wholesale.

☞ Watches repaired, and a supply of Watches and Trimmings constantly kept on hand.   *June,* 1833.

Child's Annual Advertiser, Albany, NY. 1833

STOCKMAN & PEPPER,
No. 60 CHESNUT STREET,
MANUFACTURERS

Of Gold and Silver Ever-pointed and Plain Pencil Cases. Gold and Silver Thimbles—Gold and Silver Pens—also,

NEW AND HIGHLY APPROVED METALLIC PENS.
SILVER SPOONS.—JEWELLERY, &c.

THEY HAVE ON HAND AND KEEP CONSTANTLY FOR SALE,
an extensive assortment of the above articles of their own manufacture, and also a good supply of

Brittania, Plated, and Blocktin Ware,

Leads for Ever-pointed Pencil Cases, Jackson's Superior Black Lead Pencils, Wholesale and Retail, on moderate terms. Grateful for the share of patronage which they have heretofore enjoyed, they respectfully solicit a continuance thereof, and ask particularly the attention of dealers in the above articles.

All Orders Punctually attended to.

Philadelphia Directory, 1829 (H. I. Pepper)

HE HAD A
HANG-DOG LOOK,

BECAUSE HE BOUGHT HIS
Gold, Silver, Steel and Nickel Spectacles and Eyeglasses.

Gold, Silver, Aluminum and German Silver

THIMBLES,
— AND —

SEAMLESS, GOLD FILLED, SPECTACLES AND EYEGLASSES,

BEFORE SEEING OUR LINE.
THE WINSTED OPTICAL CO.,
MANUFACTURERS OF

The BURBANK Patent Eyeglass, SEAMLESS Gold Filled Spectacles and Eyeglasses. And al other goods enumerated above. WRITE US! **WEST WINSTED, CT.**

Jeweler's Circular, September 27, 1893

H. O. HURLBURT & SONS,

Successors to McCARTY & HURLBURT,

Wholesale Agents American

WATCHES,

MANUFACTURERS OF

GOLD AND SILVER THIMBLES,

GOLD SPECS AND PLAIN RINGS,

Will **REMOVE** about May 1st to

938 MARKET STREET.

PHILADELPHIA, PA.

BEST SILVER THIMBLES MADE.

Plain.   Border Chased.   Landscape.   Octagon.

Jeweler's Circular, July, 1888

SMITH, LESQUEREUX & CO.,

SPRINGFIELD, MASS.,

MANUFACTURERS OF

Eye-Glasses, Spectacles & Thimbles

OF ALL DESCRIPTIONS.

Also BURBANK'S PATENT SELF-ADJUSTING EYE-GLASSES.

Jeweler's Circular, August, 1888

As Advertised
in the
Philadelphia Directory
1833

J. STOCKMAN,

AT THE OLD STAND, NO. 60, CHESNUT STREET,

Manufactures and keeps constantly on hand, Wholesale and Retail,

Gold and Silver Ever Pointed Pencils,

GOLD AND SILVER THIMBLES,

GOLD and SILVER Tooth and Ear-picks, Tweezers, Pens, Fountain Pens, Pen Cases, Platina Pens.

SILVER Spoons, butter knives, scissor hooks, chains, reticule clasps, purse clasps, knitting sheaths, finger shields, bodkins, tongue scrapers. Gold and Silver studs and sleeve buttons.

A general assortment of Jewelry, Britannia and Plated Ware.

Also, Jackson's superior Lead for Ever-pointed Pencils, Gilliott's Steel pens, &c. Ever-pointed pencils, and gold and silver work of every description neatly repaired. The highest Cash or Exchange prices, given for old Gold and Silver.

W. W. COOMES & CO.,
LONGMEADOW, Mass.

Successors to JACOB COLTON & CO.
ESTABLISHED 1826.
MANUFACTURERS OF GOLD AND SILVER

SPECTACLES, THIMBLES AND EYEGLASSES,

In every style and variety, with late improved facilities for Manufacturing.
We have no Traveling Agents for our Goods.

Jeweler's Circular
and Horological Review
July, 1888

Jeweler's Circular, September 7, 1892

SOMETHING · NEW.

ALUMINUM THIMBLES.

Light, Durable and will not tarnish.

In appearance similar to Silver, and at half the cost

If you want something NEW, HANDSOME and CHEAP, send, enclosing business card, for samples and prices.

KETCHAM & McDOUGALL,
198 Broadway, New York.

..A Touch And.. **IT REVOLVES**

LARGE SIZE, 10½ INCHES HIGH, HOLDS 153 THIMBLES, PRICE, $10.00

SMALL SIZE, 6½ INCHES HIGH, HOLDS 71 THIMBLES, PRICE $5.00

No. 129

THE GOLD AND SILVER **Thimble Makers of America.**

SIMONS, BRO. & CO.,

SILVERSMITHS, THIMBLE MAKERS AND MANUFACTURING JEWELERS

NEW YORK 10 MAIDEN LANE PHILADELPHIA 610 CHESTNUT STREET CHICAGO 402 COLUMBUS BUILDING
41 UNION SQUARE

Jewelers' Circular Aug. 10, 1898

Haven't you long felt the need of just such a Display Stand?

HEIGHT 10½ INCHES. PAT. PEND.

WE HAVE JUST PATENTED THE ABOVE USEFUL AND MOST ATTRACTIVE THIMBLE DISPLAY STAND IT IS MADE IN TWO SIZES EBONY FINISH 'TWILL BE A HANDSOME ADDITION TO YOUR SHOW CASE.

Ketcham & McDougall salesman's sample case.

To have made Thimbles

SINCE 1832

IS A RECORD

Yet we can conscientiously say that our firm is in direct line since 1802.

And that all the time we have MADE THIMBLES.

Trade Mark

We have added Automatic Eye-Glass Holders and make those with the same care and eye to quality as we have made thimbles.

We are up-to-date in designs and although an old house, we are *still* young in ideas.

Send for our latest illustrated price list.

KETCHAM & McDOUGALL

15-19 Maiden Lane   New York, N. Y.

Jeweler's Circular-Weekly, February 5, 1919

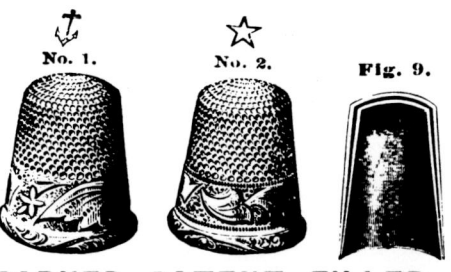

BARKER PATENT FILLED GOLD THIMBLES.

The Best Fitting, Best to Wear, and Handsomest ever made.

The Original and ONLY PATENT ever issued for a STIFFENED or FILLED GOLD THIMBLE.

AN EXCELLENT ARTICLE for the HOLIDAY TRADE.

Send for Circular.   Orders respectfully solicited from the Jobbing Trade.

JOSIAH A. WHITMAN, Sole Agent,
45 EDDY STREET,   **PROVIDENCE, R. I.**

Jeweler's Circular July, 1888

GEORGE P. PILLING,

Successor to STOCKMAN and SON,

Manufacturer of

Gold and Silver Thimbles,

SURGICAL INSTRUMENTS,

ODD-FELLOWS AND MASONIC JEWELS, MARKS, &C.,

SOUTHEAST CORNER OF DOCK AND GOLD STREETS,

(LATE BANK ALLEY.) THIRD STORY.

PHILADELPHIA.

Gold and Silver Thimbles. Cravat Hooks. Nursery Pins, Watch Hooks, Combs, Cane Heads, Whip Heads, &c.   Nursing Tubes, Reticule and Purse Clasps, Oil Stocks and Pyx, Knitting Sheaths, Finger Shields, Sleeve Buttons, Needle Cases, &c., &c.

McElroy's Wholesale Business Directory, Philadelphia, PA. 1857

Line drawings of early Dorcas thimbles.

In Great Britain, the firm of Charles Horner proudly proclaimed their silver and steel "DORCAS" thimbles, "unequaled for strength and durability." "Free exchange if rendered useless from any cause whatsoever."

These "turn of the century" advertisements show some of the beautiful designs available to Victorian women.

**LEATHER COVERED,
WITH PLUSH LINING, AND PLATE GLASS,**

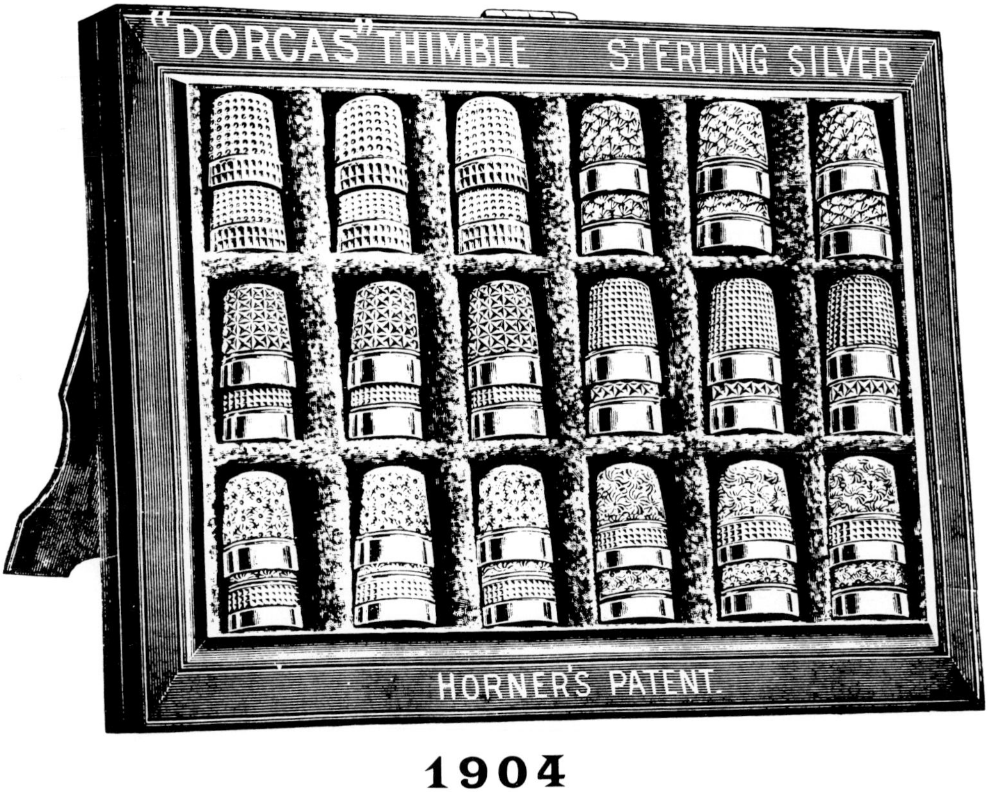

"DORCAS" THIMBLE   STERLING SILVER

HORNER'S PATENT.

1904

Early American Silversmiths
known to have made thimbles

I have made up a list of silversmiths who actually used the word "THIMBLES" in their newspaper and journal advertising. Who were these men? Did they mark their thimbles? Are there thimbles with their names or initials in your collection? We know so little about these early craftsmen, and each would be a fascinating research paper. Maybe I can spark one of you into looking up a home town thimble maker. Write it up and send it to the T.C.I. Bulletin. Here are a few clues to get you started.

John Birge 1780-1859 — Advertised in the Brattleboro, VT "Washingtonian" in 1811.

Abel Brewster 1775-1807 — Advertised in the Norwich, CT "Windham Herald" in November, 1804.

James Crooks circa 1812 — Advertised in the Northampton, MA "Hampshire Gazette" November & December, 1812.

Daniel Curtiss 1801-1878 — "Founded a shop in 1825 in Woodbury, CT." Partners with Gideon Botsford. Later with Lewis Candee, 1826-1831, and Benjamin Stiles in 1835.

Samuel Edwards 1705-1762 — Goldsmith in Boston, MA, bequeathed a "thimble stamp", etc., to nephew Joseph Edwards, Jr. Advertised in the Boston Gazette April 19, 1796.

William D. Fenno 1797-1870 — Advertised in the "Mass. Spy" between 1822 and 1824 in Worcester, MA.

Dana Payton 1803-1820 — Advertised in the "Providence Gazette" on August 10, 1805, Providence, R.I.

John Demmock circa 1798 — Listed in the Boston Directory in 1800 as a "thimblemaker," also listed in New York after 1801.

James Dunlop circa 1784 — Advertised in Bennington, VT "Gazette", March 27, 1784 "Women's Thimbles."

Joseph Dyar 1795-1851 — Advertised in the "National Standard" November 12, 1822 and in the Middlebury Free Press, Middlebury, VT.

M. Eastman circa 1816 — Advertised in the New Hampshire "Patriot" February 18, 1816, "he manufactured thimbles in Meredith."

Otis Howe 1790-1825 — Advertised in the Worcester, MA "National Aegis" November 23, 1814 and the Mass. Spy on November 30, 1814.

Francis Julius 1785-1858 — Advertised in the "Middlesex Gazette" July 8, 1806, silver thimbles, Middletown, CT.

Sidney Gardiner circa 1809 — Advertised in the Boston, MA "Patriot," January 17, 1810 under firm name of Fletcher & Gardiner. Moved to Philadelphia in 1815.

Benjamin F. Gardiner circa 1817 — Advertised in the "Nantucket Weekly Magazine" September 13, 1817, "Thimbles," Nantucket, MA.

Isaac Guild circa 1794-1854 — Advertised in the New Hampshire "Patriot" February 9, 1824.

Martin Moses circa 1793-1893 — Advertised in the "Pittsfield Sun" April, 1819. Shop in Lenox, MA. Moved to Peekskill, NY.

Edmund Hughes circa 1781-1851 — Advertised in the "Middlesex Gazette" July 8, 1806. Partnership in the Middletown firm of Hughes & Francis, of Conn.

Guy Loomis circa 1795-1874 — Advertised in the Stockbridge, MA "Berkshire Star" October 31, 1816 and the Erie, PA "Erie Gazette" October 26, 1837.

Simeon Marble circa 1777-1856 — Advertised in "Conn. Journal" 1806-22. Shop in New Haven, CT.

Apollos Rivoire circa 1702-1754 — Father of Paul Revere, Boston, MA. Advertised in the Boston Weekly News-Letter May 21, 1730.

Asa Spencer circa 1804 — Advertised in the Conn. Gazette, January 2, 1805, of his discovery of a new, improved method of making "silver thimbles with steel tops," New London, CT.

Phineas Stevens circa 1813 — Advertised in the Kennebunk, ME "Weekly Visitor" April 17, 1813.

Geer Terry circa 1775-1858 — Advertised in the Mass. Spy May 20, 1801. In partnership with Moses Wing and later with Aaron Willard in Worcester, MA.

Albert Titcomb circa 1802-1890? — Advertised in the Penobscot Journal February 28, 1832. Shop in Bangor, ME.

Isaac Townsend circa 1760-1812 — Advertised in "The Washingtonian" 1811-12. Shop in Windsor, VT.

Simeon Walton circa 1780-1862 — Advertised in the Norway Advertiser October 13, 1848. Shops in Paris and Norway, ME.

Caleb Wheaton circa 1757-1827 — Advertised in the Providence Gazette February 13, 1796. Shop in Providence, RI.

Alvan Willcox circa 1783-1870 — Listed in new Haven, CT Directory 1841 as a "thimble maker." Moved to New Jersey and then to Fayetteville, NC.

NOTE: This list is only partial; many other silversmiths made thimbles but I have not as yet come across, in their ads, any direct mention of "thimbles."

Tokens of Love

"...tis but a shiny brass thimble she proudly wears,
as if set with rare rubies in precious gold!
Now, I know she loves me, but dares not say,
for on my thimble is written 'With Love' quite bold!

"A thimble of silver is upon my love's gentle hand,
till Cupid's arrow runs its due, and she wears my golden band."

The thimble has a long tradition as a token of love and esteem. Hearts, cupids and words of endearment were often part of the design of these very special gifts.

Many young men of yesteryear gave their ladyloves a thimble as their first gift. Being practical for hand sewing, it was a basic necessity for most, and even wealthy young women were expected to do art needlework. A thimble could be received, whereas, a piece of jewelry would be inappropriate. The thimble often became a prelude to the wedding ring.

The following is a sample of some of the lovely old inscriptions found on these romantic gifts of yesterday:

Always Faithful	Love Forever	In Remembrance
God Be With You	Remember Me	I Wis It Better
Blessing Attend You	Regards	Keepsake
Charity	Perseverance	Love
Fare Well	Sincerity	Mizpah
Fare Ye Well	Forever Yours	With Esteem
Forget Me Not	Welcome	God Is Love
Always Friends	To My Love	Good Luck
Friendship	Love Is All	Happiness & Home
From A Friend	With Love	I Love You

Thimble Poetry

Thimble poems have graced our literature for over 300 years. Several publications are devoted entirely to them. Some are elegant or witty, while others bring forth a sense of nostalgia, for things which once were. This poem, by an unknown author, is one of my favorites:

MOTHER'S OLD STEEL THIMBLE

*I've been rummaging a casket, filled with relics of the past,
And I turned them idly, one by one, until I found at last,
Wrapped in a piece of homespun and laid away with care,
The dingy, old steel thimble that my mother used to wear.*

*O, that flood of memories sweeps in upon my soul,
As the course and faded covering I carefully unroll,
And dim with dust of useless years, I see before me there,
The battered old steel thimble that my mother used to wear.*

*Rough with the toil of mother love in cheerless days of yore,
It was the only ornament those dear hands ever wore,
And I tenderly caress it as a treasure rich and rare,
This precious old steel thimble that my mother used to wear.*

*Companion of her widowhood, her faithful friend for years,
Made sacred by her patient toil and sanctified by tears,
No costly gem that sparkles on the hand of lady fair,
Could buy the old steel thimble that my mother used to wear.*

*In a quiet churchyard she has slumbered many a year,
Yet in this holy hour I seem to feel her presence near,
And hear her tender benediction as I bow in grateful prayer,
And kiss the old steel thimble that my mother used to wear.*

*The memory of that mother's love shall be a beacon light,
To guide my wayward footsteps in the path of truth and right,
And the key that opens heaven's door, if e'er I enter there,
Will be the old steel thimble that my mother used to wear.*

Thimble Markings

The following is a list of maker's marks which have been found on metal thimbles and their attributions. Although this is only a partial list, with more coming to light each year, these are the ones a collector usually encounters.

American Marks

Maker	Mark
Aiken Lambert & Co. New York, N.Y.	A.L.&Co.
Barker Mfg. Co. Providence, RI	★14K gold filled only
E. & J. Bass New York, N.Y.	Ⓑ
David Brand Dayton Ohio	B
Eleanor C. Brand Dayton, Ohio	ECB
Thomas Brogan New York, N.Y.	☆
Carter, Sloan & Co. Newark, NJ & New York, N.Y.	(acorn mark)
S. Cottle Co. New York, N.Y.	ℭ
Leonore Doskow, Inc. Montrose, NY	△
Foster & Bailey Providence, RI	(flag with F&B)
David R. Hale Lowell, MA	DHALE
Goldsmith Stern Co. New York, N.Y.	S/C & anchor
A. T. Gunner Mfg. Co. Attleboro, MA	☆G
Halstead, Benjamin New York, N.Y.	B·H
Howard & Cockshaw New York, NY	H & C
Jones, Shreve, Brown Boston, MA	JSB&Co
Charles A. Keene New York, N.Y.	KEENE
Ketcham & McDougall New York, NY & Elizabeth, NJ	on sterling thimbles only — M&D ; on gold and coin thimbles only — M&D
La Pierre Mfg. Co. New York, NY	ℒ
D. J. Mahoney New York, NY	M
Metropolitan Museum of Art New York, NY	MMA
James Mix Albany, NY	J. MIX
William Moir New York, NY	Wᵐ MOIR
H. Muhr's Sons Philadelphia, PA	(crown) ; (crown with M inside) from 1887 on solid gold ; (crown with 18) and (lion) Gold filled
Joseph Muhr Philadelphia, PA	(three crowns)

Henry G. Mumford Providence, RI	H M	**Smithsonian Institute** Washington, DC	SI
Pangborn & Brinsmaid Burlington, VT	P&B	**Stern Brothers Co.** New York, NY	 1908-1912
Paye & Baker Mfg. Co. N. Attleboro, MA		**Unger Brothers** Newark, NJ	
D. C. Percival & Co. Boston, MA Made by Waite Thresher Co.		**Untermeyer Robins & Co.,** New York, NY	UR
Quincy Brothers Portland, ME	Q. BROS	**Ung, Sok** Philadelphia, PA	
William T. Rae Co. Newark, NJ	RAE & Co.	**von Hoelle, John** Philadelphia, PA	JvH
Rufus Davenport Dunbar Worcester, MA	DUNBAR		
Shepard Mfg. Co. Melrose Highlands, MA	S	**Waite-Thresher Co.** Providence, RI	
Simons Bros. Co. Philadelphia, PA		**Webster Co.** N. Attleboro, MA	
 the trefoil indicates **gold filled**		**Woodside Sterling Co.** New York, NY	

 other variations: "Quaker"

 the "A" indicated full Karat weight

 Found on nickel-silver, and oreide thimbles from 1919 to 1952.

Smith & Smith S & S
Attleboro, MA

TRADE-NAMES FOUND ON AMERICAN THIMBLES

Priscilla . . . . Simons Bros.
Pyrex . . . . Corning Glass
SBC . . . . Simons Bros.
Quaker . . . . Simons Bros.

TRADE-NAMES FOUND ON BRITISH THIMBLES

Alurine . . . . Charles Iles
Dorcas . . . . Charles Horner
Doris . . . . Abel Morral
Dorothy . . . . Charles Iles
Dreema . . . . H. Griffith
Dura . . . . Walker & Hall
Halex . . . . English
Ivorine . . . . Charles Iles
"The Spa" . . . . H. Griffith
Stratnoid . . . . Laughton & Son

British Marks

Addis, Joseph	JA
Bateman, Hester	HB
Cohen & Charles, Ltd.	C&C
Collins, James	JC
Fenton, James	JF
Foskett, Henry	HF
Foskett, Samuel	SF
Fossey, John	IF
Griffith, Henry	HG&S
Holmes, William J.	W.J.H
Horner, Charles	CH
Levi & Salaman	L&S
Massey, Samuel	SM
May, Charles	CM
Price, Joseph	JP
Rose, S. J. & Son	SJR&S
Swann, Joseph & Son	JS&S
Taylor, Alfred	AT
Taylor, Joseph	I.J.
Taylor & Perry	T&P
Turton, William	W.T.
Unite, George	GU
Walker, James	JW& Ltd
Walker & Hall	W&H Ltd
Webb, James	JW
Willmore, Joseph	JW

Iles, Charles
Birmingham, England

An enlarged British hallmark

European Marks

Gabler Brothers
Schorndorf, Germany

The Gabler symbol found on the top of their thimbles was later copied by other thimble makers, but with some variation. Modern thimbles having this mark have been made in England and Germany.

Helmut & Thorvald Greif
Creglingen, W. Germany

Greif-Prandl
Creglingen, W. Germany

J. A. Henckels
Solingen, W. Germany

Lotthammer-Eber
Pforzheim, W. Germany

David-Andersen
Oslo, Norway

Lutz & Weiss
Pforzheim, W. Germany

P. Lenain
France

O. Prudhomme
Paris, France

Soergel & Stollmeyer
Schwabisch Gmund, W. Germany

Studio Steinbock
Vienna, Austria

MISC. TRADE NAMES

Elfin	Price-Jardine, Australia
Nifty	Australia
Masta	Gabler Bros.
Alpacca	Copper-Nickel alloy
Coroza	Copper-Nickel alloy

Markings To Be Found on Porcelain Thimbles

The following is a sample of the more than one hundred marks which can be found on porcelain and bone china thimbles. Many collectors try to find at least one thimble from each manufacturer. Such a collection would be very interesting in its variety and beauty. For a more complete listing, see page 159

ROYAL ALBERT
Bone China
ENGLAND

EST 1775
AYNSLEY
ENGLAND

BONE CHINA
Hammersley
MADE IN ENGLAND

Haviland
Limoges

Noritake
JAPAN

B&G

ROYAL DOULTON
MADE IN ENGLAND
ENGLAND
BONE CHINA

1789
Royal Adderley
FINE BONE CHINA
ENGLAND

MZ
Irish Dresden

Meissen

AK
KAISER

ROYAL WORCESTER FINE BONE CHINA

HORLEY PORCELAIN

Rörstrand

HAMMERSLEY

MASON'S

HEREND HUNGARY

MOSA

JB
JOHNSON BROTHERS

ADAMS

Ginori

N
Lord Nelson

LLADRÓ

FINE BONE CHINA
CROWN
EST 1801
STAFFORDSHIRE
ENGLAND

OAC
OKURA
JAPAN

FP
FRANKLIN PORCELAIN

1814
HUTSCHENREUTHER
GERMANY

BONE CHINA
COALPORT
MADE IN ENGLAND
EST 1750

WEDGWOOD®
MADE IN ENGLAND

ROYAL TARA
FINE BONE CHINA

Bareuther
WALDSASSEN
BAVARIA GERMANY

S H
D

1877-1889—Mark used by the Derby Crown Porcelain Company.

Spode
Fine Bone China
ENGLAND

c. 1863-1935—The S. & H. stood at first for Stevenson and Hancock and later Sampson Hancock.

FUKAGAWA
PORCELAIN
ARITA JAPAN

ROYAL CROWN DERBY
ENGLISH BONE CHINA

Derby mark in use 1976 onwards.

ROYAL CROWN DERBY
TRADE MARK

DERBY CHINA
ROYAL CROWN DERBY
ENGLISH BONE CHINA

Derby mark in use 1963-1976. Sometimes combined with pattern name and number.

Franciscan

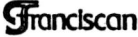

1890-1963—Mark adopted when Her Majesty Queen Victoria granted the use of the prefix "Royal" on January 3rd 1890.

In Tribute to Elizabeth Galbraith Sickels

Reprint of an article published in the April, 1984 edition of the
Thimble Collector's International's Bulletin by author

MRS. SICKELS....I PRESUME?
by John von Hoelle

No book is ever written without research and checking the facts back to their original source. Thus, I began in the summer of 1979 reading old newsletters from a half dozen early thimble groups such as the National Thimble Collectors, and the Thimble Guild, and then, the Gazette, Thimbletter and the TCI BULLETIN. Next came reading and studying the books by Lundquist, Rath and Holmes, as well as a half dozen other less well known chapters on thimbles in books published since 1887. In the meantime, I was making personal visits, writing letters and making phone calls to knowledgeable collectors and to museums for additional information. Thus, a great array of materials, scrapbooks, articles, letters, photographs, line drawings and old catalogs came forth.

During the many months it took me to read and outline this material, one name kept coming up as an original author--Elizabeth Galbraith Sickels. As I read articles on early American silversmiths - Platt, Prime, Simons, Halstead, Waite-Thresher and Ketcham & McDougall - many times I found the original source was Mrs. Sickels! Early collectors Grace Blackburn and Sarah Anne Weisbrot, as well as others, confirmed that Elizabeth Sickels, "Betty" to them, was a scholar, the most diligent researcher, and the first authority on American thimble marking. "If Betty doesn't know, nobody will", they said.

For months, I had been reading excerpts from Sarah Anne's research, but when she gave me a bundle of letters from Betty to her, written in the 1950's and early 60's, I knew I had to meet this remarkable woman. But, where was she? No one knew. Old friends had not heard from her in years and their letters had been returned by the post office. Most believed she had passed away, saying, "John, she would be in her eighties if she were still alive" . . or, "I'm sure something must have happened to her".

I became even more fascinated as I read about this determined, remarkable woman, visiting the Simons and Ketcham & McDougall factories in the 1940's to find out how thimbles were made, taking field trips to long-closed thimble makers to photograph their buildings, interviewing old craftsmen who had made thimbles, haunting museums, searching public records, and recording countless details on thimble manufacturing, designs, patents, and techniques. She did all this at a time when she knew less than 10 collectors in all the world! Who did she think would read all this? Why did she do it? Where was all this information located? What happened to it? I had to find out, but first, I had to find Mrs. Sickels.

Sarah Anne again came to my rescue and gave me Mrs. Sickels' last known address in Rochester, New York. I called information to get her number, but there was no listing. I flew to Rochester and spent a few days trying to locate her. There was no trace of an Elizabeth G. Sickels. She was not a member of any church or civic club, nor was she a patient of any doctor or dentist. She had no open bank account. Maybe she moved? I called all the moving van companies. Nothing! Next, I checked the public records. Good news--she had not died in Rochester or New York State. But where was she? Someone said she was going to give her fabulous collection to a museum. On this information, I contacted all Rochester museums and again nothing--no donations of thimbles. Mrs. Sickels had lost her husband and had no children, so thinking maybe she had made a will, I called all the lawyers in greater Rochester. At last, after what seemed like hundreds of phone calls to attorneys, I located a lawyer named Williams who had a client named Elizabeth Sickels! But his secretary said he was away on a two week vacation and could not be reached. She went on to say she could not give out any information on Mrs. Sickels without Mr. Williams approval. When asked if Mrs. Sickels was still alive, the reply was, "I'm sorry, I do not know."

The next two weeks seemed like eons, but finally 9:00 Monday morning arrived and I made a long distance call to Mr. Williams. "Yes, Mrs. Sickels had been a client". My heart sunk; I didn't like the "had been" at all. "She had a fall and hurt her back. I believe she went to live with her niece in Connecticut", Mr. Williams went on. "Do you have a telephone number or address for this niece?", I asked, holding my breath. "Yes, I do", was the reply. I wrote down the number and then dialed it immediately.

When I asked for Mrs. Sickels, I was told it was her niece, Nancy, speaking. I introduced myself and said I was doing research on thimbles for a book I wanted to write and would like an interview with Mrs. Sickels, if possible. "I think Aunt Betty would love that . . . you say you are a collector too? . . Saturday is fine . . . would you like to see her collection? . .", the conversation went on.

The next Saturday, the four hour drive from Wilmington to the western hill country of Connecticut gave me ample time to review the hundreds of questions I wanted to ask this legendary lady. About noon on this warm autumn day, I was introduced to a frail, white-haired lady with a wide, bright smile. She looked fragile in body, but so bold in spirit that she seemed much younger than her 80-plus years.

With a twinkle in her eye, Mrs. Sickels held out her hand and said, "It's time for my walk. Would you like me to hold your hand? I don't want you to have a fall". Her sense of humor got us all laughing—Nancy, Cecile, her other niece, and myself, at the sight of 5'2", 95 pound Betty Sickels holding the hand of a 6'3", 210 pound man, so he wouldn't fall! We walked and talked among the trees changing into their autumn glory.

I asked my hundred questions, and she would answer, "Yes, I did some research on that," . . . or "Mr. Holmes asked me that many years ago. I liked him; he is a true gentleman and a scholar" . . . or "No, they never made thimbles, only stamped their trademark on them." . . "You have to watch those star trademarks. Three firms used them, you know" . . .

The hours passed too quickly. I gave her warm regards from some old thimble friends and a tear came to her eye. "My hand shakes a little and I cannot write very nice. Are they mad at me?", she asked. We hugged as I thanked her for her help and advice, and I promised to see her again soon. I could see she was getting tired and we said farewell.

A month later, I received a call from Nancy asking me when I was coming up again. Betty wanted to give me some notes she had done a while back on Simons Bros. of Philadelphia, about which she knew I was very interested. I asked if I could bring along Ann Blakeslee, who had been very close to Betty for many years. The reply was, "Another collector? Please do!"

I met Ann early the following Saturday and we went together to visit Mrs. Sickels. Ann and Betty met with warm embraces and tears filled their eyes. They talked of old friends, good times and the bad, like when Betty's collection was stolen at a New York antique show, and Ann, who did not know Betty at the time, helped her get most of it back.

Late afternoon arrived, and before we parted, I was told to go to Cecile's house and look on her back porch for some material her Aunt Betty wanted me to have. When I arrived, no one was home, but a note said to take the boxes which were on the back porch. The ten cartons filled my trunk, back and front seats and each weighed about 40 pounds! Since Ann was waiting for me, I did not have time to look into the boxes. That evening was spent with Ann and her husband in her lovely, old colonial home, looking at her beautiful collection. By the time I left and arrived back in Wilmington around midnight, I was too tired to carry all the cartons into the house.

Sunday mornings around the von Hoelle house is fried eggs, waffles, sausage, newspapers, and the joys and noise of five teenagers telling their grandmother about Saturday night adventures, just to see the shock of disbelief on her face. Then, I remembered the cartons in my car and sent my two oldest boys to bring them in.

I broke the nylon tape which secured the first carton and opened it. A large note inside the top said: "Old American, English and European Thimble Catalogs and Salesman Samples". I picked up the first item, an 1889 Simons 50th Year Anniversary poster in hand-tinted color. Next came original Waite-Thresher, Simons, and Ketcham & McDougall catalogs, along with hundreds of thimble leaflets, advertisements and sample cards.

The next carton I tore open was labeled inside, "Material on Thimble Manufacturing Techniques". This box was full of line drawings and photos of thimble making machinery, U.S. and foreign patents, samples of the different stages of thimble manufacture, and how different firms used a variety of methods to make their thimbles. There were also photographs of old thimble mills and the men and women who ran them.

Another carton contained about fifty letters to and from Mrs. Sickels to Kitty Simons, who was the last Simons to run the famous thimble company, and over five hundred other letters to and from collectors all over the world from the 1940's to the 1970's. Other cartons were filled with photostats of thimble patents, an index of marks for over a thousand American silversmiths and the histories of most American thimble manufacturers. Box after box was opened and the contents explored. Now only one carton remained and I wondered what on earth was left; what topic had been missed. This box was also the heaviest. I opened it and read the now familiar note on top, "Photos of Thimble Collections". Inside was not hundreds, but thousands of large clear photos in color or black and white of the most fabulous thimbles to be found. There were pictures of the best from the legendary collections of the National Thimble Collectors, photographs from the world's finest museum collections, and photos of fabulous European collections and those belonging to French Barons and English ladies.

I was dumb struck! It would take me years to read all this. Everything was so organized, labeled, and filed as if it had been waiting to be found and published. Here was a hundred times the material I had been able to collect in three years. Here was the work of a lifetime!

The last time I saw Mrs. Sickels she was not feeling well, and there was a little sadness in her eyes. I said, "Mrs. Sickels, there is 40 years of research in those cartons. Are you sure you want ME to have it?" She answered, "Yes, John, but it is to be shared with all serious collectors and writers, and I know you will take care of it until it gets published. Some day there will be many thimble collectors, and they will want to know. In my day I had trouble getting even magazines to carry my articles. I had to get it written down before it was lost forever; now it's up to you".

I drove away with a treasure beyond value, and as she waved to me, I could see the inner joy of knowing her work was in the hands of the next generation of collectors - not the dozen she had once known in the early 1940's, but the thousands who have joined her in this unique hobby. Her work is and will be preserved in the books to come, the talks to be given, and the meetings still unplanned. Elizabeth Galbraith Sickels is that type of unique and rare person one finds in abundance among thimble collectors, and I feel priviledged to have known her.

Elizabeth G. Sickels and author, Sept., 1983

Note: The following article by H. Syer Cuming, Vice-President of the prestigious British Archeological Association, was one of the first "so-called" authoritative writings on thimbles from a historical viewpoint.

In this one article he created the myth of the legendary Roman thimbles of Herculaneum, which was quoted by British and American authors for more than a hundred years.

ON THIMBLES.

BY H. SYER CUMING, ESQ., F.S.A. SCOT., V.P.

(Read March 19, 1879.)

THE paper on sewing needles, which appeared in our *Journal* of 1877, may be fitly followed by a few remarks on thimbles, which seem to be specially called for, as a grave error respecting the antiquity of these utensils has been put forth in a popular book of information, and to which reference will again be made in the sequel.

It is natural to suppose that some scheme for the protection of the fingers was adopted almost as soon as the art of stitchery commenced, and a plate of wood, leather, or bone, bound on the finger as a shield, probably constituted one of the earliest modes of defence. But metal thimbles are of no very recent invention, for some of bronze, open at their ends, like those employed by tailors, have been discovered at Herculaneum; and two ancient bronze thimbles, exactly similar to those of modern times, are in the Geneviève collection. The thimble, in its now recognised form, may fairly claim an antiquity of some two thousand years.

The use of thimbles in this country dates in all probability from a very early period, for when we find a pure Kymreig name for any object, we may be pretty sure that the Britons possessed such an object of native contrivance. *Byswain* (finger-guard) and *gwniadur* (sewing-steel) were the appropriate titles given to the thimble by our Britannic ancestors, whose digits must have needed some strong protection whilst engaged in stitching together their pelt mantles and particoloured garbs. Bronze thimbles are said to have been exhumed with Roman remains in London, differing little in aspect from those in the Geneviève cabinet.

It is difficult to decide the exact age of antique thimbles without they be found with relics whose era is well established. The examples I now submit were recovered from the Thames, off Dowgate, Sept. 1856, and are unquestionably of very early date. They are all of golden-coloured bronze or brass, and of two distinct types. First we have one composed of a strip of metal about eight-twelfths of an inch wide, rolled round and soldered, leaving the end open in the fashion of the specimens discovered at Herculaneum. Either extremity is encircled by a plain band, the space intervening being thickly pounced with small indentations. The other thimbles from off Dowgate are of the sugar-loaf type, their tops being far more conic than those of any made within the last four hundred years. They vary from seven-twelfths of an inch to nine-twelfths in height. Their apices are smooth, with the rest of their surfaces pounced with fine indentations, with exception of a plain band round their bases.

In the fourteenth century the thimble seems to have been called a *themel,* and it is spoken of under this title by Thomas Occleve :

> "Come hider to me, sone, and loke wheder
> In this purse whether ther be any cros or crouche,
> Save nedel and threde and *themel of lether.*"[1]

Leather was certainly employed for thimbles in the middle ages, and up to a comparatively recent period leather thimbles were common among the more industrious peasants of the south of Ireland. I exhibit an example which was used in County Cork up to about the year 1820. It is tolerably neatly made of a strip of black leather sewed up one side, and the top stitched on. One who carefully examined this Hibernian thimble declared it to be made of tanned human skin, but I cannot vouch for such being the case.

The employment of leathern thimbles in the middle ages may account, in some degree, for our so seldom finding metallic ones of an earlier date than the sixteenth century, when they became comparatively common. The example I now produce has the lower band stamped with a little shield charged with a cinquefoil, the form of which will hardly permit us to assign the thimble to a later epoch than *circa* 1500. This specimen is of stout brass, ten-twelfths of an inch high; the top domed, and with the sides thickly covered with a spiral of large indentations. It was recovered from the Thames, off Dowgate, Sept. 1856, but not with the more ancient thimbles already described.

My next thimble is also of brass, nearly 1 inch high. The

[1] See Halliwell's *Dictionary of Archaic Words,* *sub* "Crouche".

ON THIMBLES.

top is much flatter than in the earlier examples; but, like them, there is no projecting rim or margin round the base, as in the modern utensil. The top and a good part of the sides are indented, and the lower part is encompassed by a band of sixteen circlets with an eleven-rayed star in each. There is likewise a small stamp bearing letters which seem to be AIN. This sixteenth century thimble was found in the Thames, near the site of Old London Bridge, May 1846; and with it was another of the same size and material, which, instead of the belt of stars, was surrounded by the words GOD SAVE THE QVENE,—a posy common on various articles made during the reign of Elizabeth, at which period such brief epigraphs were very fashionable. Among the Rarities to be seen at Don Saltero's Coffee House at Chelsea was "an ancient thimble dug out of the ruins of Stocks Market, with the motto, I WIS IT BETTER.

Allusions to thimbles are not unfrequent in the works of writers of the Elizabethan era. Thus Petrucio, in *The Taming of the Shrew* (iv, 3), says to the tailor, "Thou liest, thou thread, thou thimble"; and Grumio dares him, "Though thy little finger be armed in a thimble." In *King John* (v, 4), the "Bastard Faulconbridge" says derisively to the Dauphin,

>—— "your own ladies and pale visag'd maids,
>Like Amazons, come tripping after drums;
>Their thimbles into armed gauntlets change,
>Their needles to lances, and their gentle hearts
>To fierce and bloody inclination."

Silver thimbles of an early date are rarely met with; but they seem to have been common enough in the seventeenth century, and constituted part of the offerings made by the Puritanical ladies to Hugh Peters for the service of the Parliament. This curious fact is mentioned by Pepys in his *Diary* (sub April 3, 1663), who says that Dr. Creeton (Creighton) stated in a sermon that Hugh Peters' preaching stirred up the maids of the City to bring in their bodkins and thimbles; and allusion is also made to this circumstance in the popular ballads of the time, wherein we read,

>"And now for a fling at your thimbles,
>Your bodkins, rings, and whistles,
>In truck for your toys,
>We'll fit you with boys,
>'Tis the doctrine of Hugh's Epistles.[1]
>*   *   *

[1] *Collection of Loyal Songs.* ii. 47.

ON THIMBLES.

> "To pull down their King,
> Their plate they would bring,
> And other precious things;
> So that Sedgwick and Peters
> Were no small getters
> By their bodkins, thimbles, and rings."[1]

Keightley quotes from Howel's *Philanglus* (p. 128) that "the seamstress brought in her silver thimble, the chambermaid her bodkin, the cook her silver spoon."

The fashion of the ordinary thimble in use from the middle to the close of the seventeenth century, is well illustrated by the specimen I produce, which is more coppery than brass in aspect, and made of what was called, after its inventor, "Prince Rupert's Metal." The slightly domed top is smooth, with a ring round its margin; the upper part of the sides is indented, the lower decorated with a scroll pattern, and there is a trifling rim at the base. This thimble is really a tasteful little thing in its way.

Our lamented Associate and Secretary, Edward Roberts, Esq., F.S.A., possessed a sailor's thimble of stout brass, made probably at the end of the seventeenth century, and found at Billingsgate in August 1874. It is one inch and two-twelfths in height, and nearly one inch in diameter at the base, and with a circular aperture on the crown a quarter of an inch in diameter. The whole surface of the metal, save a band at the lower part, is covered by ten rows of large pits, the band being incised with the words BARNATTE STAR. This inscription is a novelty, and deserves record, whether it relate to the maker of the utensil, or to the ship in which it was employed.

Little more need be said about thimbles from this period. Those of silver came more and more into vogue; and the Tudor practice of inscribing a motto or posy around the lower part was vigorously followed during the eighteenth century, and traces of the old conceit may be found in the present day. "From a Friend", "A Keepsake", "A Token of Regard", "Forget me not", are among the phrases of thimble literature.

It will be seen from the foregoing remarks, that though we can neither fix the precise era nor country in which the thimble originated, it is clearly an article of very high antiquity, not alone in England, but in continental Europe, the

Collection of Loyal Songs, ii. 61.

buried city of Herculaneum proclaiming its use at least eighteen centuries since. With this well attested fact prominently before us, it is almost incredible that in a work published so late as 1855 we should find the following statement: "Thimble.—This simple, yet useful, and now indispensable, appendage to the ladies' work-table is of Dutch invention. The art of making them was brought to England by John Lofting, a mechanic from Holland, who set up a workshop at Islington, near London, and practised the manufacture of them in various metals, with profit and success, about 1695." So says Haydn in the seventh edition of *The Dictionary of Dates*. It may seem a small matter with many whether the thimble be an invention of the seventeenth or seventh century; and if the misstatement referred to had occurred in any obscure or unpretending work, it might be passed by unheeded; but when such an assertion is put forward in a book which is to be found not only in every library, but almost on every drawing-room table, and is accepted as a guide and authority by young and old, learned and unlearned, it is our duty as truth-loving archæologists to expose and denounce so gross an error.

Hitherto we have viewed the thimble as a mere inoffensive little implement designed for industrial purposes, but vile men have turned it to base and wicked ends, and given a dark side to its otherwise bright story. As the Roman *præstigiator* did the trick of the "little pea" with *acetabuli* or *paropsides*, so the modern sharper performs the nefarious game with thimbles, and many a racecourse has been the arena whereon the thimble-rigger has won the precious gold from his silly dupes. We have only to consult the letters of Seneca[1] and Alciphron[2] to see how close is the resemblance between the trickery of to-day and that of classic ages.

The World's Most Expensive Thimble

On December 3rd 1979, a London dealer, Winifred Williams bid the sum of $18,000.00 for a dentil shaped Meissen porcelain thimble, circa 1740, at Christie's auction Geneva, Switzerland.

The thimble, just over a half inch high, was painted in a rare lemon-yellow color about the band. It also had tiny harbor scenes hand painted within gold trimmed cartouches. The rim was scalloped with fired gold on its bottom edge. The thimble now belongs to a Meissen collector in Canada who wanted it for its lemon-yellow color!

How Much Is A Thimble Worth?

One of the most elusive questions a collector must face is: "How much is a thimble worth?" I recently read an article in a thimble publication which stated one simple solution; a thimble was worth what you were willing to pay. This is a simple solution, but one which could be very misleading and sometimes downright frustrating. Is a Rembrandt worth a hundred dollars because that is what one can afford, or is it worth the million dollars paid at the last auction?

A thimble, like any other object of value, is worth what a knowledgeable seller is willing to let it go for. The operative word here is *knowledgeable* seller.

We are not talking about the naive dealer who sold a friend of mine an 18th century Meissen, worth thousands, for $27, nor the poor dupe who accepted $40 for a rare gold and tortoise shell, Percey's Patent. These are lucky finds for sharp-eyed collectors based on the ignorance of the sellers. This type of transaction does not establish value, but does add to the excitement of the hunt, which we as collectors dream about.

True value is a narrow range of prices which knowledgeable buyers and sellers recognize, based on rarity and demand. It is not an absolute science, but rather an educated opinion, which is in constant change, due to inflation and market demands.

With this in mind a committee made up of three long-time astute collectors and three knowledgeable dealers, and myself have attempted to appraise the approximate current value of the thimbles illustrated in this volume. This is a task which I had wished to avoid, for it is the most difficult and subjective part of this edition. Only the overwhelming favorable response from readers of our earlier editions prompted me to include this feature again.

Some dealers said our last price list was too low, while many new collectors believed them too high. But most seasoned collectors acknowledged our estimates to be, on the whole, the most accurate available. Our last edition was recommended via their newsletter, to the members of an international appraisers association, and has been used to establish settlement of estates by the Internal Revenue Service.

To sharpen and update my own concepts on current pricing and rarity, I recently took an extended trip to the major antique markets of Great Britain, Europe and the United States. I talked to over a hundred dealers who regularly handle thimbles and reviewed the records of the major auction houses on thimble sales.

I was a bit surprised to learn how fast thimble collecting was growing, and the fact that rare thimbles such as 18th century South Staffordshire enamels, English filigrees and 19th century commemoratives have more than tripled in cost in the past three years! Not to mention the rare Meissen, Faberge, medieval and Byzantine pieces. Thus, here we go again, dancing where the angels fear to tread.

Thimble Conditions

A thimble's condition is basically its state of preservation. A well cared for thimble with beautiful detail is of more value to a collector then one which is very worn. A thimble worth $100.00 in mint condition may only be worth $5.00 in FAIR condition. A "Golden Spike" in "mint" is worth over $200.00, but in "Good" is worth less than $100.00. A thimble's grade is the buyer's opinion.

GRADES

Mint — New, never used, perfect.

Excellent — A slight degree of wear on the highest points of the design. In general, excellent condition.

Good — Used with noticeable wear all over, but all features and wording are easily readable.

Fair — Very worn, discolored, slightly bent, one hole not too noticeable, enamel cracked but not chipped off.

Poor — Damaged, two or more holes, cracked, badly bent, rusted, 50% or more of the design worn away, chipped off enamel, etc.

Index of Illustrations

(Photographed thimbles)

This index is designed to give the reader basic information on each thimble illustrated which cannot be observed from the photograph. Thus the country of origin, material used, and maker, are the first three pieces of information listed, if known. Room for any other comment usually concerns a technique of decoration.

NOTE ON PRICING

The numbers on the end of each index notation represent the approximate retail dollar value one can expect to pay for the thimble listed. The first figure is the approximate cost in "good" condition. The second figure is the approximate cost in "excellent" condition. "Mint" thimbles, especially old hand-chased and hand-painted enamels, will bring more. The same thimble in "Fair" condition should be much less.

Thimbles of plain design, but having rare maker's marks, bring a premium, as do many pre-1930 commemoratives, souvenir, and novelty thimbles.

Remember, these are current dealer "asking" prices and should in no way abate good, old-fashioned haggling, which is half the fun of collecting.

ABBREVIATIONS

ALUM = Aluminum	HP = Hand Painted	SIM = Simons Bros.
AM = Applied Motifs	JVH = by John von Hoelle	SU = Sok Ung
BC = Bone China	KMD = Ketcham McDougall	TS = Tortoise Shell
CN = Copper/Nickel	MEX = Mexico	USA = United States
FD = Fired Decal Transfer	MOP = Mother of Pearl	WT = Waite-Thresher Co.
FM = Franklin Mint	NM = No Marks	17C = 17th century
GB = Great Britain	PEW = Pewter	18C = 18th century
GER = Germany	PORC = Porcelain	19C = 19th century
GS = Goldsmith-Stern	RW = Royal Worcester	20C = 20th century
HC = Hand Chased	SIL = Silver	? = Unknown
HM = Hall Marked	SS = Sterling Silver	.800 = 80% Silver
	TURQ = Turquoise	.950 = 95% Silver

1. MEX, SIL, MOP, 20C 8-12
2. USA, SS, NM, 19C 25-35
3. IRAN, brass, HC, 19C 35-45
4. USA, SIL, Simons, M. ADAMS, 20C 35-45
5. GB, SIL, James Walker, 20C 65-75
6. USA, Brass, Scovill, Prudential 20C 2-4
7. USA, ALUM. "Milk", 20C 2-4
8. USA, Plastic, 20C 1-3
9. Austria, ALUM, Russian Ad 10-12
10. GER, Tombac, 1920s 10-12
11. Austria, Tombac, Arabic, 20C 10-12
12. GB, ALUM, Dysons, 20C 8-10
13. USA, alabaster, JVH, gold band . . 60-75
14. USA, alabaster, JVH 40-50
15. USA, amber, JVH, acorn 40-50
16. GER, ALUM, Acanthus, 20C 3-5
17. GER, ALUM, Egyptian motif, 20C 10-12
18. GER, ALUM, pine seed, 20C 3-5
19. GER, ALUM, diamond motif, 20C . . 3-5
20. GER, ALUM, swag motif, 20C 2-4
21. Austria, ALUM, floral motif, 20C 2-4
22. Austria, ALUM, chain motif, 20C . . . 2-4
23. Austria, ALUM, 20C 5-7
24. GER, ALUM, seacrests, 20C 3-4
25. GER, ALUM, engineturn, 20C 3-4
26. GER, ALUM, lazy s motif, 20C 3-4
27. GER, ALUM, remember, 20C 5-7
28. GER, ALUM, glass top, scenic, 20C 10-12
29. Austria, ALUM, palm leaf, 20C 3-4
30. Austria, ALUM, floral motif 3-4
31. GER, ALUM, Greek motif 3-4
32. USA, SIL, heart & flower, HC, 17C . . . . Unique
33. USA, GOLD, J. Hurd, HC, 18C   Unique
34. Holland, SIL, Hare & Hounds, 18C 600-750
35. Holland, SIL, cupids/hearts, 18C 600-750
36. USA, SIL, Indian, HC, 20C 15-20
37. USA, SIL, Indian, 5 turq, 20C . . . 45-55
38. USA, SIL, Niello, HC, 20C 30-35
39. USA, SIL, 5 turq, HC, 20C 25-35
40. Italy, wood, decal, 20C 8-10
41. GB, SIL, applied motif, 19C 65-75
42. Nepal, brass, 20C 6-8
43. Siam, SIL, applied motif, 20C 25-30
44. USA, SIL, Indian, 20C 35-40
45. MEX, brass on copper, 20C 25-30
46. GB, SIL, cornelian top, 19C . . . 100-125
47. GER, SIL, aquamarine stones, 20C 75-95
48. Austria, SIL, 800, 19C 300-350
49. Austria, SIL, 800, 19C 350-400
50. Austria, SIL, HC, 18C 700-800
51. Austria, brass, painted, 20C 8-10
52. Austria, brass, painted, 20C 6-8
53. Austria, brass, painted, 20C 6-8
54. Austria, brass, painted, 20C 6-8
55. Austria, MOP, J. Schwarz, 19C 400-450
56. Austria, 800 SIL, cast 45-60
57. Austria, 800 SIL, cast 45-60
58. Austria, 800 SIL, cast 45-60
59. Persia, SIL, Angushtahne, 19C . 250-300
60. India, bamboo, painted 8-10
61. GER, SIL, HC, 19C 35-45
62. GB, PORC, Wedgwood, basalt . . . 10-12
63. USA, Pewter, cast, battersea 15-18
64. USA, bone, JVH, pierced 35-40
65. USA, bone, JVH, SIL top 60-75
66. USA, bone, scrimshaw, JVH 60-75
67. USA, bone, gold band, 8 turq, JVH 50-60
68. USA, bone, JVH, SIL top 35-45
69. USA, bone, onyx & gold motif, JVH 40-50
70. USA, bone, horn top, JVH 45-50
71. USA, bone, pierced, JVH 30-40
72. USA, bone, MOP top, JVH 35-45
73. USA, Narwhale, HC, 19C 40-50
74. USA, bone, TURQ & pearl, JVH . 75-90
75. China, bone, 2 PC, 19C 75-90
76. ?, bone, pierced 50-60
77. ?, bone, pierced 40-50
78. USA, bone, JVH, scallop rim 40-45
79. ?, bone, crenellated 50-60
80. Spain, brass gilt, glass, 20C 8-10
81. Spain, brass gilt, TURQ, 20C 8-10
82. USA, SIL, brand, 20C 20-25
83. USA, brass/copper, brand, 20C . . . 12-15
84. India, brass, HC, 20C 12-15
85. ?, brass, 19C 8-10
86. GER, brass, 20C 8-10
87. ?, brass, 19C 8-10
88. ?, brass, 19C 8-10
89. GB, brass, Her Majesty, 19C 15-20
90. ?, Oriede, 19C 10-12
91. India, brass, 20C 8-10
92. Austria, brass, 20C 8-10
93. USA, brass, applied anchor, 20C 6-8
94. Austria, brass, 19C 8-10
95. Austria, brass, floral band 10-12
96. GER, brass, Greek Key, 19C 8-10
97. GER, brass, triangle indents, 20C . 10-12
98. Austria, brass, 20C 7-9
99. GER, brass, 20C 6-8
100. Poland, gold, lapis & pearls, 19C 600-700

#	Description	Price
101	USA, brass, Bonewell, opal 20C	45-50
102	USA, SIL, Muhr, 19C	25-30
103	GB, PORC, Wedgwood, 20C	20-25
104	Italy, gold, cameo	250-300
105	GER, SIL, Cornelian top, 19C	45-60
106	GER, SIL, Gabler, 19C	45-50
107	GB, SIL, Dormon-Brailsford, 20C	45-50
108	MEX, SS, man & donkey, 20C	10-15
109	MEX, SS, geometric design, 20C	10-15
110	Guatemala, SS, HC, floral motifs	18-25
111	MEX, SS, flowers in relief, 20C	10-15
112	MEX, SS, flowers in relief, 20C	10-15
113	MEX, Alpaca, inlaid MOP/abalone	7-10
114	MEX, copper, inlaid MOP, 20C	7-10
115	MEX, SS, applied wire W/TURQ	18-25
116	MEX, SS, applied wire, HC	12-15
117	MEX, alpaca, multi enamel	7-9
118	Guatemala, SS, HC, floral, 20C	15-18
119	MEX, SS, abalone rim, 20C	7-9
120	Guatemala, SS w/orange opal, 20C	45-50
121	MEX, SS, abalone rim, HC	10-12
122	MEX, SS, HC, 20C	10-12
123	MEX, alpaca, HC, applied wire	5-7
124	MEX, alpaca, HC, applied wire	5-7
125	MEX, alpaca, HC, applied wire	5-7
126	MEX, alpaca, HC, applied wire	5-7
127	MEX, alpaca, HC, applied wire	5-7
128	MEX, SS, abalone rim w/TURQ	18-22
129	MEX, SS, abalone inlaid, 20C	7-10
130	MEX, SS, abalone inlaid rim	15-18
131	MEX, SS, floral motif in relief	12-15
132	MEX, alpaca, applied wire, 20C	3-5
133	MEX, SS, applied wire, work, 20C	7-10
134	MEX, SS, applied wire work, 20C	7-10
135	MEX, SS, applied wire work, 20C	8-10
136	MEX, SS, plain sides applied wire	7-10
137	MEX, SS, applied wire work	8-10
138	MEX, SS, abalone inlaid, 20C	8-10
139	MEX, alpaca, abalone inlaid	4-6
140	MEX, alpaca, abalone inlaid	4-6
141	MEX, alpaca, abalone inlaid	4-6
142	MEX, alpaca, abalone inlaid	4-6
143	MEX, SS, HC w/applied wire, 20C	8-10
144	MEX, SS, HC w/applied wire, 20C	8-10
145	MEX, SS, applied hearts motif	8-10
146	MEX, SS, applied wire work, 20C	8-10
147	MEX, SS, w/abalone shell rim	8-10
148	GB, PORC, FD, Caverswall	10-12
149	GB, PORC, FD, Caverswall	10-12
150	GB, PORC, FD, Caverswall	10-12
151	GB, PORC, FD, Caverswall	10-12
152	USA, SS, Chalmer's, 20C	20-25
153	China, cloisonne-cinnabar, 20C	10-12
154	China, cloisonne-cinnabar, 20C	10-12
155	China, cloisonne-cinnabar, 20C	10-12
156	China, cloisonne domed top	12-15
157	China, cloisonne band, SQ indents	12-15
158	China, cloisonne, multicolor	15-18
159	China, cloisonne, BLK ground	8-10
160	China, cloisonne, DK GR Multicolor	10-12
161	China, cloisonne, w/pink flowers	12-15
162	China, cloisonne, ivory	12-15
163	China, cloisonne, multicolor	10-12
164	China, cloisonne, orange bird	8-10
165	China, cloisonne, w/multicolor	10-12
166	China, cloisonne, flowers	10-12
167	China, cloisonne, multicolor	10-12
168	USA, Brass gilt, applied motif	7-9
169	India, SIL, HC, 19C	100-125
170	Italy, gold, cupids, 18C	1200+
171	USA, brass, child's thimble	5-7
172	GB, SS, HC, HM	40-45
173	GER, SIL, chrysoprase stones, 20C	60-75
174	USA, coal, hand carved, 20C	8-10
175	USA, SS, Simons, Chicago Expo 1892	300-325
176	France, SIL, Lanain, 19C	45-60
177	France, SIL, Lanain, 19C	45-60
178	GER, SIL gilt, 20C	40-50
179	France, SIL, Lanain, 19C	40-50
180	USA, glass, Corning, 20C	40-50
181	Italy, copper, applied mini pennies	10-12
182	USA, brass, Joseph Muhr, 19C	25-35
183	Swedish, SIL, crenellated, 18C?	250-300
184	GB, SS, HM:HG&S, 1953	60-75
185	GB, SS, Albert & Victoria, 19C	300-400
186	GB, SS, Eliz, II 1953	100-125
187	GB, SS, Victoria 1837-1897	350-450
188	GB, SS, HM:HG&S, 1953	60-75
189	GB, SS, George V 1911, gilt crown	200-250
190	GER, glass, lead crystal, 20C	15-18
191	GER, glass, pine tree motif, 20C	15-18
192	GER, glass, gilt band, 20C	10-12
193	GER, glass, diamond faceted, 20C	15-18
194	GER, SIL, gold damascene, 19C	400-500
195	France, SIL, Lanain, 20C	45-60
196	France, SIL, Lanain, 19C	100-125
197	France, SIL, Lanain, 20C	45-80
198	GB, SS/steel, Dreema	60-75
199	GB, SS/brass, Dorothy	125-145
200	GB, SS/steel, Doris	75-85
201	GB, SS/steel, Dorcas	35-45
202	GB, SS/steel, Dura	45-60
203	Israel/USA, SS, J. Demirjian	20-25
204	Israel/USA, SS, J. Demirjian	20-25
205	Israel/USA, SS, J. Demirjian	20-25
206	Israel/USA, SS, J. Demirjian	20-25
207	GB, SS/steel, Dorcas	35-45
208	GB, SS/steel, Dorcas	35-45
209	GB, SS/steel, Dorcas	35-45
210	GB, SS/steel, Dorcas	35-45
211	GB, SS/steel, Dura	45-60

#	Description	Price
212	GB, SS/steel, Dura	45-60
213	GB, SS/steel, Dura	45-60
214	GB, SS/steel, Dura	45-60
215	GB, SS/steel, Dreema	60-75
216	GB, SS/steel, Dreema	60-75
217	GB, SS/steel, Dreema	60-75
218	GB, SS/steel, Dreema	60-75
219	GB, SS/steel, Doris	75-85
220	GB, SS/steel, Doris	75-85
221	GB, SS/steel, steel-clad	50-60
222	GB, SS/steel, steel-clad	50-60
223	GB, SS/steel, Little Dorcas	45-60
224	GB, SS/steel, Little Dorcas	45-60
225	GB, SS/steel, Little Dorcas	45-60
226	GB, SS/steel, Little Dorcas	45-60
227	Dutch?, brass, cast, 17C	100-125
228	Dutch, brass, cast, 17C	125-145
229	Dutch, brass, cast, 18C	135-150
230	Dutch, SIL, 4 Cupids in ovals, 18C	400-450
231	USA, brass/leather, 20C	10-15
232	USA, Italian alabaster, HC, 20C	30-40
233	USA, SS, Simons	40-50
234	GB, gold, 6 rubies, HM, 20C	350-400
235	India, SIL, HC, 19C	100-125
236	GER, SIL, Gabler, 19C	60-75
237	GER, SIL, Gabler, 20C	100-125
238	Norway, SIL-gilt, HC, 20C	125-145
239	GER, SIL, HP, 20C	25-30
240	GER, SIL-Plate brass, AM, 20C	8-10
241	GB, SS, enameled, HM	35-40
242	GER, SS, enameled, 20C	25-30
243	GB, SS, decal, 20C	15-20
244	GER, SS, Gabler, scenic	35-45
245	USA, SS, Simons, 20C	60-75
246	USA, SS, KMD, HP, 20C	100-125
247	Spain, SS, enameled band, 20C	35-45
248	GB, enameled brass, Crummles, 20C	35-40
249	Austria, brass, Steinbock	18-25
250	GER, SIL-plated brass, enameled	8-10
251	GB, brass, Stitch-In-Time	25-35
252	USA, SS, KMD, HP, 20C	100-125
253	Dutch, SS, 75 anniv.	40-50
254	GB, SS, Swingler, Mother's Day	75-90
255	GER, SS, decal on enamel, 20C	35-40
256	GB, enameled brass, Halcyon, 20C	40-45
257	Dutch, enameled brass, "1976"	8-10
258	GB, enameled brass, Halcyon, 20C	40-45
259	GER, SIL-plated brass, Hummel, 20C	8-10
260	GB, SS, decal on enamel, 20C	25-35
261	GER, SIL, HP on enamel, 20C	25-35
262	Norway, SIL-gilt, HP, 20C	75-80
263	GER, SIL, HP on enamel, 20C	45-50
264	GB, SIL, decal on enamel, 20C	35-40
265	Spain, SS, decal on enamel, 20C	35-45
266	GB, SIL, decal on enamel, 20C	35-45
267	GB, SS, decal on enamel, 20C	35-40
268	GB, brass, chevron motif, 16C	600-750
269	GB, SIL, chevron motif, 16C	1000+
270	GB, brass, chevron motif, 16C	600-750
271	GB, SS, HM:JS&S, 20C	45-60
272	GB, SS, HM:JF, 19C	45-60
273	GB, SS, HM:WHW, 19C	50-65
274	GB, SS, jade top, HM:CH	60-75
275	GB, SS, HM:AB&CO	45-60
276	GB, SS, HM:CM	60-75
277	GB, SS, HM:SF	60-75
278	GB, SS, HM:AI	50-65
279	GB, SS, 1851 Expo	300-350
280	GB, SS, Lichfield Cathedral	300-350
281	GB, SS, Brighton, 19C	300-350
282	GB, SS, Newstead Abbey, 19C	300-350
283	GB, SS, Silver Jubilee, HM:JS&S	40-45
284	GB/Holland?, brass, Lofting?, 17C	100-125
285	GB/Holland?, brass, Lofting/, 17C	100-125
286	GB, SS, HM:JF, 19C	25-35
287	GB, SS, HC, 18C	45-55
288	GB, SS, HM:SF, 19C	35-45
289	GB, SS, pierced scallop, 19C	60-75
290	GB, SS, Comm. HM:JS&S, 20C	35-40
291	GB, SS, agate top, HM:CH, 19C	45-55
292	GB, SS/steel, Dorcas, Pat, 19C	30-35
293	GB, SS, HM:HG&S	25-35
294	GB, SS, Eliz. II Jubilee, 1977	35-45
295	GB, SS, enameled, 20C	35-40
296	GB, SS, enameled, 20C	25-35
297	GB, SS, Swingler, 20C	75-95
298	GB, Gold, HC, 19C	125-145
299	GB, Gold, 15 TURQ, 19C	275-300
300	GB, Gold, 15 TURQ, 19C	300-325
301	GB, Gold, 6 TURQ, 19C	275-300
302	GB, Gold, applied buds, 19C	175-200
303	GB, SS, Birmingham, w/bottle, 18C	600-700
304	GB, SS, Birmingham, 18C	400-450
305	GB, SS, Victoria & Albert, 19C	400-450
306	GB, SS, HC, HM:JF, 20C	35-45
307	GB, SS, Mary Rose Comm., HM:JS&S	35-45
308	GB, SS, HC, HM:JF, 20C	45-55
309	GB, SS, Royal SPA, HM:HG&S, 20C	45-55
310	GB, SS, Blk berry Pat., HM:AB&CO	45-55
311	GB, SS, HC, NM, 20C	35-40
312	GB, SS, James Walker, 20C	40-50
313	GB, SS, Moss agate top, JS&S, 20C	40-50
314	GB, SS, HM:JS, 19C	35-45
315	GB, SS, HM:HG&S	40-45
316	GB, SS, HM:CH, 19C	75-85
317	GB, SS, HM:GG, 19C	75-85

#	Description	Price
318	GB, PORC, NM, HP, 19C	125-150
319	GB, PORC, NM, HP, 19C	200-225
320	GB, PORC, NM, HP, 19C	100-125
321	GB, PORC, NM, HP, 19C	100-125
322	GB, PORC, NM, HP, 19C	125-150
323	GB, PORC, NM, HP, 19C	100-125
324	GB, PORC, NM, HP, 19C	200-250
325	GB, PORC, NM, HP, 19C	150-175
326	GB, PORC, NM, HP, 19C	250-300
327	GB, PORC, NM, HP, 19C	200-250
328	GB, PORC, NM, HP, 19C	250-300
329	GB, PORC, NM, HP, 19C	250-300
330	GB, PORC, NM, HP, 19C	150-200
331	GB, PORC, NM, HP, 19C	200-225
332	GB, PORC, NM, HP, 19C	200-225
333	GB, PORC, NM, HP, 19C	200-225
334	GB, SS, HM:JS&S, Prince WM.	35-40
335	Canada, stone, Eskimo, 20C	40-45
336	Canada, stone, Eskimo, 20C	30-35
337	USA, brass, brand, 20C	15-18
338	USA, brass, brand, 20C	15-18
339	GB, SIL, HC, NM, 16C	1200+
340	GB, SIL, Be True to God, 1575	1500+
341	GB, SIL, ? Love Me Ever, 16C	1200+
343	GB, SS, HM:JF, 19C	40-50
344	GB, SS, HM:JF, 19C	40-50
345	GB, SS, HM:JF, 20C	40-50
346	GB, SS, HM:JF, 19C	40-50
347	?, plastic, molded, 20C	3-5
348	USA, chrome/brass, Howser, 20C	5-7
349	GB, copper/nickel, 19C	40-50
350	GB, SS, HM, 19C	45-55
351	GB, SS, dated 1804, filigree	450-500
352	GB, SS, early filigree, 18C	750-800
353	GB, SS, early filigree, 18C	1500+
354	Portugal, SS, filigree, 20C	15-18
355	GB, SS, Birmingham, 18C	400-450
356	Persia, gold, filigree, 18C	1200+
357	Portugal, SIL-gilt, enameled, 20C	25-35
358	Philippines, SS, filigree, 20C	18-20
359	Philippines, SS, filigree, 20C	18-20
360	Israel, SS, filigree, 20C	35-40
361	Israel, SS, filigree, 20C	35-40
362	Peru, SIL, Indian filigree, 20C	35-40
363	Peru, SIL, Indian filigree, 20C	35-40
364	Peru, SIL, Indian filigree, 20C	35-40
365	Portugal, SIL-gilt, 20C	18-20
366	GB, SS, HC, HM:JF, 20C	40-50
367	USA, horn, C. Fisher, 20C	18-25
368	GB, SS, HM:SJR, 20C	35-45
369	China, fossilized bone, pearls	60-75
370	GB, SS, HM:SF, 19C	40-50
371	GB, SS, HM:SF, 19C	40-50
372	GB, SS, HM:SF, 19C	40-50
373	GB, SS, HM:HF, 19C	40-50
374	USA, SS-gilt, FM, fidelity, 20C	55-60
375	USA, SS-gilt, FM, peace, 20C	55-60
376	USA, SS-gilt, FM, Steadfastness	55-60
377	USA, SS-gilt, FM, Friendship	55-60
378	USA, SS-gilt, FM, Courage	55-60
379	USA, SS-gilt, FM, Perfection	55-60
380	USA, SS-gilt, FM, Love	55-60
381	USA, SS-gilt, FM, Hope	55-60
382	USA, SS-gilt, FM, Loyalty	55-60
383	USA, SS-gilt, FM, Virtue	55-60
384	USA, SS-gilt, FM, Wisdom	55-60
385	USA, SS-gilt, FM, Health	55-60
386	USA, pewter, FM, Grimms, 20C	12-15
387	USA, pewter, FM, Grimms, 20C	12-15
388	USA, pewter, FM, Grimms, 20C	12-15
389	USA, pewter, FM, Grimms, 20C	12-15
390	France, 950, P. Lenain, HM	45-60
391	France, 950, P. Lenain, Alfonso XVI	40-50
392	France, 950, P. Lenain, Paris Expo	45-60
393	France, 950, P. Lenain, stork & wolf	45-60
394	France, 950, P. Lenain, Lyon Expo 1914	45-60
395	France, SS, applied chain, 19C	45-55
396	France, 950, P. Lenain, shell motif	35-45
397	France, 950, P. Lenain "Joan De Arc"	45-60
398	France, 950, O. Prudhomme	45-60
399	France, SIL unknown, HM	35-45
400	France, 950, P. Lenain, Crab, HM	35-50
401	France SS w/gold band lacework	35-50
402	France, 950, P. Lenain	45-60
403	France, 950, P. Lenain	35-40
404	France, 950, O. Prudhomme	45-60
405	France, SS, Madonna & child	50-60
406	France, SS, Vain Beauty	45-55
407	France, SS, flower girl	45-60
408	France, SS, P. Lenain, Notre-Dame	35-45
409	France, SS, "Noublions Jamais!" 1914	45-60
410	USA, SS, FM, 20C	40-50
411	USA, SS, FM, 20C	40-50
412	USA, SS, KMD, 19C	18-20
413	USA, SS, Webster, 19C	25-30
414	USA, pewter, Donohue, 20C	12-15
415	USA, pewter, Donohue, 20C	12-15
416	Italy, glass, HP, 20C	8-10
417	GB, glass, Royal Brierly, 20C	35-40
418	GER, glass, gold dots, 20C	10-12
419	GER, glass, hand cut, 20C	10-12
420	GER, 800 SIL, Gabler, 19C	45-55
421	GER, 800 SIL, Gabler, 19C	30-35
422	GER, SS, Gabler, glass top	25-30
423	GER, SS, Gabler, 20C	25-30
424	GER, 800 SIL, Gabler, 20C	25-30
425	GER, 800 SIL, Gabler, 19C	50-55
426	GER, SS, Gabler, 20C	25-30
427	GER, 800 SIL, Gabler, stone top	35-45
428	GER, SIL, Gabler, 19C	45-50
429	GER, SIL, Gabler, AM, 19C	35-40
430	GER, SIL, Gabler, AM, 19C	50-60
431	GER, SIL, Gabler, 19C	40-50

432 GER, SIL, Gabler, AM, 19C 50-60
433 GER, SIL, Gabler, 19C 60-75
434 GER, SIL, Gabler, 19C 50-60
435 GER, SIL, Gabler, 19C 50-60
436 USA, brass, tobacco tap, 20C 15-20
437 ?, brass, cutter, 1904 PAT. 30-35
438 ?, brass, for long nails 20-25
439 Denmark, CN, pipe thimble 12-15
440 GB, SIL-plate, Iles, cutter, 19C . . . 25-35
441 Austria, CN, gripper 35-45
442 ?, CN, w/magnet 30-40
443 GER, steel, blind threader 15-20
444 GB, brass, Stanhope lens, 19C . 100-125
445 GB, CN, Iles, ventilated 45-50
446 GB, CN, non-slip, 20C 30-35
447 GB, SS, PAT. non-slip 35-45
448 USA, brass, cutter, 20C 10-12
449 USA, brass, w/magnet top 5-7
450 USA, brass, w/needle gripper 5-7
451 USA, brass, w/needle threader . . . 18-25
452 ?, brass, quilter top, 20C 3-5
453 GER, brass, Gagiana find, 16C . 300-350
455 USA, SS, Simons St. Louis
    1904 300-350
456 GER, glass, HP, green, 20C 15-18
457 ?, SS, red glass top 18-20
458 GER, SS, glass top 18-20
459 Austria, ALUM, glass top, 20C . . . 10-12
460 Austria, ALUM, glass top, 20C . . . 10-12
461 France, gold 72 pearls, hair
    19C 700-750
462 Persia, gold, HP, 18C . . . . 1200+
463 GB, gold TURQ/pearls, 19C . . . 275-300
464 USA, SS w/gold band 45-50
465 USA, SS w/gold band 45-55
466 USA, SS w/gold band 45-55
467 USA, SS w/gold band 45-55
468 USA, SS, GS 20-25
469 USA, SS, GS, swimmer, 20C . . 100-125
470 USA, SS, GS, scenic 40-50
471 USA, SS, GS, cupids 100-125
472 USA, SS, GS, 20C 20-25
473 Greek, SIL, enameled, 20C 12-15
474 Greek, SIL, enameled, 20C 12-15
475 Greek, SIL, AM, 20C 12-15
476 Greek, SIL, enameled, 20C 12-15
477 Greek, SIL, enameled, 20C 12-15
478 GER, SS, Greif, braid, 20C 40-45
479 GER, SS, Greif, Rembrandt 70-75
480 GER, SS, Greif, Gabler Mill 70-75
481 GER, SS w/gold band, Greif 60-75
482 GB, SS, HM:HG&S, 20C 40-50
483 GB, SS, HM:HG&S, 20C 35-45
484 GB, SS, HM:HG&S, 20C 30-35
485 GB, SS, HM:HG&S, 20C 30-35
486 GB, SS, HM:HG&S, 19C 40-45
487 GB, SS, HM:HG, 19C 45-55
488 GB, SS, HM:HG, 19C 45-55
489 GB, SS, HM:HG, 19C 45-55

490 USA, Gutta-Percha, 19C 12-15
491 GB, plastic, Halex, 20C 15-18
492 USA, SIL w/steel top, BH, 18C 200-250
493 USA, SIL w/steel top, BH, 18C 200-250
494 GB, SS, HM:GG, 19C 40-50
495 China, SIL, HC, 19C 40-45
496 MEX, SIL, AM, 20C 8-10
497 GER, SIL, Henckels, 20C 15-20
498 USA, SIL, B. Halstead, 18C . . . 300-350
499 France, PORC, Haviland, 20C . . . 12-15
500 France, PORC, Haviland, 20C . . . 12-15
501 France, PORC, Haviland, 20C . . . 12-15
502 France, PORC, Haviland, 20C . . . 12-15
503 Hungary, PORC, Herend, 20C . . . 20-25
504 Hungary, PORC, Herend, 20C . . . 20-25
505 Hungary, PORC, Herend, 20C . . . 20-25
506 USA, iron & ivory, hem roller 60-75
507 Scotland, Horn, 20C 15-18
508 South America, Horn 20C 10-12
509 USA, horn, HP, Thompson, 20C . 20-25
510 India, Horn, 20C 8-10
511 GB, SS, HM:CH, agate, 19C 45-55
512 GB, SS, HM:CH, pierced, 19C . . . 60-75
513 GB, SS, HM:CH, blood stone,
    19C 75-85
514 GB, CN, Iles, 20C 20-25
515 GB, SS, Mary Rose, HM:JS&S . . . 35-45
516 GB, iron, Iles, 19C 7-9
517 GB, brasss, Iles, Remember Phila . . . 5-6
518 GB, Alum w/glass top, Iles, 20C 6-8
519 GB, Alum, Iles, Adver, 20C 6-8
520 GB, Alum, Iles, Adver, 20C 6-8
521 GB, Alum, Iles, Adver, 20C 6-8
522 India, SIL, HC, 19C 75-90
523 India, SIL, HC, 19C 75-90
524 India, SIL, HC, 19C 125-150
525 India, SIL, HC, 19C 75-90
526 India, SIL, HC, 19C 60-75
527 India, SIL, HC, 19C 70-80
528 India, SIL, HC, 19C 70-80
529 India, SIL, HC, 19C 70-80
530 India, SIL, HC, 19C 75-90
531 India, SIL, HC, 19C 100-125
532 India, SIL, HC, 19C 100-125
533 India, SIL, HC, 19C 125-150
534 India, SIL, HC, 19C 250-300
535 India, SIL, HC, 19C 125-150
536 India, SIL, HC, 19C 200-225
537 India, SIL, HC, 19C 125-150
538 USA, ivory, JVH, 20C 125-145
539 USA, ivory, "I love Ann", 20C 25-35
540 China, ivory, 20C 25-35
541 China, ivory, 19C 50-60
542 USA, ivory, JVH, 20C 40-45
543 USA, ivory, JVH, 20C 25-30
544 China, ivory, 19C 30-40
545 USA, ivory, scrimshaw, 20C 15-18
546 USA, ivory, JVH, 20C 50-60
547 USA, ivory, JVH 45-50

#	Description	Price
548	USA, ivory, ARA/JVH, 20C	75-85
549	USA, ivory, JVH, coral/gold	85-100
550	USA, ivory, JVH	50-55
551	USA, ivory, JVH	60-65
552	USA, ivory, JVH, lattice	85-100
553	USA, ivory, JVH	60-65
554	USA, ivory, JVH	40-50
555	France, ivory w/gold band, 19C	150-175
556	China, ivory, 19C	60-70
557	?, ivory, 19C	75-90
558	China, ivory, 19C	75-90
559	China, ivory	60-75
560	China, ivory, 19C	100-125
561	GB, ivory, 19C	100-125
562	GB, ivory, 19C	100-125
563	GER, ivory, 20C	35-40
564	USA, ivory, scrimshaw, 20C	30-35
565	USA, ivory, JVH/ARA, 20C	45-50
566	China, ivory, 20C	35-40
567	Africa, ivory, hand carved, 20C	40-50
568	Africa, ivory, hand carved, 20C	40-50
569	France, ivory, gold band, 19C	150-175
570	USA, ivory, JVH, 20C	60-65
571	USA, ivory w/stones, JVH	50-75
572	USA, ivory w/stones, JVH	50-75
573	USA, ivory w/stones, JVH	50-75
574	USA, ivory w/stones, JVH	50-75
575	USA, ivory w/stones, JVH	50-75
576	USA, ivory w/stones, JVH	50-75
577	USA, ivory w/stones, JVH	50-75
578	USA, ivory w/stones, JVH	50-75
579	USA, ivory w/stones, JVH	50-75
580	USA, ivory w/stones, JVH	50-75
581	USA, ivory w/stones, JVH	50-75
582	USA, ivory w/stones, JVH	50-75
583	USA, ivory w/stones, JVH	50-75
584	USA, ivory w/stones, JVH	50-75
585	USA, ivory w/stones, JVH	50-75
586	USA, ivory w/stones, JVH	50-75
587	USA, ivory w/stones, JVH	50-75
588	USA, ivory w/stones, JVH	50-75
589	USA, ivory w/stones, JVH	50-75
590	USA, ivory w/stones, JVH	50-75
591	USA, ivory w/stones, JVH	50-75
592	USA, ivory w/stones, JVH	50-75
593	USA, ivory w/stones, JVH	50-75
594	USA, ivory w/stones, JVH	50-75
595	USA, ivory w/stones, JVH	50-75
596	USA, ironstone, JVH, 20C	12-15
597	USA, ironstone, JVH, 20C	12-15
598	USA, ironstone, JVH, 20C	12-15
599	USA, ironstone, JVH, 20C	12-15
600	USA, ironstone, JVH, 20C	12-15
601	USA, ironstone, JVH, 20C	12-15
602	USA, ironstone, JVH, 20C	12-15
603	USA, ironstone, JVH, 20C	12-15
604	USA, ironstone, JVH, 20C	12-15
605	USA, ironstone, JVH, 20C	12-15
606	USA, ironstone, JVH, 20C	12-15
607	USA, ironstone, JVH, 20C	12-15
608	USA, ironstone, JVH, 20C	12-15
609	USA, ironstone, JVH, 20C	12-15
610	USA, ironstone, JVH, 20C	12-15
611	USA, ironstone, JVH, 20C	12-15
612	USA, ironstone, JVH, 20C	12-15
613	USA, ironstone, JVH, 20C	12-15
614	USA, ironstone, JVH, 20C	12-15
615	USA, ironstone, JVH, 20C	12-15
616	USA, ironstone, JVH, 20C	12-15
617	USA, ironstone, JVH, 20C	12-15
618	USA, ironstone, JVH, 20C	12-15
619	USA, ironstone, JVH, 20C	12-15
620	USA, ironstone, JVH, 20C	12-15
621	USA, ironstone, JVH, 20C	12-15
622	USA, ironstone, JVH, 20C	12-15
623	USA, ironstone, JVH, 20C	12-15
624	USA, ironstone, JVH, 20C	12-15
625	USA, ironstone, JVH, 20C	12-15
626	USA, ironstone, JVH, 20C	12-15
627	USA, ironstone, JVH, 20C	12-15
628	GER, SIL, Gabler, 19C	60-75
629	GER, SIL, Gabler, 19C	40-50
630	GER, SIL, Gabler, 19C	60-75
631	USA, SS, KMD, 20C	60-70
632	USA, SS, KMD, 20C	60-70
633	USA, SS, KMD, 20C	45-55
634	USA, SS, KMD, 20C	25-35
635	USA, SS, KMD, 20C	40-45
636	USA, SS, KMD, gold band, 20C	45-60
637	USA, SS, KMD, embroidery 20C	45-50
638	USA, SS, KMD, 20C	20-25
639	USA, SS, KMD, Greek Key, 20C	20-25
640	USA, SS, KMD, 20C	18-22
641	USA, SS, KMD, 20C	18-22
642	USA, SS, KMD, 20C	45-50
643	USA, SS, KMD, 20C	20-25
644	USA, SS, KMD, 20C	20-25
645	USA, SS, KMD, 20C	18-22
646	USA, SS, KMD, 20C	15-18
647	USA, ceramic, lava glaze, 20C	10-12
648	India, leather, HP, 20C	10-12
649	USA, SS, Simons, Lib. Bell 1976	45-55
650	USA, SS, HC, 19C	18-22
651	France, SIL, Lanain, 19C	60-75
652	France, SIL, Lanain, 20C	45-55
653	France, SIL, Lanain, 20C	45-55
654	France, SIL, floral motif	45-55
655	USA, SS, KMD, Salem witch	300-325
656	GER, SIL, Lott Stutzel	45-55
657	USA, SS, KMD, 19C	45-50
658	GER, PORC, Meissen, 18C	4000+
659	GER, PORC, Meissen, 18C	4000+
660	GER, PORC, Meissen, 18C	4000+
661	GER, PORC, Meissen, 18C	4000+
662	GER, PORC, Meissen, 18C	4000+
663	GER, PORC, Meissen, 19C	1200+
664	USA, SS, KMD, 19C	45-50
665	Turkey, Meerschaum, brass top	30-35

666 GER, PORC, Meissen, 20C 125-135
667 GER, PORC, Meissen, 20C 115-125
668 GER, PROC, Meissen, 18C ..... 4000+
669 GER, PROC, Meissen, 18C ..... 4000+
670 GER, PROC, Meissen, 18C ..... 4000+
671 GER, PROC, Meissen, 18C ..... 4000+
672 GER, PROC, Meissen, 18C ..... 4000+
673 GER, PROC, Meissen, 18C ..... 4000+
674 USA, SS, Muhr, 19C 25-30
675 USA, SS, Muhr, 19C 25-30
676 USA, SS, Muhr, 19C 35-40
677 USA, SS, Muhr, 19C 25-30
678 USA, SIL/brass, Simons
   displayer 250-300
679 Iraq, SIL, Niello, 20C 60-75
680 MEX, SIL, Niello, 20C 20-25
681 Iran, SIL, Niello, HC, 19C 50-60
682 Russian, SIL, HC, Niello, 19C .. 200-250
683 Norway, SIL, enamel
   w/moonstone 100-125
684 Norway, SIL, enameled 85-100
685 GER, SIL, enameled 50-60
686 Norway, SIL, enamel
   w/moonstone 75-95
687 Norway, SIL, enamel
   w/moonstone 60-75
688 Norway, SIL, enamel
   w/moonstone 125-150
689 Norway, SIL, enamel
   w/moonstone 150-175
690 Norway, SIL, enamel
   w/moonstone 100-125
691 Norway, SIL, enamel
   w/moonstone 85-100
692 USA, pewter, Gish, 20C 12-15
693 USA, pewter, Gish, 20C 12-15
694 USA, pewter, Gish, 20C 12-15
695 USA, pewter, Gish, 20C 12-15
696 USA, pewter, Gish, 20C 12-15
697 USA, pewter, Gish, 20C 12-15
698 USA, pewter, Gish, 20C 12-15
699 USA, pewter, Gish, 20C 12-15
700 USA, pewter, Gish, 20C 12-15
701 USA, pewter, Gish, 20C 12-15
702 USA, pewter, Gish, 20C 12-15
703 GER, brass, clover mark, 16C .. 100-125
704 GER, brass, latch mark, 16C ... 200-250
705 GER, brass, latch mark, 16C ... 150-175
706 GER, brass, latch mark, 16C ... 200-225
707 GER, brass, latch mark, 16C ... 200-225
708 GER, brass, latch mark, 16C ... 200-225
709 GER, brass, Nuremberg, 16C... 200-225
710 GB, steel, OA&S, 19C 12-15
711 USA, SS, tailor's, 19C 30-35
712 USA, SS, Simons 100-125
713 USA, Oreide, SBC, 20C 15-20
714 India, papier maché, HP, 20C 10-12
715 GB, SS/steel, Dorcas, 19C 25-35
716 GB, CN, peephole, 20C 12-15
717 GB brass, peephole, 20C 12-15
718 USA, SS, H. Muhr 25-35
719 USA, SS, Muhr, 19C 25-35
720 USA, SS, Muhr, 19C 25-35
721 USA, brass, J. Muhr, 19C 25-35
722 USA, SS, GS, 19C 30-35
723 USA, SS, Muhr, 19C 35-45
724 USA, SS, Simons, 20C 35-45
725 USA, SS, G&S, 20C 35-45
726 USA, SS, Simons, 20C 20-30
727 USA, SS, Simons, 19C 30-35
728 USA, SS, Simons, 20C 20-25
729 USA, SS, WT, 20C 20-25
730 USA, SS, Simons, 20C 20-25
731 USA, SS, KMD, 20C 20-25
732 USA, SS, GS, 19C 35-40
733 USA, SS, GS, 20C 20-25
734 USA, SIL, Peters, 19C 150-175
735 Pewter, 20C 8-12
736 Pewter, 20C 8-12
737 Pewter, 20C 8-12
738 Pewter, 20C 8-12
739 Pewter, 20C 8-12
740 Pewter, 20C 8-12
741 Pewter, 20C 8-12
742 Pewter, 20C 8-12
743 Pewter, 20C 8-12
744 Pewter, 20C 8-12
745 Pewter, 20C 8-12
746 Pewter, 20C 8-12
747 Pewter, 20C 8-12
748 Pewter, 20C 8-12
749 Pewter, 20C 8-12
750 Pewter, 20C 8-12
751 Pewter, 20C 8-12
752 Pewter, 20C 8-12
753 Pewter, 20C 8-12
754 Pewter, 20C 8-12
755 USA, plastic, personals, 20C ...... -0-
756 USA, plastic, personals, 20C ...... -0-
757 USA, plastic, personals, 20C ...... -0-
758 USA, plastic, personals, 20C ...... -0-
759 USA, plastic, personals, 20C ...... -0-
760 Pewter, 20C 8-12
761 Pewter, 20C 8-12
762 Pewter, 20C 8-12
763 Pewter, 20C 8-12
764 Pewter, 20C 8-12
765 Pewter, 20C 8-12
766 Pewter, 20C 8-12
767 Pewter, 20C 8-12
768 Pewter, 20C 8-12
769 Pewter, 20C 8-12
770 Pewter, 20C 8-12
771 Pewter, 20C 8-12
772 Pewter, 20C 8-12
773 Pewter, 20C 8-12
774 Pewter, 20C 8-12
775 Pewter, 20C 8-12

776 Pewter, 20C 8-12
777 Pewter, 20C 8-12
778 Pewter, 20C 8-12
779 Pewter, 20C 8-12
780 Austria, brass, petit-point, 20C 5-7
781 Austria, brass, petit-point 8-10
782 GER, SIL-gilt, Pforzheimm, 20C . . 35-45
783 USA, SS, SU, 20C 40-45
784 USA, ivory, SIL, band, JVH . . . 150-175
785 USA, SS, Simons 100-125
786 USA, ivory, TURQ, JVH 35-45
787 USA, ivory, gold rim, emeralds,
    JVH 150-175
788 GB, SS, Atlantic cable, 19C 60-75
789 USA, SS, Simons, pierced 100-125
790 GB, SS, HM:CH 100-125
791 USA, SIL-gilt, Simons, repro, 20C . 35-40
792 GB, TS, gold pique, 19C 150-175
793 ?, brass/w steel top, 18C 35-40
794 GER, iron, enameled, AM,
    1944 150-175
795 USA, SS, L, Doskow, 20C 40-45
796 Austria, ALUM, God Damn
    England 12-15
797 Austria, ALUM, God Damn Italy . . 12-15
798 Austria, ALUM, Durch, Kampf 12-15
799 Austria, ALUM, Heil & Sieg 12-15
800 GB, BC, Adams, FD, 20C 15-18
801 Italy, PORC, Agostinelli, FD, 20C . . . 5-8
802 GB, BC, Ashleydale, FD, 20C 8-10
803 USA, PORC, Avon, FD, 20C 5-7
804 GB, BC Highland, FD, 20C 12-15
805 GER, Bareuther-Waldsassen, 20C . . . 6-8
806 USA, BC, BEL, FD, 20C 6-8
807 France, PORC, Bernardaud, FD,
    20C 8-10
808 Denmark, PORC, Bing & Grondahl,
    HP 20-25
809 GB, BC, Birchcraft, FD, 20C 5-7
810 Canada, BC, Canadian Classic, FD . . 6-8
811 Canada, BC, Canadian Superior,
    FD 6-8
812 GB, BC, Caverswall, FD, 20C 6-8
813 MEX, PORC, Ceramic Artistica,
    20C 7-9
814 GB, BC, Coldport, 20C 15-18
815 USA, PORC, Coral, HP, 20C 15-18
816 GB, BC, Countess, FD, 20C 6-8
817 GB, BC, Crown Staffs, FD, 20C . . 10-12
818 USA, PORC, Delorea, HP, 20C . . 15-18
819 GB, BC, Fenton, FD, 20C 5-7
820 GB, BC, Finsbury, FD, 20C 7-9
821 USA, ceramic, Franciscan, HP,
    20C 12-15
822 USA, PORC, Franklin, FD, 20C . . 12-15
823 Japan, PORC, Fukagawa, 20C 8-10
824 Italy, PORC, Ginori, FD, 20C 12-15
825 GB, BC, Golden Crown, FD, 20C . 10-12
826 USA, BC, Gorham, FD, 20C 15-18
827 USA, PORC, Gridley, 20C 10-12
828 GB, BC, Goebel, FD, 20C 7-10
829 GER, PORC, Goebel, FD, 20C 7-10
830 GB, BC, Hammersley, FD, 20C . . . 12-15
831 France, PORC, Haviland, FD,
    20C 10-12
832 GB, BC, Nealacraft, HP, 20C 18-20
833 USA, PORC, Heirloom, HP, 20C . 12-15
834 Hungary, PORC, Herend, HP,
    20C 15-18
835 Hungary, PORC, Hollohaza, FD,
    20C 12-15
836 USA PORC, Hurley, HP, 20C 15-18
837 GER, PORC, Hutschenreuther, FD 10-12
838 Ireland, PORC, Irish Dresden, 20C 12-15
839 GB, ironstone, Johnson Bros, FD . 12-15
840 GER, PORC, Kaiser, FD, 20C 5-7
841 Japan, PORC, Knobler, FD, 20C . . . 5-7
842 GER, PORC, Lindner, FD, 20C . . 10-12
843 Spain, Parian, Lladro, 20C 18-20
844 GB, BC, Lord Nelson, FD 10-12
845 GB, BC, Lysander, FD, 20C 10-12
846 Japan, PORC, Maruri, FD, 20C . . 10-12
847 GB, ironstone, Masons, FD, 20C . . 12-15
848 GER, PORC, Meissen, HP, 20C 115-135
849 Holland, PORC, Mosa, 20C 15-18
850 GB, BC, Newhall, FD, 20C 12-15
851 Japan, PORC, Noritaki, 20C 20-25
852 Japan, PORC, Okura, FD, 20C . . 15-18
853 GB, BC, Palissy, FD, 20C 8-10
854 Norway, PORC, Porsgund, 20C . . 20-25
855 GB, BC, Queen, FD, 20C 8-10
856 GER, PORC, Reutter, FD, 20C 5-7
857 MEX, PORC, Roman, HP, 20C . . 10-12
858 Sweden, PORC, Rostrand, FD,
    20C 20-22
859 GB, BC, Royal Adderley, FD, 20C 15-18
860 GB, BC, Royal Albert, FD, 20C . . 15-18
861 Denmark, PORC, Royal Copen . . . 18-20
862 GB, BC, Royal Doulton, FD, 20C . 15-18
863 Ireland, BC, Royal Tara, FD, 20C . 15-18
864 GB, BC, Royal Worcester, 20C . . . 18-22
865 GB, BC, St. George, FD, 20C 8-10
866 GB, ceramic, Staffordshire, FD 5-7
867 GB, BC, Sutherland, FD, 20C 10-12
868 GB, BC, Spode, FD, 20C 15-18
869 GB, BC, Theo-Paul, FD, 20C 6-8
870 Portugal, PORC, Vista Allegre, FD . 20-25
871 GB, PORC, Wedgwood, Wht on
    lilac 25-30
872 New Zeland, BC, Wht, Heron, FD . 12-15
873 USA, PORC w/rubies, 20C 25-35
874 GB, BC, Royal Worcester, HP,
    20C 40-50
875 GB, BC, North Lodge, 20C 8-10
876 GB, BC, Ottignons, HP, 20C 20-25
877 Ireland, PORC, Belleek, 20C 20-25
878 Denmark, PORC, B&G, HP, 20C . 20-25
879 USA, PORC, HP, Knoettner, 20C . 10-12

880	USA, PORC, HP, Thome, 20C	8-10
881	USA, PORC, HP, B. Kinch, 20C	10-12
882	USA, PORC, HP, Knoettner, 20C	10-12
883	USA, PORC, HP, Stines, 20C	8-10
884	USA, PORC, HP, Roba, 20C	8-10
885	USA, PORC, HP, C. Stines, 20C	8-10
886	USA, PORC, HP, JK, 20C	6-7
887	USA, PORC, HP, M. Stines, 20C	8-10
888	USA, PORC, HP, Knoettner, 20C	10-12
889	USA, PORC, HP, JK, 20C	6-7
890	USA, PORC, HP, Knoettner, 20C	10-12
891	USA, PORC, HP, J. Geertz, 10C	8-10
892	USA, PORC, HP, Teri, 20C	6-8
893	USA, PORC, HP, Nickland, 20C	6-8
894	USA, PORC, HP, Lynn, 20C	10-12
895	Portugal, SIL-plate, 20C	5-7
896	Portugal, SIL-plate, 20C	5-7
897	Portugal, SIL-plate, 20C	5-7
898	Portugal, SIL-plate, 20C	5-7
899	Portugal, SIL-plate, 20C	5-7
901	Portugal, SIL-plate, 20C	5-7
902	Portugal, SIL-plate, 20C	5-7
903	Portugal, SIL-plate, 20C	5-7
904	Portugal, SIL-plate, 20C	5-7
905	Portugal, SIL-plate, 20C	5-7
906	Portugal, SIL-plate, 20C	5-7
907	Portugal, SIL-gilt, filigree, 20C	18-20
908	Portugal, SIL-gilt, filigree, 20C	25-35
909	Portugal, SIL-gilt, filigree, 20C	15-20
910	USA, SS, Simons, Priscilla	18-22
911	USA, brass, Scovill, Prudential	2-4
912	France, SIL, Prudhomme	35-40
913	France, SIL, Prudhomme	35-40
914	Pseudo, thimbles	10-12
915	Pseudo, thimbles	10-12
916	Psuedo, thimbles	10-12
917	GB, pewter, Lord's Prayer	10-12
918	USA, pewter, Lord's Prayer	10-12
919	USA, pewter, 23rd Psalm	10-12
920	USA, pewter, 10 COM.	10-12
921	GER, SIL, removable top	400-450
922	Portugal, SIL-plate	5-7
923	Brazil, SS	30-35
924	Portugal, SIL-plate	5-7
925	Italy, gold, Athena, 18C	800-900
926	Portugal, brass	3-4
927	Portugal, brass	3-4
928	Siam, SIL, Buddha	30-40
929	GB, SS, St. Peter's	40-45
930	GER, alum, Mary	10-12
931	France, SIL, Madonna	50-60
932	GER, SIL, Madonna	50-60
933	Israel, 22, "Ruth"	35-40
934	USA, SS, FM	35-40
935	France, SIL, Joan D'Arc	45-50
936	Ireland, SS, HM, St. Brennon, 20C	35-45
937	Spain, SS, AM, Santiago, 20C	45-55
938	GB, SS, L. Redl, 20C	65-75
939	GB, SS, L. Redl, 20C	65-75
940	GB, SS, L. Redl, 20C	65-75
941	GB, SS, L. Redl, 20C	65-75
942	GB, SS, L. Redl, 20C	65-75
943	USA, plastic, red top, 20C	2-4
944	USA, plastic, red top, 20C	2-4
945	USA, "?", AM, Reed & Barton	20-25
946	USA, gold, P. Revere, 19C	Rare
947	GB, SIL, Constantine, 1909	100-125
948	GB, SIL, Constantine, 1909	100-125
949	GB, PORC, R. Worcester, 19C	1200+
950	GB, PORC, R. Worcester, 19C	1200+
951	GB, PORC, R. Worcester, 19C	300-400
952	GB, PORC, R. Worcester, 19C	300-400
953	GB, PORC, R. Worcester, 20C	20-35
953	GB, PORC, R. Worcester, 20C	20-35
954	GB, PORC, R. Worcester, 20C	20-35
955	GB, PORC, R. Worcester, 20C	20-35
956	GB, PORC, R. Worcester, 20C	20-35
957	GB, PORC, R. Worcester, 20C	20-35
958	GB, PORC, R. Worcester, 20C	20-35
959	GB, PORC, R. Worcester, 20C	20-35
960	GB, PORC, R. Worcester, 20C	20-35
961	GB, PORC, R. Worcester, 20C	20-35
962	GB, PORC, R. Worcester, 20C	20-35
963	Russia, SIL, enameled, 19C	600-700
964	Russia, SIL, enameled, 19C	750-850
965	Russia, SIL, Niello, 19C	200-250
966	Russia, SIL, enameled, 19C	600-700
967	Russia, SIL, enameled, 19C	600-700
968	Russia, SIL, enameled, 19C	750-850
969	Russia, SIL, Niello, 19C	200-250
970	France, SIL, AM, 19C	45-55
971	India, SIL, ruby top, 19C	45-55
972	USA, gold, KMD, 20C	85-100
973	GB, SS, HM:EJC, 20C	35-40
974	USA, SS, HC, NM, 19C	35-40
975	USA, SS, Simons, 19C	50-60
976	USA, SS, Muhr, 19C	30-35
977	USA, SS, NM, 19C	35-40
978	USA, SS, NM, 19C	30-40
979	USA, SS, NM, 19C	30-40
980	USA, SS, Simons, 19C	30-40
981	USA, SS, NM, 19C	30-40
982	USA, SS, WT, 19C	35-45
983	USA, SS, NM, 19C	35-45
984	USA, SS, Sterns, 19C	40-50
985	USA, SS, Simons	30-40
986	USA, SS, Simons	30-40
987	GB, SIL, steel-top, HC, 18C	100-125
988	GB, SIL, steel-top, HC, 18C	100-125
989	GB, SIL, steel-top, HC, 18C	100-125
990	GB, SIL, steel-top, HC, 18C	100-125
991	USA, CN, Simons, SBC, 20C	3-6
992	USA, CN, Simons, SBC, 20C	3-6
993	USA, CN, Simons, SBC, 20C	3-6
994	USA, Oreide, Simons, SBC, 20C	15-20
995	Philippines, Shell, 20C	8-12
996	Philippines, lip shell, 20C	10-12

#	Description	Price
997	Philippines, blk coral, 20C	10-12
998	MEX, MOP, 20C	8-10
999	USA, SS, KMD, Hanging rim, 20C	175-200
1000	Korea, silk, 20C	5-7
1001	Korea, silk, 20C	6-8
1002	Korea, silk, 20C	5-7
1003	USA, SS, Simons, "Stitch," 20C	300-325
1004	USA, SS, Simons, "Spike," 20C	300-325
1005	USA, SS, Simons, 1892 Chicago	350-400
1006	USA, SS, Simons, gold band	40-50
1007	USA, SS, Simons, grapes	35-40
1008	USA, SS, Simons	45-60
1009	USA, SS, Simons, HC	25-35
1011	USA, SS, Simons, panelled	20-25
1012	USA, SS, Simons, grapes & leaves	75-90
1013	USA, SS, Simons, love birds	30-40
1014	USA, SS, Simons, chased scene	35-45
1015	USA, SS, HC	18-22
1016	USA, SS, Stitch-in-Time	300-325
1017	USA, SS, Simons, Chicago World's Fair	350-400
1018	USA, SS, Simons, Cherubs & Garlands	100-125
1019	USA, SS, Simons, scenic	30-40
1020	USA, SS, Simons, gold band	45-55
1021	USA, SS, Simons, die stamped	25-35
1022	USA, SS, Simons, California thimble	25-30
1023	USA, SS, Simons, gold band	45-50
1024	USA, SS, Simons, chased band	20-25
1025	USA, SS, Simons, panelled	35-40
1026	USA, SS, Simons, egg & dart rim	15-20
1027	USA, SS, Simons, circled florals	25-30
1028	USA, SS, Simons, Liberty Bell 1976	45-55
1029	USA, SS, Simons, Walls of Troy	15-20
1030	USA, SS, Simons, HC	20-25
1031	USA, SS, Simons, egg & dart	15-20
1032	USA, SS, Simons, Priscilla	20-25
1033	USA, SS, Simons, Rose	15-20
1034	USA, SS, Simons, leaf design	20-25
1035	USA, SS, Simons, scenic	35-50
1036	USA, SS, Simons, panel	20-25
1037	USA, SS, Simons, panel	40-50
1038	USA, SS, Simons, golden spike	300-325
1039	USA, SS, Simons, DAR thimble	30-35
1040	USA, SS, Simons, embroidery	40-50
1041	USA, SS, Simons, diamond pattern	25-30
1042	USA, SS, Simons, geometrics	20-25
1043	USA, SS, Simons, flowers & diamonds	18-22
1044	USA, SS, Simons, embossed flowers	35-40
1045	USA, SS, Simons, die stamped	20-25
1046	USA, SS, Simons, HC	18-25
1047	USA, SS, Simons, enameled band	60-75
1048	USA, SS, Simons, HC	18-25
1049	USA, SS, Simons, pierced band	100-125
1050	USA, SS, Simons, large ovals	50-65
1051	Peru, SIL, Indian, 20C	35-40
1052	Peru, SIL, Indian, 20C	35-40
1053	Peru, SIL, Indian, 20C	35-40
1054	Argentina, SIL, HC, 20C	35-40
1055	Argentina, SIL, stone, 20C	40-45
1056	Argentina, SIL, stone, 20C	40-45
1057	Argentina, SIL, 19C	60-75
1058	Argentina, SIL, 20C	40-45
1059	Argentina, SIL, 20C	30-35
1060	Argentina, SIL, 20C	30-35
1061	South Amer, SIL, 20C	25-30
1062	South Amer, SIL, 20C	25-30
1063	Argentina, SIL, 20C	25-30
1064	Argentina, SIL, 20C	25-30
1065	South Amer, SIL, 20C	10-15
1066	Paraguay, silk, Bicho-Canasto	-0-
1067	GB, enameled brass, 18C	750-850
1068	GB, enameled brass, 18C	750-850
1069	GB, enameled brass, 18C	750-850
1070	GB, enameled brass, 18C	500-600
1071	GB, enameled brass, 18C	400-500
1072	GB, enameled brass, 18C	500-600
1073	GB, enameled brass, 18C	400-500
1074	GB, enameled brass, 18C	100-125
1075	GB, enameled brass, 18C	400-500
1076	USA, ALUM, steel pier, 20C	3-5
1077	?, nickel-plated brass, 20C	4-5
1078	GER, SIL-plate, AM, 20C	7-9
1079	?, nickel-plated brass, AM, 20C	3-5
1080	?, pewter, AM, 20C	3-5
1081	USA, SS, Simons, 20C	300-325
1082	USA, spun PORC, F. Gridley, 20C	15-18
1083	USA, SS w/steel top, BH, 18C	100-125
1084	GB, SS w/agate top, JS&S, 20C	35-45
1085	USA, SS	35-45
1086	USA, SS	35-45
1087	USA, SS, Sterns, 19C	35-45
1088	USA, marble, JVH, gold band	30-35
1089	USA, marble, JVH	20-25
1090	USA, gold, KMD	85-100
1091	GB, ALUM, Laughton	8-12
1092	India, stone, unique	25-40
1093	India, stone, unique	25-40
1094	India, stone, unique	25-40
1095	India, stone, unique	25-40
1096	India, stone, unique	25-40
1097	India, stone, unique	25-40
1098	India, stone, unique	25-40
1099	India, stone, unique	25-40
1100	India, stone, unique	25-40
1101	India, stone, unique	25-40
1102	India, stone, unique	25-40
1103	India, stone, unique	25-40
1104	India, stone, unique	25-40
1105	India, stone, unique	25-40
1106	India, stone, unique	25-40

#	Description	Price
1107	India, stone, unique	25-40
1108	GB, SS, HM:JS&S, 20C	35-45
1109	GB, SS, HM:JS&S, 20C	30-35
1110	GB, SS, HM:JS&S, 20C	30-35
1111	GB, SS, HM:JS&S, 20C	30-35
1112	GB, PORC, Sutherland, 20C	10-12
1113	GB, PORC, Sutherland, 20C	10-12
1114	GB, PORC, Sutherland, 20C	10-12
1115	GB, PORC, Sutherland, 20C	10-12
1116	South Amer, Tagua nut, 20C	2-3
1117	USA, SS, tailor's, 19C	15-18
1118	USA, brass, 19C	20-25
1119	USA, SS, w/gold band	35-50
1120	USA, coin SIL, 19C	20-25
1121	USA, SS, Simons, "Dorcas"	40-45
1122	USA, SS, Simons, NTC	60-75
1123	USA, SS, JVH, BATS	45-50
1124	USA, SS, Simons, PTS	25-30
1125	USA, SS, BATS	25-30
1126	Spain, brass, Toledo, 20C	3-5
1127	GB, SIL, Dover Castle, 19C	300-350
1128	GER, Tombac, glass top, 20C	10-12
1129	Italy, glass, gold ribbons, 20C	40-50
1130	USA, gold w/Neillo, Tiffany, 19C	200-250
1131	GB, TS w/gold pique, 19C	300-350
1132	GB, TS w/gold, Pierey's PAT, 19C	1200+
1133	China, TS, hand carved, 19C	220-250
1134	Brazil, gold on blk wood, 20C	150-200
1135	GB, wood, Tunbridge, 19C	100-125
1136	GB, wood, Tunbridge, 19C	100-125
1137	USA, SS, SU, 20C	30-35
1138	USA, SS, SU, 20C	30-35
1139	USA, SS, SU, 20C	30-35
1140	USA, SS, SU, 20C	30-35
1141	GB, V. ivory, 19C	30-35
1142	USA, V. ivory, JVH, 20C	30-35
1143	GB, V. ivory, 19C	50-60
1144	GB, V. ivory, 19C	40-50
1145	USA, V. ivory, JVH, 20C	30-35
1146	Italy, glass, Latticino, 20C	40-50
1147	France, SIL-gilt, 20C	18-22
1148	Portugal, PORC, Vista Alegre	20-25
1149	USA, SS, Webster	25-30
1150	GER, iron, Von der Becke	300-350
1151	USA, SS, WT	35-45
1152	USA, SS, WT	35-45
1153	USA, SS, WT	25-30
1154	USA, SS, WT	25-30
1155	USA, SS, WT	20-25
1156	USA, SS, WT	35-40
1157	USA, SS, WT	25-30
1158	USA, SS, WT	30-35
1159	USA, SS, WT	25-30
1160	GB, PORC, Wedgwood	10-15
1161	GB, PORC, Wedgwood	10-15
1162	GB, PORC, Wedgwood	10-15
1163	GB, PORC, Wedgwood	10-15
1164	GB, PORC, Wedgwood	10-15
1165	USA, ALUM, whistle	25-30
1166	France, wood, 19C	200-250
1167	France, wood, steel studs, 19C	300-350
1168	France, wood, gold rim, 19C	350-400
1169	India, wood w/brass, 20C	8-10
1170	USA, wood, Braatz, 20C	12-15
1171	GB, wood stick-ware, 20C	8-10
1172	India, wood, HP, 20C	3-5
1173	GB, wood, lathe, 20C	8-10
1174	USA, wood, Carradus, 20C	8-10
1175	USA, wood, Fisher, 20C	12-15
1176	France, wood, 20C	10-12
1177	USA, corncob w/brass top	3-4
1178	India, bamboo, HP, 20C	5-6
1179	Hungary, wood, carved, 20C	7-8
1180	India, bamboo, HP, 20C	5-6
1181	USA, wood, Ozarks, 20C	1-2
1182	Israel, SS, Yemini, 20C	25-35
1183	Israel, SS, Yemini, 20C	25-35
1184	Israel, SS, Yemini, 20C	25-35
1185	GER, zinc, Gabler 1943	25-30
1186	Iraq, SIL, Niello, 20C	100-125
1187	Iraq, SIL, Niello, 20C	100-125
1188	Russian, SIL, Niello, 19C	400-450
1189	Iraq, SIL, Niello, 20C	100-125
1190	Turkey, SIL, Niello, 19C	65-80
1191	Turkey, SIL, Niello, 19C	65-80
1192	Turkey, SIL, Niello, 19C	65-80
1193	Egypt, SIL, Vienna, 19C	100-125
1194	Egypt, SIL, Vienna, 19C	100-125
1195	Egypt, SIL, Vienna, 19C	100-125
1196	Spain, Brass enameled	5-7
1197	Spain, SS, applied band, HC	35-50
1198	Spain, SS, yellow enamel band	35-45
1199	Spain, brass love birds	5-7
1200	Spain, SS, applied shell, HC	35-45
1201	Spain, SS, AM, gold ducks	40-50
1202	Spain, SS, applied shell & band	35-45
1203	Spain, SS, applied shell enameled	35-45
1204	Spain, SS, yellow enamel band	35-45
1205	Spain, SS, HC band	35-45
1206	Spain, SS, HC band	35-45
1207	Spain, SS, HC band	35-45
1208	Spain, SS, red enameled cross	40-50
1209	Spain, SS, red enameled cross	40-50
1210	Spain, SS, red enameled cross	40-50
1211	Spain, SS, red enameled cross	40-50
1212	Spain, SS, HC band	30-35
1213	Spain, SS, HC band, red stones	35-40
1214	Spain, SS, HC band, stone top	35-50
1215	Spain, SS, HC band, TURQ	40-45
1216	England, SS, JS, leaves & flowers	60-75
1217	USA, SS, Stern Bro.	25-35
1218	USA, SS, Simons, arrow motif	45-55
1219	USA, SS, Untermeyer-Robbins Co.	30-40
1220	USA, SS, Goldsmith-Stern, HC	35-50
1221	GER, 800S, Gabler, Amethyst	45-55
1222	English, SS w/gold letters	50-75

#	Description	Price
1223	USA, SS, Lachine rapids-Montreal	80-100
1224	England, SS, SF, finger shaped	45-55
1225	England, SS, C. Horner, HM, HC	45-60
1226	USA, SS, Simons scenic (poor)	10-15
1227	USA, SS, Simons scenic (exc)	25-45
1228	England, SS, HG&S, HC	40-55
1229	England, SS, Royal Spa, HG&S	35-45
1230	GER, 800S, Gabler, filigree	125-150
1231	USA, SS, Simons	25-35
1232	England, SS, HG&S, HC	60-75
1233	USA, Simons, fleur-de-lis	35-40
1234	USA, KMD, 3 cherubs	150-175
1235	GER, 800S, Gabler, amethyst	50-65
1236	USA, SS, GS, 22 cherubs	45-60
1237	USA, coin silver, AL&CO	20-25
1238	Persia, SS, HC	20-30
1239	GER, 800S, Gabler enameled	35-50
1240	Navajo Indian, SS, HC	20-25
1241	USA, SS, KMD, "Salem Witch"	200-250
1242	USA, SS, Webster, "Salem Witch"	200-250
1243	USA, SS, Chalmers' pearls	20-25
1244	GER, SS, Gabler, amethyst	35-50
1245	Unknown, SS, Topaz top	50-65
1246	USA, SS, Simons "Atlantic City"	45-55
1247	USA, SS, Simons enameled	40-50
1248	Unknown, SS, NM	50-60
1249	India, SS, NM, 19C	100-125
1250	India SS, HC, NM, 19C	100-125
1251	Persia, SS, HC, NM, 19C	85-100
1252	English, gold, HM, pearls/TURQ	225-250
1253	France, gold w/TURQ, 19C	250-300
1254	English, gold w/8 TURQ, NM	200-250
1255	English, gold, HC, NM, 19C	250-300
1256	France, SS, 19C	75-90
1257	France, gold, 12 gems	300-350
1258	India, SS, HC, NM	100-125
1259	USA, SS	100-125
1260	English, SS, Birmingham, filigree	400-450
1261	Unknown IRON w/gold motifs	130-150
1262	GER, SS, Cornelian top	60-75
1263	English, SS, thistle, HM, JS&S	40-50
1264	GER-Spain, steel, gold inlay, Gabler	150-175
1265	England, SS, Wellington 1852	400-450
1266	England, SS, HM, JF, moss agate	60-75
1267	Swedish, SS, amethyst top	45-55
1268	USA, SS, Muhr, HC	35-40
1269	Java, 800 SIL, HC, 20C	30-40
1270	Iran, SS, gold inlay	50-60
1271	Iran, SS, HC	20-25
1272	Austria, 800, Niello	35-40
1273	USA, SS, Simons, farm	35-45
1274	England, S. TURQ/gold	175-200
1275	Greek, 800, cast	12-15
1276	GER, 800, 4 hens	30-40
1277	USA, Oreide, Simons, SBC	15-20
1278	GER, 800, redstone top	35-45
1279	GER, amber	30-45
1280	GB, brass, Bilston, HP, 18C	1200+
1281	Persia, enameled gold, HP, 19C	1200+
1282	GB, brass, Bilston, HP, 18C	1200+
1283	GB, brass, Bilston, HP, 18C	1000+
1284	GB, brass, Bilston, HP, 18C (poor)	100-125
1285	GB, brass, Bilston, HP, 18C	1000+
1286	GB, brass, Bilston, HP, 18C	1200+
1287	Persia, enameled gold, HP, 19C	1500+
1288	USA, enameled gold, HP, 19C	250-300
1289	GER, gold, Gabler, 19C	200-250
1290	France, gold, HC, 19C	250-300
1291	China, gold, HC, 19C	250-300
1292	France, gold, 18 Lapis pearls, 19C	300-350
1293	GB, gold, Lapis & pearls, 19C	400-450
1294	GB, gold, pearls, 19C	350-400
1295	GB, gold, Coral & pearls, 19C	350-400
1296	GB, gold, 21 pearls, 19C	700-750
1297	GB, gold, rubies & pearls	600-650
1298	GB, gold, pearls & coral, 19C	350-400
1299	GB, gold, 15 TURQ, 19C	350-400
1300	GB, gold, 15 TURQ, 19C	350-400
1301	?, gold, diamonds & enamel, 19C	450-500
1302	?, gold, 30 diamonds, 4 pearls, 19C	2500+
1303	GER, gold, sapphires & diamonds, 19C	750-850
1304	GB, gold, diamonds & rubies, 19C	450-500
1305	GB, gold, HC, rubies, 19C	450-500
1306	GB, gold, 80 TURQ, 19C	350-400
1307	Persia, gold, filigree, 18C	1200+
1308	GB, gold, HC, NM, 19C	300-350
1309	GB, gold, 8 TURQ, NM, 19C	250-300
1310	France, gold, 12 TURQ, 19C	350-400
1311	USA, gold, 5 rubies, NM, 19C	400-450
1312	USA, gold, 5 diamonds, 19C	500-550
1313	USA, gold, 14 rubies, 19C	400-450
1314	France, gold, HC, 19C	250-300
1315	GB, gold NM, 19C	200-250
1316	?, gold, NM, 19C	175-200
1317	GB, gold, Victoria & Albert, 19C	1000+
1318	GB, gold, 4 TURQ, NM, 19C	300-350
1319	So. Amer, gold, HC, 20C	150-200
1320	Russia, gilt, enameled, 19C	700-800
1321	France, gold, 12 gems, 19C	400-500
1322	France, mult. gold, applied, 19C	400-500
1323	USA, gold, jade, JVH, 20C	200-250
1324	GB, gold, 6 rubies, HM, 20C	400-450
1325	USA, gold, Simons, rubies & emeralds	250-300
1326	USA, gold, 3 roses, JVH, 20C	200-250
1327	India, gold, HC, 19C	450-500
1328	Italy, gold, marked GM, 18C	800-900
1329	Italy, gold, marked GM, 18C	800-900

1330 France, 2-tone gold, 18C 600-700
1331 France, gold, 17 pearls, 19C ... 400-500
1332 USA, gold, 6 rubies, JVH, 20C . 200-250
1333 GB, enameled, Bilston, HP, 18C . 1200+
1334 Poland, gold, lapis & pearls,
  19C 600-750
1335 USA, gold, KMD, 19C 150-175
1336 USA, gold, diamond, KMD,
  19C 350-400
1337 Persia, gold filigree, 18C .... 1200+
1338 USA, gold, Tiffany, enamel,
  1870s 200-250
1339 GB, gold, TURQ & pearls, 19C 200-225
1340 GB, gold, applied motifs, 19C .. 275-300
1341 USA, gold, enameled, 19C 275-300
1342 GB, gold, HC, 19C 250-275
1343 GER, gold, stone-top, TURQ,
  19C 250-300
1344 GB, gold, 24 pearls, 19C 250-300
1345 GB, gold, 16 pearls, 19C 250-300
1346 GB, gold, pearls, 19C 200-225
1347 GB, gold, pearls & tiger eye,
  19C 250-300
1348 GB, gold, coral, 19C 250-270
1349 GB, gold, pearls & TURQ, 19C . 200-225
1350 GB, gold, coral, 19C 300-350
1351 GB, gold, TURQ, 19C 250-275
1352 GB, gold, TURQ, 19C 200-225
1353 GB, gold, TURQ, 19C 200-225
1354 GB, gold, TURQ, 19C 250-300
1355 USA, ivory, gold rim, JVH,
  gems 150-175
1356 USA, ivory, gold rim, JVH,
  gems 150-175
1357 USA, ivory, gold rim, JVH,
  coral 200-225
1358 USA, ivory, gold rim, JVH,
  gems 150-175
1359 USA, Ivory, gold band, emeralds,
  JVH 200-250
1360 USA, ivory, SIL, coral rose,
  JVH 200-225
1361 USA, ivory, gold rim, emeralds/
  opals, JVH 200-225
1362 USA, ivory, SIL rim, jade, JVH . 150-175
1363 USA, ivory, lapis/TURQ, JVH .. 100-125
1364 USA, ivory, gold rim, amethyst,
  JVH 200-250
1365 USA, ivory, pearls & coral,
  JVH 100-125
1366 USA, ivory, gold rim, gems,
  JVH 150-175
1367 Russia, gilt, enamel, HM, 19C .. 700-800
1368 Russia, SIL, Niello, 19C 150-200
1369 Russia, SIL, enamel, HM, 19C . 700-800
1370 Russia, SIL - gilt, enamel, HM,
  19C 700-800
1371 Russia, SIL - gilt, enamel, HM,
  19C 700-800

1372 USA, gold, KMD, blue enamel
  19C 225-250
1373 Russia, 84 SIL, enamel, HM,
  19C 700-800
1374 GER, iron/gold Damascene,
  Gabler 250-300
1375 Russia, SIL - gilt, 84, HM, 19C . 700-800
1376 China, TS, NM, 19C 200-250
1377 GB, TS & gold, Piercy's Patent,
  19C .... 1200+
1378 GB, TS & gold pique, 19C 300-350
1379 GB, SIL - gilt, filigree, 19C 500-600
1380 France, MOP, gold pansy, 19C . 400-500
1381 USA, gold, KMD, HP, 19C 250-300
1382 France, multi-gold, 19C 600-750
1383 France, multi-gold, 18C .... 1200+
1384 Sweden, gold, HC, 19C 200-250
1385 GB, SIL, 17C .... 1000+
1386 GER, SIL/enamel, 3 pc .... 1500+
1387 GB, SIL, 16C 800-950
1388 France, sandlewood, cut iron,
  19C 300-350
1389 GB, TS, gold pique, 19C 300-350
1390 France, sandlewood, gold rim,
  19C 300-350
1391 India, SIL, HC, 19C 250-300
1392 India, SIL, HC, 19C 300-350
1393 GB, SIL, filigree, 19C 700-800
1394 GB, gold, HC, 19C 200-250
1395 USA, gold, HC, 19C 250-275
1396 ?, gold, HC, 19C 300-350
1397 USA, gold, HC, 19C 200-225
1398 ?, gold, HC 200-250
1399 USA, gold, HC, 19C 200-225
1400 France, multi-gold, 19C 250-300
1401 France, multi-gold, steel-top 350-400
1402 GB, gold, HC, 19C 200-250
1403 USA, gold, enameled, 19C 250-300
1404 USA, gold, Niello, 19C 125-150
1405 USA, gold, enameled, NM, 19C 150-175
1406 USA, gold, blk enamel, NM,
  19C 200-250
1407 USA, gold, blk enamel, NM,
  19C 200-250
1408 USA, gold, blk enamel, NM,
  19C 200-250
1409 GB, gold blue/wht enamel, 19C 200-250
1410 France, gold, steel top, 19C 600-750
1411 GB, gold, enameled, 19C 700-800
1412 to 1438 — At recent international auctions, Meisen thimbles have been selling from $3,000 to 5,000 in U.S. dollars. Most Meissen thimbles with scenes were painted during the eighteenth century.
1439 England, enameled brass, 18C ... 1200+
1440 England, enameled brass, 18C .. 700-800
1441 ?, gold, 72 pearls, braided hair ... 1200+
1442 Persia, gold, HP, 18C .... 1200+
1443 English gold, multi-gold deco ... 250-300

1444 Persia gold filigree, 18C .... 1200+
1445 USA, gold, HP, 19C 200-250
1446 Unknown, gold, multi-gold deco 250-300
1447 Ireland bog oak, "Erin" 100-125
1448 Iran, SIL, HC 60-75
1449 Israel, SS, Neillo, Bethlehem 35-45
1450 Iran, Silver, HC 60-75
1451 USA, SS, Simons, HC 45-60
1452 USA, SS, Victoria & Albert 400-500
1453 USA, SS, KMD, bikers 150-175
1454 Unknown, SS, NM 60-75
1455 GER, 935S, green stone-top 35-50
1456 GER, SS, Gabler, blue flowers 75-90
1457 GER, SS, Gabler, HP, flowers 50-75
1458 GER, 800S, Gabler, HP, roses 50-75
1459 France, SS, NM, 18C 50-75
1460 France, SIL, Taillepied 1750-56 . 175-250
1461 France, Vermeil, ornate pattern ... 50-75
1462 France, Vermeil, gold flowers 60-75
1463 USA, 14K gold, HC 100-125
1464 USA, gold, HC 100-125
1465 USA, 14K gold, Simons, scenic . 100-125
1466 USA, 14K gold, Simons, scenic . 100-125
1467 USA, SS, Simons, waffles & swirls 60-75
1468 England, SS, JF, HM, HC 40-50
1469 USA, SS, KMD, applied motif 30-40
1470 England, SS, JS, diamond & floral 45-60
1471 Sweden, gold, stone-top, 19C .. 150-200
1472 Sweden, gold, stone-top, 19C .. 150-200
1473 Sweden, gold, stone-top, 19C .. 175-225
1474 Sweden, gold, stone-top, 19C .. 125-150
1475 USA, gold, scenic, 19C 100-135
1476 USA, gold-filled, HC, 19C 35-45
1477 USA, gold, blk enamel, 19C ... 150-175
1478 USA, gold-filled, 19C 35-45
1479 GB, BC, HP, 21-4-86 15-18
1480 GB, BC, Falklands, G. Payne 15-18
1481 USA, PORC, HC, Delorea 15-18
1482 GB, BC, G. Payne, LW, 20C 10-15
1483 Argentina, SIL, 19C 25-35
1484 GB, SS, HC, 18C 150-175
1485 USA, gold, scenic, NM, 19C ... 100-135
1486 USA, SS, gold band, 20C 45-60
1487 USA, ALUM, KMD, 19C 45-50
1488 USA, SS, NM, 19C 30-35
1489 USA, SS, KMD, 19C 45-60
1490 USA, SS, KMD, 19C 25-35
1491 GER, SS, enameled, Madrid 75-90
1492 GER, SS, Juliana 1909 150-175
1493 USA, SS, Simons, HP 75-95
1494 USA, SS, Simons, HP 75-95
1495 France, iron, 19C 100-125
1496 Portugal, brass pierced 25-30
1497 USA, SS, HC, 19C 30-35
1498 USA, SS, Columbia Expo 1892 100-125
1499 Dutch, SIL - plate, AM, 20C 10-12
1500 USA, SS, Stern, 19C 150-175
1501 Israel, SS, Yemini, 20C 35-40
1502 GB, Polymer, Last Supper, 20C .. 10-12
1503 Iran, SIL, HC, 20C 25-35
1504 Afghanistan, SIL, 11 TURQ, 19C . 75-90
1505 Iraq, SIL, Niello, 20C 100-125
1506 Iran, SIL, Niello, 20C 100-125
1507 Israel, SS, w/garnets, 20C 25-35
1508 Israel, SS, Yemini, 20C 30-40
1509 Israel, SS, cast filigree, 20C 25-30
1510 Israel SS, cast, 20C 20-25
1511 GB, agate-ware on brass, 20C 12-15
1512 Hungary, SS - gilt, green enam, 20C 30-35
1513 Turkey, SIL, blue enamel 100-125
1514 GER, green malachite w/gilt SIL .. 30-35
1515 GER, SS, rabbits, 20C 30-35
1516 GB, SS, HC, 18C 75-85
1517 Spain, SS, AM, TURQ, 20C 35-45
1518 USA, brass, Hollis, 20C 15-18
1519 English, PORC, HP, 19C 200-300
1520 Unknown, PORC, HP, 19C 75-100
1521 Unknown, PORC, HP, 19C 60-75
1522 Unknown, PORC, HP, 20C 40-60
1523 Unknown, PORC, HP, 20C 40-60
1524 Unknown, PORC, HP, 19C 75-95
1525 GER, Meissen, HP, 18C .... 3500+
1526 GER, Meissen, HP, 18C .... 3500+
1527 GER, Meissen, HP, 18C .... 3500+
1528 GER, Meissen, HP, 18C .... 3500+
1529 GER, Meissen, HP, 18C .... 1500+
1530 GER, Meissen, HP, 18C .... 1500+
1531 Unknown, PORC, HC 45-60
1532 English, enameled brass, HP, 18C 600-700
1533 English, enameled brass, HP, 18C 700-750
1534 English, enameled brass, HP, 18C 700-750
1535 English, PORC, R. Worcester, 20C 40-75
1536 English, PORC, R. Worcester, 20C 40-75
1537 English, PORC, R. Worcester, 19C 250-300
1538 English, PORC, R. Worcester, 19C 250-300
1539 English, PORC, R. Worcester, 19C 250-300
1540 English, PORC, R. Worcester, 19C 250-300
1541 English, PORC, R. Worcester, 19C 250-300
1542 English, PORC, R. Worcester, 20C 40-75
1543 Unknown, PORC, HP, 20C 30-65
1544 English, PORC, HP, 20C 40-75
1545 English, PORC, HP, 20C 40-75
1546 English, PORC, HP, 20C 40-75
1547 English, PORC, HP, 20C 40-75
1548 English, PORC, HP, 20C 40-75

1549	English, PORC, HP, 20C	40-75
1550	English, PORC, HP, 20C	40-75
1551	English, PORC, HP	40-75
1552	English, PORC, HP	40-75
1553	English, PORC, HP, 19C	100-150
1554	English, PORC, HP, 19C	60-75
1555	English, PORC, HP, 19C	150-200
1556	English, PORC, HP, 19C	200-225
1557	English, PORC, HP, 19C	100-125
1558	English, PORC, HP, 19C	100-125
1559	Unknown, PORC, HP	35-50
1560	Unknown, PORC, HP	35-50
1561	Unknown, PORC, HP	35-50
1562	English, PORC, HP	100-125
1563	English, PORC, HP	125-150
1564	English, PORC, HP	50-75
1565	English, PORC, HP	50-75
1566	English, PORC, blank	10-12
1567	English, PORC, HP, 20C	60-75
1568	English, PORC, HP, 19C	75-85
1569	English, PORC, HP	100-125
1570	English, PORC, HP	100-125
1571	English, PORC, HP	40-60
1572	English, PORC, HP	75-85
1573	English, PORC, HP	150-200
1574	English, PORC, HP	200-250
1575	English, PORC, HP	40-60
1576	English, PORC, HP	200-225
1577	English, PORC, HP	100-125
1578	English, PORC, HP	200-250
1579	English, PORC, HP	150-175
1580	English, PORC, HP	150-175
1581	English, PORC, HP, R. Worcester 20C	40-75
1582	English, PORC, HP, R. Worcester	40-75
1583	GER, PORC, Meissen, HP, 18C	3500+
1584	GER, PORC, Meissen, HP, 18C	3500+
1585	GER, PORC, Meissen, HP, 18C	3500+
1586	GER, PORC, Meissen, HP, 18C	3500+
1587	GER, PORC, Meissen, HP, 18C	3500+
1588	GER, PORC, Meissen, HP, 18C	3500+
1589	GER, PORC, Meissen, HP, 18C	3500+
1590	GER, PORC, Meissen, HP, 18C	3500+
1591	GER, PORC, Meissen, HP, 18C	3500+
1592	GER, PORC, Meissen, HP, 18C	3500+
1593	GER, PORC, Meissen, HP, 18C	3500+
1594	GER, PORC, Meissen, HP, 18C	3500+
1595	GER, PORC, Meissen, HP, 18C	3500+
1596	GER, PORC, Meissen, HP, 18C	3500+
1597	GER, PORC, Meissen, HP, 18C	3500+
1598	GER, PORC, Meissen, HP, 18C	3500+
1599	GER, PORC, Meissen, HP, 18C	3500+
1600	GER, PORC, Meissen, HP, 18C	3500+
1601	GER, PORC, Meissen, HP, 18C	3500+
1602	Unknown, PORC, HP	100-125
1603	Unknown, PORC, HP	10-12
1604	Unknown, PORC, HP	100-125
1605	Unknown, PORC, HP	100-125
1606	Unknown, PORC, HP	25-35

Reproductions, Restrikes, and Replicas

1607	USA, pewter, liberty bell	8-10
1608	US, SIL - gilt, Simons, SI	35-40
1609	Israel, SIL, 84 Fake Russian	25-35
1610	Unknown, SIL, Salem witch	35-40
1611	USA, SS, SU, w/emerald	50-60
1612	USA, SS, SU, Nuremberg	30-35
1613	USA, SS, SU, India type	30-35
1614	USA, SS, SU, cast	30-35
1615	USA, SS, SU, cast	30-35
1616	USA, SS, SU, cast	30-35
1617	USA, SS, SU, cast	30-35
1618	USA, SS, SU, cast	30-35
1619	USA, SS, SU, cast	30-35
1620	USA, SS, SU, cast	30-35
1621	USA, SS, SU, cast	30-35
1622	USA, SS, SU, cast	30-35
1623	Unknown, bronze, "Roman copy"	8-10
1624	Unknown, bronze, "Roman copy"	8-10
1625	GB, brass Mary Rose copy	10-12
1626	Unknown, brass, "Roman copy"	10-12
1627	Unknown, SIL - gilt, MMA	35-40
1628	USA, SS, SU, cast	30-35
1629	USA, SS, SU, cast	30-35
1630	USA, SS, SU, cast	30-35
1631	USA, SS, SU, cast	30-35
1632	Israel, SS, cast	30-35
1633	Unknown, bronze, "Roman"	8-10
1634	USA, SS, SU, cast	30-35

Bibliography

ALDRIDGE, E. — *Thoughts on Thimbles,* T.C.I. 1983-86
ALDRIDGE, E. — Collecting Thimbles, Journal of Antique Collecting, Nov. 1973
AMERICAN SCHOOL OF CLASSICAL STUDIES — Archives, Athens, Greece.
ANDERE, MARY — *Old Needlework Boxes and Tools,* New York, 1971
BELFORD, R. — COLLECTORS CIRCLE GAZETTE, 1975 to 1983
BERTRAND, C. — Brass Thimbles, Research Paper, 1982
BETENSLEY, B. — *52 Thimble Patents,* Indiana, 1980
BISHOP, CARL W. — Personal Research Papers
BLACKBURN, G. — Personal Research Papers
BOND, S. — *History of Sewing Tools,* London, 1967
BULLETIN OF T.C.I., 1980-1986
CARPENTER, C. H. & M. G. — *Tiffany Silver,* New York, 1978
CHAMBERLAIN, G. S. — "Hand-wrought Silver Thimbles of Guatemala," Hobbies, March 1947
CROSBY, L. M. — Thimbletters, 1973-1986
D'ALLEMAGNE, H. R. — *Les Accessories du Costume et du Mobilier,* Paris, 1928
DAVIDSON, G. R. (WEINBERG) — "Corinth," Vol. 12, The Minor Objects ASCS 1952.
DER MARDEROSIAN, A. — "Bakelite Plastics and Their Use in Thimble Manufacture," Thimbletter, Jan. 1978, and "Celluloid Plastics Used in Thimble Manufacture," Thimbletter, Nov. 1977
DER MARDEROSIAN, E. — Personal Research Papers on Thimbles
EARLE, A. M. — Samplers with Thimbles, The Century Illustrated Monthly Magazine, Nov. 1911 to April 1912, New York
EUBANKS, E. — Advertising Thimbles, American Collector's Magazine, June 1975
EUBANKS, E. — Personal Research Papers
FINGERHUT MUSEUM — Archives, Creglingen, Germany
FRANK, B. — Celluloid, Plentiful and Still Affordable, Antiques News, June 1982
GARDNER, K. — Personal Research Papers on Royal Worcester
GERMAN NATIONAL MUSEUM — Archives, Nuremberg, Germany
GREIF, H. — *Gesprache uber Fingerhute,* Austria, 1983
GREIF, H. — "Talks About Thimbles," Dine-American, Wilmington, Del., 1984
GREIF, H. — Personal Research Papers
HOLTHUIZEN, H. — Research Papers on Dutch Thimblers, Amsterdam, 1984-85
HOLMES, E. F. — *"Thimbles,"* Dublin, 1976
HOLMES, E. F. — *History of Thimbles,* 1985
HOWELL, D. — Thimble Lore, London, 1973
HUGHES, B. & T. — *The Collector's Encyclopedia of English Ceramics,* London, 1968
ILES & GOMMS, LTD., CHARLES — Company Records, Birmingham, England
LUNDQUIST, M. — *The Book of a Thousand Thimbles,* 1970. *Thimble Treasury,* 1975, *Thimble Americana,* 1981, Des Moines, Iowa

LUNDQUIST, M. — Personal Research Papers on Thimbles
MAGER, M. — Research Papers on Advertising Thimbles, 1979-1980
METROPOLITAN MUSEUM OF ART — Archives, N.Y.C.
NAPIER, C. — Decorative Thimbles, Antique Collector, Dec. 1979
NATHAN, H. — Personal Research Papers on Thimbles
NATIONAL MUSEUM OF ARCHEOLOGY — Archives, Madrid, Spain
NEW YORK HISTORICAL SOCIETY — Archives, N.Y., N.Y.
NUREMBERG CITY LIBRARY — Archives, Nuremberg, Germany
PERKINS, M. — Personal Research Papers
PIGGOTT, S. — *"The Dawn of Civilization,"* McGraw-Hill 1961
PRINCETON UNIVERSITY MUSEUM — Archives, Princeton, N.J.
RAINWATER, D. T. — *Encyclopedia of American Silver Manufacturers,* New York, 1975
RATH, J. A. — *Antique and Unusual Thimbles,* New York, 1979
RHODE ISLAND HISTORICAL SOCIETY — Archives, Providence, R.I.
ROBERTS, F. H. — Research Papers, Smithsonian Institute
ROBERTSON, W. A. — Research Papers on Ancient and Medieval Metallurgy
SERFASS, R. — *Porcelain,* New York, 1979
SICKELS, E. G. — New York Thimble Makers from Huntington, Long Island. The Antique Journal, Sept., Oct., Nov. 1964
SICKELS, E. G. — Personal Research Papers on Thimbles
SICKELS, E. G. — Thimble Makers in America, Antiques, Sept. 1967
SMITH, M. E. — Thimbles to Collect, Spinning Wheel, April 1972
SMITHSONIAN INSTITUTE — Archives, Washington, D.C.
SYER, CUMING H. — "On Thimbles," Journal of the British Archaeological Assoc., London 1879
THUBRON, C. — *The Venetians,* Alexandria, VA, 1980
UNDERHILL, P. J. — Research Paper on American and Foreign Thimble Marks, 1982
UNIVERSITY OF CALIFORNIA — Archives
UNIVERSITY OF CHICAGO — Archives
UNIVERSITY OF PENNSYLVANIA — Archives
UNIVERSITY OF MISSOURI — Archives
UNTRACHT, O. — *Metal Techniques for Craftsmen,* New York, 1968
VON TRAITTEUR, I. — Personal Papers on Needle-Pushers
WHITING, G. — *Tools and Toys of Stitchery,* New York, 1928
WYLER, S. B. — *Book of Old Silver, English, Foreign and American,* New York, 1937
YALE UNIVERSITY — Archives
ZALKIN, E. — Research Papers on Dorcas Thimbles

Epilogue

We hope you have enjoyed this new international edition as much as we enjoyed bringing it to you. We believe this encyclopedia represents the largest collection of facts, illustrations, and learned opinions ever devoted to collectors' thimbles. It also represents the shared knowledge of hundreds of fellow collectors. This work seeks to correct many of the past errors, odd opinions, and false assumptions found in some earlier works on the subject. However, we are not so vain as to believe this work is without its own errors, and there is still much to be learned and published.

We, therefore, request that you send any corrections to us. Only in this way can we continue to grow and learn. We also would welcome suggestions for additional data that you feel should be included in the next edition. These suggestions may be forwarded to the author via the publisher. We thank you for your support and wish you warm regards and success in all your endeavors.

"Deep Creek Plantation," author's family homestead

About the Author

John von Hoelle was born in Miami, Florida, and reared in rural Virginia and Wilmington, Delaware. He attended Boston University while stationed with the Air Force in Bedford, Massachusetts. After special training at Hanscome Field, he was assigned to British Royal Air Force in the Intelligence and Security field. Over the next several years, he was sent on missions to Europe, Asia, North and Central Africa. He finished his education at the University of Cambridge, England and returned to the United States. For the next twenty years, he was associated with the international marketing and distribution of art needlework and sewing merchandise.

His interest in thimbles began quite accidentally while he was Director of Advertising of a division of the McCall Pattern Company. He began using antique thimbles, scissors and sewing boxes as background props for photographing new sewing products for ad campaigns.

The intrisic beauty and skilled craftsmanship of the tiny sewing aid intrigued him. Once bitten by the collecting bug, he threw his personal and corporate resources into acquiring a collection of great diversity. Mr. von Hoelle is a member of the Philadelphia Thimble Society and Thimble Collectors International. He helped attribute the National Thimble Collection at the Smithsonian Institute and has been a key speaker at many regional and international conventions. In 1986 he received the coveted "Troy-New York Award" for scholarship and research from T.C.I. This is his seventh work on this sewing collectible.

*The beginnings of Thimble Collector's Encyclopedia
Author's dining room table, September 21, 1979*

An early American trade card

An American trade-card advertising Willimantic thread, circa late 19th century. Note thimble, needle, and two spools of thread guarded by the original "Knight of Ye Silver Thimble."